Liberal Politics in the Age of Gladstone and Rosebery

Liberal Politics in the Age of Gladstone and Rosebery

A Study in Leadership and Policy

D.A.Hamer
Formerly Professor of History, Victoria University of Wellington, New Zealand

EER
Edward Everett Root, Publishers, Brighton, 2019.

EER
Edward Everett Root, Publishers, Co. Ltd.,
30 New Road, Brighton, Sussex, BN1 1BN, England.

edwardeverettroot@yahoo.co.uk

Liberal Politics in the Age of Gladstone and Rosebery
A Study Leadership and Policy

D.A.Hamer

Classics in social and economic history series, no. 10.

© the estate of the late David Hamer, 1972, 2019.

This work first published in 1972.
This edition © Edward Everett Root Publishers 2019.

ISBN: 978-1-911204-71-8 Paperback.
ISBN: 978-1-911204-70-1 Hardback.

The rights of the author and of the author's estate have been asserted under the Copyright, Designs and Patents Act 1998 as the owner of this work.

All rights reserved. No part of this publication may be reproduced, stored in a retrieval system or transmitted, in any form or by any means, electronic, mechanical, photocopying, recording or otherwise, without the prior permission of the copyright owner.

Cover design by Pageset Limited, High Wycombe, Buckinghamshire.

FOR BEA

Contents

	Abbreviations	viii
	Introduction	ix
I	Sections and Interests in Liberal Politics	1
II	Liberalism and Radicalism, 1867–1877	34
III	Gladstone and the Unity of Liberalism	57
IV	The Second Gladstone Government, 1880–1885	79
V	The Crisis of 1885	99
VI	The Irish Preoccupation and Liberal Politics, 1886–1890	124
VII	The End of the Irish Preoccupation	154
VIII	The Liberal Government of 1892–1895	185
IX	The Debate on the Future of Liberal Politics	208
X	The Liberal Leaders and the Reconstruction of Liberal Politics	237
XI	Imperialism and Liberal Politics	263
XII	Reconstruction and Recovery, 1902–1906	291
	Epilogue: Liberalism after Gladstone and Rosebery	315
	Appendix: Biographical Notes	330
	Select Bibliography	343
	Index	357

Abbreviations

C.R.	*The Contemporary Review*
F.R.	*The Fortnightly Review*
N.C.	*The Nineteenth Century*
N.L.F.	National Liberal Federation
N.L.F. Report	Annual Report presented to the meetings of the Council of the National Liberal Federation, together with the account of the proceedings at these meetings. For details see Bibliography. The report of the inaugural conference in 1877 is referred to as *Proceedings Attending the Formation*.
N.L.W.	National Library of Wales
Ramm, *1868–1876*	A. Ramm (ed.), *The Political Correspondence of Mr Gladstone and Lord Granville 1868–1876*. Camden Third Series, vols. lxxxi–lxxxii, 1952.
Ramm, *1876–1886*	A. Ramm (ed.), *The Political Correspondence of Mr Gladstone and Lord Granville 1876–1886*. Oxford, 1962.

All books referred to in footnotes were published in London, unless otherwise indicated.

Introduction

THE historian of the Liberal party in the period 1867 to 1905 is faced, when he comes to survey the work that has already been done on this subject, by a very incomplete mosaic. Scattered fragments exist, often of a high quality, but there is a total lack of synthesis. A general pattern is discernible in some of these fragments, but nobody has yet tried systematically to work it out. Between the two outstanding syntheses of John Vincent's *Formation of the Liberal Party 1857–1868* and Trevor Wilson's *Downfall of the Liberal Party 1914–1935* stretches a long expanse of Liberal political activity, the activity of the party in its prime, after it had been formed and before its downfall commenced, on which most of the basic interpretative work still has to be done. It is, perhaps naturally, the years of power which are the least thoroughly studied. No adequate surveys exist of the governments of 1868–74 and 1880–5 or the political crisis of 1885–6, and since Halévy no historian has succeeded in rising above the level of narrative for the Liberal government of 1905–14. It is true that Vincent's book illuminates much about the Liberal politics of the 1870s; but unfortunately one of the few weaknesses of Wilson's book is that he gives almost no consideration to the history of the party before 1914. Undoubtedly, of the books about the period 1867–1905 R. T. Shannon's *Gladstone and the Bulgarian Agitation 1876* and H. J. Hanham's *Elections and Party Management* are outstanding, the latter being the only work that has dealt substantially with Liberal sectionalism. P. Stansky's work on the leadership struggle in the 1890s, *Ambitions and Strategies*, has little to say on policy or on the party itself, and Donald Southgate's *Passing of the Whigs* is conventional and uninspired. Astonishingly enough, apart from Shannon's book and J. L. Hammond's classic *Gladstone and the Irish Nation*, serious work on Gladstone's post-1868 career is conspicuous by its absence. Sir Philip

Magnus's biography certainly cannot be placed in this category. Most of the leading Liberals of the period were the subjects of official biographies. These seldom rise above a decent competence; and few revisionist studies have been attempted. The best known of the more recent biographies, R. Rhodes James's *Rosebery* and Roy Jenkins's *Sir Charles Dilke*, show an insubstantial understanding of the general context of Liberal politics.

It is not the purpose of this book to provide a complete synthesis of the kind to which I have already referred. I explore certain themes, and discuss certain aspects, of Liberal politics in the period 1867 to 1905; but the study is selective and is not designed to be either a history of the Liberal party or a comprehensive assessment of all aspects of Liberal political activity and thought. It is perhaps inevitable that at this point any attempt to write a work of this kind will result in its being compared closely with Vincent's *Formation of the Liberal Party*. But what follows is in no sense intended to serve as either a sequel or a complement to that book. It will be obvious that my approach, and the subjects on which I concentrate, are very different from Vincent's and that the kind of work which he does, exploring grass-roots Liberalism and Liberal feeling in the country at large, remains to be done for the period after 1868. Nevertheless, no one who studies the history of the Liberal party in the second half of the nineteenth century can now fail to become in the process deeply indebted to Vincent. The reader will soon become aware of the extent to which my thinking on Liberal politics has been stimulated and guided by his work.

This book is concerned mainly with Liberal politicians. It is my aim to examine what they understood the purpose of Liberal political activity to be and what were the reasons and assumptions which led to their supporting or promoting particular policies. I also study at length and in detail the various styles of leadership which were offered to the Liberal party. I examine the philosophies and strategies of Joseph Chamberlain, Gladstone, Sir William Harcourt, Lord Rosebery, and Sir Henry Campbell-Bannerman and try to reveal the basic beliefs about the purpose and direction of Liberal politics which underlay each man's conduct as Liberal (or Radical) leader. A third object of this book is to analyse the major organizing and controlling themes in Liberal politics and to show how certain policies were taken up, or at least exploited, not merely because of belief in them as solutions to certain problems but also because concentration on them was expected or was seen to have a beneficial ordering and cohering influence on Liberal politics. Among the themes which I shall be examining are the conflict between, on the one hand, the advocates and promoters of reform programmes and, on the other, those who preferred concentration on one great issue or cause at a time, and the preoccupation of Liberals with real or alleged 'obstructions to progress' such as the Irish question and the House of Lords. Other organizing principles that occur in the history of the Liberal party in this period include the 'umbrella' of democratic party organization, reliance on Gladstone's authority, the Liberal Imperial idea, and the 'Broad Church' interpretation of the nature of the party. I shall also discuss how the Liberals defined their political purpose and identity in relation to their Conservative opponents and what influence a concern with 'anti-Toryness' had over the course of Liberal politics. I am concerned with Radicalism as well as Liberalism and shall trace how and with what success Radicals, led by Chamberlain and Henry Labouchere in particular, endeavoured to transcend the politics of sectional interests and 'fads' on which so much militant Radical activity was based.

An assumption underlying much of the argument in this book is that Liberal politics in the late nineteenth century were not controlled by any single and generally accepted system of thought, any set of ideas, creed, or philosophy relevant to contemporary needs and situations and capable of guiding political practice. Liberals were not held together by any strong sense of common purpose. There was not seen to exist any central core of principle and belief to which were related and in which were cohered all the particular things that Liberals did and all the particular reforms in which they were interested. John Vincent writes concerning the Radicals of the 1860s:

> What they lacked was any theory as to *what* they were dealing with, what their principles had to be applied to, and what forces were at work in history. This lack was serious and fraught with consequences: between 1860 and 1920 it was generally accepted that, whatever actually happened in politics, the 'principles of

Liberalism' were a miscellany of vaguely humanitarian enthusiasms, chiefly for the relief of the individual from metaphysical rather than material distress.

Vincent goes on to describe Cobden as having alone among Victorian Liberals 'bound the whole miscellaneous information of his age into a few guiding generalities'.[1] But by the 1880s only a small minority of Radicals and Liberals accepted these generalities as the controlling influence over their political practice, and they were being increasingly subjected to criticism as conservative and unprogressive. In my book *John Morley, Liberal Intellectual in Politics* I have examined very closely the awareness of one leading Liberal of the absence of system and the remedies which he sought for this problem. In this present study the consequences of confusion and incoherence in Liberal politics are a recurrent theme, perhaps the basic theme of the entire work.

In this book I concern myself very much with the *form* of Liberal policy. In other words, I investigate the place which particular policies and causes were given in the total structure of Liberal politics and their relationship to other policies. It is my opinion that for most Liberal politicians and especially the leaders such considerations were just as important as were beliefs concerning the *content* of policies. Questions were often taken up not only because those who did so believed in them but also because the very process of taking them up and concentrating on them was expected to have beneficial consequences for Liberal political life in general. Few historians have either recognized that this latter motive has often operated in connection with the promotion of reform policies or analysed in any detail the way in which it has operated. M. Ostrogorski made some suggestions on the topic in his *Democracy and the Organization of Political Parties*, but no one has followed these up or used his concepts as tools of analysis. In his study of the Anti-Corn Law League Norman McCord discusses the appeal for Radicals of the 1830s and 1840s of concentration on the one issue of repeal of the Corn Laws. But otherwise, in so far as Liberal and Radical policies have been studied, the emphasis has been almost entirely on their content.

The danger of concentrating on the study of form and

[1] J. Vincent, *The Formation of the Liberal Party 1857–1868*, 1966, pp. 30, 34.

relationship is that, partly perhaps because of the novelty of such an approach, one will be accused of paying too little attention to the content of reform questions and, above all, of eliminating conviction and conscience from the range of influences that affect political conduct. One can easily appear to be cynical about the role of genuine belief. I have been aware of this danger, and where, as in the sections on Home Rule or Liberal Imperialism, I omit detailed consideration of views on the content of policy, this should not be taken as implying that I consider that such views had little influence in determining whether or not Liberals committed themselves to particular causes. It has been my principal aim, however, to draw attention to the ways in which Liberals defined and understood the relationship between their own particular reform interests and the wider scheme of things, this wider scheme being, for example, the position and purpose of the Liberal party, the belief in progress, the desire to promote social improvement, and the need for a system of thought. An example of this approach is my analysis of the Home Rule issue in terms of the 'obstruction' theory.

My particular interest is in the leaders and their role in the organization of policy. It is my contention that a man justified himself as a leader exactly in so far as he did have this concern with the form as well as the content of policy. A sectionalist may perhaps be said to have been more interested in content than in form. He was strongly attached to a certain cause and gave the promotion of it priority over the promotion of all other reform questions, even if this meant disorganizing the entire pattern of Liberal political activity. But the leader could not afford to take up a policy in this way, thinking only of its content. When he recommended courses of action or concentration on certain policies to his party, he had to devise, and try to enable his followers to see, some positive and organic relationship between what he was recommending and *all* the elements of Liberal politics. Gladstone was outstanding as a leader because of his ability to do this. His rhetoric fused form and content, and in adopting a policy he never blindly considered only its content. The belief that he did so has, in my opinion, led to a considerable misunderstanding of his conduct in 1885–6.

My interest in leaders of this kind has resulted in my not saying a great deal about the Whigs as a separate force in Liberal politics. John Vincent has shown that the notion, derived from Chamberlain's rhetoric, of 'the Whigs' as a large bloc of M.P.s, balancing 'the Radicals' as the other half of the party in the Parliaments of the pre-1885 era, does not stand up to analysis. The Whig tradition was one of leadership, and by this period the tradition of disinterested and liberal control is wearing very thin. With Hartington, Spencer, and even Rosebery the impression of natural disinclination to engage in an active career of political leadership struggling against a historically derived and inbred sense of duty is very marked; and Rosebery's career and his abandonment of the responsibilities of leadership can be seen as exemplifying the irrelevance of the Whig tradition in the conditions of the late nineteenth century. Rosebery had to force himself to be what he did not want to be, what tradition—and Gladstone—nevertheless indicated that he ought to be, and what the circumstances of the time made almost futile any attempt to be.

My subject is the period between the late 1870s and 1905. It is a period in which the Liberals found themselves mostly in opposition or, if in power, as in 1880-5, 1886, and 1892-5, able to achieve very little. My theme is therefore the phenomenon of powerlessness. In my Epilogue I make a briefer analysis of what happened after 1905. But I am interested there principally in the relationship of the themes and problems of the pre-1905 era to the record of the Liberal government of 1905-14. The history of that government itself is a large and complicated subject which merits separate treatment.

This work is based largely on manuscript collections, and I am indebted to numerous people who have assisted me in my research in these. I wish in particular to express my gratitude to Earl Spencer for giving me access to the papers of the fifth Earl at Althorp, to Viscount Harcourt for allowing me to work on the Harcourt papers at Stanton Harcourt, and to Mr. and Mrs. W. B. Morrell for their help in connection with the papers of Robert Spence Watson. Among the staff of the numerous libraries at which I worked I should mention in particular Mr. D. Porter of the Bodleian Library, Oxford, and Mr. A. Bell of the National Library of Scotland, Edinburgh, for their very valuable assistance in guiding me through the complex arrangements of the Bryce and Rosebery papers. The help which I received at the National Library of Wales, Aberystwyth, the University Libraries at Sheffield and Birmingham, and the British Museum Department of Manuscripts also eased my task considerably.

I wish to express my gratitude to the Cambridge University Press for permission to use in this book portions of an article of mine on 'The Irish Question and Liberal Politics, 1886–1894' which they published in *The Historical Journal* in 1969.

D. A. HAMER

Victoria University of Wellington
New Zealand
April 1971

I Sections and Interests in Liberal Politics

THE Liberal party was a coalition throughout its existence as an alternative-government party, and, of course, any party that aspires to fill, or already does fill, such a role in a large and diverse country must assume such a form. Since 1867 at least no party in Great Britain has had any hope of attaining the status of alternative government unless it has been something more than a section or interest group, unless it has been able to command political support from across a wide spectrum of attitudes and beliefs, interests, and aspirations.

To many people today such an observation must seem so much of a truism as to be scarcely worth repeating. But, in fact, as a description of the ideal and desirable, as distinct from the actual and practical, nature of a political party it cannot be said even yet to have won general acceptance. There are still adherents of the Labour party who demand a return to definite, clear-cut principles of 'socialism' as the basis of its policy and action, just as there are Conservatives who, for example, wish to see Conservative party politics based on the particular kind of Conservatism associated with *laissez-faire* and minimal State intervention. It is not surprising that such an attitude towards party was widespread in a period when the phenomenon of the domination of parliamentary politics by two alternative-government parties was new. In the late nineteenth century there were many Liberals who regarded the existence of so many sections and pressure-groups, so many different points of view and demands for reforms, in Liberal politics as a weakness and a handicap. To them it seemed that the Liberal party ought itself to be like the sections for which it served as an 'umbrella'—a movement with a solid, single basis, devoted to the promotion of a single cause or the propagation of a single set of principles. Only gradually was it seen that the situation had been transformed by the voters using their electoral power primarily to exercise control over government. The Liberals thus became, when in opposition, simply the leverage that the voters could exert, if they so wished, to get rid of the men who were governing them. Such a status meant that it was not necessary for the Liberals to have a definite, single cause to promote, that they could survive and periodically enjoy office while continuing to be a coalition of miscellaneous interests and sections and causes. But the realization of this came over Liberals only slowly.

For the period after 1867 is a period of transition in reform politics.[1] For about a hundred years the politics of the promotion of reform had been the politics of great single-cause movements, operating mainly outside Parliament and with no expectation or desire themselves to constitute the government. Henceforward reforms were to come through the legislative programmes of governments chosen by the voters through the medium of alternative-government parties to which candidates in the particular constituencies professed adherence. But it took time for the former pattern of reform activity to be absorbed into the latter, and the process of absorption was, as we shall see, one of much confusion and misunderstanding.

In considering the coalition nature of the Liberal party, we need to distinguish between two types of sectional opinion. On the one hand, there were the great permanent blocs of regional, occupational, or religious interest which had become attached to Liberal politics and which had a status which did not depend merely on the advocacy of a particular programme or reform policy. Such were, for example, the interests of Wales, Scotland, and, to a rapidly diminishing degree after about 1870, Ireland, and also 'Labour' or 'Lib-Labism', and Nonconformity. On the other hand, there were the reform organizations, the pressure-groups and lobbies, which resembled the Anti-Corn Law League in being concerned solely for the securing of some particular reform and in being therefore only of a provisional nature, destined, like the League, to disappear once the reform had been secured. Numerous examples of this kind of section

[1] J. Vincent, *The Formation of the Liberal Party 1857–1868*, 1966, p. xxxiii.

will appear in the course of this book. The most notable of such movements in the late nineteenth century were the United Kingdom Alliance which pressed for temperance reform and had been founded in 1853, the Liberation Society (or Society for the Liberation of Religion from State Patronage and Control) which had been founded in 1844 by Edward Miall as the British Anti-State-Church Association and acquired its permanent title in 1853, and the Association for the Repeal of the Contagious Diseases Acts which achieved its goal in 1886. These sections were the very stuff of activist Liberal politics. They embodied the causes to which rank-and-file Liberals were attached and in which many men found the reasons for calling themselves Liberals. Each particular cause—temperance reform, women's suffrage, disestablishment, a secular education system, repeal of the Contagious Diseases Acts, the promotion of international peace—had its own set of adherents, and in their overlapping and their pressure on Liberal politicians was woven the fabric of Liberal political activity.

Of course, there was in practice no rigid division between the permanent and provisional types of section, for the former were fertile breeding-grounds for sectionalism of the provisional, particular-cause variety. The desire to promote reforms, or to press the promotion of them upon the Liberal leaders, was by no means necessarily associated with adherence to a major permanent interest. Nonconformity or Lib-Labism was not a political programme but rather a frame of mind, a viewpoint as to status, which could from time to time inspire in a section of those adhering to it a desire to form an organization for some special cause. In order to understand the context within which the reform causes and 'fads' were promoted we must therefore examine first of all the major 'frames of mind' which were to be found within Liberalism.

To many people it seemed that Liberal politics were, or had to be as a consequence of the electorate created by the 1867 Reform Act, an alliance between two great interests, Nonconformity and Labour.[1] Recent analyses of Liberal politics, notably by John Vincent, have indeed shown the extent to

[1] Cf. J. L. Garvin, *The Life of Joseph Chamberlain*, vol. i, 1932, p. 219. D. A. Hamer, *John Morley, Liberal Intellectual in Politics*, Oxford, 1968, p. 110.

which this alliance represented an organic whole. Nonconformity was as important a factor in the culture of the artisan as it was in that of the provincial industrialist; and the frame of mind which became known as Lib-Labism represented attitudes about the capitalist system as a whole which were held also by many Liberal employers.[1]

The days when Nonconformity could have formed a coherent programmatic section within Liberal politics were now passed. As their historic struggle for legal and social emancipation and for the reduction of the privileges of the Established Church drew to a close, the political action of Nonconformists became increasingly diversified. Their energies and religious and social impulses were channelled into a variety of 'good causes' no one of which was obviously of pre-eminent importance to the interests of Nonconformists as Nonconformists. Nonconformity scarcely ever now expressed itself with one voice or on behalf of any one particular cause, but nevertheless, at the level of myth and tradition and common beliefs about the historic evolution of political Liberalism, it remained of fundamental importance in the creation of the Liberal frame of mind.[2]

The 'Nonconformist conscience' remained a vague concept, and the cohesiveness of Nonconformity as a political force was weakening with the disappearance of distinctively Nonconformist and therefore unifying causes. The reverse was the case with Labour. Here the unifying causes and influences were emerging, not disappearing, and the potential for a Labour party was developing as that for a Nonconformist party was being eroded. Apart from the Irish, Labour seemed the best placed of all the sections in the Liberal coalition to have its own M.P.s elected and thus secure the basis on which a full-scale parliamentary party could be established. And yet for a remarkably long time after 1867 this development did not take place. At times Labour behaved, or showed signs of wanting to behave, in a sectional way; that is, spokesmen for 'Labour' tried to mobilize and organize it as a more distinct section within Liberal politics. But behind them were not yet those forces which alone would enable Labour to transcend sectionalism and to begin to take a stand outside, and not just as a

---

[1] Vincent, *Formation of the Liberal Party*, pp. 76–80.
[2] Ibid., p. xxix.

component part of, Liberalism: consciousness of the existence of a unified working class, a trade-union movement which could be plausibly regarded as representing that class, and an ideology which presented an alternative to the system of attitudes towards capitalism on which the integration of Labour into Liberal politics was based.

Nonconformist sectionalism reached its peak with the National Education League. A Nonconformist-dominated movement, this was one of the single-cause reform organizations which had been active before the emergence of a national Liberal party.[1] In post-1867 parliamentary politics its members naturally were Liberals rather than Conservatives, but this was not seen as necessitating any subordination of its interests to those of the Liberal party. It is scarcely accurate to refer to the League's campaign against certain provisions of the 1870 Education Act as a 'revolt' against the Liberal party. For 'revolt' implies that they were casting off a well-established connection with that party, and no such connection existed. Nevertheless, in the campaign the League did appear to undergo a fundamental change which perhaps first revealed to supporters of particular reform causes the limitations of a completely autonomous stance in the new political circumstances. For between 1868 and 1873 the League's function appeared to change from the positive one of promoting educational reform to the negative one of obstructing a government because it had brought in a reform different in some respects from what the League had advocated. Its actions betrayed its weakness in the new circumstances, its dependence on an organization which had the parliamentary majority which it itself, as a minority single-cause movement, could never hope to secure on its own. The majority had the power: all that the League could do was to threaten to detach its portion of that majority and thus in all probability bring about the accession to majority status of the Conservatives who were much less likely to give them what they wanted in any respect whatever. What clearly had now to be done for the sake of the stability of Liberal politics *and* for the sake of minority

[1] F. H. Herrick, 'The Origins of the National Liberal Federation', *Journal of Modern History*, vol. 17, no. 2 (June 1945), pp. 121-3. D. Read, *The English Provinces, c. 1760–1960. A Study in Influence*, 1964, p. 169.

reform causes was to establish some more positive and organically integrated relationship between minorities and majority.

Liberals who supported the League in its opposition to the Education Act were urged to put this particular viewpoint of theirs first and let it determine their whole political conduct as Liberals. This was a typical sectionalist attitude that we shall find being expressed again and again by sectionalist Liberals in the next twenty to thirty years. Two attitudes to party came into conflict. If the party ought to have a definite, clear-cut basis of policy, then that basis ought to be whatever reform cause you as a Liberal happened to believe in most enthusiastically. Since Liberals did not agree on what was the most important reform cause, the one deserving priority of attention, there was no hope of securing a stable majority through the application of this attitude. But the other attitude, that the role of a party was primarily to support a governing or potentially governing leadership, seemed to leave dangerously little scope for effective sectionalist influence. When in 1870 a second Liberal candidate was put up at a by-election in opposition to the 'official' Liberal who supported the Education Bill, the leading Nonconformist clergyman, R. W. Dale, approved of this as a way in which Nonconformist Liberals could show that there were 'certain terms' by which their allegiance to the party 'stands or falls'.[1] The two candidates represented two different attitudes towards the party. The conflict between these can be seen also in the Bath by-election in 1872 when the League was surprised that the local Liberal leaders, even though they seemed to be 'wholly at one with the League in principle', nevertheless 'denied the right of the League to make any requisition on the subject of their candidate's opinions'.[2] For what was at stake was the right of any minority to control the action of an organization that sought to win a majority of the electorate.

Dale represented one extreme point of view as to the relationship that Nonconformists should establish, or should threaten to establish, between their own political influence and general Liberal politics. He once commented on the possibility that the National Education League's tactics might 'lead to the breaking up of the Liberal party': 'When the Liberal party is false to its

[1] A. W. W. Dale, *The Life of R. W. Dale of Birmingham*, 1898, p. 281.
[2] F. Adams, *History of the Elementary School Contest in England*, 1882, pp. 292-4.

noblest principles, it is time that it should be broken up.'[1] But not all Nonconformists were so sure that these were the best tactics to pursue for the promotion of their own interests. The crucial question for this as for all other sections that were involved in Liberal politics was whether more was to be gained from aggressive and even obstructive behaviour, utilizing whatever electoral leverage the section happened to possess, or from trying to earn the gratitude of the party leadership by full loyalty to it. In other words, was it the most loyal or the most militant and assertive section that stood the greater chance of having its demands accepted by the leaders? An example of a Nonconformist who believed that the primary need was to maintain the strength of the party even if this meant soft-pedalling Nonconformist questions is J. J. Colman, the great mustard manufacturer and Liberal magnate who was M.P. for Norwich from 1871 until 1895. Almost as soon as he entered Parliament, he found himself supporting a resolution of Edward Miall's in favour of disestablishment but with the feeling that the promotion of the question at this juncture was impolitic since 'the Liberal Party for another Election on the new Franchise needs consolidation and not an element of division'. 'I am a Nonconformist,' he said, 'but I am a Liberal too, and I fear the latter will lose more than the former will gain.'[2] The events of 1870–4 revealed the weaknesses of Nonconformity as a would-be independent section. Its resources for organization and agitation were not great, and it entirely lacked the means and potential for growth through influence over outside opinion that alone could make it practically effective if it wished to operate apart from, and even in opposition to, the Liberal party. Nonconformity needed the Liberal party a good deal more—to get a parliamentary majority on its side—than Liberalism needed it. The Liberal débâcle of 1874 was undoubtedly a shock to many Nonconformists, and feeling that it might be better in their own interests to work within rather than against the party became fairly general among them.[3]

The National Education League cannot, in any event,

---

[1] Ibid., pp. 272–3.
[2] H. C. Colman, *Jeremiah James Colman. A Memoir*, 1905, p. 260.
[3] H. J. Hanham, *Elections and Party Management. Politics in the Time of Disraeli and Gladstone*, 1959, pp. 118–21.

accurately be called representative of Nonconformity, even at its peak: as Hanham observes,[1] militant agitation had little attraction for the majority of Nonconformists. And from the high point at about 1873-4 the sectionalism of even the militant minority began to wane. Most of the pressing, practical, and directly felt grievances of Nonconformists had by now been remedied, and what was left as the major issue—the ultimate cause, disestablishment itself—lacked both urgency and practicality, and was too fundamental a change and too much a matter of doctrine and theory to appeal to middle-class people who were politically increasingly conservative.[2] In addition, of course, once the Liberals had left office, the education issue was much less inflammatory, and the Liberal leaders were able to contribute to this diminution of friction by making gestures of conciliation—without being under any pressure to translate these into legislative action.[3]

The revised Nonconformist attitude to sectionalist conduct is well illustrated by an article written by the leading Nonconformist, the Revd. J. Guinness Rogers, which appeared in the *Nineteenth Century* for April 1880. In this Rogers, whom we shall have occasion frequently to cite as a shrewd and perceptive commentator on Liberal politics, describes and condemns the kind of sectionalism which, as in 1874, produces the disruption of, and renders impotent, the only agency which can procure for the section the changes which it demands. Once again, he remarks, Nonconformists could find excuses for behaving sectionally, for they have received little in the way of pledges from the Liberal leaders. 'In truth, if Dissenters were at all disposed to look to sectional interests, and to forget that they are an integral part of the Liberal party, they might have found in the omission of distinct reference to questions of religious equality in the manifestoes of the Liberal leaders some excuse for taking independent action.' But they will not do so

[1] Hanham, op. cit., p. 121.
[2] R. T. Shannon, *Gladstone and the Bulgarian Agitation 1876*, 1963, p. 35. Contemporary comment on this change in the position of Nonconformity is quoted in S. M. Ingham, 'The Disestablishment Movement in England, 1868-74', *Journal of Religious History*, vol. 3 (1964), p. 40.
[3] Thus on 10 June 1874 Hartington, Goschen, Lowe, and Mundella were among those who voted for the second reading of Henry Richard's Elementary Education Act (1873) Amendment Bill. The motion was lost by 373 to 128, and Forster voted against it. Cf. Ingham, 'The Disestablishment Movement', p. 40.

for they recognize that their principle of religious equality is, 'after all, only one element of their Liberalism, and it would be folly indeed were they to sacrifice all the rest because the immediate triumph of that one in which they may be specially interested is impossible'. 'Such action', he writes in terms very similar to those used by Colman in 1871, 'could not advance their special end, and it would imperil much which is as dear to them as to other Liberals.' Special organizations constitute 'a serious evil' when they 'endeavour to extort by menace' commitments which 'they cannot secure by reason'. Their proper role is to be 'auxiliaries to the Liberal party'. Nonconformists should be 'Liberals first, Nonconformists afterwards', recognizing that Liberalism is 'a consistent whole' and that 'they have no hope of securing the triumph of one element in it by pressing it on to the exclusion of all others'.[1]

With 'Labour' the reverse process can now be seen to have taken place in the thirty years after 1867—a growing away from integration in Liberal politics. But this was a very slow evolution, and there were very few signs of it until at least the late 1880s. In 1868 Labour appeared to be very willing to be thoroughly integrated into Liberalism. The idea of separate working-class political action did not appeal at all to George Howell and his colleagues in the Reform League.[2] As Royden Harrison has shown, they did a great deal to promote the electoral interests of the Liberal party in 1868 and contributed greatly to the cohering of Liberal political activity while neither receiving nor even expecting a reward for these services in the shape of candidatures for the section that they claimed to represent.[3] The Reform League behaved in fact as the Liberal leaders always wished that sections would behave, stressing party unity and suppressing divisive tendencies.[4]

At this time, and for a considerable period thereafter, Labour seemed to be the best integrated of all the sections in the great

[1] J. Guinness Rogers, 'A Nonconformist's View of the Election', *N.C.*, no. 38 (April 1880), pp. 632–5. See below, pp. 82–3.
[2] R. Harrison, *Before the Socialists: Studies in Labour and Politics 1861–1881*, 1965, p. 142.
[3] Ibid., pp. 148, 151–3, 162, 170, 175, 188, 205.
[4] Ibid., pp. 166, 172, 176–8, 186, 197, 205.

Liberal coalition. Perhaps the reason was that, whereas in the other cases undisciplined sectionalism was attributable to the absence of a controlling and generally accepted system or 'school' of Liberal thought and principles,[1] in the case of Labour there was an ideology, a system of ideas and assumptions generally accepted, that underlay and justified its relationship to, and integration in, the total pattern of Liberal politics. Recent writers have stressed the extent to which the articulate working-class leaders of the day were involved in the same political culture as the Liberal employing and capitalist class. John Vincent, for example, argues that 'the working class was genuinely Liberal in the same way—and with the same complications from religious and social causes—as the middle class'.[2] Labour was kept integrated in Liberalism—or Lib-Labism—by a genuine belief in an alliance of interests between working men and employers and also by the Liberals' political fixation on the non-industrial class enemy, the landed class. T. R. Tholfsen has analysed the association of working-class radicals with middle-class Liberals in the development of the Liberal 'caucus' in Birmingham.[3] Caution may be needed in generalizing from the Birmingham experience because of the special features of Birmingham's socio-economic structure to which Asa Briggs has drawn attention;[4] but Vincent has shown how a political culture that covered both middle and working classes was an important factor contributing to the formation of a national base for the parliamentary Liberal party. He suggests that even in the 1860s and 1870s the working class could have found separate political expression. The funds and the organizational basis for this were present, but the awareness of factors in common with the Liberal middle class was as yet far stronger than any awareness of fundamental differences. The principal working-class voters of the pre-1885 period, the artisans and the trade unionists, were close to the middle class in their social values and aspirations. The feeling of identification, rooted in the structure and ethos of mid-Victorian industrial capitalism, was given political expression, crystallized into

[1] Hamer, *John Morley*, p. 64.
[2] Vincent, *Formation of the Liberal Party*, p. 77.
[3] T. R. Tholfsen, 'The Origins of the Birmingham Caucus', *Historical Journal*, vol. 2, no. 2 (1959), pp. 161 ff.
[4] A. Briggs, *Victorian Cities*, 1963, Chapter 5.

a broad national political culture that became known as Liberalism, by the varied rhetorical and opinion-forming efforts between 1860 and 1880 of John Bright, John Stuart Mill, and Gladstone.[1]

Some of the leading spokesmen for 'Labour' really did seem to have as much confidence as their middle-class Liberal contemporaries in Birmingham in the possibility of the evolution of a genuinely organic 'democratic' polity, that is a situation in which through Liberal politics a unified community interest transcending classes was expressed.[2] George Howell repudiated rule by any one class: 'I want a government of the entire people —where wealth and intellect will have its fair share of power— no more.'[3] It was his hope that a general Liberal political organization would develop in which 'the working men shall be consulted and called into active political life'.[4] To ensure that the danger of an anti-working-class reaction was minimized, and in view of the unrevolutionary character of the British working-class movement which made independent action unlikely to be effective, he and others wanted the working men to seek their advancement through an alliance with middle-class Liberals and radicals. They had full faith in the practicability of such an alliance, and that faith was represented by the 'Lib-Lab' M.P.s who spoke for Labour in the House of Commons until the early twentieth century.

Labour naturally had rather higher ambitions and a more exalted view of its own status than other sections. The term 'Lib-Lab' implied a special relationship, and there were those who called upon the old concept of Parliament as a forum of interests—a concept recently refurbished by Bagehot in his *English Constitution*—to justify a claim for a representation of the 'Labour interest' in the Commons 'proportionate to the other interests and classes'.[5] Advocates of independent Labour politics, such as Alexander MacDonald, the pioneer of Labour representation, were in fact not doing much more than seeking a greater emphasis on the 'Lab' side of 'Lib-Labism'. 'Labour' politicians were far more reluctant sectionalists than were the

[1] Vincent, *Formation of the Liberal Party*, pp. 76–82, Chapter 3.
[2] For examples of this confidence in Birmingham see Briggs, *Victorian Cities*, pp. 194–201.
[3] Harrison, *Before the Socialists*, p. 144.
[4] Ibid., p. 163.
[5] Ibid., p. 141.

Nonconformists and the 'good-cause' militants. In 1869 Howell declared his abhorrence of 'the old Chartist practice' of 'opposing all parties except those pledged to labour questions'.[1] In 1871 an attempt was made by the T.U.C. Parliamentary Committee to mobilize 'Labour' in the constituencies against M.P.s who failed to support the legislative demands of the trade unions.[2] But the moves that were made in 1872–3 to found a new party based on, or primarily involving, Labour came mainly from middle-class radicals and intellectuals and collapsed once these people had concluded that 'a mere working class, Trade Unionist platform' was 'not enough' and 'too classy'. Most trade-union leaders were not enthusiastic about the idea of a 'Labour party'.[3] Radicals such as Chamberlain who wished to appeal to 'Labour' as a political force, far from having any intention of stimulating Labour sectionalism, sought the harnessing of Labour to, and its absorption into, a wider and primarily middle-class-controlled 'general' radicalism. Until the late 1880s Labour sectionalism, if in evidence at all, gave little concern to the Liberal leaders. It was well submerged in the great wave of Gladstonian feeling after 1876,[4] and strongly Gladstonian 'Lib-Labs' such as Broadhurst, Burt, and Arch had few rivals until well into the 1890s as political spokesmen for Labour. In 1886 Labour was the most loyal and least divided of the sections. 'Lib-Labs' accepted the orthodox Gladstonian-Liberal position on most major policy issues and were quite content with their status as a section within Liberalism. A distinctive Labour political creed was lacking, and the Socialist creed of challenge to the liberal capitalist system, within which the trade unions were being accorded, it seemed, a secure place and an accepted role, was slow to gain converts in the ranks of organized Labour. Indeed, the trade-union leaders' opposition to the interference of the State in industrial questions which they regarded it as their business to attend to, their fear that such interference would undermine the trade-union movement

---

[1] Harrison, *Before the Socialists*, p. 207.
[2] H. W. McCready, 'British Labour's Lobby, 1867–75', *Canadian Journal of Economics and Political Science*, vol. 22, no. 2 (May 1956), p. 154.
[3] Harrison, *Before the Socialists*, p. 300. H. W. McCready, 'The British Election of 1874: Frederic Harrison and the Liberal Labour Dilemma', *Canadian Journal of Economics and Political Science*, vol. 20, no. 2 (May 1954), pp. 168–73.
[4] Shannon, *Gladstone and the Bulgarian Agitation*, pp. 234–5.

itself, meant that it was not from them that the promotion of a strong programme of distinctive legislative demands on behalf of the working class was likely to come. Their involvement in Liberal politics was not programmatic. It was a reflection of an attitude to status.

This being so, if any disintegration of the Lib-Lab relationship was to occur, it would most probably be closely associated with indications of a change in the socio-political status of Labour. To understand how such a change did in fact begin to appear we have to examine the ways in which Liberals regarded the involvement of Labour in their politics. There were three possible ways in which Liberals could respond to the creation of a working-class electorate. The most favoured way was to ignore distinctions of class and to refer and appeal to working men as individuals, voting units in a liberal parliamentary democracy. One difficulty here, of course, especially before 1885, was that democracy did not yet exist, that social and property-owning distinctions were made between voters and non-voters, so that it was not easy to validate an individualistic interpretation of the role of working men in the political system. Secondly, Labour could be regarded as a section within the Liberal coalition and its interests considered in the same way as those of the Nonconformists or the temperance reformers. Thirdly, Labour could be acknowledged to have a status that was more than sectional, to be the ally of capital in a broad fusion of interests that was one of the basic principles of Liberalism. This last concept of Labour was the one held and put into practice by many of the great employers and capitalists who were active in Liberal politics and of whom A. J. Mundella and Samuel Morley were outstanding examples. These men were the proponents of an enlightened capitalism in which Labour had an accepted and stable role. They saw a balance between labour and capital as the essential source of industrial harmony and stability. To them the meaning of political Liberalism was the representation of the wider community interest, the spirit of a unified industrial capitalist system in which labour and capital were organically interrelated and interdependent. The role of government was to ensure that the balance was kept even and to create conditions in which an organic harmony could most freely emerge. Theirs was the

Liberalism of opposition to class war, and in pursuing policies designed to promote social and industrial stability they were expressing what we shall again and again be seeing was one of the most deep-rooted concepts that Liberals had of their role in politics. The philosophy, the ideology even, to which these men adhered and which they sought to put into practice had been developing throughout the nineteenth century. It had received its first major expression in the pre-1832 agitation for parliamentary reform, was used to justify the failure to enfranchise working men in 1832 as well as their employers, underlay much of the rhetoric and propaganda of the Anti-Corn Law League and of the campaign for working-class enfranchisement in the 1860s, and had indeed become the ideology, the justification for existing, of popular radicalism and Liberalism.[1] It was that between working men and employers there was a fundamental identity of interest, that prosperity or lack of prosperity in industry affected all alike, that working men benefited if capitalists prospered. All belonged to 'the industrious class', and in so far as there was a class division in British society it was between working men and their employers, on the one hand, and the parasitic, non-'industrious' land-owning class, on the other. Until the First World War this theme of the struggle of the 'industrious class' against inherited, aristocratic, and landed privilege continued to provide a unifying emotionalism for a popular radicalism that transcended class boundaries. And a 'Lib-Lab' alliance remained a practical concept so long as there was a trade-union leadership that shared with the employers a dislike of State control over industrial life, that preferred voluntary, negotiated settlements of industrial issues to settlements imposed by governments, and that desired that the State should confine itself to providing conditions—legal security for trade unions, machinery for arbitration—in which such voluntary arrangements could be most easily effected.

Royden Harrison has shown the confidence of the great 'New Model' Liberal employers in their ability to stabilize the industrial system through the conciliation of, and co-operation

[1] G. Kitson Clark, *The Making of Victorian England*, 1962, pp. 123–32, 144. A. Briggs, 'Thomas Attwood and the Economic Background of the Birmingham Political Union', *Cambridge Historical Journal*, vol. 9, p. 191. A. Briggs, *Victorian Cities*, pp. 188–91. H. Perkin, *The Origins of Modern English Society 1780–1880*, 1969, pp. 216, 312, 372.

with, Labour.¹ The great themes of their political activity—and of the activity of many other Liberals who interested themselves in industrial matters—were arbitration, conciliation, the maintenance of harmony and connection and constant contact with Labour, regarded as an integral component of an organic capitalist order. The career of A. J. Mundella, the Nottingham hosiery manufacturer who represented Sheffield constituencies for nearly thirty years, shows a remarkably sustained effort to put into practice these principles of a liberal capitalism and capitalist Liberalism. He opposed men who had attitudes to industrial problems which seemed to him 'too one-sided'. He expressed succinctly *his* philosophy as a Liberal when he commented on one man who appeared to be looking at a problem entirely 'from the [trade] Unionist point of view': 'He and some others are just as unfair to the masters as Roebuck is to the men, and I don't mean to do or say anything *unfair to either*.'² Mundella worked throughout his political career, in and out of office, to develop both the machinery of, and the habit of resorting to, industrial arbitration and conciliation.³ The careers of many prominent Liberals in the late nineteenth century show a similar interest in the principles and practice of arbitration. Samuel Morley devoted himself to increasing the number of Boards of Conciliation and Arbitration and facilitating the adjustment of differences between capital and labour.⁴ Robert Spence Watson, who was President of the National Liberal Federation from 1890 to 1903, served as arbitrator in over one hundred trade disputes in the North of England. In the period after 1886 Lord Rosebery, A. H. D. Acland, and Sidney Buxton were among prominent Liberal practitioners of arbitration.⁵

The practice of Liberals such as Mundella and Morley was

---

¹ *Before the Socialists*, p. 37.
² W. H. G. Armytage, *A. J. Mundella 1825–1897. The Liberal Background to the Labour Movement*, 1951, p. 69.
³ He wrote to R. Leader, 29 October 1871, concerning local Boards of Arbitration: 'Consider the influence of these Associations whenever they are provided. I believe they have more influence in the tranquillity of a district than any legislation we can adopt.' Mundella MSS., folio IX.
⁴ E. Hodder, *The Life of Samuel Morley*, 3rd edition, 1887, p. 359.
⁵ For Watson, Acland, and Buxton, see the articles on them in the *Dictionary of National Biography*. For Rosebery's mediation in the coal strike of 1893, see R. Rhodes James, *Rosebery. A Biography of Archibald Philip, Fifth Earl of Rosebery*, 1963, p. 292.

to associate themselves with Labour as much as possible so as to prevent it from becoming or appearing to be an isolated force. Mundella would attend meetings of the T.U.C. and 'do his duty' and be very pleased to note how much 'more forbearance and moderation' would result. His message to the T.U.C. was that an alliance between labour and capital was a necessity for labour since their own welfare depended on the welfare of capital.[1] Morley insisted strongly on the importance of direct personal contact and 'intimacy between masters and men'.[2] Large employers of labour, he believed, should not 'shut themselves within their own circle' but should 'be willing to hear all that can be said by the advocates of the working class'.[3] Many of these Liberal capitalists in fact made a practice of personally meeting and cultivating the Labour leaders of the day.[4] 'I think it highly desirable', wrote Mundella in 1873, 'that the members of the T.U. Congress should not be left in a state of isolation. At the recent meetings of Nottingham and Leeds they were entertained by the Mayors of those towns, and a considerable number of employers attended the dinner, etc. and gave a moderate tone to their meetings, and deprived them of that exclusive class character which they are too prone to take if left to themselves. I think, moreover, that Liberal and sensible employers should manifest their sympathy with this labour Parliament in all efforts of a reasonable and laudable character tending to improve their class.'[5] When Mundella discovered that the Sheffield middle class was not prepared to display towards the T.U.C. a similar 'kindly feeling', he resolved that, 'rather than it should be wanting' and class antagonisms be hardened as a result, 'poor as I am, I will do it myself. I can give them a breakfast at the Victoria [Hotel] without any very great extravagance.' To middle-class people who were apprehensive of being swamped in any movement that aimed at combining the two classes Mundella would argue that 'the power and influence of men of your class does not consist in *numbers*. Only mix with the people, go amongst them

[1] Mundella to R. Leader, 10 January 1872, 15 October 1874, Mundella MSS., folio IX. Armytage, *Mundella*, p. 111.
[2] Hodder, *Samuel Morley*, p. 397.
[3] Ibid., p. 251.
[4] Harrison, *Before the Socialists*, pp. 38–9, 147. Armytage, *Mundella*, pp. 117, 120.
[5] Mundella to R. Leader, 31 December 1873, Mundella MSS., folio IX.

and gain their confidence, and every one of you counts for a thousand.' Mundella believed that 'the people' could be a political force, and he would draw a contrast between the politics of 'working up some enthusiasm amongst the people' and the politics of 'the separation of classes'. He had faith that the former could be made to predominate over the latter. Not surprisingly, therefore, he was one of the most active and enthusiastic organizers of the Bulgarian agitation from 1876 on. 'I believe in the Democracy', he once wrote. 'The people are less selfish and more open to conviction than interested sections of the Community, whether squires, farmers, parsons, manufacturers or any other select class.'[1] He worked hard during the 1868–74 Liberal government to make the alliance a practical reality, keeping Labour in contact with the government and organizing deputations on industrial matters which contained both leading Liberal employers and workers' delegates.[2] It was his conviction that 'the workmen prefer being led to leading themselves'.[3]

The concept of a balance between capital and labour implied, of course, recognition of Labour as a distinct and even equal force, and there were Liberals, whose economic and political creed was individualistic, who found this very uncongenial.[4] Liberal politicians who were not employers of labour seldom went as far as Mundella and his associates did in making the labour–capital alliance the central fact of their Liberal politics. Furthermore, there was a potential source of difficulty in the idea of a balance in that it did imply the possibility of the adoption by the Liberals of an anti-Labour stance—if they as guardians of the community interest should decide, or the employers on the other side of the balance should claim, that the balance had swung too far in the other direction and needed to be brought back into equilibrium by

[1] Mundella to R. Leader, 2 January 1874, 1 and 3 November 1875, Mundella MSS., folio IX. Mundella to H. J. Wilson, 6 October 1875, H. J. Wilson MSS., Sheffield Univ. Library, Box 2. For a similar expression by John Morley of faith in the influence of middle-class people who mix with the masses, see his article, 'An Address to Some Miners', *Fortnightly Review*, N.S., no. 123 (March 1877), pp. 392–3. Hamer, *John Morley*, p. 79.
[2] Armytage, *Mundella*, pp. 96, 132.
[3] Mundella to H. J. Wilson, 22 March 1878, H. J. Wilson MSS., Sheffield Univ. Library, Box 2.
[4] Hamer, *John Morley*, p. 109.

measures reducing the rights and powers of the trade unions.[1] Another danger threatening Labour's sense of status within Lib-Lab politics was that Labour would interpret as indications of class prejudice and lack of genuine belief in the idea of balance between labour and capital the failure of Liberal politicians to promote reforms that would facilitate the entry of working men into Parliament and of local middle-class-dominated Liberal associations to make candidatures available to working-class Liberals. Labour's status within the Liberal coalition was always insecure. Liberals did not agree among themselves as to what it was, and many feared what it was growing to become during the last quarter of the nineteenth century—a class. Yet to treat Labour merely as a section on a par with temperance reformers became more and more difficult to justify and maintain as the cohesiveness of the working class, the strength and representativeness of its institutions, and its electoral preponderance grew. Liberalism as it had developed in the nineteenth century was founded on the denial of fundamental class division within the industrial community. Liberals shrank now from acknowledging a class. 'Lib-Labism' and the concept of a balanced relationship within an organically unified capitalist system represented stages of Liberal thought and practice that were uneasily and ambiguously suspended between treating 'Labour' as a section and admitting that it must be dealt with as a class. The time would come when Labour itself would demand an end to the ambiguity.

Ambiguity and uncertainty of status, a hovering between integration and independence, also characterized the relationship to the Liberal party of the great national blocs of opinion—the Irish, the Welsh, and the Scots. For, like Labour, none had any hope of attaining on its own a majority in the House of Commons. Permanent minority status could only be overcome by association with that electoral force which was able to gain that majority—the Liberal party. But, as against this fact of practical parliamentary politics, the growth of national consciousness impelled the representatives of the Irish, the Welsh, and, to a much smaller extent, the Scots, to aspire to the status of independence—as the growth of class consciousness was in

[1] See below, p. 225.

time to impel the spokesmen of Labour. In all these cases the tension between the practical necessity of sectional dependence and the emotional impulse towards independence was to grow and to create serious strains within the Liberal coalition. Another complicating factor was that the Welsh and Scots appeared to be strongest within the Liberal movement at the very times when the Liberals did not have power. It was English constituencies which made the crucial difference in elections because the Liberal vote there was so much less solid. The Welsh and Scots had to struggle hard and shout very loudly in order to establish a connection between their loyalty to Liberalism and Liberal possession of power.[1] The 'Celtic Fringe' came to be regarded with some contempt as a phenomenon of opposition.

Even the Irish seemed for a period after 1867 to be just another section in the coalition, though a section that was able to elect its own M.P.s.[2] The Irish had two great strengths as a section. Their distinct geographical base enabled them to secure this direct representation in Parliament, and then after the mid-1870s the growing force of Irish nationalism and the alliance between the parliamentary movement and the Fenians and agrarian radicals gave this representation a strength, permanence, and inner coherence that went far beyond what a section was normally able to develop. Secondly, the Irish Home Rulers also had many supporters—the Irish migrants—scattered over the industrial constituencies of England, Scotland, and Wales who, though in a minority in nearly all these constituencies, if mobilized (as they so effectively were) could be a very powerful sectional influence on Liberal politicians. To all appearances the Irish had become by 1885 a distinct party consisting of a solid bloc of M.P.s welded into unity by Irish national feeling. But, of course, the Irish were not and could not be a parliamentary party of the same kind as the Liberals and Conservatives. As a permanent minority with a very definite limit on their scope for expanding their numbers in Parliament, they were in no position to constitute an alternative government and therefore in order to have any kind of contact with the source of power in the system had to establish a relationship

[1] Cf. Vincent, *Formation of the Liberal Party*, pp. 47–52.
[2] E. R. Norman, *The Catholic Church and Ireland in the Age of Rebellion 1859–1873*, 1965, p. 409. D. Thornley, *Isaac Butt and Home Rule*, 1964, pp. 51, 56–7, 62.

with one of the parties that were in this position. Thus after 1885 the Irish appeared to have returned to the Liberal coalition. What they did constitute was an alternative government to the British authority for Ireland itself, and the consciousness of this status did confer on them a quite unique ability to resist the pressures for integration to which most other sections were in the end obliged to succumb.[1]

'Wales' and 'Scotland' also formed sections within Liberalism and turned it into what Vincent has described as a 'federal alliance'.[2] Welsh and Scottish M.P.s were normally predominantly Liberal. But their influence as representatives of sections within the party tended to be weakened by the conflict between on the one hand the pressure and desire to express a distinctive Welsh or Scottish nationalism and radicalism, and on the other hand the pressure and opportunity, accentuated by personal ambition, to be involved in general Liberal and radical politics. They did not constitute, and did not aspire to constitute, the potential alternative governments of their own countries, and the prospect of the achievement of Welsh or Scottish self-government was remote enough for none of them to be prepared to forgo because of it the attractions of fully integrated political careers within the *British* political system. Under pressure from their constituencies, they did however intensify and complicate the clash of sectionalisms in Liberal politics by promoting particular Welsh and Scottish causes which often had the effect of splitting and thus weakening certain general radical movements, especially those connected with Nonconformity. For example, during this period the general disestablishment agitation was more and more fragmented into particular national agitations. The disestablishment of the Irish Church in 1869 both reflected Gladstone's desire to strengthen the general position of the Establishment by eliminating the indefensible and peripheral anomalies which rendered it vulnerable to criticism, and provided an incentive for Welsh and Scottish Nonconformists to concentrate on the situations in their own

---

[1] For an example of how the Irish were felt to be different from the other sections, see a letter written by H. J. Wilson to his family, 13 January 1886: '*they* are the only set who are really a "party" & a *force*. Other people, Temperance, & Liberationists, &c., including Repealers [of the C.D. Acts], are a rope of sand. There is no cohesion.' H. J. Wilson MSS., Sheffield Central Library, M.D., 2615-4. [2] Vincent, *Formation of the Liberal Party*, p. 47.

countries. This they did with the effect that, given the disproportionate strength of Wales and Scotland in Liberal politics, the general influence of Nonconformity tended to be weakened. For disestablishment was the one absolute overall aim in politics that Nonconformists could still have in common, that could still cohere them. But the temptation to aim first of all at the easier Scottish and Welsh targets was obviously hard to resist. The same thing tended to happen in the sphere of temperance reform with the increased promotion of Welsh and Scottish licensing bills.[1] All Liberal sectional causes naturally depended very heavily on support from the ranks of Welsh and Scottish Liberal M.P.s. Nationalism was a potent force cutting across the involvement of these M.P.s in general sectionalism.

In a study of British Liberalism, Welsh and Scottish Liberalism provide interesting points of contrast. The Liberalism of each country did not in fact constitute a microcosm of the total Liberal position, first because it was not directly related to the achievement and use of governmental power, and secondly because it became the medium for the expression of national feeling which provided a unifying emotionalism such as British Liberalism as a whole seldom enjoyed the advantage of.

Scotland lacked the strong national feeling that suffused Welsh Liberalism. Scottish Liberals played a prominent part in British Liberalism, and no leaders of calibre were willing or available to concentrate on the organization of an effective Scottish section.[2] Scottish Liberalism was itself very sectional and lacking in cohesion: rival party organizations were constantly springing up, and Scottish Liberals were notorious for the large number of surplus candidatures in which they indulged.[3] Intricate ecclesiastical conflicts and tensions disrupted Liberal harmony.[4] It has been suggested that, nevertheless, Scottish

---

[1] Sometimes as a deliberate manœuvre on the part of the leaders. Cf. Campbell-Bannerman to Spencer, 12 December 1899: 'Edward Buxton, Algie West, & Co . . . wd. like us to give up Local Veto. *We cannot do it*: all we can do is to delay or postpone it in England, under cover of passing it for Scotland & Wales.' Spencer MSS., 1899 A–R.
[2] J. G. Kellas, 'The Liberal Party in Scotland, 1876–1895', *Scottish Historical Review*, vol. 44, no. 137 (April 1965), pp. 14–15. Hanham, *Elections and Party Management*, p. 157.
[3] Kellas, 'Liberal Party in Scotland', pp. 8–9.
[4] J. G. Kellas, 'The Liberal Party and the Scottish Church Disestablishment Crisis', *English Historical Review*, vol. 79 (January 1964), pp. 31–45.

Liberals managed to cope with this kind of tangled sectionalism much better than English Liberals did when harassed by sections because large Liberal majorities enabled them to be more relaxed and to tolerate a loose party structure and numerous rival candidatures. The electors could choose between the candidates of the sections, and at the end a Liberal would still win the seat.[1] Certainly, Gladstone was in the habit of treating Scottish parliamentary elections as opinion polls of Liberals.[2] One consequence, however, of this loose order was to reduce the coherence and effectiveness of 'Scotland' as a sectional force within Liberalism. It set the Scots at the opposite pole to the Irish with their tight party control and discipline at both the parliamentary and constituency levels.

In Wales after 1868 there was more and more emphasis on separate Welsh questions. Parts of general issues were detached and agitated about separately. As far as disestablishment was concerned, the Liberation Society opposed this trend, but it was really opposing the force of developing Welsh national feeling, the breaking down of the Welsh Church Establishment being seen as symbolizing the emancipation of Wales from English domination.[3] In 1868 Liberalism in Wales had seemed to be a fully integrated part of general Liberal politics: little reference was made by Welsh Liberals to distinctively Welsh issues.[4] For a while thereafter many Welsh M.P.s favoured a general disestablishment campaign rather than one about the Welsh Church in particular, and the Liberationists who had done so much to develop Liberal electoral organization in Wales seemed 'virtually opposed to recognition of Wales as an entity for separate treatment'.[5] But gradually Liberal politics became the medium for the expression of Welsh nationalism, and disestablishment itself was subsumed in that nationalism, especially as more and more Churchmen became involved and the agitation for it became national rather than denominational.[6]

---

[1] Hanham, *Elections and Party Management*, p. 167.
[2] See below, p. 139.
[3] K. O. Morgan, *Wales in British Politics 1868-1922*, Cardiff, 1963, pp. 66-7.
[4] Ibid., p. 28.
[5] Ibid., pp. 30-1. F. E. Hamer (ed.), *The Personal Papers of Lord Rendel*, 1931, p. 304.
[6] 'We *must* be sure in Wales to render it a Welsh question pure & simple and to deny effectively that it is from our point of view the thin end of the wedge of the Liberation Society.' Stuart Rendel to T. Gee, 16 March 1887, Thomas Gee Papers, N.L.W. MS. 8308 C, p. 257.

In the 1880s 'secular' Liberal organizations were set up in Wales, and 'the Welsh' were now regarded as a distinct section in the parliamentary party. The idea of a completely independent Welsh party naturally had some appeal after 1886, particularly in view of the success of the Irish in getting the Liberal leaders to take up their cause. But the basis of a desire for political separation was lacking. Welsh Home Rule was very weakly supported. Few Welsh Liberal M.P.s would go so far as to demand a complete break with the Liberal party, and so the status of section had to be accepted. The term 'party' was used, but in fact 'party' decisions were not and could not be made binding on Welsh M.P.s. K. O. Morgan observes that the Welsh were really like one of the loose radical groups of the pre-1867 era, 'incoherent in empirical action'.[1] In 1888 at the time when the term 'Welsh party' was beginning to be used quite freely by some Welsh M.P.s John Morley made a comment which very accurately summed up the realities of the situation: 'After all, need we make too much fuss about "Welsh Natl. Party"? They will find us the only people who will touch or look at the things they care for. Why shd. they not be a party, if they like—for their own purposes? Nothing will come of it.'[2] Like other sections, the Welsh came to recognize that, short of a determination, for which feeling in Wales provided no basis, to behave like the Irish and accept frustration in the present for the prospect of power in their own country in the future, they could hope to achieve anything only by remaining within the Liberal coalition for it alone could involve them in majority status.[3] The in-betweenness and ambiguity which the Welsh felt to characterize their political status is well illustrated by a letter written by a leading Welsh Liberal, J. Herbert Lewis, to Tom Ellis when Ellis was making up his mind whether to become one of the Liberal Whips in the House of Commons:

> I feel I dare not advise you. Like yourself, I am in great perplexity. Sometimes I oppose it, sometimes I am in favour of it. I know not what to say.
> ... the great question is—have we most to gain from co-operation, or from independence?

[1] *Wales in British Politics*, pp. 106, 115–16.
[2] J. Morley to Rendel, 27 September 1888, Rendel MSS., 2nd Series, folio 574.
[3] Morgan, *Wales in British Politics*, p. 164.

If the former, will you, as a member of the Ministry, be allowed to preach Welsh Home Rule?[1]

There now remains to be considered the other kind of section—the single-cause movement, the organization of men devoted to the achievement of a certain specific reform or reforms in a certain specific area. To their critics these movements were 'fads' or groups of impractical fanatics; and yet without their existence Liberal politics would have been largely devoid of 'movement' and of vitality. The 'fads' filled an essential function for many Liberals in providing them with the means of giving concrete expression, and bearing practical witness, to their Liberalism. The sections probably made most impact on Liberal politics and were most organically involved in the fabric of Liberal political activity, not because of the cause which they advocated, but because they provided rallying-points for radicals and Liberals who sought some way of 'focalizing' their general political attitudes.[2] Indeed, sections had to make this kind of appeal if they were to have any hope of getting on to their side the support of the majority of Liberals. They had to make their causes symbolic representations of a wide range of Liberal attitudes. In the absence of a generally accepted 'school' or system of Liberal thought and practice each cause attracted Liberals who wanted their Liberalism to be coherent and expressible in some definite form and saw in the specific reform cause the only way of achieving this. The 'faddists' were all Liberals, seeing in their cause a practical application of general Liberal principles and assumptions. To its adherents each particular reform proposal seemed to represent the key that would unlock the door to certain social progress, the means of striking at the root of all social ills, the wedge that would bring down the whole edifice of privilege. Many were Liberals because of their commitment to one or other of these causes; others had moved from a general Liberal position to one that was more particularized and specific. Reform causes were connected with the politics of all Liberal M.P.s, of course, but in widely varying ways. There were those such as Sir Wilfrid Lawson or W. S. Caine or James Stansfeld who devoted themselves to one cause for most of their careers;

[1] 19 May 1892, Ellis MSS., folio 1400.
[2] Cf. Hamer, *John Morley*, pp. 90–2, and *passim*.

there were 'general' Radicals such as John Morley who calculatedly attached their Radicalism to 'single great questions';[1] there were those such as H. J. Wilson or A. J. Mundella or J. E. Ellis who seemed to be involved in nearly every cause.[2] Liberal politicians were often under the strongest sectionalist pressure at the local level, especially when the promoters of a particular cause succeeded in getting control of the party machinery or when some interest or pressure-group—such as the Irish—was well enough organized to represent an electoral force which could not safely be ignored. There were as a result Liberal M.P.s whose support of some particular cause could be directly related to constituency pressures. For example, a major factor in bringing James Stansfeld to devote himself to the cause of repealing the Contagious Diseases Acts would appear to have been the pressure put on him in his Halifax constituency by the anti-C.D. Acts agitators in the early 1870s.[3] Of course, this kind of pressure usually had the effect of crystallizing in one particular commitment Liberal convictions which could just as well have taken half a dozen other different forms at least. Temperance reformers, with their experience of electoral mobilization considerably pre-dating 1867, were well known for their efforts to take over local organizations and restrict Liberal candidatures to sympathizers with their cause.[4] There were two kinds of response favoured by Liberal politicians who wished to protect themselves in such a situation, especially when there were several competing sections. On the one hand, there was the technique of the blanket refusal, based on the belief that safety lay only in refusing to give any pledges or commitments to anyone and elevating this into a constantly reiterated principle. Pledges meant not only trouble in the future for the politician if he found himself unable to fulfil them

---

[1] Ibid.
[2] For a comment by H. J. Wilson on the breadth of his own interests, see his letter to A. J. Mundella, 22 March 1873, H. J. Wilson MSS., Sheffield Univ. Library, Box 1. 'Now it happens I am a full-blown Radical, . . . ready to go any length with any man or party you could wish, and a good deal beyond you in one or two points.' The problem, he wrote, was not 'that we are "men of one idea" as the phrase goes', but that 'in truth we have too many'.
[3] J. L. and B. Hammond, *James Stansfeld, A Victorian Champion of Sex Equality*, 1932, pp. 182–6.
[4] Cf. L. A. Atherley-Jones, *Looking Back, Reminiscences of a Political Career*, 1925, p. 21.

but also the arousing against him of jealousies and resentments from the adherents of those causes to which he had not given any pledge.[1] By contrast, many Liberal M.P.s were in the habit of expressing sympathy in general terms with every cause or even of voting cheerfully in favour of every local-option or disestablishment resolution that came up in the House of Commons.

The problem of sectionalism which so harassed the Liberal leaders stemmed not only from the large number of such reform causes which competed for their attention but also from the tendency of the supporters of each cause to feel convinced that it was the most fundamental and important of all and therefore to be very annoyed and resentful if any other cause was given priority over it. A sectionalist would be even more suspicious if the leaders did nothing at all about his cause. To him the cause represented *true* Liberalism: he had adopted it because this was how he felt about it. Anyone, therefore, who opposed it or did not help to promote it and yet claimed to be a Liberal was showing that there was something false about his Liberalism. We have already seen that many Nonconformists came to feel this about the Liberal leaders in the early 1870s. The basic problem for the Liberal leaders was that people so often were Liberals because they had some sectional enthusiasm, some 'fad' to promote. The party became increasingly dependent on enthusiastic voluntary workers at the constituency level, especially after the 'elimination' of 'corrupt practices' and the defection of so many of its wealthy and socially influential members; and many were prepared to be activists only because of their militant interest in some particular reform that they looked to the party to adopt. Somehow this sectional militancy and enthusiasm had to be harnessed to and made to serve the general Liberal cause but in such a way that in the process the vitality and desire to be active were not drained away.[2] There

---

[1] For examples of politicians who refused pledges, see Colman, *Jeremiah James Colman*, pp. 234, 337–8, 343; E. F. Rathbone, *William Rathbone. A Memoir*, 1905, p. 289; and Mundella to R. Leader, 4 July 1874 [the reference is to pressure from the Irish]: 'I am resolved that no section of my constituents shall ever squeeze me again. I mean to act perfectly square and independent and follow out my own convictions.' Mundella MSS., folio IX.

[2] Cf. Mundella's comments on H. J. Wilson: 'There can be no doubt of the desirability of having Wilson & Co. as friends instead of enemies, for they are indomitable workers, and give time and money without stint to promote anything

had to be some reason why, if the Liberal leaders were not handling his particular cause in the way that he would like it to be handled, a sectionalist would nevertheless feel some attachment to the Liberal party and leadership and some willingness to help them. Establishing such a reason was all the more difficult because there was little tradition of party 'loyalty'. Sectional organizations had been a familiar feature of the political scene for much longer than the Liberal party, and the subsuming of loyalties to them was not an easy process.

The sections and single-cause movements did not fit comfortably into any scheme of general Liberal politics or accommodate themselves easily to the strategies and programmes devised by the Liberal leaders. This was largely because of their tendency to adopt very extreme and absolute positions and their great unwillingness to contemplate any compromise alternative. Discussion of detail, which has to be the basis of any compromise, was entered into very reluctantly, for such discussion, and all the admission of qualifications and blurring of hard lines which would ensue, were very likely to kill off the enthusiasm stemming from direct commitment to simple, clear, moral positions which was the life-blood of the sectional organizations and the basis of their influence within Liberal politics. Internal disagreements, which reduced the strength and effectiveness of a section and provided the party leaders with a reason for not doing anything about its demands, were kept to a minimum, and recruitment of supporters was maximized, by an extreme simplification of aim.

We shall see how difficult the sections made life for Liberal governments. A Liberal legislative programme had to be constructed from the range of reform questions in which members of the party took an interest. In most areas of reform there was at least one organization active, very often more than one. The extremism of the sectionalists, their habitual unreadiness to settle for anything less than one hundred per cent of what they demanded, made accomplishment by Liberal governments of practical reforms in the areas covered by the

they take in hand. If these fiery spirits can be harnessed by our friends, I think we shall manage to hold our own in the Borough.' 'He is a capital fellow *in harness*, and is only dangerous when he has nothing to do.' Mundella to J. D. Leader, 18 January 1874, and to R. Leader, 2 March 1876, Mundella MSS., folio IX.

sections very difficult. Indeed, to try to do anything at all in these areas involved a serious risk of conflict with one or other of the sections which would insist on a great deal more being attempted and try to wreck moderate proposals.[1]

Some Liberals saw a danger that the sectionalists' manipulation of party organization and electoral machinery might cause the leaders to accept and even to put into legislation a reform policy to which public opinion had not yet been converted. The consequences might be not merely embarrassment in then trying to put the new law into effect, but even an electoral rebuff for a party which had thus shown itself to be out of line with public opinion. It was dangerous to let the kind of 'opinion' which the sections represented become through party political processes a substitute for 'educated' and 'matured' public opinion in the devising of reform legislation. Lord Hartington made this point in 1877 when he warned advocates of local option that their main task was to convince the majority of their countrymen. Advocates of this reform must recognize that 'no amount of party pressure, no amount of pledges extracted from their representatives will avail them one iota' until this had been accomplished.

Do you suppose [he asked them] that if by any skilful manipulation—Parliamentary or electioneering manipulation—you were to secure a majority in favour of the Permissive Bill at this time, and if you have not also persuaded the people of the country that such legislation would be for their benefit, do you believe for one moment that the passing of the Permissive Act would be received by the country with that universal acceptance which, I am thankful to say, always characterizes the acceptance of our legislation?[2]

Similar warnings were given to Nonconformist sectionalists by J. Guinness Rogers. Reforms, he told them in 1880, were permanent only if they followed public opinion. 'Those who would pursue a contrary course, and fancy that they can force an unpopular measure on the country by the dexterous management of electoral minorities, forget that any temporary success would produce a reaction which would probably go further than

---

[1] Cf., e.g., Hanham, *Elections and Party Management*, p. 120; Hammond, *James Stansfeld*, p. 174; H. Carter, *The English Temperance Movement: A Study in Objectives*, vol. 1, 1933, pp. 147–63.

[2] Carter, *Temperance Movement*, pp. 195–6.

the undoing of the premature reform they had so unfairly pressed.' Nonconformists must 'understand that they have to convert the nation, not to manage a party'.[1]

Observations of this kind reflect the way in which, as the nature and permanence of the new party system became more evident, the sections came to work much more within the party machinery. This was not, as we shall see, altogether to the good as far as the party was concerned. Hartington and Rogers draw attention to one of the resultant disadvantages of the trend, that it involved a retreat from concentrating on converting public opinion, irrespective of party. The 'conversion' of a party to a particular reform might in fact represent only a very small increase in genuine public conviction in favour of it. One of the great principles of Joseph Chamberlain's reform of party organization was to make party opinion as accurate and full a reflection of public opinion as possible so that the leaders would not be misled by it into taking up reforms which then involved them in great difficulty or unpopularity in the country at large.[2]

As we have already noted in connection with the Nonconformists, all sectionalists had sooner or later to make a choice of tactics. They had to decide whether they could gain their end more quickly and more easily by forcing themselves on the attention of the party and its leaders and making a great nuisance of themselves or by behaving 'loyally' and 'responsibly' and so strengthening the party as a whole. In Parnell's time the Irish could succeed with the former strategy because of their discipline and cohesion. At the other extreme were the 'integrated' sectionalists, those who were clearly aware of the limitations on a section's freedom to manœuvre and shaped their political conduct accordingly. Guinness Rogers is obviously a notable example of this. But undoubtedly the Liberal who most thoroughly, consistently, and clear-sightedly put into practice an understanding of an organic relationship between Liberal sections and Liberal party was Stuart Rendel, the Welsh parliamentary leader of the 1880s and early 1890s. The two great purposes of Rendel's career were the integration of sectional politics into general Liberal politics and the achievement within this basic condition of integration of a particular

[1] *N.C.*, no. 38 (April 1880), pp. 633–4.   [2] See below, pp. 50–1.

sectional aim, in his case Welsh disestablishment. Rendel in his own ideas and practice linked the two worlds of general and sectionalist Liberal politics, and his correspondence represents a very useful commentary on the relationship between them.

Rendel came to constitute such a link because he had not only crossed the boundary between general and sectionalist politics but kept on moving to and fro across it, thus becoming acutely aware, and being constantly reminded as few other Liberals were, of the nature of the connection between them. He was an Englishman, a member of the great armaments firm at Elswick near Newcastle upon Tyne. But in 1880 he became M.P. for Montgomeryshire, and he played a leading role in Welsh politics both in Wales and at Westminster from then until he received a peerage in 1894. He devoted himself to the strengthening of Welsh Liberalism as the vehicle for the expression of Welsh national feeling and took up the cause of Welsh disestablishment, seeing in it the best way of representing or symbolizing this feeling within the general framework of Liberal politics. But, while doing all this, he remained closely connected with *British* Liberalism through his friendship with Gladstone. Frequently he would leave Wales and Welsh politics to visit Gladstone and would report to him what were the desires and attitudes of the Welsh Liberals. Gladstone would then tell Rendel how he saw the position of Welsh disestablishment in relation to the general state of Liberal politics and would instruct him concerning the restrictions on his action in regard to particular sectionalist causes. Rendel would then return to his Welsh colleagues and advise them on their strategy in accordance with the insight which he had gained into the state of Gladstone's mind and the shaping of general Liberal politics. In this way Rendel became, perhaps uniquely, a transmitter of Gladstone's 'sense of measure', an agent for communicating to a section Gladstone's understanding of the relationships that went to make up the organic fabric of Liberal political life. Rendel once referred to himself as being for the Welsh 'an English link with English statesmen'; and his own closest link was with Gladstone.[1]

---

[1] Rendel to Thomas Gee, 26 December 1890, Gee MSS., N.L.W. MS. 8308 C, folio 265. Rendel to A. C. Humphreys-Owen, 13 March 1886, Glansevern Collection, N.L.W.: Letters to Humphreys-Owen, folio 234.

In his correspondence with other Welsh Liberals Rendel constantly wrote of the Welsh M.P.s not as an isolated group but as a section within a much greater whole. Thus, when Welsh Liberals complained that their questions were not being adequately attended to, Rendel would reply that in his opinion they had been fairly treated by the Liberal leaders 'in relation to our numbers & to the numbers behind us and to the steadiness & reliability of the contingent we can offer to the Liberal Army'.[1] Here we see a remarkable assessment of the place of a section within general Liberal politics and of the limitations which that place entails.

The ideal which he always upheld and in relationship to which he wanted Welsh sectionalist behaviour to be determined was that of Liberalism as an organic alliance which could be disrupted by the 'selfish', the exclusively self-regarding, conduct of any one section. This comes out very clearly, for instance, in a letter which he wrote to Thomas Gee at the time of the Parnell divorce crisis in response to a suggestion that the Welsh should use the opportunity of the weakening of the Irish cause to push their own to the front. Such 'selfish' action would, Rendel argued, disintegrate the entire fabric of Liberal political relationships and replace a regime of co-operation by one of rivalry, tension, and frustration for all sections of the party. 'At this moment', he wrote, 'we [the Welsh] have the 3 sister democracies with us. Each of them has its own special grievances and programme. All had agreed to fix to one the 1st place, to another the 2nd place.' For the section which had thus secured through common agreement the second place to rush in 'and openly seek profit for ourselves' out of the difficulties of another section 'would, surely, be as mean & contemptible as it would be injudicious & intemperate'. The result would be to encourage everyone to act selfishly, 'to justify the Irish democracy in forgetting all our services in the past, the English democracy in withdrawing its vy serious & unselfish liability to us, and the Scotch in claiming priority over us'.[2] In other words, a minority section had to recognize that the achievement of its goal was very greatly dependent on the maintenance of the principle

[1] Rendel to A. C. Humphreys-Owen, 21 July 1888, Glansevern Collection: Letters to Humphreys-Owen, folio 402.
[2] 26 December 1890, Gee MSS., N.L.W. MS. 8308 C, folio 265.

of unselfishness in Liberal politics. Another principle of sectional behaviour on which Rendel always insisted was that a section must at all costs avoid setting itself up in rivalry to, or antagonizing, another section. He would warn his colleagues of the folly of 'running Welsh Disestnt. against Scotch Disestnt'. This would create the kind of atmosphere in Liberal politics in general which could only harm the long-term prospects for the accomplishment of Welsh disestablishment itself.[1] One sectional cause should be kept entirely clear of another—Welsh disestablishment and the activities of the Liberation Society, for example.[2]

Rendel saw his own task as the construction of an organic and fruitful relationship with the Liberal party itself. When in the early 1890s younger Welsh Liberals such as Lloyd George began to behave 'selfishly' and think only of Wales without any concern for the effect of their conduct on Liberal politics in general, he was in despair. 'It is sad for me', he wrote, 'to see my laboriously built up house tumbling down like a pack of cards.'[3]

Rendel's strategy was founded on an awareness of the limitations of sectional action. 'The real & only question' he defined as the impossibility of Wales venturing 'to say like Italy "Italia fara da se"' or trying to 'accomplish alone & unaided & in defiance of her friends as well as of her opponents her own deliverance'.[4] It was, he told Welsh M.P.s, 'idle to talk of carrying our measure by our own strength, or in any other way than by securing the whole force of the English Liberal party'.[5] That being so, the interests of the Welsh would best be served by striving at all times to keep that force on which they were dependent 'whole'. They must do nothing whatever to embarrass the Liberal party or weaken its capacity to maintain and develop its total strength. One of his main aims in openly and with as much publicity as possible severing the links

[1] Rendel to A. C. Humphreys-Owen, 16 October 1890, Glansevern Collection: Letters to Humphreys-Owen, folio 499.
[2] Rendel to A. C. Humphreys-Owen, 22, 23, February 1891, Glansevern Collection: Letters to Humphreys-Owen, folios 523–4.
[3] Rendel to A. C. Humphreys-Owen, 28 May 1892, Glansevern Collection: Letters to Humphreys-Owen, folio 593.
[4] Rendel to Gee, 26 December 1890, N.L.W. MS. 8308 C, folio 265.
[5] 12 March 1887, Rendel MSS., N.L.W. MS. 19458 E.

between Welsh disestablishment and the Liberation Society was to ensure that the Welsh agitation would not damage the Liberal party by stirring up the much more formidable and complicated issue of disestablishment in England itself.[1] It is significant that this attitude to Welsh tactics was shared by another Englishman who represented a Welsh constituency, William Rathbone, the Liverpool merchant and philanthropist who, after representing Liverpool in the 1870s, became M.P. for Caernarvonshire in 1880. Rathbone wrote to Rendel that the Welsh must take care not to do anything which would 'have the effect of irritating & weakening the Liberal party on whose strength & cordial assistance we can alone reckon to carry Welsh Disestablishment'.[2]

Because the Welsh were so dependent on the Liberal party, they had to cultivate and help and appeal to it. Intimidation and rebelliousness were futile tactics because they had the effect of disrupting and making less coherent and therefore less effective the general Liberal political strength. Instead Wales must act so as to 'invite the confidence of the Liberal Party'. 'It is for Welsh Liberalism', Rendel wrote, 'to shew that the Liberal Party can safely do business with it.'[3] Rendel consistently deprecated 'throwing doubt on the pledges of the Liberal Leaders & Liberal Organization'.[4] It was for the Welsh to show themselves worthy of Liberal aid, not for the Liberal leaders to be expected constantly to conform to the demands of that or any other section. It was the difference between giving practical effect to an ideal of harmony and organic unity within which the advance of the whole would mean also and naturally the advance of the particular units in that whole, and creating a regime of selfishness and anarchy within which no section would be able to get what it desired because of the collapse of that general force on which such an accomplishment had to depend.

[1] Rendel to Gee, 16 March 1887, Gee MSS., N.L.W. MS. 8308 C, folio 257. Rendel to A. C. Humphreys-Owen, 21 July 1888, 27 November 1889, Glansevern Collection: Letters to Humphreys-Owen, folios 402, 474.
[2] 23 August 1893, Rendel MSS., N.L.W. MS. 19454 E, folio 467.
[3] Rendel to A. C. Humphreys-Owen, 21 July 1888, Glansevern Collection: Letters to Humphreys-Owen, folio 402.
[4] Rendel to A. C. Humphreys-Owen, 9 January 1890, Glansevern Collection: Letters to Humphreys-Owen, folio 478.

II Liberalism and Radicalism 1867–1877

WHEN Gladstone took office after the general election of 1868, he referred to 'the moral union of the majority' which that election had produced for the Liberal party.[1] The contrast with the state of the party before the election was certainly startling. In the Reform Bill debates of 1865–7 the Liberals had been outmanœuvred repeatedly, and the leaders had seemed incapable of exercising control over their 'followers'. Disraeli's tactics had skilfully exploited and intensified the divisions in the Whig-Liberal ranks, to such an extent indeed that the prospect of a stable tenure of power by the Liberals for any period of time must have seemed remote.[2] Why was it that the election wrought such a dramatic change? One of the main reasons was Gladstone's success in gaining a new kind of power based on a direct relationship with the electorate which then disciplined the House of Commons in a way that mere arts of parliamentary management had never been able to achieve.[3] Before the election the Duke of Argyll had sensed what was about to happen when he noted that, although the party was at that time 'disorganized' and thoroughly estranged from Gladstone, there would be 'a great change in the new Parliament'. For not only would the 'disorganizing influence' of the Reform question be abated, but there would also be felt the effect of Gladstone's 'hold over the country', which was 'a very different thing' from his hold over 'the present House of Com-

[1] Gladstone to Granville, 18 July 1869, Ramm, *1868–1876*, i, p. 36.
[2] Cf. M. Cowling, *1867 Disraeli, Gladstone and Revolution. The Passing of the Second Reform Bill*, Cambridge, 1967, *passim*.
[3] John Vincent, discussing the careers of Palmerston and Russell, remarks on 'the difficulty of controlling a Parliamentary party on the basis of Parliamentary support alone', and then observes that 'Gladstone made a synthesis by using his standing with the electorate to control and guide the Parliamentary party from inside'. *Formation of the Liberal Party*, p. 142.

mons'.[1] In the election Gladstone's 'hold over the country' was a powerful factor, and the focusing of Liberal electoral efforts on his political personality[2] and the way in which candidates identified themselves as 'supporters of Mr. Gladstone' forged a 'moral union' in the party at the opening of the new Parliament.

Gladstone was clearly anxious that the Liberal leaders should not risk the loss of this asset and a return to the anarchical situation of 1866–7 by, for example, making excessively large concessions to the Tories for the sake of achieving a settlement of major issues—concessions which the Tories' control over the House of Lords threatened to make a frequent practical necessity. Thus he wrote in 1869 concerning the Irish Church Bill: 'I take it for granted we do not mean to carry this Bill against our friends by the votes of our opponents. That is an alternative quite possible, but plainly I think to be rejected.'[3] And yet a year later this was the course which he found his government following over the Education Bill. By late 1871 John Bright was sending him this warning: 'The Reform Govt. of 1832 went to ruin by trying to please or placate its enemies; the Education Bill has pleased the Church, but the Church will not maintain the Govt.'[4] For in the Education Bill the government had aimed at securing a stable, durable settlement of the education question, and this alienated the Nonconformist militants who found distasteful the compromises with existing educational arrangements which such a settlement had to entail. The Liberal leaders were anxious to conciliate the Nonconformists[5] but they did not go nearly far enough. To many Nonconformists the Liberal leaders' behaviour seemed to offer ample grounds for genuine indignation and accusations of 'betrayal'. The refusal of W. E. Forster and his colleagues to make their policy conform to the views and wishes of their most militant

[1] The Eighth Duke of Argyll, *Autobiography and Memoirs*, vol. ii, 1906, p. 241. Cf. also Gladstone to Lord John Russell, 2 November 1867, G. P. Gooch (ed.), *The Later Correspondence of Lord John Russell, 1840–1878*, vol. ii, 1925, pp. 362–3.

[2] A. F. Thompson, 'Gladstone's Whips and the General Election of 1868', *The English Historical Review*, vol. 63 (1948), pp. 189–90, 197. Thompson stresses the contrast with the undisciplined situation in the party in 1867.

[3] Gladstone to Granville, 18 July 1869, Ramm, *1868–1876*, i, pp. 35–6.

[4] Bright to Gladstone, 24 November 1871, Gladstone MSS., B.M. Add. MS. 44112, folio 194.

[5] Cf. T. Wemyss Reid, *Life of the Right Honourable William Edward Forster*, 4th edition, 1889, p. 277.

party supporters was a cause of great surprise and incomprehension. But this very lack of understanding reveals to us what was the fundamental reason for the refusal and for the clash between Liberal government and Liberals in the country—that all were affected by a very new and as yet unanalysed political phenomenon.

Like all governments henceforward—except for coalition governments produced by agreement and intrigue among politicians of various parties—the Liberal government of 1868-74 had a dual basis to its existence and purpose. It consisted of the leaders of a party who had been placed in office not by that party but by the votes of the electorate. It had acquired power because many voters who were not members or active supporters of the Liberal party had nevertheless expressed a wish to see the leaders of that party in control of the government. It was almost inevitable that at times there would be conflict between these two ingredients in the government's identity—its party 'colour' and the broader national source of its governmental authority. For stemming from this duality were two alternative ways of handling a major policy issue. On the one hand the government could aim primarily at a national settlement which would have to involve compromises and modifications to conciliate non-party interests and viewpoints. This is what happened with the Education Bill. On the other hand, the legislation could be devised primarily to meet the views of party members or of the section within the party which was particularly interested in the question. The former kind of settlement obviously had a greater chance of gaining general acceptance and of being reasonably stable and durable. But there was also the risk that it would upset the Liberal activists and thus weaken the party both internally and in its impact on the electoral community with not so much voluntary party work being undertaken and a bad 'image' of discord being created. As we shall see, in nearly every reform undertaken henceforth by the Liberal leaders a calculation had to be made between party and what might be called 'consensus' interests, and very seldom could the balance be made so even that no adverse reaction was provoked from either party or electorate.

The 1868-74 government made serious attempts at legislation

in numerous areas of reform, and a high proportion of these aroused anger and vigorous and often obstructive opposition from the sections whose 'causes' were involved. Besides the Education Bill and the Nonconformist agitation that that stirred up, there was conflict with the Irish over the Irish University question, with the United Kingdom Alliance over Bruce's Licensing Bill, and with the agitators for the repeal of the Contagious Diseases Acts. Why was it that nevertheless this was such a successful government, the most successful of Gladstone's four administrations in terms of legislative achievement? One reason may be found in the very obstructiveness and hostility of the sections in so far as these can be taken as indicating that their relationship to the Liberal party was still to some extent an external one. The sections were not yet as fully integrated into Liberal politics as they were to be at the time of Gladstone's later administrations, and therefore conflict between them and the Liberal leadership did not have quite the character of *internal* disorganization that it was felt to have in the 1890s, for example. In the 1868–74 administration the process of the formation of the Liberal party had been so recently completed and the pattern of relations between sections and party was as yet so unformed that the Liberal leaders were not so inhibited as they were later to be in the shaping of their legislative programme by consideration of the need to satisfy 'the party' and the sections. Furthermore, a high proportion of the leaders were still either Whig aristocrats or Peelites and others who had been accustomed to govern in circumstances where their own estimation of the national interest was the primary factor and governmental action was not expected to be directed 'from below'.

It could also be argued that the 1868–74 government was successful because there was a theme underlying its work, the theme of 'liberation' and the curbing of privilege, which unified, inspired, and directed. In the 1880s and 1890s Gladstone was to look back to this uncomplicated 'era of liberation' in reform politics and to contrast it with the era of confusion and empiricism which had followed.[1] The mood was set and a 'moral union' created by the Irish Church campaign of 1868 which satisfied vicariously so many different interests and

[1] See below, pp. 218–19.

viewpoints and served as a symbol of emancipation. Also important was the long period before 1868 of preparation of the reforms which this government undertook. Reform of the civil service, especially of recruitment to it, reform of the organization and staffing of the British army, elimination of the more anomalous and less defensible aspects of the Anglican Establishment—these and much else had been planned and debated since at least the early 1850s and notably during the period of the Crimean War, that great catalyst for the formation of criticisms of rule by aristocracy.[1] In addition, the great Reform Bill controversy of 1865-7 had stimulated thinking on the uses of the vote and the implications of an extended franchise. The way in which this was seen as producing definite ideas about practical reforms was and is reflected in the widespread acceptance of Robert Lowe's alleged statement that 'we must educate our masters' as indicating the basic inspiration of the Education Act. The contrast between this preparation of ideas and policies and the situation in 1880, for example, when Gladstone took office for the second time, is very striking.

Our study of the Liberal party in the years between 1874 and 1906 will show how necessary it is for the leaders of a party, if they are to retain reasonably effective control of the political situations within which they have to operate, to try to prepare the future, to discern what large issues are coming up and plan responses to them, or to decide what questions they think should be prominent and then prepare opinion on them so that they will be. The experience of the Liberal leaders was often to illustrate the danger of a policy vacuum, of having no means of checking the accelerating momentum of drift and disorganization caused by the pressure of sudden crises and demands for action when they were in office.

The decline and fall of the government of 1868-74 were seen as involving a crisis in the relations between the leaders and the party. The great issue for Liberals in the next few years was the establishment of some kind of organic and stable relationship. What we have now to examine are the various solutions which were thought of for this problem. We must, however, bear in

[1] A. Briggs, *The Age of Improvement 1783-1867*, 1959, pp. 433-4. O. Anderson, *A Liberal State at War. English Politics and Economics During the Crimean War*, 1967, Parts i and ii.

mind that there were two different meanings to the term 'the party' and the role of the leaders was not the same in relation to each. On the one hand, there was the parliamentary party, the Liberal M.P.s among whom the leaders worked and on whom their voting power depended. But on the other hand, there was the Liberal party 'in the country' which acquired a more and more definite form during the 1870s with the establishment of local Liberal 'caucuses' and the foundation of the National Liberal Federation in 1877. The question of the exact relationship of the leaders of the parliamentary party to this other Liberal 'party' was to be the subject of much controversy in the next thirty years.

After the election defeat of 1874 the condition of the Liberal party in the House of Commons seemed to the party leaders to be little better than 'anarchical', and they felt themselves incapable of establishing any meaningful control over it. Goschen commented on the parliamentary session of 1874 that, if the leaders did not 'settle the direction to be given to a debate on a given question', they 'were accused of neglecting [their] duty', of effacing themselves; but, if they did try to give a lead, they then were 'taunted' with 'attempting to lead where we had no authority'.[1] Many of the Liberal leaders believed that leadership should do no more than reflect the condition of the party. If the party was in a state of confusion and indiscipline, leadership should be 'light and negative' until such time as order re-emerged in the party itself.[2] Lord Hartington took repudiation of positive leadership to an extreme when on Gladstone's retirement in 1875 he proposed that the real state of Liberal politics be recognized in a new arrangement of three leaders—Whig, Radical, and Irish—instead of one.[3] An alternative approach to the problem of Liberal disorganization was that of Sir William Harcourt who argued that, if the leaders recommended a definite course to the party, and did so 'with decision', 'I believe it would be accepted cheerfully'.[4] The effect

[1] Goschen to Granville, 5 January 1875, Lord E. Fitzmaurice, *The Life of Granville George Leveson Gower, Second Earl Granville K.G. 1815–1891*, 2nd edition, vol. ii, 1905, p. 138.
[2] See below, pp. 60–1.
[3] Hartington to Granville, 21 January 1875, Fitzmaurice, *Granville*, ii, p. 150.
[4] B. Holland, *The Life of Spencer Compton, Eighth Duke of Devonshire*, vol. i, 1911, p. 142.

of negative leadership was felt to be that party action became dictated and policy moulded by the unco-ordinated initiatives taken by individuals and groups within the party. In April 1878 Lord Granville wondered whether anything could be done about a state of things in the House of Commons whereby, after 'the ex-officials' had decided, and Gladstone had advised, against a Liberal amendment on a particular issue, 'a crotchetty member' could nevertheless sponsor one himself and thus compel other Liberals to '*vote*, some one way, some another'. This kind of incident was 'destructive to the unity and influence of a party'.[1] Hartington, who led the party in the Commons from 1875 to 1880, would occasionally rebuke private Members for bringing forward motions without consulting the leaders, thus prejudicing their actions.[2]

Leadership alone could hardly be relied upon as a means of establishing order and discipline in Liberal politics. Strong leadership depended on the leaders having confidence in themselves and having some clear understanding of the purpose of their action. What was needed most of all was obviously some general philosophy or system of Liberal politics that most Liberals would accept as relevant to contemporary political circumstances and as a guide for their own political practice. In so far as they were a party of reform, Liberals needed to possess some common understanding as to the nature of the 'improvement' and 'progress' that they were to work to promote. Within such an over-all understanding leaders would lead and followers would follow, associated in a common purpose and organic unity of action. But no single system of Liberal politics was now available to fill this role. There were numerous different

[1] Granville to Gladstone, 9, 11 April 1878, Ramm, *1876–1886*, i, pp. 69–70. Cf. A. J. Mundella's account of what happened after the 'crotchetty individual', Sir Wilfrid Lawson, put his amendment on the notice paper: 'The Radicals felt that if they refused to vote they would be charged with cowardice, especially as, in a two night's discussion, not one in ten would get the chance of speaking. So we voted, Gladstone and Bright voting with us, Hartington and the rest infinitely disgusted at the want of reason and discipline in our ranks. All this is very sickening, and makes great demands on our faith and patience.' Mundella to J. D. Leader, 14 April 1878, Mundella MSS., folio IX. Mundella was one of those Liberals who became very ready to accept whatever line the leaders decided to recommend. See below, p. 76.

[2] e.g. Hartington to P. Rylands, 14 April 1879, L. G. Rylands, *Correspondence and Speeches of Mr Peter Rylands, M.P. With a Sketch of his Career*, vol. i, 1890, p. 273.

'schools of thought' and ideas as to where and by what means 'progress' should now be sought, but Liberalism now no longer possessed a coherent and unifying, because generally accepted, ideological base. What we are to analyse in this book are the various substitutes for 'system' which were offered and to which Liberals had recourse in their quest for order and cohesion in their politics.[1]

For Radicals in particular a basic problem was the absence of any system of principles such as was believed to have guided, and bestowed practical effectiveness on, previous generations of Radicals, for example, the Benthamites and the Manchester School. John Morley, chief ideologue of the 'general' Radicals, that is those who wanted a Radicalism broad and general enough to sustain a Radical party and a Radical government, often lamented the lack of a 'system' relevant to the issues of his own time.[2] These Radicals sought in the disunity and fragmentation of Radicalism and the excessive individualism of both its theory and its practice the reason why, instead of triumphing after 1867, as had been widely predicted—and feared—Radicalism remained so weak and ineffective. Joseph Chamberlain in particular felt that effective Radicalism could only be concentrated and unified Radicalism and that power for Radicals such as himself would depend on finding some means of creating this concentration.[3] The problem as he saw it was that there were 'only individual Radicals, each specially interested in some part of the whole, but with no connected organization or idea of united action'. Chamberlain's ambition was to create a general Radicalism, to 'choose out the most important of all the questions debated' by the 'individual Radicals' and 'weld them into a connected scheme'. It was his belief that, until this were done, Radicals would continue to make little impression because each was advocating 'some favourite reform' and so their agitation lacked 'uniformity or consistency'.[4]

---

[1] For the idea of the 'substitute for system', see the fuller discussion in Hamer, *John Morley*, pp. 86–93.
[2] Ibid., p. 64.
[3] H. W. Lucy (ed.), *Speeches of the Right Hon. Joseph Chamberlain, M.P. With a Sketch of his Life*, 1885, p. 74.
[4] Garvin, *Chamberlain*, i, p. 161. J. Chamberlain, 'A New Political Organization', *F.R.*, N.S., no. 127 (July 1877), p. 127; 'The Caucus', *F.R.*, N.S., no. 143 (November 1878), p. 737.

There was clearly a need for some principle or policy or creed that would provide a means of focusing and cohering Radical politics.

The cohering factor, the substitute for system, most often favoured and resorted to by Liberals was some single issue or cause around which the diverse elements in Liberal politics would be induced to rally by being persuaded that it was of such overriding importance that their own various interests ought to be subordinated to it. The most serviceable kind of single issue—and one which we shall encounter frequently in this study—was one that involved reform of Parliament or of some other part of the political machinery or arrangements of the country. For Liberals and Radicals were most likely to agree to work together for a single cause if that cause could be interpreted as improving the machinery through which every reform in which they had a special interest would have to be secured. For instance, one finds Sir Charles Dilke writing to a Radical colleague in 1871 about the question of parliamentary reform that people who urged that other questions ought to be settled first should be told that 'to try to do so is to try & put cart before horse': 'we are being destroyed on every kind of question because of the falsity of representation.'[1] We shall see this emphasis on the improvement of political machinery in connection with such major issues as the extension of the franchise, Home Rule for Ireland, the House of Lords, and even imperialism. Co-operation was much less easy to obtain if what was being proposed was some particular *use* of the machinery, for Liberals and Radicals had many different such uses to promote, and there were widely differing views as to which should get priority.

Sometimes general unification of reform politics was sought by Radicals through 'adoption' of one of the sectional interests or causes. Normally such causes were too narrow to be the

---

[1] 'For instance [he goes on] the minority in Fowler's division on the Contagious diseases acts; the minority on the Lords Amendments to the Trades Unions Bill, & the minority on the Election expenses clause of the ballot bill represented as I am prepared to prove the *majority* of voters in each case.' Dilke to Mundella [September 1871], Mundella MSS., folio II. Mundella argues in the same way for the primacy of parliamentary reform over particular sectional causes in letters to H. J. Wilson, 21 March 1873, and 6 October 1875, H. J. Wilson MSS., Sheffield University Library, Boxes 1 and 2.

basis of a general Radicalism—unless it was possible to develop them as focuses. Radicals were in fact often attracted to particular questions not so much on account of their merits as because of the potential felt to be in them as focusing areas for Radical political activity. For each sectional cause was potentially a substitute for system, having, after all, attracted people who continued to regard themselves as Liberals, because it seemed to them to represent particularly well the essential Liberal principles. The model for such a concentrating movement was the Anti-Corn Law League which not only had unified Radicalism very well in the 1840s after a period of great confusion and individualistic conduct but had been intended by some of its promoters, notably Cobden, to have this effect. The campaign against the Corn Laws was seen both as an important cause in itself and as a means of cohering and disciplining the Radicalism of the day. Cobden himself chose this issue to concentrate on partly because it seemed the best available focus for Radical politics.[1] He had maintained that 'the English people cannot be made to take up more than one question at a time with enthusiasm';[2] and the success of the League had a powerful effect in establishing this 'one great question' tradition among Liberal politicians.[3] Cobden and his colleagues opposed the programme-favouring Radicals of the time the dispersive effect of whose simultaneous pursuit of several questions they deplored.[4] Attitudes of this kind towards the form of political action reappear very strongly in the political thought and practice of Cobden's biographer, John Morley. Indeed, much of Morley's career was to involve the search for, and selection of, particular reform questions on the basis of their being potential unifying influences in Liberal politics.

Might some reform movement once again become a rallying-point for various kinds of Radicals and thus provide the coherence which alone could make Radicalism an effective force? Just as Cobden had discarded the question of the secret ballot for the repeal of the Corn Laws in his search for such a rallying-point, so Chamberlain and other Radicals were in the 1870s

[1] N. McCord, *The Anti-Corn Law League 1838–1846*, 1958, pp. 16–20.
[2] Ibid., p. 20.
[3] Hamer, *John Morley*, pp. 94–5. D. A. Hamer, 'The Irish Question and Liberal Politics, 1886–1894', *Historical Journal*, vol. 12, no. 3 (1969), p. 518.
[4] McCord, *Anti-Corn Law League*, p. 17.

to try one question after another to see whether they could be a focus for Radicals. They tried to generalize and widen each question. One of the main difficulties, as always, was to find a question which would be accepted by persons interested in other questions as meriting priority of attention. For a while Chamberlain believed that one of the Nonconformist 'causes', 'national education' or disestablishment, might provide a focus for the formation of a more general Radicalism. Writing in October 1874 about the problem of 'the prominence of special questions' in the elections of 1874, he pointed out that when at an election there was a 'larger issue' the voices of the sectionalists were silent—as, for instance, in 1868 when 'the question on which the verdict of the electors was wanted was felt to be of sufficient magnitude to justify the postponement of all minor subjects'. What was now necessary, therefore, was that once again one of 'the many practical applications of Liberal principles' should 'be selected as the next rallying cry of the Liberal party'. His own choice was disestablishment, the 'only one great question of immediate interest to Radical politicians on which the party may be summoned to unite or to re-form'. It should be 'the first article of the new Liberal programme'.[1] Chamberlain and John Morley hoped to make the agitations for 'national education' and disestablishment as comprehensive as possible, appealing to a very wide range of Liberal opinion. But eventually they had to conclude that neither 'cause' had, or could develop, a wide enough base. The crucial new feature in the situation was, as Chamberlain appreciated, that a Radical movement had to appeal to working men if it was to have any hope of gaining real electoral strength.[2] Some Labour leaders did associate themselves with the National Education League;[3] but in the main it was an agitation of middle-class people, and there was considerable feeling among them against making any particular appeal to working men.[4] Chamberlain

[1] Chamberlain, 'The Next Page of the Liberal Programme', *F.R.*, N.S., no. 94 (October 1874), pp. 413, 418, 420–2.
[2] Chamberlain, 'The Liberal Party and its Leaders', *F.R.*, N.S., no. 81 (September 1873), p. 293. Garvin, *Chamberlain*, i, p. 146.
[3] Herrick, 'Origins of the National Liberal Federation', p. 123.
[4] Hamer, *John Morley*, p. 109. A. T. Bassett, *The Life of the Rt. Hon. John Edward Ellis, M.P.*, 1914, p. 30. The same is true of the Liberation Society. For the involvement of working men in its agitation and the extreme unwillingness of middle-class Nonconformists to welcome or encourage this, see Ingham, 'The Disestablishment

looked for something wider than the League when he appreciated how little working-class involvement there was in its campaign, and for a time he believed that disestablishment could be made into a cause that would attract working men. But it too soon came to appear irredeemably narrow and sectional.¹

In fact, this interest in a single question as the means of unifying Radicalism was not typical of Chamberlain. Fundamentally he was a 'programme' politician, and for most of his career he acted as such. In other words, he usually advocated a reform programme as the best mode of Radical action. He believed that Liberal and Radical politics could and should be about the simultaneous promotion and agitation of numerous reform topics. This confidence as to the efficacy of 'programme' politics he may well have derived from the political atmosphere of Birmingham where there was such a strong unifying sense of community and 'democracy'; and it may have been reinforced by his own experience as Mayor of Birmingham in successfully putting through a large programme of municipal reforms. His first major programme appeared in 1872-3 when he took up several issues and presented them as connected through a general theme of opposition to class privilege: 'Free Land', 'Free Church', 'Free Labour', and 'Free Schools'. He declined at first to single out any one as the most important.² Although after the débâcle of 1874 he did veer towards concentrating on 'Free Church', he remained aware of the inadequate and increasingly anachronistic nature of the 'single question' approach to organizing reform politics. The Anti-Corn Law League was not so suitable as a model for Radical agitation in an era when power depended on association with a party that aspired to the attainment of a parliamentary majority. Such a party had to operate beyond the confines of a single question

Movement', pp. 47–50. Cf. Chamberlain's approach: '. . . as to the "respectables" I neither expect nor want their aid. I am a working man's representative, if I am anything, & it is to ensure fair consideration for their claims* that I chiefly care to enter Parliament. . . . *as to all questions—not merely on special labour legislation.' Chamberlain to H. J. Wilson, 25 December [1873], H. J. Wilson MSS., Sheffield University Library, Box 1.

¹ Chamberlain, 'The Next Page of the Liberal Programme', pp. 422–7. Hamer, *John Morley*, pp. 109–11.

² Chamberlain, 'The Liberal Party and its Leaders', pp. 294–300. P. Fraser, *Joseph Chamberlain Radicalism and Empire, 1868–1914*, 1966, pp. 12–13.

in order to build up majority support. It had to contain and appeal to numerous sections and minorities and could not afford to be itself exclusively identified with just one of these.

Chamberlain was interested in power. His rejection of the 'single question' mode of concentrating and organizing Radical political activity was related to a growing awareness of the need to make both the form and the content of that activity appropriate to the changed nature of the parliamentary system. The organizational form of the National Education League, deriving from the pre-1867 era, was replaced under his influence after 1874 by the new programmatic and 'democratic' form of Radical organization, the National Liberal Federation.

The National Liberal Federation, as organized in 1877, was Chamberlain's answer to the problem of avoiding disorder and incoherence in programmatic Radical politics. Its purpose was to provide an institutional umbrella within which priorities could be fixed among the numerous reform questions of the day. At the outset one of the aims of the Federation was stated to be 'to aid in concentrating upon the promotion of reforms found to be generally desired the whole force, strength, and resources of the Liberal party'. Under its auspices would occur 'the selection of those particular measures of reform and of progress to which priority shall be given'.[1]

It would be able to fulfil this function because it would incorporate within itself, and allow full expression to be given to, the spirit of the new 'democratic' age. The ideal on which both the local Liberal 'caucuses' of this period and the N.L.F. were based was that of securing the institutionalized expression of the will of the majority. Thus unity would be secured by a transcending of the Radicalism of particular reform causes that appealed only to minorities. The broad aim was to create a new kind of Liberal politics relevant to a new era, what might be called 'majority Liberalism', with the old reformism of minority interests subordinated and controlled. The 'caucuses' —which were federated in the N.L.F.—were designed to create a majority feeling or will that would override the activities of the 'crotchet-mongers'. Francis Schnadhorst wrote of them as courts of appeal for M.P.s who were 'worried by crotchety

---

[1] Hanham, *Elections and Party Management*, p. 138.

individuals' and harassed by 'attempts at dictation' by 'cliques'.[1]

Chamberlain was very confident that a coherent majority will could be arrived at in such organizations and could thus enable Radicalism to become at last really practical and effective. The source of this confidence was obviously Birmingham where 'democracy as an organized whole' had long been felt by Liberals to be a political reality.[2] In defending the 'caucus' Chamberlain defined his aim as to ensure 'that the will of the people should find fuller, more adequate, more effective expression in the legislation of the country'. The basis of his creed was the assumption that 'the force of democracy' and 'the will of the people' really did exist and could be made supreme in the political life of the nation.[3] The application of the democratic principle—that the majority should rule— would not merely be a convenient way of developing order in Radical and Liberal politics; it would also give a moral unity to Radicalism and make it conform to the spirit of the post-1867 political system. The N.L.F. was to select for prior attention and recommend to the party leaders those questions which, after their advocates and the advocates of other questions had been listened to and all the questions had been discussed, the majority decided were ripe for action. The sections and the reform groups were told that their task was to convince the majority that their questions deserved to be placed in this category. Those who failed to do so must abide by the will of the majority but were at liberty to continue working to change it. In this way the anti-Whig attitude of the leaders of the N.L.F. was consistent with their basic political principles, for the Whigs were opposed as a minority section who tried by the use of non-democratic political influence and without the support of the majority of Liberals to control the party. Chamberlain wrote that the 'caucus' system was 'designed to relieve majorities from the disabilities under which they have so long laboured' and to end the power that minorities had hitherto had in 'determining the course of English politics'.[4] Addressing

[1] Ibid., p. 133. F. Schnadhorst, 'The Caucus and its Critics', *The Nineteenth Century*, no. 65 (July 1882), p. 24.
[2] Briggs, *Victorian Cities*, Chapter 5.
[3] Lucy, *Speeches of Joseph Chamberlain*, p. 74.
[4] Chamberlain, 'The Caucus', pp. 726-7.

the 1880 N.L.F. Council, he told the sectionalists in the party that their proper role was to 'maintain your several opinions and claim full liberty to discuss them, and if possible to convert a majority to them'. What was not tolerable was insisting on the immediate adoption of these opinions as 'an indispensable point in your programme', irrespective of whether or not this conversion had taken place. The decision of the majority as to which reforms were to be taken up first must be accepted.[1] In return what was offered to the sections? Nothing less than the prospect of what the advent of a two-party alternative-government system seemed to be rendering so difficult—the attaching to a minority cause of the support of the democratic majority.[2]

But how was the will of the majority to be arrived at, and how were minorities to be persuaded to accept and recognize and subordinate themselves to it? The answer was found in the classic liberal ideal, the faith that out of the free play of ideas and opinions, out of free and open discussion with all points of view being expressed and heard, order and agreement and a sense of 'truth' would organically emerge. A consensus would impress itself on all who participated in the debate, so long as that debate was completely open. The sections, being involved in this free play of ideas and opinions, would feel part of the organic ordering that would emerge from it and would voluntarily defer to the consensus of opinion. This was the ideal that was again and again held before the N.L.F. by its organizers. Through it would develop what Chamberlain referred to as a system of 'perfect loyalty' in which all would respect one basic principle: 'each to do whatever the others think best'.[3] Chamberlain argued that divisions in the party were most effectively prevented, 'not by stifling the expression of opinion, but by courting it, and by convincing every individual member of the party of the openness and fairness of the process by which

[1] *N.L.F. Report 1880*, p. 17.
[2] Thus at the inaugural conference of the N.L.F. William Harris drew a contrast between 'arousing special political agitations for every political subject', e.g. the Education League, the Reform Union, the Liberation Society, and the Land Reform Association, and forming 'a general political organisation', 'a federation which, by collecting together the opinions of the majority of the people in all the great centres of political activity, should be able to speak on whatever questions arose with the full authority of the national voice'. *Proceedings Attending the Formation*, p. 22.
[3] Chamberlain to Jesse Collings, 27 July 1876, Chamberlain MSS. JC 5/16/57.

its decision is obtained'. If all are 'heard and consulted', then 'all show much readiness to concede in matters of minor importance'. The 'caucus' type of Liberal organization 'accepts, solicits, nay, almost extorts' the expression of 'shades of feeling'. Because every point of view is heard, a minority finds that it can 'defer to the general sentiment' 'without loss of self-respect or sense of injustice'.[1] When Robert Spence Watson became President of the N.L.F. in 1890, the description of its ideals which he gave to its members could have come straight out of the pages of Mill's *On Liberty*. There should be, he said, 'the widest and freest discussion':

> They encouraged in every way the fullest collision of mind; some of them advocated, and always had advocated, the freest course for that which they believed to be error . . . he could not conceive that any true Liberal could in any way oppose the preaching and the teaching even of that which he believed to be error. Let him do as we had all had to do in our time—let him, if he held a question truly, not endeavour to carry it in the way which is becoming a little popular in certain quarters at the present time—not endeavour to force things forward by threats—but take the sensible, the practical, and the only true way of, by argument and persuasion, converting his minority into a majority. Honest and earnest men might be convinced, but they never would be coerced. What they wanted was really in all their political movements the agreement and unity which sprang from conviction, and that alone.[2]

The ideal is that of an organic unity, of a system of thought which is at once comprehensive, taking into account all aspects of the situation, and ordered through the growth of 'conviction'.

There was to be the maximum of openness and fluidity in the discussion of policy so that the conclusions arrived at would be a reflection of the real, the *whole*, state of opinion and feeling. According to the Revd. R. W. Dale, one of the leading Birmingham Liberals, the N.L.F. was 'an attempt to form a political church without a creed, and without a bishop, and without a synod'.[3] There would be no artificial organizing factors. Another basic principle that was often insisted on was that of comprehensiveness. For the only way to arrive at a genuine expression of the will of the majority was to ensure that it was

[1] Chamberlain, 'The Caucus', pp. 730, 734.
[2] *N.L.F. Report 1890*, pp. 49–50.   [3] Dale, *Life of R. W. Dale*, p. 422.

a majority related to a genuine whole, that no section was excluded from the process of forming the majority will, that there was full toleration of diversity of opinion. Indeed, in 1877 Chamberlain insisted that the N.L.F. should not have a formal creed or statement of principles to which delegates would have to adhere. The only 'passport to admission' that delegates should have to have was 'representative character'.[1] It was the democratic principle that would provide the unifying force in Liberal politics. Schnadhorst said that no matter what a man's creed or position or opinion on any particular question was 'he was not excluded'. All that was asked of him was that he should abide by the principle that the minority should defer to the majority.[2] In December 1878 Chamberlain assured the Whig leader, Hartington, that Whigs were not automatically excluded. The N.L.F. was intended to be 'thoroughly representative of all sections of the party', and, 'with a view to this, no Shibboleth in the shape of a formal programme' was to be required. Membership was open 'to all who accept the name of Liberals'.[3] Gladstone, when he expressed approval of the 'Birmingham system', made much of this feature of it. 'A man is not bound', he said, 'by the Birmingham plan to subscribe to any list of political articles. . . . At Birmingham you know they are tolerably advanced, but they don't attempt to exclude the most moderate.'[4]

In 1879 Chamberlain told Liberals at the N.L.F. that its basis was 'its truly representative character': 'It is a condition of success that every section of the party should be represented —that none should suffer from exclusion.'[5] What did he mean by this? Why was observance of this principle in particular to make Radicalism a 'success'? A year later he gave one answer: 'Until that is effected the organisation fails of its purpose—it is no longer the voice of the whole party, and its decisions cannot be accepted as indicating what would be the result of the appeal to those with whom in the end the appeal must lie—viz., the electors.'[6] In other words, if the N.L.F. accurately reflected

[1] *N.L.F. Report 1879*, p. 26.
[2] Quoted in M. Ostrogorski, *Democracy and the Organization of Political Parties*, vol. i, 1902, p. 183.
[3] Holland, *Devonshire*, i, p. 247.
[4] Ostrogorski, *Democracy and the Organization of Political Parties*, i, p. 183.
[5] *N.L.F. Report 1879*, p. 26. [6] *N.L.F. Report 1880*, pp. 14–15.

public opinion—and Chamberlain and his followers were sure that Liberal opinion and public opinion were synonymous[1]—then the Liberal leaders would find that they could rely, indeed had to rely, on the Federation to tell them what policies to adopt and put before the electors. And so Radicalism would at last control the party. Another way in which the comprehensiveness, the great 'width of the base' on which the 'caucus' and the N.L.F. rested, would help Radicalism was through minimizing the disruptiveness of any single sectional group.[2]

Throughout Chamberlain was concerned to forge a relationship between Radicalism and power. His aim was to change the traditional Radicalism of opposition to and suspicion of government into a Radicalism concerned primarily with acquiring and using governmental power. He had also, therefore, to replace individualistic Radicalism by a disciplined Radicalism characterized by co-operation. The traditional Liberal view of the proper relationship of the House of Commons to the executive, as inherited from the Whigs and as expounded very recently by both Mill and Bagehot, was that it should be a detached critic and scrutineer of governmental action. The 'House of Commons Radicals' of the 1870s, for whom the Chamberlainites felt such contempt,[3] were very much in the old tradition, individualistic both in their ideas and in their behaviour, suspicious of government and concerned to restrain it and reduce its influence. That the main role of Radicals ought to be to provide a government with a firm majority so that it could use its powers strongly and positively was indeed a major departure from several aspects of the British Radical tradition. But it was a departure that Chamberlain was determined to bring about.

The National Liberal Federation did not in itself effect this new departure. It helped to begin it. But in several ways it did represent a compromise with more traditional practices and attitudes, and its role in Liberal politics remained ambiguously

---

[1] Cf. Chamberlain's hope that the N.L.F. might evolve into 'a really Liberal Parliament outside the Imperial Legislature, and, unlike it, elected by universal suffrage, and with some regard to a fair distribution of political power'. *Proceedings Attending the Formation*, p. 16.

[2] Hanham, *Elections and Party Management*, p. 135. Chamberlain, 'A New Political Organization', pp. 128–9.

[3] Vincent, *Formation of the Liberal Party*, p. 28. Hamer, *John Morley*, pp. 100–3.

defined in certain crucial respects. The theory on which the N.L.F. was based represented something of great significance for the development of Liberal politics, an attempt to reconcile the *liberal* idea of the free 'collision of minds' and tolerance of diversity of opinion with the *democratic* idea of making the will of the majority effective in political life. What remained to be proved was whether out of the application of the former could come the order of a firm consensus of opinion.

It was unclear also what would be the relationship between the N.L.F. and the party leaders. Chamberlain seems to have envisaged a partnership in which the N.L.F. would not coerce, or impose its will on, the leaders but would by its representativeness be able to get them voluntarily to take up the policies which it recommended to them. Chamberlain certainly did not regard the N.L.F. as a permanent substitute for the party leadership as the directing force in the party, nor did he want it to be any kind of extra-parliamentary opposition to it. He was by nature and ambition basically a leader himself. His was not a Radicalism of perpetual opposition and criticism. He wanted the N.L.F. to strengthen leadership, not to replace or weaken it. His attitude was that 'it is only when leaders cease to lead that their followers are driven to attempt a campaign on their own account'.[1] This is what had happened during the 1870s. But the crisis which had led to followers having to take the initiative themselves was, he hoped, only a temporary one. He clearly looked forward to the day when new men such as himself would once more be giving the party strong leadership. Addressing the inaugural conference of the N.L.F. in 1877, he pointed to two ways in which the party's policy and strategy could be determined. Either the leaders would select some great question 'as the next object of our exertion' or, 'failing this', 'the rank and file should choose for itself'. He gave examples of both: the 1867 Reform Bill had resulted from 'popular pressure', but the Irish reforms of 1868–70 had been Gladstone's responsibility. Since 1874 the leaders had been divided and inactive and it was therefore necessary for the party itself to take the initiative once again.[2]

The implication was clear: it was primarily the responsibility

---

[1] Chamberlain, 'The Next Page of the Liberal Programme', p. 413.
[2] *Proceedings Attending the Formation*, p. 17.

of leaders to decide on what questions should be taken up and when. Like Harcourt in 1875, Chamberlain believed that what really mattered were boldness and decisiveness in leadership. This was what followers mainly wanted. An organization such as the N.L.F. could advise and influence, but in the last resort there had to be a leader-follower relationship. But among the Liberals of the N.L.F. there existed and was to keep on recurring a different attitude, one of permanent suspicion of leadership, and of desire to reduce its scope and minimize its independence. Thus there were those who took Chamberlain's democratic rhetoric one stage further and argued that, now that democracy had come, it was 'the people' who should rule. William Harris told the N.L.F. in 1877 that in this new era the direction of party policy and the determination of questions 'on which the people should be asked to agitate' should no longer be confined to the leaders. 'The people themselves ought to decide what the agitation should be, and when it should begin.' Hence the creation of the N.L.F.[1] In 1883 a Liberal conference was held on the issue of parliamentary reform. When it was proposed that the conference demand that the Liberal leaders should now give a Reform Bill priority over all else, some Liberals present opposed this on the ground that they should have trust in their leaders to be able to decide from their superior knowledge of the circumstances in what order questions were to be taken up. R. W. Dale called the implications of this 'dangerous'. The leaders, he wrote, could not be trusted, because they were inclined to take too narrow a view and 'to exaggerate the importance of measures belonging to their own departments'. Their judgement needed to be 'corrected and controlled, not merely by the opinion of their colleagues, who have their own schemes to carry, but by the opinion of the party in the country'.[2] But, as Chamberlain appreciated, party organization was only strong *vis-à-vis* the party leaders in so far as it did represent the real state of opinion—and of opinion, not merely within the Liberal party, but in the country at large. For otherwise the Liberal leaders could not afford automatically to carry out the demands of the N.L.F., even if they wanted to. For they had to operate in a wider context and seek to win power through

[1] Ibid., pp. 20–1.
[2] R. W. Dale, 'The Leeds Conference', *C.R.*, vol. 44 (November 1883), pp. 759–63.

getting the votes of people who were not members of the Liberal party as well as of people who were. Their success in doing this gave them an authority, and a greater claim to be representative of 'the people' and of the will of the majority, than any that the N.L.F. could ever hope to possess. If Radicalism was to be connected with power, it had to come to terms with this kind of authority, with this source of power. The history of the N.L.F. was to be one of identifying itself with power by carrying out the strategies and policies decided on by the leaders while doing its best to get the leaders to employ their power also on behalf of the policies which 'the party' favoured.

For Chamberlain the N.L.F. was essential for giving effectiveness and coherence to Radicalism, but for the securing of power it was not enough. It was not itself a parliamentary party, and it was in Parliament that power had to be sought. The crucial question was what kind of party he would work to develop. With the apparent break-up of the Liberal party in the early 1870s at least three possibilities were open to him. He could work for an entirely new, that is, a third, party. He could develop a new second party that would replace the Liberals when their disintegration was complete. Or he could concentrate on permeating and trying to take over the Liberal party while it continued to exist. Chamberlain, who naturally did not want to close any of these options prematurely, wavered continually from one strategy to another. In mid-1873 he declared that he was in despair of getting any good 'from the Liberal party in its demoralised decrepitude'. The party, 'as it is, is not worth holding together'; it should be broken up or at least reconstructed with a new programme and possibly new leaders. On another occasion he wrote that he wanted to 'smash up this gigantic sham called a Liberal party, and to secure reorganization on a new basis', and referred to the possibility of having Radicals oppose official Liberal candidates at elections.[1] All three strategies are discernible here. In March 1874 he said that he wanted not 'the reconstruction of the Liberal party upon the old basis' but 'the formation of a new Liberal—a new Radical party'.[2] The language remained very uncertain, very fluid.

[1] Garvin, *Chamberlain*, i, p. 155. Fraser, *Joseph Chamberlain*, p. 18.
[2] Fraser, *Joseph Chamberlain*, pp. 20–1.

Chamberlain's Radicalism, his characteristic urge to seek a complete reconstruction, a clean sweep, conflicted with his equally characteristic striving for power which would necessitate some kind of accommodation with the organs of power that already existed. One can see this conflict in his attitude to the Liberal party. One can see it also in his attitude to Parliament. On the one hand, his Radicalism led him to tell the inaugural meeting of the N.L.F. of his hope of seeing develop 'a really Liberal Parliament outside the Imperial Legislature, and, unlike it, elected by universal suffrage, and with some regard to a fair distribution of political power'.[1] But, on the other hand, he had himself become a member of the 'Imperial Legislature' in 1876. He was not the man to postpone all hope of power and influence until such time as an ideal situation had been attained. In practice he moved towards an accommodation with the Liberal party. When he first entered Parliament, he had some hopes of being able to organize his own Radical 'party' there. But this 'party' scarcely grew beyond an initial nucleus of about six. The 'House of Commons Radicals' proved far too individualistic and resistant to efforts to organize them.[2] By 1878 Chamberlain was deciding to change his strategy. He told Jesse Collings that he now saw the Birmingham Radicals' best chance of success as lying 'rather in a hearty alliance & attempt to influence our present leaders, than in the formation of any new party. There is no party of Radicals below the gangway; their only point of agreement is the fact that each one differs in some respect or another from the leaders; but their differences among themselves are really greater than those which separate them from the front bench.'[3]

Chamberlain's decision to neglect, to stop trying to organize, the rank-and-file Radical M.P.s was to have important consequences for his own career later on: in 1886 he was to take with him a very small following from among the Liberal M.P.s. What had happened, above all, to cause him to take this decision was Gladstone's campaign against the Conservative government's Eastern policy. For not only had this revealed by

---

[1] *Proceedings Attending the Formation*, p. 16.
[2] Fraser, *Joseph Chamberlain*, pp. 23–4. S. Gwynn and G. M. Tuckwell, *The Life of the Rt. Hon. Sir Charles W. Dilke, Bart., M.P.*, vol. i, 1917, pp. 214–15.
[3] Chamberlain to Collings, 26 February 1878, Chamberlain MSS. JC 5/16/78.

1877 Gladstone's great hold over Radical opinion; it showed also that in Gladstone there was a force that could bring that opinion into a positive, constructive relationship with power as obtainable through the parliamentary system. Association with Gladstone promised to provide abundance of unifying emotionalism for Radical politics. Chamberlain showed his awareness of this by securing Gladstone to 'float' the N.L.F. with his oratory at its inaugural conference in 1877. It was indeed tempting to employ this way of unifying at the outset the new national Radicalism. But as a result Radicalism became dangerously dependent on Gladstone for its emotional coherence. And the mood of 1877–80 was too negative for the good of the N.L.F. It relied too much on feeling against 'Beaconsfieldism' in its first few years, and these were not used adequately for the working out of the policy and the developing of a more positive and constructive 'general sentiment' among Radicals. R. T. Shannon has drawn attention to the unfortunate consequences for Chamberlainite Radicalism of Gladstone's re-emergence from retirement in 1876: what seemed the 'natural destiny' of the Liberal party, to become a Liberal-Radical party under Chamberlain's leadership, was thereby frustrated.[1] It is now necessary, therefore, to examine Gladstone's political personality and assess what there was about this that continued to make it the dominant influence in shaping the development of the Liberal party.

[1] Shannon, *Gladstone and the Bulgarian Agitation*, p. 273.

III Gladstone and the Unity of Liberalism

WE have seen what a great problem sectionalism became for Gladstone's first administration. No one was more conscious of this problem or more concerned to find ways of overcoming it than Gladstone himself, and his career from the mid-1860s on is indeed scarcely intelligible unless interpreted in terms of his constant preoccupation with unifying Liberal political action against what he—and many of his contemporaries and colleagues—regarded as a natural, inherent tendency to disorganization.

To Gladstone the nature of the Liberal party was to be the party of action and movement. He wrote to Granville in 1877: 'My opinion is & has long been that the vital principle of the Liberal party, like that of Greek art, is *action*, and that nothing but action will ever make it worthy of the name of a party.'[1] He expounded the same theory to the inaugural meeting of the N.L.F. Conservatism, he said, represented, like Egyptian art, the 'principle of repose', whereas 'in our Liberal party we have got the Greek idea of life and motion'. This was why the problem of maintaining order and discipline was much more serious in Liberal than in Conservative politics.[2] For 'life' manifests itself in innumerable ways, and these manifestations must be spontaneous. Any attempt to force Liberals into patterns of conformity and orthodoxy must destroy vitality. But how to ensure that vitality does not mean anarchy, and that a devotion to the principle of 'movement' can be associated with agreement on the direction which that movement should be taking?

Gladstone saw sectionalism as a specifically Liberal disease because it represented a misapplication, a turning into wrong

[1] 19 May 1877, Ramm, *1876–1886*, i, p. 40.
[2] *Proceedings Attending the Formation*, pp. 46–7.

channels, of the Liberal party's 'superior force of healthy individuality, without which its energy of movement, and its generous love of improving changes, could not be maintained'.[1] He strove constantly to maintain a distinction between healthy and unhealthy manifestations of individuality. When in 1888 two young Liberals, R. B. Haldane and Edward Grey, voted against a motion of his concerning a Land Purchase Bill, and Haldane wrote to him that he felt that they ought to resign their seats for having thus opposed their leader, Gladstone replied: 'Incidents of this kind do not in any way shock or shake me. I have a comfort in referring them very much to the nature of the Liberal party, & the laws under which it exists, laws on the whole so healthful and beneficial and free.'[2] On the other hand, 'the sects, which nestle within the party, cannot', he wrote in an article published in 1878, 'be treated quite so tenderly'. The 'divisive courses of sectional opinion' caused a 'loss of collective working power', a very serious diminution in 'the aggregate energy' of the party. The evil effects of sectionalism he described thus:

> Their [the sects'] characteristic is a liability, far from uniform, yet too frequent, to make out of particular and isolated questions, which from any cause have a special hold upon their conscientious attachment, a kind of *idola fori*, for the sake of which the whole mass of the general public interests are to be sacrificed. . . . Under these sectarian or local influences it happens, more frequently than the Liberals at large are aware, that on the occurrence of parliamentary vacancies, and likewise at General Elections, the party, instead of settling its subaltern differences within itself by a judicious organisation, advisedly severs itself into two or more sections, and contends against the political adversary as if with one hand free and the other bound. The consequence is that a majority is broken up into two or three minorities; and Liberal constituencies, because they can only secure agreement with a Liberal candidate on nine points out of ten, make over the seat to a Tory, who on all the ten is against them. No more ingenious recipe could be found in a self-governing country for solving the problem, apparently so hopeless, how to devise a method under which, where the majority prevails by law, the minority shall be in fact supreme.[3]

[1] W. E. Gladstone, 'Electoral Facts', *N.C.*, no. 21 (November 1878), p. 961.
[2] Gladstone to Haldane, 21 November 1888, Haldane MSS. 5903, folio 112. [Lord Haldane], *Richard Burdon Haldane. An Autobiography*, 1929, pp. 111–12.
[3] 'Electoral Facts', pp. 960–1.

Three points in particular should be noted about this. First, his objection is clearly to sectarianism, to the influence of organizations, obstructing through their negative influence as minorities the achievement of the will of the majority. Secondly, one notes that like Chamberlain Gladstone is addressing himself to the problem of how to secure coherent majority force in British politics. For him too this was a matter of power: governments now depended for stability and accomplishment on the existence of such a force in the constituencies. Like Peel, Gladstone believed that strong parties were essential as a basis for strong governments;[1] but for him, much more than for Peel, owing to the changes in the electoral system and his own synthesizing efforts from the 1860s on, the source of this strength and discipline had to be discovered and nurtured in the nation itself and not solely or even mainly within the confines of the Houses of Parliament. Thirdly, there is evident Gladstone's belief—to which he constantly gave expression[2]—that the Liberal party was the national party, the party which had behind it the support of the majority of the nation, and which, unlike the Tories, looked to the national interest. If the Liberals were defeated, as in 1874, it was not because they had ceased to be the party of the majority, but because the internal divisions created by sectionalism frustrated the expression of this basic reality. The achievement and retention of political power by the Liberals must depend therefore on the overriding or subduing of sectionalism and the creation of a unified majority feeling in the country. As we shall see, Gladstone believed that it was in the achievement of this feeling that lay the key to the solution of the problem of obstructive sectionalism.

One way of dealing with sectionalism which Gladstone never employed was expulsion, the use of the authority of the leader to restore order in the party by intervening in its affairs to secure the removal of the disruptive or discordant element. Force was never in any sphere Gladstone's remedy for disorder. Order, if it was to be strong, durable, and dependable, must be organic, must develop from within, not imposed by strong acts

---

[1] Morley, *Gladstone*, i, p. 541. For Peel's attitude to party, see N. Gash, 'Peel and the Party System', *Transactions of the Royal Historical Society*, 5th Series, i, pp. 56–7.

[2] Cf. Morley, *Gladstone*, ii, p. 368.

of 'leadership'. Gladstone's attitude towards the Liberal party was one of deliberate and calculated detachment, even, indeed all the more, when it was in a state of disunity. He was not a believer in close organizational ties between leaders and followers. They had their own respective spheres of action, and no relationship should be established which involved the imposition of particular courses of action either by leaders on followers or by the party on their leaders.[1] His own habit was to take the initiative with regard to the promotion of a particular line of policy when *he* judged the time to be 'ripe'—without first cultivating and consulting the party or even, as in 1886, his closest colleagues. His attitude was that they could follow if they wanted to; the decision must be voluntary and based on conviction.

The only order that he wished to see in the party was order that resulted from spontaneous action within the party, though that spontaneous action might develop as a response to an initiative taken by himself. If the party was in disorder or was giving trouble to the leaders, Gladstone's reaction was normally to insist that it be left alone as much as possible to make its own adjustment.[2] Thus in November 1867 he wrote concerning the paralysis in the party resulting from 'internal dissensions': 'I think that time will apply a remedy by a spontaneous action from within the bosom of the party, but for myself I think the best course is to avoid all acts of leadership which can be dispensed with.'[3] After the election defeat of 1874 he adopted a similar attitude, declaring that he would not resume the leadership of the Liberal party 'unless that party had settled its differences'. He felt that 'it is absolutely necessary to party action that they should learn that all the duties and responsibilities do not rest on the leaders, but that followers have their obligations too'.[4] He then assumed a position of detachment

---

[1] Hanham, *Elections and Party Management*, pp. 203-4.

[2] Cf. his attitude in 1872 as reported by H. A. Bruce: 'He [Gladstone] is vexed at the ingratitude of men for whom he has done such great things, which would have been simply impossible without him, and would not be unwilling to leave them for a while to their own guidance...' *Letters of the Rt. Hon. Henry Austin Bruce G.C.B. Lord Aberdare of Duffryn*, vol. 1 (printed for private circulation), Oxford, 1902, pp. 339-40.

[3] Gladstone to Lord John Russell, 2 November 1867, Gooch, *Later Correspondence of Lord John Russell*, ii, pp. 362-3.

[4] *Letters of Lord Aberdare*, i, p. 361.

and waited for the party to move of its own accord 'towards effective union'. Calls for his own resumption of the leadership seemed to him attributable to the fact that 'men feel that the party is in the ditch, and they want to have somebody responsible for getting them out of it'.[1] Such a responsibility he refused to undertake. By January 1875 he had reached the conclusion that 'the party can do for a time without a leader in the Commons'. 'The truth is, it has peccant humours to purge, and bad habits to get rid of, and it is a great question whether this can or cannot be best done without first choosing a leader.'[2] What he had in mind was clearly an independent and voluntary restoration of order to the party by itself. When, after Gladstone had formally resigned, the party did select a new leader, Lord Hartington, Gladstone's advice to him was 'that the leadership of the Liberals in both Houses ought to be and cannot help being, light and negative rather than positive, in a degree unknown at least in the House of Commons for the last forty-five years'.[3]

Gladstone thus had a very special view as to the proper role of a party leader. This deliberate detachment, this belief in spontaneous internal reorganization without the intervention of the leader, is seen also in his great unwillingness to interfere in what he regarded as 'ordinary' party matters—organization, settlement of disputes. If there were a dispute and sections were forming within the party, it was not his role to settle the issue by taking one side or the other. In July 1873 he wrote: '... if there is to be a great schism in the liberal party, I hope I shall never find it my duty to conduct the operations either of the one or of the other section.' In 1874 he wrote that he might resume the leadership if some great issue arose, but 'always with the understanding that as between section and section I could not become a partisan'.[4] His leadership must itself be supra-sectional, must express a superior force. Lord Selborne once observed of Gladstone: 'For the *arts* of political management, he trusts too implicitly, I think, to whippers-in and other men inferior in political earnestness and insight to himself....'[5]

[1] Gladstone to Granville, 7 December 1874, Ramm, *1868–1876*, ii, p. 461.
[2] Gladstone to Granville, 27 January 1875, ibid. ii, p. 468.
[3] Gladstone to Hartington, 2 February 1875, Holland, *Devonshire*, i, p. 149.
[4] Morley, *Gladstone*, ii, pp. 66, 107.
[5] Selborne to Sir A. Gordon, 6 September 1874, Roundell Palmer, Earl of Selborne, *Memorials, Part II—Personal and Political 1865–1895*, vol. i, 1898, p. 334.

But it can be argued that the force and integrity of this 'earnestness and insight' depended, and were felt by Gladstone himself to depend, on preserving detachment from the details of 'political management'. For the effect, whether calculated or not, of his detachment was that his political authority seemed to be in reserve, as belonging to some superior concept of the nature of politics, and was therefore more effective, less contaminated and corrupted, when it was thrown into the political balance. His more perceptive colleagues encouraged him to stay aloof for this reason, and many Liberals saw value for their party in this aspect of Gladstone's behaviour. For example, Lord Wolverton told Gladstone in October 1874 that he was finding, when discussing the disunity of the party with rank-and-file Liberals, that some went 'so far as to think that the true policy is that your strength should be kept in reserve'.[1] Gladstone himself knew how much the authority on which his power rested would be diminished by involvement in intra-party disputes. His practice was always to strive to keep his authority based on national feeling rather than merely party or sectional opinion. A. F. Thompson has shown how between 1866 and 1868 Gladstone did not concern himself at all closely with matters of party organization, while the party managers exploited and developed his national personality.[2] It was this that Gladstone sought to preserve and which became indeed one of the party's main assets in establishing its own links with national opinion.[3]

Gladstone's view that the time for strong party leadership was only after the party had restored order to itself was not shared by all his colleagues. The alternative attitude was well expressed by Granville in a letter to Gladstone in January 1875. In this Granville argued that what was 'the party of progress' had particular need of constant strong control. He did not agree with Gladstone that the spontaneous upsurge of feeling within the party, or 'sudden enthusiasm for a cause, or for an individual', could of itself overcome the disorganization and 'habits of indiscipline' which, he insisted, were in fact created

[1] Wolverton to Gladstone, 30 October 1874, Gladstone MSS., B.M. Add. MS. 44349, folio 39.
[2] Thompson, 'Gladstone's Whips and the General Election of 1868', pp. 189-91, 197.
[3] Cf. Vincent, *Formation of the Liberal Party*, p. xxxii.

by absence of leadership. Gladstone's own 'worthy causes' had to be carried through by a party machine. His refusal to concern himself with the maintenance of this would lead to his finding it 'completely out of gear' when the need for it arose.[1]

But after the election débâcle of 1874 Gladstone seems to have determined that he would not again act as an 'ordinary' party leader. He made a distinction now between not henceforth being 'able to give any material aid in the adjustment of [the] difficulties' of the Liberal party and, on the other hand, remaining willing to 'enter into counsel' if it was a question of 'arresting some great evil or procuring for the nation some great good'.[2] It is of great importance for interpreting the course of Gladstone's subsequent career to remember that he now saw his duty as to nation, not to party. Nevertheless, as we shall also see, he was not to be unmindful of the possible beneficial effects for the party of intervention by himself in a national issue.

For Gladstone came to believe that one of the best ways of establishing organic order in Liberal politics was to attach them to some great cause that would so impress Liberals with its importance that they would voluntarily subordinate to it their special, divisive interests. The aim was the same as that which is to be found underlying so many aspects of his political life, the striving to create wider frames of reference which would enable individuals or sections or classes or even nations to transcend the narrow limits of their own 'selfish' interests. One can indeed find a parallel between his response to the behaviour of the sections and his attempt in his agitation on the Eastern question to stop the setting up of Britain's own interests 'out of place, in an exaggerated form, beyond their proper sphere' and to show how Britain could rise above 'the motives of a narrow selfishness'.[3] We may take his behaviour in 1873 as an example of his belief in this kind of remedy for party disorganization. A letter to John Bright of 17 April shows him trying to sort out 'large matters' of policy and remove entanglements and 'inferior associations' from them. By August he is reaching the conclusion that in 'finance' lay an issue that might raise Liberals 'to a higher & firmer level' where 'they wd. have more disposition to abate severally what they could honourably

[1] 5 January 1875, Ramm, *1868–1876*, ii, p. 463.
[2] Morley, *Gladstone*, ii, p. 107.   [3] Ibid. ii, p. 186.

part with in their schemes [or?] their opinions, as they wd. feel there wd. be a real value in agreement if once attained, & that it was worth while to make some effort to attain it'.[1]

Furthermore, the great cause which would unify Liberalism had to be national. Because the Liberals were or ought to be the national party, the only issue which really could foster an organic unity among them was one on which national feeling was aroused, and not merely party feeling. The source of coherence and strength in Liberal politics, the only force that could transcend and also subdue the divisive influences of sectionalism, was national opinion. It was characteristic of Gladstone to work in this direction, to approach the situation of the party via a national issue, not to approach a great national problem in 'the spirit of party'. Positive leadership was possible for the Liberal party only if the party were associating itself with a great national cause. When in 1875 Gladstone advised Hartington that leadership in the Commons ought to be 'light and negative', he pointed out that this had also been the case 'in 1867 after the important defeat' but that in 1868 leadership had 'altered its character, solely because the great Irish question came up in force'.[2] In connection with the crisis over the Eastern question in 1876–7 Gladstone wrote that he had come to the conclusion that, 'as in so many other cases, the Liberal party alone is the instrument by which a great work is to be carried on'.[3] The key word here is 'instrument'. A great cause arose and found in the Liberal party, the only truly national party, its instrument: the party did not itself create and exploit great causes.[4] In discussing one such cause, the county franchise, in an article in November 1877, Gladstone made it plain that he believed that 'the interests of party' could not and should not be the controlling influences over it. 'Party', he wrote, 'is a legitimate and necessary, but essentially a secondary and sub-

---

[1] Gladstone to Bright, 17 April, 27 August, 1873, Gladstone MSS., B.M. Add. MS. 44113, folios 41, 68.
[2] Gladstone to Hartington, 2 February 1875, Holland, *Devonshire*, i, p. 149.
[3] Gladstone to Granville, 23 May 1877, Ramm, *1876–1886*, i, p. 42.
[4] Gladstonian Liberals generally accepted this interpretation of the nature and purpose of their party. Thus A. J. Mundella wrote to H. J. Wilson, 3 December 1876, concerning a proposed conference on the Eastern question: 'We put aside Party for National duty, and if Liberalism reaps the advantage it is the fault of those who persist in misunderstanding and misrepresenting the Nation.' H. J. Wilson MSS. Sheffield Univ. Library, Box 2.

ordinate, instrument for promoting the public good.'[1] It followed from this that party considerations must not be permitted to restrict or inhibit a Liberal's response to the emergence of an issue that involved the public good. In 1878 Gladstone wrote after having voted with a minority of Liberals for Sir Wilfrid Lawson's motion condemning the calling out of the reserves: 'On these great questions, which cut so deep into heart and mind, the importance of taking what they think the best course for the question will often seem, even to those who have the most just sense of party obligation a higher duty than that of party allegiance.'[2] It is not surprising to find Lord Acton writing in June 1880 that, 'taking party in the practical and popular sense, of an instrument for holding office, people are uneasily conscious that Mr. Gladstone will sacrifice it to loftier purpose sooner than they would like'.[3] These were indeed prescient words. In a few years 'people' were to find that their uneasiness had ample justification. But from Gladstone's point of view what he was to do in 1886 was to help create a different kind of party, to effect a transmutation of the Liberal party from 'party in the practical and popular sense' to party that was the 'instrument' of 'lofty purpose'. And in the process he believed that he was creating a stronger, more coherent, more unified party.

Gladstone's search for a great cause is constantly associated with thoughts of the advantages which such a cause might confer on Liberal politics. For a great national issue might so impress Liberals with its importance that they would be willing to subordinate their special questions to it. In a letter to Bright in August 1873 Gladstone defined what was needed, some issue that would generate 'a *positive* force to carry us onward as a body' and that, if 'worked into certain shapes', 'may greatly help to mould the rest, at least for the time'.[4] In the period before the 1874 general election he analysed numerous questions to see whether they were of this kind.[5] W. H. Maehl in a detailed

---

[1] W. E. Gladstone, 'The County Franchise and Mr Lowe Thereon', *N.C.*, no. 9 (November 1877), pp. 538–9.
[2] Gladstone to Granville, 12 April 1878, Ramm, *1876–1886*, i, p. 70.
[3] Acton to Mary Gladstone, 1 June 1880, H. Paul (ed.), *Letters of Lord Acton to Mary, Daughter of the Right Hon. W. E. Gladstone*, 2nd edition, 1913, p. 12.
[4] Morley, *Gladstone*, ii, p. 87.
[5] Gladstone to Granville, 8 January 1874, Ramm, *1868–1876*, ii, p. 960.

study of Gladstone's political strategy in 1873-4 has shown how Gladstone was looking for some 'mechanism, consistent with political principle, by which to obscure the issues that were dividing the liberals and to unite the party once more on a measure of overriding importance', and how he believed that he had found this in the issue of financial and taxation reform. He wanted to show people what a great national issue 'finance' was, and then, when the Liberals had responded to it in these terms, to appeal to the country in a general election. But Parliament was dissolved prematurely, before this process could be followed through. Nevertheless, Gladstone did hope that one of the benefits of the election campaign and his proposal for the abolition of the income-tax would be the absorption of the sections in the party into 'a question of universal and commanding interest'.[1] On this occasion, as Maehl shows, Gladstone failed. After the election he had to conclude that there did not exist 'any great positive aim (the late plan having failed) for which to co-operate', any end that was 'desired by the entire party, or by any clear and decisive majority of it'.[2]

The Conservatives came back into office. Gladstone now sensed that the party might be rallied in negative as well as positive ways. The alternative possibilities were 'a cause: or such portentous blundering [on the part of the government] as is almost beyond hope or fear'.[3] His great achievement after 1876 was, of course, to combine these, to turn denunciation of 'blundering' in foreign and imperial policy into a great 'cause'. But the opportunity for doing this was not at first available. He resigned the Liberal leadership in 1875, complaining that 'we have no public object on the pursuit of which we are agreed'.[4] It was the campaign over the 'Bulgarian atrocities' which was to revive Gladstone's interest in rallying Liberals around a great 'public object'. R. T. Shannon has written of how during the 'Bulgarian agitation' Gladstone became possessed by 'an almost compulsive need to concern himself with the encouragement of developments "very beneficial to the party as such" ', developments that could make the party 'more

[1] W. H. Maehl, 'Gladstone, the Liberals and the Election of 1874', *Bulletin of the Institute of Historical Research*, vol. 36 (1963), pp. 53-69.
[2] Morley, *Gladstone*, ii, pp. 106, 111.
[3] Gladstone to Granville, 25 November 1874, Ramm, *1868-1876*, ii, p. 461.
[4] Gladstone to Granville, 7 December 1874, ibid. ii, p. 462.

practical and astute' in 'shaping means with a view to ends than, perhaps, it has been of late years'.[1] But Gladstone was now the leader only of Liberal opinion in the country, not of the party in Parliament, and the caution of the Parliamentary leaders seemed to him to be wasting a very good opportunity. Writing to Granville in May 1877 about the agitation, he remarked that in his opinion 'to carry it on freely would have been very beneficial to the party as such' but, regrettably, 'the action of the party as a whole within the House does not come up to its action and feeling in the country at large'. He wished 'that there were some other question of real magnitude likely to unite' Liberals; 'but', he added, 'I do not see any'.[2] As he warned the inaugural conference of the N.L.F., before Liberals were going to be able 'to prevail and to conquer', they would have to 'learn much of the sacrifice of private and secondary opinion for the sake of great general objects'.[3] He believed that nothing would produce a Liberal revival 'but some great question', and again and again he returned to the potential for this that had seemed to be inherent in the Eastern question.[4] In an article in *The Nineteenth Century* in November 1878 he claimed that feeling in the country over the Eastern question had not only caused the Liberal party to gain seven seats since the beginning of 1876 but had produced a new coherence and discipline in the party. Of the fifty-four votes cast by Liberals against their party in the four great divisions on the government's Eastern policy, only three had been cast by members elected since 1 January 1876.[5] The concentration of Liberal feeling in the country around this great national issue was producing a new kind of Liberal M.P. and forging a new bond between Liberalism in Parliament and that Liberalism in the nation from whence alone unity could come.

During his great campaign of 1879–80 against 'Beaconsfieldism' Gladstone made it quite plain that it was national, not party, opinion to which he was addressing himself and which he wished to foster. Since he was not at this time leader of the Liberal party, he was able to assume with more freedom than

[1] Shannon, *Gladstone and the Bulgarian Agitation*, p. 267.
[2] Gladstone to Granville, 23 May 1877, Ramm, *1876–1886*, i, p. 42.
[3] *Proceedings Attending the Formation*, p. 47.
[4] Holland, *Devonshire*, i, p. 176. [5] 'Electoral Facts', pp. 964, 968.

usual this role of leader of national opinion. Indeed, in his Midlothian speeches he makes a point of setting party action over against the development of national feeling on the evils of Beaconsfieldism. For example, in his speech of 25 November 1879 he claims that the feeling which arose against the government's Eastern policy and to which he responded came from the nation as a whole and not from the Liberal party whose leaders had been so cautious and so unwilling to come out strongly on the issue. Anti-Beaconsfieldism was not created by, nor did it reflect, mere party feeling; it transcended 'the old question between Whig and Tory' and expressed national feeling concerning the conduct of the nation's affairs.[1] Yet at the same time, of course, Gladstone's campaign did greatly help the interests of the Liberal party and he was by no means unwilling to express his awareness of how it was doing so. He would remind Liberals that, as they were the true national party, they ought to be able to find unity when there emerged such a great national issue. It was an issue which was so important, so all-embracing in its scope and implications, that it naturally overrode the various interests of the sections of the party. All these were absorbed and united within the transcending need to overturn this system of government.

... what I beg to insist upon before you and before all is this—it is not now a question of this or that particular measure. We are all of us, or most of us here, I take it, of Liberal politics, and have a great interest in many particular measures. There are a great many things that we wish to be done. ... Some of us are very anxious for one thing, and some for another, and some for all. But it is a great deal more than that. It is a system and a method of Government with which we have to deal.[2]

One of the most outstanding features of Gladstone as political leader was his very acute sense of proportion and relationship. He once defined his own most 'striking gift' as 'an insight into the facts of particular eras and their relation to one another', and noted that the result of this was the moving of public opinion towards some 'particular end'.[3] His mind was ceaselessly at work arranging, ordering, assessing the 'weights' of political

---

[1] W. E. Gladstone, *Political Speeches in Scotland, November and December 1879*, Edinburgh, 1879, pp. 21–2, 26.   [2] Ibid., pp. 94, 11–12.
[3] Quoted in P. Magnus, *Gladstone. A Biography*, 1954, p. 190.

subjects and defining their relationships to one another. This ceaseless striving to organize, systematize, and order the diverse materials of his existence was, as we can now appreciate more clearly from the publication of his diaries,[1] a characteristic of Gladstone's mind that was not confined to his political interests. His diary shows him to have been constantly at work from an early age compiling lists and trying to organize what he felt to be the excessively fragmented and uncoordinated aspects of his life into compartments and schemes of relationship.[2]

Gladstone once formulated his great complaint about the Liberal sectionalists in these terms: 'Tenacity of predilection is made to stand instead of paramount weight in the object itself, and all proportion of judgment is lost.'[3] Appreciation of 'weight in the object', and 'proportion of judgment', were the qualities that he so pre-eminently possessed or strove to obtain. Gladstone's style of leadership was in this, as in so much else, clearly modelled on that of Sir Robert Peel whom Gladstone admired for his 'sense of measure' and for having 'generally an exact sense of the proportion between one Bill, and the general policy of the Government; also of the proportion between the different parts of the same Bill; and of the relation in which the leaders of his party stood to their followers'.[4] Now it is true that many of Gladstone's contemporaries considered that his leadership was of exactly the opposite kind from this, that one of his main weaknesses was lack of a 'sense of measure'. They observed his 'one idea at a time faculty',[5] and believed that he did not see

[1] M. R. D. Foot (ed.), *The Gladstone Diaries*, vols. i and ii, *1825–1839*, Oxford, 1968.
[2] Cf. Morley, *Gladstone*, i, pp. 76–7. He once described a diary as 'an account-book of the all-precious gift of Time'. Ibid. i, p. 205.
[3] 'Electoral Facts', p. 961. The sectionalists expressed similar complaints about *his* lack of 'proportion of judgment'. Mrs. Josephine Butler, one of the foremost campaigners for the repeal of the Contagious Diseases Acts, wrote in 1872: '... *we have nothing to hope from Mr. Gladstone in respect of repeal*. . . . My impression is that he is convinced we are right, but that he has no conception of the vital nature and vast importance of the subject. . . . It is most true that he has no sense of proportion.' Quoted in Hammond, *James Stansfeld*, pp. 179–80. This attitude should be compared with that of the National Education Leaguers who were astonished that Bath Liberals should be 'wholly at one with the League in principle' and yet deny the League a say in the determination of the Liberal candidate's policy. See above, pp. 6–7.   [4] L. A. Tollemache, *Talks with Mr Gladstone*, 1898, p. 116.
[5] Lord Houghton, quoted in J. L. Hammond, *Gladstone and the Irish Nation*, 1938, p. 184. Houghton described this faculty as 'at once his weakness and his strength'.

beyond the particular great issue in which he was for the time absorbed. Lord Selborne once criticized him for having a mind that was 'too one-sided and vehement' and that lacked 'accuracy, equability, the sense of proportion, and breadth'. He referred to Gladstone's tendency to become totally preoccupied with a single question: 'He can hardly be brought to interest himself at all in matters (even when they are really great matters) in which he is not carried away by some too strong attraction; and, when he is carried away, he does not sympathize, or take counsel with, those whose point of view is at all different from his own.' But Selborne then went on to acknowledge, although he saw this as ground for complaint, that it was only when 'it is the time for some "heroic" measures, for which he can excite public enthusiasm', that Gladstone's mind became 'a centre, round which other minds can revolve' and which harmonized and regulated the thoughts, interests, and action of other men.[1] For Selborne the main problem was Gladstone's deficiencies as an 'ordinary' party leader, but in analysing these he had stumbled on what were in fact Gladstone's great positive powers as a leader, the secret of his 'extraordinary' ability to unify Liberal politics where 'ordinary' leadership, whether his own or that of other Liberals, perpetually failed. In his own political personality, and in his personal approach to the problem of relationship and order in reform politics, he was the best substitute for a creed, a system of thought, that the party possessed. Until old age, he possessed both the open mind, sensitive to the emergence of new ideas and influences, which John Stuart Mill so valued, and the ability to systematize and cohere these ideas and influences. As a recent historian has observed, he had 'an extraordinary capacity for holding a wide range of materials in view' and was forever investigating, responding to, and endeavouring to absorb new ideas.[2] As late as 1890 he was making a comparison between 'those who have been so happy that they have been born with a creed that they can usefully maintain to the last' and persons such as himself, 'a learner all my life'.[3] But at the

---

[1] Selborne, *Memorials, Part Two*, i, p. 334.
[2] R. Kelley, *The Transatlantic Persuasion, The Liberal-Democratic Mind in the Age of Gladstone*, New York, 1969, pp. 166–7.
[3] Morley, *Gladstone*, i, pp. 812–13.

same time he seemed to have been able to escape the 'dispersive' and 'anarchical' consequences of open-mindedness of which mid-Victorian Liberal thinkers were increasingly conscious. His mind seemed to be generating what John Morley argued that his generation craved, the 'union of the advantages of an organic synthesis, with the advantages of an open mind and unfettered inquiry'.[1] Gladstone showed himself conscious both of living in a state of perpetual flux and intrusion of new influences and of the need for the establishment of new frameworks of comprehension. 'The horizon enlarges, the sky shifts, around me', he wrote in his diary in 1860. 'It is an age of shocks; a discipline so strong, so manifold, so rapid and whirling that only when it is at an end, if then, can I hope to comprehend it.'[2] He longed to 'get sufficiently out of myself to judge myself, and unravel the knots of being and doing of which my life seems to be full'.[3]

Gladstone's 'sense of measure' made him the means of conferring order on Liberalism, and this 'sense of measure' was expressed through the very concentration on single great causes that Selborne so deplored and thought so typical of Gladstone's lack of such a sense.

One of the best commentaries on the kind of political leadership which Gladstone offered is a criticism which he made in 1873 of Robert Lowe as a politician. 'Is not your light too much concentrated?' he asked Lowe. 'Does not its intensity darken the surroundings?' Gladstone argued that the 'light' which is generated by a politician's intellect should illuminate 'the surroundings', by which 'I mean the relations of the thing not only to other things but to persons'.[4] Thus did Gladstone in his concentration on great causes *at the same time* expose and illuminate the relationship between them and 'other things' and 'persons'.

Always in his absorption in single great questions Gladstone was acutely aware of the relationship to them of all other questions, a relationship that was normally one of organic subordination. And this relationship he constantly referred to and impressed on Liberals' minds. Gladstone had the imaginative—and the rhetorical—power to convert his single questions

[1] Hamer, *John Morley*, pp. 86–7.
[2] Morley, *Gladstone*, i, p. 726.
[3] Ibid. ii, pp. 84–5.
[4] Ibid. ii, p. 72.

into 'centres' around which other questions and interests revolved. In part this was because of what Robert Kelley refers to as 'the key fact about Gladstone's intellectual development', 'the way in which his mind instinctively reached for wider frames of reference': 'Whatever was limited in scope could never satisfy him; universalism was always the keynote. His mind ... was not penetrating, it was capacious; its impetus was centrifugal, not inward-turning.'[1] But it is also true that this impetus itself was expressed within his intense concentration on single great causes or 'missions'. This concentration, the intensity with which it was organized, and the rhetorical power with which he presented it to others, can be seen as a product of the constant conflict which he felt within himself between his extremely emotional and excitable temperament, which inclined him to become deeply interested in many different matters simultaneously, and his craving for order and concentrated purpose in his life. His Evangelical upbringing helped to instill in him an extreme sense of duty and mission, but his temperament seemed likely to prevent him from fulfilling any particular duty. In 1830, when he was considering what profession to take up and writing of his desire to 'set before the eyes of man ... the magnificence and the glory of Christian truth', he observed that 'I feel that my temperament is so excitable, that I should fear giving up my mind to other subjects which have ever proved sufficiently alluring to me, and which I fear would make my life a fever of unsatisfied longings and expectations.'[2] As a politician, Gladstone was constantly worried by 'distraction'. He would complain that business 'follows and whirls me day and night', that the many committees of which he was a member 'distract and dissipate my mind', that his life had become 'broken this way and that into a thousand small details, certainly unfavourable to calm and continuity of thought'.[3] By 1856 he was writing of himself as 'enclosed in the invisible net of pendent steel', 'a network ... woven out of all that the heart and all that the mind of man can supply'. His life was 'full of calls and duties' and 'charged with every kind of interest', but 'these interests are for ever growing and grown too many and powerful'.[4]

[1] Kelley, *Transatlantic Persuasion*, p. 171.
[2] Morley, *Gladstone*, i, p. 83.
[3] Ibid. i, pp. 187, 219, 191.
[4] Ibid. i, p. 557.

Out of this state of mind came the ever more intense craving to subdue the tumultuous and distracting details and interests of his life, to concentrate them within some single great and overriding duty. And in the process of achieving this concentration he was able to perform a similar ordering service for the chaotic multitudinousness of Liberal and reform politics. The intimate connection between Gladstone's state of mind and his characteristic mode of political action can be seen, for example, in his remark, after taking up the great issue of Irish Home Rule in 1886, that since he felt the Liberals' political position to be now 'broader as well as more solid than that of others' the general effect of the 'hurly burly that whirls round about us' was 'to incline me to a great tranquillity in my inner self'.[1] All else was subordinated to his single questions. One area in which contemporaries particularly felt the force of this was that of personal friendship. It was observed that Gladstone selected and adapted his friendships according to the requirements of the issue in which he was absorbed; and reactions to this are an eloquent commentary on the great ordering force which Gladstone's personality had become. H. F. Cowper, for instance, once referred to Gladstone's 'egoism of genius': 'a great cause would so absorb him as to make him view his friends and colleagues almost exclusively in the lights of instruments for the attainment of the end he had at heart.'[2] And Sir Algernon West, who was for some time his private secretary, wrote:

> The intense enthusiasm with which he entered into the subject and the object of the moment was apt to dim, if not obliterate, the little loves and affections which crowd the life of smaller men. The execution of his great work was the one thing in his eyes, and the instruments and tools he used were dearer to him than anything else; and the men associated with him at the moment were always greater than the men who had passed away.[3]

Gladstone always and very calculatedly moved on a plane of his own. One result of his deliberate aloofness from internal

---

[1] Gladstone to Harcourt, 30 December 1886, Harcourt MSS.
[2] J. Bailey (ed.), *The Diary of Lady Frederick Cavendish*, vol. ii, 1927, p. 285 (entry for 30 April 1881).
[3] Sir A. West, *Recollections 1832 to 1886*, vol. ii, 1899, pp. 33–4. Gladstone himself once observed that: 'I am a man so eager upon things as not to remember always what is due to persons.' Magnus, *Gladstone*, p. 194.

party disputes and sectionalism was that he never became completely committed to either radical or conservative positions. But nor did he become committed against them. His commitments always followed out, and were seen to follow out, a logic peculiar to his own political personality and attitudes. One reason for his unifying influence in Liberal politics was the ambivalence that this produced in his relationship towards and as between radicals and conservatives in the party. It was an ambivalence that unified, partly because it mirrored the essence of Liberal politics—a complex pattern in which radicalism and conservatism were not clear-cut positions, involving the same people on all issues, but varied endlessly according to the eye of the beholder and the particular issue that was involved.[1]

In his book *The Public Life* J. A. Spender observes that 'Gladstone's remarkable success in keeping extremists and moderates within the one fold of the Liberal party' was the result of the 'theory of party leadership' that he put into practice. This theory is defined by Spender as a refusal to commit himself on any question until he was convinced that it was 'ripe for action'. Consequently, while the extremists could live in hope 'that, if only they were patient, Mr. Gladstone would be converted', the moderates could also hope 'that, if they held on, they would prevent his conversion'.[2] What Gladstone made plain was that he would never allow party or sectional considerations to force him into commitments. He would make up his own mind. As a result no section could feel that its point of view was automatically excluded. Gladstone's political mind operated as the promoters of the National Liberal Federation hoped that *it* would operate—the free play of ideas, the determination not to exclude or be sectional, but at the same time the constant process of ordering and of moving towards conviction.

Even when Gladstone did commit himself to 'advanced' measures, conservatives were very ready to see conservative reasons for his having done so. There is an excellent assessment of the duality of Gladstone's policies, as seen from a conserv-

---

[1] For a comment on the at least potentially unifying effect of 'the ambiguity of Gladstone's position' in the mid-1860s, see M. Cowling, *1867 Disraeli, Gladstone and Revolution. The Passing of the Second Reform Bill*, Cambridge, 1967, p. 120.

[2] J. A. Spender, *The Public Life*, vol. i, 1925, p. 72.

ative's point of view, in a letter written by the Duke of Argyll to Lord Selborne in 1874. Gladstone, he suggested, was becoming increasingly sympathetic towards disestablishment because of 'his dislike of the sort of legislation to which the Church would be exposed by a "Liberal" Parliament'. But Gladstone might find the policy of disestablishment 'the best card to play' not merely 'for the resistance of liberalism in ecclesiastical affairs' but also 'for the leadership of the Liberal party in politics'— because of his awareness that it appealed to Radicals but could be made to appeal to conservatives as well.[1]

Gladstone was very conscious of the ambivalence of his position, of how his views did not correspond precisely with those of any one section but had an organic unity of their own.[2] Thus he told Goldwin Smith in 1877 that, while in matters of Church policy he was too much of a 'stiff denominationalist' to be in harmony with the 'average feeling of the party', on civil questions 'my opinions and leanings are too popular for the larger part of the aristocratic section of the party'.[3] Gladstone developed a very strong hold over Radical opinion without having to become the leader of the Radical section of the party. In 1873 he observed that, while on many questions his sympathies were with 'the advanced party', he could never lead it because of 'other and general grounds'.[4] But this refusal did not matter to the Radicals, indeed it was an advantage to them because it enabled Gladstone to preserve that wider authority and appeal which the Radicals so needed to assist their drive for power. The Radicals felt that there was enough common ground between them and Gladstone to give them hope of achieving under his leadership of the party as a whole some part of what they desired; and his hold over the electorate, particularly the actual and potential Radicals within it, naturally made them reluctant to break with him. The kind of calculation, or rather, as it turned out, miscalculation, that

---

[1] Selborne, *Memorials, Part Two*, vol. i, p. 360.
[2] In 1852 Gladstone had referred to his desire to be 'on the liberal side of the conservative party, rather than on the conservative side of the liberal party'. Morley, *Gladstone*, i, p. 431.
[3] Gladstone to Goldwin Smith, 14 November 1877, A Haultain (ed.), *A Selection from Goldwin Smith's Correspondence Comprising Letters Chiefly To and From His English Friends, Written Between the Years 1846 and 1910*, [1913], p. 62.
[4] Morley, *Gladstone*, ii, p. 65.

Radicals made about Gladstone is illustrated by Chamberlain's remark in 1876 that he was 'our best card': 'if he were to come back for a few years (he can't continue in public life for very much longer) he would probably do much for us, & pave the way for more.'[1] R. T. Shannon has summed up the implications for the Liberal party of the re-emergence of Gladstone from retirement after 1875 as 'the ruin of Radicalism'. The party was diverted from what seemed its logical development towards 'predominantly Radical inspiration and control'. The factor which 'most debilitated Radicalism' was Gladstone's command of the loyalty of most Radicals even although he was 'fundamentally alien to their outlook'. Radicalism 'could neither do with Gladstone nor do without him so long as he remained a force in public life'.[2]

One asset on which Gladstone could rely increasingly and which he could exploit to foster unity in the party was the existence in it of a substantial body of Liberals who were prepared to put complete trust in him and accept whatever he might propose or do, even if it were something that they would not on other grounds have agreed with. The Duke of Argyll referred in 1881 to Gladstone's 'authority in proposing *anything*'.[3] Hartington saw Gladstone's power as resting on the fact that 'the party are ready to take anything from him'.[4] A. J. Mundella may serve as an example of the kind of Liberal who had this attitude to Gladstone. In 1869 Granville reported to Gladstone that Mundella had declared 'that the confidence felt in you by him & others enabled you to do what you liked'.[5] In the crisis after the 1885 general election one finds this attitude recurring with Mundella writing to Gladstone that most Liberals, including himself, would accept whatever course on Ireland Gladstone chose to prescribe.[6] The existence of this feeling in the party was clearly one major reason why both Radicals and Whigs were so anxious to keep in contact with Gladstone and not to force a break that would leave them isolated with him

---

[1] Chamberlain to Dilke, 10 October 1876, Dilke MSS., B.M. Add. MS. 43885, folio 49.
[2] Shannon, *Gladstone and the Bulgarian Agitation*, pp. 273-4.
[3] Magnus, *Gladstone*, p. 298.   [4] Holland, *Devonshire*, ii, p. 73.
[5] Granville to Gladstone, 22 July 1869, Ramm, *1868-1876*, i, p. 38.
[6] Mundella to Gladstone, 15 December 1885, Gladstone MSS., B.M. Add. MS. 44258, folios 211-15.

against them. Radicals had good reason to fear the disruptive effects on Radicalism of a rift with a man who had such a hold over Radical opinion. Whigs saw in Gladstone's influence above all a guarantee against the assumption by the Radicals of complete control over the party; they feared too that their own rejection of his leadership might leave his political power and influence altogether at the disposal of Radical causes.[1]

More and more did the Whigs make their assessment of the situation in Liberal politics in terms of ensuring that Gladstone was not 'captured' by the other side through their own default. 'If you separate from him', Harcourt had warned Roundell Palmer as early as 1868, 'you will weaken the *right* and proportionately strengthen the *left* of the Liberal party; you will drive Gladstone by the force of circumstances into the hands of the Liberationists.'[2] Hartington saw that it was necessary for the Whigs to acquiesce in Gladstone's becoming Prime Minister in 1880 because of the probable dangerous consequences of the 'constant pressure' to which, if out of office, he would be subjected 'from the more extreme section of the party'. Sooner or later, wrote Hartington, Gladstone would criticize or even oppose what the Whig-led government was doing, and such was his hold over Liberal opinion that this would suffice to bring it down. He would then 'from the nature of the case be called to power, relying on the support of the more advanced section of the party, whereas, at the present time, if called on by Her Majesty to form a Government it would be necessary for him to obtain the support of as large a number as possible of its more moderate members'.[3] Until late 1885 Hartington, leader of a section which he knew and admitted to be a minority in the party, was most anxious that his section should not do anything 'to split up the party against Gladstone'. 'There is no doubt', he argued, 'that, if a split is to come, it will be much better that it should be caused by the Radicals against the Whigs and Gladstone, than by the Whigs against the Radicals and Gladstone.'[4] Gladstone's hold over Radical opinion paradoxically made it all the more necessary for Whigs to work to

---

[1] On this point, cf. Cowling, *1867*, pp. 89–90.
[2] A. G. Gardiner, *The Life of Sir William Harcourt*, vol. i, 1923, p. 179.
[3] Holland, *Devonshire*, i, p. 274.
[4] Hartington to the Duke of Devonshire, 14 January 1884, ibid. i, p. 404.

strengthen his position and authority. Hartington felt that 'the advanced section' would accept more moderate measures from Gladstone than they would require from any other Liberal leader, including himself.[1] Granville expressed this point of view when he rebuked one Whig peer, the Duke of Argyll, who did break with Gladstone. This mode of 'preventing Liberalism running off on tracks which you think false and dangerous' might well, he warned, 'have the contrary effect' for Gladstone as a political leader was in reality 'a *Conservative* power which will not be replaced by Salisbury, Churchill, or some of the best Whigs'.[2]

Lord Acton summed up very well how many saw Gladstone's position in Liberal politics when he wrote that the party was held together, 'not by forces within, but by a force above it'. It consisted of 'two wings and a head'. Were Gladstone's 'ascendency and the lustre of his fame' to be removed, insubordination, incohesion, and inability to govern because of internal friction would quickly come to characterize Liberal politics.[3] But the feelings which focused on Gladstone as the rallying-point in Liberalism were themselves 'forces within'. There *was* an impulse towards unity, a desire for cohesion and system. All depended on whether Gladstone was able to 'institutionalize' his influence, to translate it into some more objective and durable formula or institution.

[1] Hartington to Gladstone, 12 November 1882, Gladstone MSS., B.M. Add. MS. 44146, folios 103–4.
[2] Granville to Argyll, 11 July 1885, Fitzmaurice, *Life of Granville*, ii, p. 450.
[3] Acton to Mary Gladstone, 10 July 1880, 27 October 1881, Paul, *Letters of Lord Acton to Mary Gladstone*, pp. 20, 84–6. John Vincent's analysis of Gladstone's leadership is very relevant here: 'So quickly did he evolve, that differing impressions of him, mutually exclusive in the long run, but all favourable, were co-existent in the minds of great classes, and Gladstone obtained that support of the general interest he looked for, from a party which was a confederation of all classes, each acting in their own interests. By the velocity of his evolution towards many-sidedness, he temporarily squared the political circle.' *Formation of the Liberal Party*, p. 228.

IV The Second Gladstone Government, 1880–1885

GLADSTONE's second administration was beset constantly by crises in Irish and imperial affairs. These took up a very great part of the time and attention of Ministers and Parliament and are obviously a major reason for the very unhappy record of this government in the field of domestic legislation. Certainly the Liberal leaders themselves, and Gladstone in particular, frequently resorted to the explanation that they would have been attending to domestic reform actively and on a wide front had it not been for the perpetual diversion or obstruction which Irish and imperial problems created. This explanation was so often used that it became one of the basic assumptions of Liberal politics, and this assumption had a profound effect on the subsequent history of the party. The reality of the crises, the urgency of the problems which they raised, the necessity for the devotion of a great deal of time to them, cannot be disputed. But what is questionable is whether here alone is adequate explanation for the near paralysis which afflicted this government so far as reform was concerned for much of its time in office. Was the underlying state of Liberal and reform politics from which attention and effort were thus diverted itself healthy and orderly and capable of generating and sustaining vigorous reform activity? What kind of reform impulse *was* being obstructed?

It could be argued that much of this government's weakness stemmed in fact from the nature of the process which led up to what seemed at the time such a great electoral triumph for the Liberals in 1880. The election campaign was very negative both in atmosphere and in result. Gladstone involved the Liberals in a great emotional crusade against a tendency of policy—'Beaconsfieldism' in foreign and imperial policy—the ending of which would not constitute any kind of positive programme or scheme of legislative action. It was almost impossible to derive from what went on in 1879 and 1880 any impression as to what the voters wanted doing in domestic affairs. In a letter to Dilke at the end of 1879 Harcourt discussed how difficult it was to find a positive basis for electoral action:

> I really find nothing new to say. . . . I never felt it so difficult to mix a prescription good for the present feeling of the constituencies. . . . Depend upon it, if we are to win (as we shall), it will not be on some startling cry, but by the turning over to us of that floating mass of middle votes which went over to the Tories last time, and will come back from them in disgust at the next election. It is much easier to persuade the public that the Government are duffers than that we are conjurers.[1]

The Liberal leaders campaigned on no reform programme worthy of the name.[2] There was no clear action that had to follow from such an election. Therefore, unlike in 1868, the Liberal leaders, once elected, had to start from scratch and construct a legislative programme with very little benefit from prior discussion and preparation of specific topics.

Another problem was the lack of pressure and of activity in preparing reforms from the 'advanced' section of the party. Their vehicle, the National Liberal Federation, had moved almost at once into a primarily 'anti-Beaconsfield' stance, symbolized by Gladstone's being invited to address the inaugural conference mainly on account of the hold which his Bulgarian agitation had given him over Radical opinion. One of the aims of the promoters of the N.L.F. had been to achieve an ordering of priorities among reform questions. But between 1877 and 1880 all that was done in this direction was to subordinate everything else to the cause of turning out the government and ending 'Beaconsfieldism'. This kind of ordering was to be of no benefit after the election had been won. In the annual report of the N.L.F. presented in January 1879 it was admitted that the 'disturbed state of public feeling' on issues of foreign policy had 'diverted attention from questions of domestic

[1] Gwynn and Tuckwell, *Life of Dilke*, i, pp. 296–7.
[2] T. Lloyd, *The General Election of 1880*, 1968, p. 54.

legislation'; and Chamberlain told delegates that not only 'personal claims' and 'crotchets of all descriptions' but also 'some deep-seated convictions and long-cherished hopes of important reform' would have to give way to the supreme cause of getting rid of the Beaconsfield government.[1] Evidence of how the willingness of Radicals to work out policies and take a constructive attitude was affected by the atmosphere which Gladstone's campaigns created can be found in correspondence in the Bryce Papers which resulted from a suggestion by James Bryce in late 1878 that a new Liberal league or organization should be set up to construct and promote a programme of Radical reform.[2] John Morley, editor of the *Fortnightly Review* and close associate of Chamberlain, replied opposing the idea. 'The great object of all public effort at present', he wrote, 'should be, in my judgment, to drive home to our people the mischievous effects of the foreign policy of the government; both as to its results, and as to its methods.' He even thought that 'this ought to be for the present the substantive part of a new movement among the workmen', a section for whom Bryce had particularly believed a Radical programme to be necessary. Morley argued that all Liberal politics ought to be concentrated on 'the particular object of erecting such a vehement hostility to our bad foreign policy as will turn the government out':

If people cannot be aroused by the flagrant misdemeanours of the govmnt. in foreign affairs, they are not likely to be stirred by the dim hope of the changes so usefully enumerated in the Programme.

We shall make no way until the present govmt. is displaced. Will they not be more surely (and more justly) displaced on the issues of the hour, than on the prospect of reforms wh. are for the moment of indisputably secondary interest.[3]

This attitude of preferring concentration on some one great cause to a programme of reforms was characteristic of Morley and was ultimately to be one factor in the disruption of his

[1] *N.L.F. Report 1879*, pp. 13, 27.
[2] J. Morley to Bryce, 14 December 1878; H. Fawcett to Bryce, 29 December 1878; H. Broadhurst to Bryce, 10 January 1879; G. Howell to Bryce, 11 January 1879, Bryce MSS., P5.
[3] Yet four years earlier Morley had written to Chamberlain (12 March 1874, Chamberlain MSS.): 'What moves me is the notion of preparing Liberal Reactions, *and making sure that it shall mean something when it does come*' (my italics).

association with Chamberlain.¹ Especially significant is the appearance of the theme of an obstruction to progress in the accomplishment of reform programmes. Morley's negative approach to the situation was echoed by Henry Fawcett who likewise rejected Bryce's scheme.

I feel it to be of such vital importance [he wrote] to displace the present Government that I think it will be the duty of all Liberals at the next Election to sink minor differences. However united we may be it will be sufficiently difficult to effect that object, & there will be no chance of doing so, if among any section of Liberals in the Constituencies a feeling should arise against supporting a candidate unless he accepted the articles of a particular programme.

Another Radical who adopted this attitude during 1878 was A. J. Mundella. He argued that, since, 'if we go to War, all reforms, great and small, will be postponed indefinitely', it was very important, 'in a *radical sense* as well as a party sense', to work 'to strengthen the party': 'I am in that style of mind that Joseph Hume once was in when he said he would vote black to be white to get rid of a Tory Government.'² On the other hand, Henry Broadhurst, the prominent Lib-Lab, wrote to Bryce approving the programme and deploring the way in which 'the Liberal Party seems to want to return to power without being pledged to Liberal work'. The labour people with whom he was in contact were anxious to get rid of the Conservative government; but they were asking as well, 'What is the programme of the Liberals when they get into office?'

Sectionalism was remarkably subdued in 1880, Gladstone's crusade against Beaconsfieldism being almost universally accepted as an overriding cause.³ Lady Frederick Cavendish, who had complained bitterly in 1874 that the party was 'suffering for its innumerable hobby-riders and crotchet-mongers', now noted with surprise that the party seemed 'absolutely united; many questions are sometimes asked as to drink, disestablishment, etc., but there seems no fear of losing any votes

¹ Hamer, *John Morley*, pp. 160–1.
² Mundella to J. D. Leader, 26 February 1878, Mundella MSS., folio IX. Mundella wrote to R. Leader, 2 March 1876: '... as you say, a Tory Government gets rid of Liberal Crotchets and cements us together as a party.' Mundella MSS., folio IX.
³ Lloyd, *General Election of 1880*, pp. 51, 114, 148.

by these differences, and we fly into the arms of rabid Dissenters and teetotallers, all as gentle as sucking-doves.'[1] Nonconformist leaders refused to raise the disestablishment issue because they saw the defeat of the government as more important than any particular reform cause.[2] After the election at a meeting of Nonconformists the influential and veteran M.P., Henry Richard, promised that they would not withdraw confidence from the new Liberal government if it did not proceed to try to incorporate their demands in legislation; they accepted Gladstone's argument that the government had first to deal with its inheritance of Tory blunders, complications, and crimes.[3] But this subduing of sectionalism, which looked on the face of it to be such an advantage for the party, was perhaps not really an unmixed blessing. For with the voices of the sectionalists stilled there was little discussion of policy even of the 'faddist' variety. There was no urgent pressure from anyone on the Liberal leaders for the formulation of domestic policy. One contemporary analyst of the election argued that the men of 'isms', of 'special measures', were essential contributors to the vitality of the party.[4] If this was so, Liberal politics in 1880 were not in quite such a healthy state as superficial appearances suggested. There was a notable absence of controversy over reform policy in 1880; but it was soon only too obvious that the calm had been the calm of a vacuum. Nothing solid was being prepared that might have enabled the second Gladstone administration to withstand the impact of repeated Irish and imperial crises and preserve some semblance of order and purpose in domestic policy.

It did not withstand them. Year after year the government's legislative programme was in large part abandoned. Although Irish and imperial crises were obviously primarily responsible

[1] Bailey, *Diary of Lady Frederick Cavendish*, ii, pp. 168, 244 (entries for 11 February 1874 and 29 March–4 April 1880).

[2] Dale, *Life of R. W. Dale*, p. 428. J. Guinness Rogers, *An Autobiography*, 1903, p. 214. Hanham, *Elections and Party Management*, p. 124: Hanham quotes Gladstone's praise of the 'noble example' which this section of the party was setting: 'They are putting their own views into the shade in order that they may not interfere with the success of the cause in which they believe their particular idea is included and absorbed.'

[3] C. S. Miall, *Henry Richard, M.P. A Biography*, 1889, pp. 319–20.

[4] W. Saunders, *The New Parliament, 1880*, 1880, pp. 180–1.

for this, it is clear that lack of planning and co-ordination also contributed substantially to the creation of such a situation. One of the most detailed analyses of this government's weaknesses is that by Agatha Ramm in her introduction to the Gladstone–Granville correspondence.[1] She shows that there was a basic condition of disorder and confused thinking which the emergencies of the period aggravated but did not create. There was very little planning done through Cabinet meetings at any stage, and the government drifted from one session to another without adequate preparation of plans for the use of parliamentary time and the organization of parliamentary business. A major weakening factor was Gladstone's failure to provide over-all control and sense of direction and long-term purpose. He was often ill, and in any case did not feel any great pressure of concern about the future of the party as he—and many other Liberals—assumed that he was on the verge of retirement.[2] Sir Edward Hamilton was to note how Gladstone's judgement was increasingly affected by his 'yearning to retire' which caused him to try to stand aside from debates about future Liberal policy.[3] The Cabinet failed to function as an effective co-ordinator of policy and strategy. Decisions were taken by 'conclaves' or 'quasi-cabinets', votes were taken, and there was a marked tendency to 'leakiness' and unauthorized initiatives by members of it.

At the outset, before Ireland or Egypt had begun seriously to take up the government's time, some Liberals were very concerned about the need to forestall the advent of drift and cumulative frustration. Robert Lowe warned in 1880 that 'the first moments of a Government were golden' and must be seized. Questions could then be settled which, 'if delayed, it might afterwards be impossible to settle for ten years'. As time passed, the government's 'essence and power' were bound to be eroded by 'cabals and weakness within it'. The government should therefore not waste time in bringing forward measures of secondary importance but should grasp the opportunity to 'deal with matters of the first and greatest importance'.[4] But

[1] Ramm, *1876–1886*, i, pp. xxxviii–xlvi.
[2] Hammond, *Gladstone and the Irish Nation*, pp. 165–6.
[3] Sir E. Hamilton's Diary, B.M. Add. MS. 48640, folio 49 (5 May 1885).
[4] Quoted in Saunders, *The New Parliament*, p. 114.

here was the problem. The Liberal leaders came into office with no programme of measures at all, let alone any understanding of degrees of importance; and the extra-parliamentary organization had not fulfilled its purpose of working out priorities. One of the younger Liberals, G. O. Trevelyan, wanted the county franchise tackled at once: 'They must not fritter away their vast strength in minor questions, or even consume it in salutary reforms which will bear one or two sessions' delay.'[1] But no detailed scheme had yet been worked out: the Liberal leaders in 1880 were plainly not yet ready to concentrate on this reform.

James Bryce, who, as we have seen, was so worried in 1878 about the absence of preparation of policy, now sensed what troubles the government was likely to run into and prepared a 'Memo. on the Imperfection of the Arrangements of the Government and of the House of Commons For the Work to be Done'. In it he foreshadowed the process of disorganization that was to occur over the next few years, although his purpose was to comment more generally on the unsatisfactory nature of relations between the House of Commons and the government, whatever party was in control of it.

The absence of any systematic arrangement of the work expected from a Parliament, carefully considered beforehand, and publicly announced, seems to those accustomed to business or other organisation a serious defect.

The procedure is strangely unmethodical, unbusinesslike, and altogether inadequate to the needs of modern legislation. Measures are brought in each session far beyond the possibilities of either completion or discussion; Ministers appear to be left to scramble in the Cabinet or out of it for the precedence of their own progeny....

His remedy was for a government when elected to announce the main subjects of legislation to be dealt with by it over the next five or six years and the order in which they would be taken up, making it clear 'that no pressure should induce them to attempt to pass too many Bills at once'. He then proposed a programme for the new Liberal government.[2] Of the items in this only one was in fact to have been at all satisfactorily dealt

---

[1] Quoted in ibid., p. 148.
[2] This printed memorandum is to be found in Bryce MSS., P5. It is unsigned and undated, but is clearly by Bryce and refers to the 1880 election.

with by 1885—franchise reform and redistribution of seats. On most of the rest nothing was to be achieved at all.

Chamberlain too had a plan—and a presentiment of trouble. He warned Harcourt in April 1880 that 'a solid meal must be provided for the Liberal lions—if they are to be kept from rending one another'. It was essential to 'keep the present fire alive' and to be able to go to the country again 'before the present wave has spent its force'. He therefore wanted the government to concentrate on the production of two 'exhaustive' 'omnibus Bills' dealing with 'the Land and the Franchise'.[1] But no such strategy was adopted. In September 1880 Gladstone did admit that there was a need to get some thinking done on 'the relative advantages and disadvantages of the greatest legislative subjects before us for the chief work of next Session— such as, Land, suffrage, local Government'. But already there was an ominous note. The 'gravity of the Candahar affair', was, he wrote, tending to put such matters 'out of my head'.[2] Gladstone had, after all, in his opinion and that of most Liberals as well, been elected primarily to deal with the legacy of 'Beaconsfieldism', and the 'Candahar affair' was very representative of that legacy. The spirit of Midlothian remained strong, and Liberals continued to be influenced by it to make allowances and curb their impatience. In May 1881 Chamberlain wrote: 'It looks possible that next year we may at last be free from the complications of the Tory policy and able to devote ourselves absolutely to Home legislation and reform.'[3]

But no preparation was being undertaken for this situation. The Cabinets of 1880-1 and the parliamentary session of 1881 were largely given over to Ireland. When it looked as though 1882 was going to be equally unplanned for, Harcourt wrote to Gladstone demanding a decision on whether or not the reform of London government was to be dealt with as time was needed for the preparation of so complex and contentious a measure: 'It is one of the disadvantages of the postponement of the Cabinet that the decisions not being taken as to which Bills are to be undertaken the preparation of them is delayed.'[4]

[1] Chamberlain to Harcourt, 10 April 1880, Chamberlain MSS., JC 5/38/119.
[2] Gladstone to Granville, 13 September 1880, Ramm, *1876–1886*, i, pp. 172–3.
[3] Chamberlain to J. T. Bunce, 6 May 1881, Chamberlain MSS., JC 5/8/56.
[4] Harcourt to Gladstone, 15 December 1881, Gladstone MSS., B.M. Add. MS. 44196, folios 253–4.

Gladstone envisaged a large scheme of reform of parliamentary procedure and devolution of functions of government as the great work of 1882;[1] but the pressure of Irish business—a major cause in itself of Gladstone's mounting interest in such reform—forced even a very limited part of this scheme off the parliamentary agenda. Reform of local government, including that of London, had to be 'thrown over for the year'.[2] No planning of any importance was done for 1883, and what was meant to be the main measure of that year, London government reform, was not even submitted to Parliament.[3] Liberals such as Harcourt and Dilke who put a great deal of hard work into the preparation of Bills naturally became intensely frustrated;[4] and the party in the House of Commons grew increasingly uneasy at the wholesale jettisoning every year of entire legislative programmes which contained measures that had been previously described by government spokesmen as of great urgency.[5] 'Moderate' Liberals had their own reason for impatience: the desire to see major issues dealt with by this Parliament, not one elected under an extended franchise in which Radicals might have greater influence.[6]

Bryce had appreciated that the only alternative to planning and establishing priorities was the anarchy resulting from the simultaneous and uncontrollable pushing of the numerous reform causes in which Liberals had special interests. A firm commitment at the outset to a five- or six-year programme, a firm statement as to the order in which issues would be dealt with, and an expression of determination not to be deflected from this programme and order, would keep the sections happy by giving them something to hope for while making them

[1] Gladstone to Granville, 2 November 1881, Ramm, *1876–1886*, i, p. 308.
[2] Gladstone to Granville, 8 April 1882, ibid. i, pp. 356–7.
[3] Ibid. i, p. xxxi. On 7 July 1883 the Cabinet abandoned eight Bills and decided to persist with six, of which only three reached the statute book.
[4] Harcourt wrote to Chamberlain, 19 January 1883: 'The worst of it is that we have no programme settled nor likely to be settled for the Q.'s speech of the work of the Session. And the most singular thing is that I can't get anyone to see the seriousness of this want especially after the expectations which will be raised by the passing of the Procedure Rules.' Harcourt MSS. For Dilke, see Gwynn and Tuckwell, *Life of Dilke*, ii, pp. 10–14.
[5] e.g. the complaints voiced by H. H. Fowler on 4 July and Jesse Collings on 10 July 1884. *Hansard*, 3rd Series, vol. 290, cc. 37,743.
[6] Cf. Childers to Gladstone, 21 December 1884, 14 January 1885, Gladstone MSS., B.M. Add. MS. 44131, folios 247–9; 44132, folio 29.

realize that intimidatory or obstructive pressure would be futile.[1] Instead, what happened was the very reverse of this. The 1880 election having produced no firm commitment by the leadership to any scheme or arrangement of policy and not having enabled *them* to point to any mandate from the electors beyond the overthrowing of Beaconsfieldism, sectionalists were able to step in and make claims that were as hard to disprove as they were to substantiate, that under the surface their questions had really been the ones that the electors were interested in. The truce of 1879–80 was soon broken. The sections began clamouring for priority of attention, and the Liberal leaders soon seemed to be spending more time in finding excuses for inaction than in getting things done. Apologizing for impotence was ominously becoming the hallmark of the Liberal leader.

There was such a variety of reform causes being promoted that choice was bound to be very difficult and invidious. What made matters worse was that there was no cause which was clearly and unmistakably popular in the country or which had an overriding importance that was apparent not only to the leaders but also to the adherents of all the other causes and interests. Licensing reform is a good example of an issue which, on the one hand, was very popular among Liberal activists, but, on the other, was bound to stir up against the government a great deal of hostile feeling. The advantages and the disadvantages of taking it up were both very considerable, and so the government fell into its increasingly habitual state of paralysis. As soon as the new Parliament met, Sir Wilfrid Lawson's local option resolution began securing the support of a majority of the House. In June 1880 it was carried for the first time ever with 133 English Liberal M.P.s for and only 35 against.[2] It was clear that here was a question on which rank-and-file Liberals felt strongly, and there could be no doubt that the election *had* made a difference. From this it was a short step to saying that this was what the election had been all about.[3] Although Gladstone himself abstained in this vote, he

[1] 'Memo. on the Imperfection . . .', p. 5.
[2] Carter, *Temperance Movement*, p. 200.
[3] For examples of this claim, see ibid., p. 199, and J. Newton, *W. S. Caine, M.P. A Biography*, 1907, pp. 83, 102.

did promise that licensing reform would be among 'the great subjects to which the attention of the Executive Government shall be directed as early as the pressure of business will allow'.[1] Eighteen members of the government, including Harcourt, Bright, and Chamberlain, voted for the resolution.

There was no reference, however, to licensing reform in the Queen's Speech of 1881. Lawson's resolution once more received a majority, but the government was divided on it, twenty ministers voting for and five against. The five included Gladstone who was by this time becoming alarmed about sectionalism and was clearly determined to discourage it. On 10 June 1881 he intervened in a debate on a motion calling for the introduction of land reform to state that the government should not and would not try to earn popularity by entering into general commitments when it had no immediate intention of giving these legislative effect.[2] But the sectionalists began to press hard. Introducing his resolution, Lawson made a number of points which were soon to become familiar themes with Radicals. He warned against paying too much attention to the problems of five million Irish and neglecting the thirty-five million 'people of this Island', and demanded action on the liquor question as soon as 'the time shall have come when the attention of the Government can be turned to anything else than Irish affairs'.[3] Threats of rebellion began to be heard. James Stansfeld, leading campaigner for the repeal of the Contagious Diseases Acts, indicated that his patience was running out: '. . . no one has ever been able to say that I put personal objects above my allegiance to my party's cause. But for myself the time has come for something more than this, and I here declare that upon this subject, I owe, henceforth, no allegiance whatsoever save to my conscience and the higher law.'[4] Efforts by party leaders to secure an indefinite prolongation of the truce of 1880 began meeting with resistance. In November 1881 Dr. Rainy, one of the leaders of the Scottish disestablishment movement, complained directly to Gladstone about this. He agreed that 'decisive legislative action on the

---

[1] Carter, *Temperance Movement*, pp. 200–1.
[2] Ibid., pp. 201–2. *Hansard*, 3rd Series, vol. 267, cc. 304–5.
[3] *Hansard*, 3rd Series, vol. 267, cc. 524–5.
[4] Hammond, *James Stansfeld*, p. 224.

subject is not to be looked for in this Parliament' because the disestablishers had 'concurred in the policy of forbearing to push the question at [the] last general election'; but now they wanted it freely and fully discussed so that it could be an issue at the next election and settled by the Parliament then chosen. Gladstone declined to receive a deputation on Scottish disestablishment, however, giving the characteristic excuse that all other matters were for the time 'thrown into the background' by one great issue, in this instance the reform of parliamentary procedure.[1]

In a speech in October 1881 Gladstone reminded Liberals that sectional divisions had caused defeat in 1874 and urged them to maintain a state of 'healthy union'.[2] But such warnings were not now adequate. Gladstone's 'sense of measure' impelled him to seek a basic cause, a comprehensive explanation, for the disintegration and drift which were overtaking Liberal politics once more. The explanation at which he arrived was that the machinery of government was being blocked or obstructed. At the end of 1882 he wrote advising a colleague to reply to an impatient promoter of the interests of a particular section that 'the joint effect of emergencies in Ireland & the block in the H of C has been almost absolutely to cancel the available power to make progress in public affairs for a period of two years: hence state of arrear in all legislative & organic business'.[3] 'Arrears of legislation' is from this time on to be a phrase that is used again and again by Gladstone and the other Liberal leaders. They seem to become obsessed with the problem, to feel it overwhelming them, and there is more and more talk of 'obstructions to progress' and the need for all Liberals, whatever particular reforms they were concerned for, to concentrate on clearing these out of the way. Gladstone himself became preoccupied with the question of 'unblocking' Parliament. Ireland constituted an obstruction because its affairs needed such constant attention; the answer was to make the House of Commons better able to deal with the business which did come before it, while at the same time 'devolving' as much business as possible,

---

[1] P. C. Simpson, *The Life of Principal Rainy*, vol. ii, 1909, pp. 10–12, 15.
[2] *Speeches Delivered by the Rt. Hon. W. E. Gladstone, at Leeds, October 7th and 8th, 1881*, [1881], pp. 6–7.
[3] Gladstone to Granville, 26 December 1882, Ramm, *1876–1886*, i, p. 478.

and especially that of Ireland, on to other regional and local bodies. Hence the grand schemes which now begin forming in his mind and in which reform of parliamentary procedure, 'devolution', local government reform, and the introduction of some kind of 'home rule' for Ireland, and if possible Scotland and Wales as well, are indissolubly connected.[1] Institutional reform came to seem, and to be presented to impatient Liberals as, the key that alone could secure the restoration of order and the resumption of progress in Liberal politics. To all Liberals who wanted particular reforms attended to the word which was from now on to be used to explain why they were not being attended to was 'obstruction'. The will to progress, a clear and agreed understanding as to what 'progress' now meant and in what direction it now led—these might or might not in fact exist. But the need to discover whether they did could now be obscured. Liberals were being drawn away from debating the nature of 'progress' to removing obstacles to 'progress', whatever their particular understandings of its meaning might be.

Throughout the nineteenth century the removal of obstructions had been one of the predominant themes of Liberalism, but there was a significant change in the way in which it was now being interpreted. The repeal of the Corn Laws and all the other restrictions on, and legislative and governmental interferences with, economic activity, the overthrowing of privilege and the opening up to men of talent and ability of access to positions of power—all reforms of this kind were not preludes to progress but themselves represented what Liberals understood progress to be. Progress was equated with freedom, with the 'liberation' of the individual and the minimizing of control by the State over the development of society and the organization of economic activity. But now the obstructions that Liberals were concerned with were merely forces preventing the extension of State interference, the passing of reform legislation, the use of political power to enact certain demands for 'progress' Progress had ceased to be implicit in the process by which the obstructions were removed. It was now to depend on what use was made of the situation after that removal had been effected. The change reflects the transition from enthusiasm for

[1] For examples, see Hammond, *Gladstone and the Irish Nation*, pp. 183, 198–204, 259–62.

dismantling of governmental power to demands for the positive use of such power. This is why the obsession with the clearance of obstructions becomes much more genuinely negative. It no longer springs out of a philosophy of progress but now unites Liberals only in so far as it represents to all of them an essential preliminary to the putting into effect of the various interpretations of the principles of progress to which the sections among them are devoted.

Even if the government did have time to attend to reform legislation, there was no simple means of deciding to which of the numerous reform demands this very limited amount of time should be given. Nor could the sections see any convincing reasons why any particular reform question should receive priority over their own. A typical attitude was that of W. S. Caine as expressed in the debate in April 1883 on Lawson's local option resolution. He complained bitterly about the continuing absence of legislation on the liquor question: 'We felt we had a right to expect, in a Session devoted to useful social measures, that we should have had a prominent, if not the first, place, and that the Queen's Speech would have contained some intimation from the Government of their intention to deal with a question which interests the public more deeply than any other.'[1] Ministers, aware that they would achieve nothing at all if they tried to legislate on everything at once, sought anxiously for some ordering principle. In March 1883 Harcourt wrote to Gladstone about his London Government Bill that he had a 'great horror' of a Minister who obstinately urged the claims of his own department 'at the expense of the general interests of the whole'. Perhaps, therefore, it would be well to give priority to the Tenants Compensation Bill because it 'interests a larger area (though hardly a larger population) in the country'.[2] Gladstone typically began trying to isolate from among the mass of reform proposals some single great measure in which the expression of Liberalism could be concentrated. In May 1883 he wrote to Harcourt that he placed 'rather high the political expediency, or necessity, of going forward with the London Bill during the present year': 'The Liberal party as a

[1] *Hansard*, 3rd Series, vol. 278, c. 1296.
[2] 22 March 1883, Gladstone MSS., B.M. Add. MS. 44198, folios 19–20.

SECOND GLADSTONE GOVERNMENT, 1880–1885

rule draws its vital breath from great Liberal measures. Sometimes it can afford an interval of rest; sometimes it cannot. It so happens that at present we have many good Bills in hand; but they are not understood as distinctively Liberal Bills.'[1]

By this time a means of satisfying this requirement and establishing order was appearing as government spokesmen began to stress that the extension of the county franchise, 'above all, is the measure of the greatest importance which this Parliament was elected to accomplish', and supporters of particular questions began to note how 'the shadow of this great business was already exercising a paralysing influence upon legislation' because of the belief expressed by Ministers that 'reforms in other directions must be deferred till the agricultural population were enfranchised'.[2] That the Reform Bill became a provisional solution for the whole problem of sectionalism can be seen in Harcourt's announcement to M.P.s in July 1884 that the government were dropping everything else except it because of the great difficulty of dropping some Bills in which people 'took a special interest' and not others. 'There is a good rule in bankruptcy that there is to be no favour shown to any creditor, and it would be a species of fraudulent preference to favour any particular Bill in our present state of bankruptcy of legislation.'[3]

In little more than a year Harcourt had veered from one extreme to the other—a veering that is characteristic of the history of Liberal policy throughout this period. In May 1883 he had told Gladstone that he and several of his Cabinet colleagues believed 'that it is absolutely necessary in order to rehabilitate the Party and the Govt. and most of all the H. of C. that we should announce a determination to go on with all our measures and take an Autumn Session for the purpose'.[4] Yet by July 1884 he was urging the Cabinet 'to *throw overboard everything in the way of legislation*': 'If we attempt to drag on with

---

[1] 18 May 1883, Harcourt MSS.
[2] *Hansard*, 3rd Series, vol. 277, cc. 1,131, 1,143 (Arthur Arnold and Harcourt, 30 March 1883). Cf. 'Home and Foreign Affairs', *F.R.*, N.S., no. 199 (July 1883), p. 148: 'The consciousness that this [a Reform Bill] is the real remaining business of the Government reacts with a distinctly mischievous and debilitating influence upon their policy. The shadow of the eclipse, which can only be delayed by eighteen months, or of the circumstances which will precede that eclipse, paralyses action in just the same degree as it quickens conjecture.'
[3] *Hansard*, 3rd Series, vol. 290, c. 751.
[4] Harcourt to Gladstone, 24 May 1883, Harcourt MSS.

a selection of second and third rate measures we shall have a terrible wrangle over the choice and give great offence to the friends of those which are omitted.'¹ Chamberlain himself now began to describe parliamentary reform as 'the subject which is the root of all others and the settlement of which will give the greatest possible stimulus to all the reforms which the Liberal party have in their heart to carry'.² With concentration on a Reform Bill all sections could be treated alike, and none could have cause for complaint about having been passed over. A sectionalist such as James Stansfeld was willing to make allowances in 1884 and not press for the legislation that he wanted. But by 1885 the pressure was beginning to build up again. Early in the year he declared that the government no longer had an excuse for its inaction regarding the Contagious Diseases Acts and that of the measures before Parliament only the Redistribution Bill had any just claim for precedence over the repeal of these Acts.³ Sir Wilfrid Lawson wrote to Harcourt in December 1884 that he did not complain of the absence of governmental action on the liquor question 'during the peculiar Session of last summer—although individually, I believe that legislation in the interests of public morality is quite as important as measures to extend political freedom'. But, while conceding that the circumstances of that Session had been 'abnormal', he urged on Harcourt that 'now the *very time* for action appears to have arrived'. If Harcourt did not give assurances at the beginning of the next Session that the government intended to deal with the liquor question, Lawson would try to move a resolution 'affirming that there should be no further delay in the matter'. He was sure that most Liberal M.P.s would support this, for they could see 'the new constituency looming in the distance' and 'know well enough that the new Reform Bill enfranchises hardly any publicans, but thousands and thousands of the publicans' enemies'.⁴

'General', i.e. supra-sectional, Radicalism was in as great a state of disorganization and confusion of purpose as was

---

¹ Harcourt to Gladstone, 9 July 1884, Harcourt MSS.
² Lucy, *Speeches of Joseph Chamberlain*, p. 47.
³ Hammond, *James Stansfeld*, pp. 244–5.
⁴ 17 December 1884, Harcourt MSS.

'official' Liberalism and had little to contribute to Liberal politics at this stage that was either positive or constructive. Its dependence on Gladstone had been highlighted by the 1880 election campaign when the Radicals had not even tried to adopt any kind of independent position. There were very few Radical leaders, and the best from these were, albeit after some show of reluctance on Gladstone's part in particular, creamed off into the party leadership. The party leaders treated Radicalism as akin to the hydra, chopping off its heads whenever these appeared.[1] After 1880 there was a growing divergence between those Radicals who held office and had to share responsibility for the decisions and actions of the government and those who remained outside the government and did not like aspects of government policy and behaviour in which their erstwhile leaders were thus acquiescing.[2] Increasingly it was more than just a split between office-holders and back-benchers; there was also a rift of philosophies, between 'constructive' Radicals such as Chamberlain and Dilke who wanted to make full use of the power of the State and the more traditional Radicals whose position was based on suspicion of government and desire to minimize its activity. The rift in Radicalism that finally did occur in 1886 had been in preparation for some time.

Chamberlain was as usual full of a quite unjustified confidence that a strong and concentrated Radicalism did exist in the country and the party and was only waiting to be utilized by leaders such as himself whenever they wished to do so. Thus in 1880 he threatened that, if he were omitted from the government, he would organize a 'pure left' party in the House and in the country.[3] To Dilke and Chamberlain the problem was much more one of finding leaders than of finding followers: the followers were assumed to be there waiting to be led. In 1880 Dilke wrote that if the Radicals were to break with 'Whiggery' they would need to 'have the great names of Gladstone and Bright' upon their side. They had no 'men to officer our ranks': 'really, besides Mr. Gladstone, who was an old man, there was only Chamberlain.' The others seemed dismal—'windbags' or

[1] Cf. *Letters of Lord Aberdare*, i, p. 357; ii, p. 90.
[2] Hamer, *John Morley*, pp. 134–5. E. H. Fowler, *The Life of Henry Hartley Fowler, First Viscount Wolverhampton, G.C.S.I.*, 1912, p. 168.
[3] Chamberlain to Collings, 27 April 1880, Chamberlain MSS., JC 5/16/93.

'good third-rate men' at best.¹ In October 1885 Chamberlain complained that, although 'the rank and file are all right', 'there is an awful lack of Generals, and even of non-commissioned officers'.² He and Dilke might profitably have spent less time worrying about the quality of leadership—a concern which reflects their primary interest in using governmental power —and more time investigating whether the rank and file really were 'all right', as well as considering whether the shortage of Radical leaders might not have been related to the predominant Radical ideology of the time.

They were, however, becoming aware of doctrinal divisions. Dilke came to feel that one of the main obstacles to the formation of 'a solid party' of Radicals was the holding by Chamberlain and himself of 'strongly patriotic and national opinions in foreign affairs'.³ During this period an anti-imperialist, 'little England' school of Radicals was diverging more and more from imperialist Radicals. Clearly involved in this were attitudes towards the role of the State. The imperialists, as Chamberlain's Irish policy shows, found no discrepancy between constructive reform politics at home and an imperial policy based on the desire to construct and improve abroad. Resolute Cobdenites, on the other hand, tended to be as opposed to State intervention at home as they were to the 'meddling' of the State in the affairs of other peoples and its aggrandisement through the growth of a territorial Empire. Nowhere is the distinction more clearly seen than in the career of John Morley who, beginning in the early 1870s as one of Chamberlain's closest advisers and colleagues on the basis of traditional anti-State Radicalism (disestablishment, 'free church, free schools, free land, free labour'), breaks with him in the 1880s when his Radicalism evolves in the direction of a more 'constructive' use of State power at home and abroad.⁴ In his speeches justifying

¹ Gwynn and Tuckwell, *Life of Dilke*, i, p. 347. R. Jenkins, *Sir Charles Dilke. A Victorian Tragedy*, 1968 edition, p. 148.
² Chamberlain to Labouchere, 20 October 1885, A. L. Thorold, *The Life of Henry Labouchere*, 1913, p. 240. On 12 October 1885 he wrote to Collings: 'I wish we had more help & more backbone. As it is we have a splendid army but no non-commissioned officers.' Chamberlain MSS. JC 5/16/109.
³ Gwynn and Tuckwell, *Life of Dilke*, i, p. 364. Cf. Morley to Chamberlain, 16 December 1882, and Chamberlain to Morley, 29 November 1883, Chamberlain MSS. JC 5/54/464, 524.
⁴ Hamer, *John Morley*, pp. 141–76. They even began to diverge over the question

the greater use of State power Chamberlain was not only attacking Conservative and Whig opposition but also advocating a new departure in Radical attitudes to the State:

> When Government represented only the authority of the Crown or the views of a particular class, I can understand that it was the first duty of men who valued their freedom to restrict its authority and to limit its expenditure. But all that is changed. Now Government is the organized expression of the wishes and the wants of the people, and under these circumstances let us cease to regard it with suspicion. Suspicion is the product of an older time—of circumstances which have long since disappeared.[1]

As Chamberlain was to discover, not all Liberals shared his confidence that 'the people' were or could be a force in politics that would transcend the interests of particular classes in shaping the attitudes of the new voters.

The Liberal leaders appreciated that what was needed above all was the concentration of Liberal political activity, the uniting of Liberals behind some one standard or in the pursuit of some particular objective. The alternative, of trying to deal with all their demands at once, was clearly the recipe for disaster. Harcourt in particular now began to assume the role which he was to play in Liberal politics for the next ten years, of being the member of the leadership most insistent that reforms should be taken up to appease 'the party' and make amends to them for the long periods of frustration that they were being required to suffer. In January 1883 he wrote to Granville that 'we must have at least one political measure from a Party point of view' and suggested 'either Liquor or County Franchise'.[2] Gladstone was, as usual, the most sympathetic of Harcourt's colleagues. When in April 1883 Harcourt told him that 'I feel sure that if we do

of disestablishment about which Chamberlain was already becoming much less enthusiastic. A more profound disagreement on the role of the State is revealed. Morley to Chamberlain, 17 June 1883, Chamberlain MSS., JC 5/54/506: 'Your doctrine about keeping the priests &c. under the grip of the state, is bad—in my sober and daylight judgment. It is the Whig and Erastian plea for Establishment: viz. that it enables sensible politicians to keep fanatical fools in order. Leave the spiritual power alone, I say. You will only get into a hopeless mess, as Bismark has done. I'm all against your "autoritaire". I don't believe in it, and I never did. Your Cromwells and Fredericks don't do their work half as well as slow sober free American citizens.' [1] Lucy, *Speeches of Joseph Chamberlain*, pp. 131, 188.
[2] Gardiner, *Life of Harcourt*, i, p. 470.

not give Lawson[1] a substantial support there will be great dissatisfaction in the Party', Gladstone expressed his agreement.[2] 'It is certainly desirable', he wrote in May, 'to have this year some one measure to rouse and rally the party.'[3] Harcourt kept pressing, and now formulated his argument, in which he was to persist for at least the next ten years, that the reform of liquor licensing was the key to the 'rallying' of the party. He had reached the conclusion that 'the Temperance Party' was 'an important perhaps the most important section of the Liberal Party'. By 1885 they had much cause, in his opinion, for feeling aggrieved at their neglect by the leadership. The customary excuses—'that we have too much else to do', and that the electorate should have its say before anything was done on the question—were inadequate to appease them. 'What are we to do?'[4]

One possibility was that local government reform might be made to serve as a great 'umbrella' covering simultaneous attention to a wide range of problems such as Ireland, local option, and parliamentary 'arrears'. This idea began to develop in the minds of Gladstone, Chamberlain, and Dilke;[5] but the drawback was that the Liberal leaders needed quick results, and local government reform of this kind was altogether too vast a subject to yield short-term legislative achievement. Another cause that might 'rally' and also be an 'umbrella' was an attack on the House of Lords which seemed to some Radicals an obvious next step after the extension of the franchise.[6] The problem here is summed up in John Morley's phrase about 'mending or ending' the Lords which H. H. Fowler described as representing the two horns of an '(already) classical dilemma'.[7] Many moderate Liberals shrank from the extreme policy of abolition, and it was clear that abolitionist Radicals could not hope to carry the party on this; but 'mending' might well have the effect of strengthening the Lords' position by making it a more representative institution.

[1] i.e. Sir Wilfrid Lawson's local option resolution.
[2] Gardiner, *Life of Harcourt*, i, pp. 480–1.
[3] Gladstone to Granville, 17 May 1883, Ramm, *1876–1886*, ii, p. 51.
[4] Harcourt to Gladstone, 21 January 1884, 18 January 1885, Gladstone MSS., B.M. Add. MS. 44199, folios 3, 174–5.
[5] For Gladstone see his letter to Harcourt, 19 January 1885, Gladstone MSS., B.M. Add. MS. 44547, folio 164.   [6] Hamer, *John Morley*, pp. 147–50.
[7] Fowler, *Life of Viscount Wolverhampton*, pp. 161–3.

V The Crisis of 1885

IN Liberal politics in the late nineteenth century there was continual oscillation of enthusiasm between the two modes of action—the single great 'concentrating' question and the programme. 1885 marks one of the high points of support for programme politics. For Chamberlain's Radical campaign of that year is based explicitly on the principle that the programme is now the right and proper form of organization in reform politics. *The Radical Programme* was offered as something 'upon which the energies of Radicals may be concentrated, and which may form a rallying ground for the party'.[1] This assumption, that concentration and 'rallying' were possible by means of a programme, was always repudiated by 'single question' Liberals. But Chamberlain's view was that the wider the electorate was, the more necessary it was to have a large programme to satisfy the increased range of sections, interests, and wants within that electorate.[2] The more 'planks' there were in a programme, the more support the party proposing it would receive: to him programme politics were this simple. His attitude is well illustrated by a memorandum which he was to send to Lord Salisbury in 1894 advocating the adoption by the Unionists of 'a large and generous programme': 'I need hardly point out how greatly the strategic effect of any policy of this kind would be increased by the cumulative influence which would be gained by dealing not merely with one or two isolated questions, but with a great number of important points forming together a complete scheme of reform which would be likely to appeal to the popular imagination.'[3]

---

[1] *The Radical Programme. With a Preface by the Right Hon. J. Chamberlain, M.P.* 1885, p. 20. On 14 June 1885 Sir Edward Hamilton recorded in his diary after a talk with Chamberlain: 'He has he says programmes enough and to spare.' B.M. Add. MS. 48640, folio 110.

[2] *The Times*, 9 September 1885, p. 6.

[3] J. L. Garvin, *The Life of Joseph Chamberlain*, vol. ii, 1933, p. 616.

At first in 1885 Chamberlain said that his Radical proposals were simply for discussion. But during the course of the year they evolved into being his conditions for participating in any future Liberal government. He and his colleagues would stand aside, he declared, if Gladstone—or any other Liberal leader—failed to incorporate the main planks of the Radical programme in the government's own legislative programme.[1] The ending of the stage of discussion certainly came very rapidly: in terms of the ideal of the National Liberal Federation it could be argued that Chamberlain had not allowed sufficient time for the 'ripening' of his questions, that he had turned instead to trying to force the adoption of them on the party leadership by means other than the growth of conviction within the party as a whole. Clearly, of course, what he was trying to do was to make sure that the next Liberal government, unlike the last, did have a programme of legislative work ready to get on with. If his demands were accepted, there would be much less chance that the post-1880 experience of drift and absence of practical achievement would be repeated. As it was, Gladstone's election manifesto was again ominously unclear as to the legislation that the next government would try to put through. A determination to prevent a recurrence of the frustrations of 1880–5 undoubtedly accounts in part for the haste with which Chamberlain forced on his proposals.

A striking feature of Chamberlain's behaviour in 1885 is his confidence as to the strength of Radicalism, its ability to stand on its own, to do without Gladstone, even to sweep the country. By September he was declaring that, 'if we cannot convince our allies of the justice and reasonableness of our views, then, with whatever reluctance, we must part company. We will fight alone; we will appeal unto Caesar; we will go to the people from whom we came.' Liberal union might not be necessary now, he argued, for surely among the new voters there would be few Whigs or 'armchair politicians' (moderates). 'If we had to fight out this battle as between Radicals and Tories, I think we should give a very good account of our adversaries, even without the assistance of the moderate Liberals.'[2] By early October he was threatening 'to run a

---

[1] Chamberlain to Gladstone, 26 October 1885, Garvin, op. cit., ii, pp. 114–15.
[2] *The Times*, 9 September 1885, p. 6; 16 September 1885, p. 7.

Radical in every constituency', and saying of Gladstone that 'if we chose to go into direct opposition we might smash him'.[1] There is no evidence that in 1885 Radicalism was anywhere near as coherent or organized a political force as this suggested. To a certain extent Chamberlain was obviously trying by his rhetoric to foster into existence a force which he alleged already existed. But clearly what we see once again is his tendency to generalize on the basis of his Birmingham experience, to believe that there could be a 'democratic' Radicalism as real and coherent and productive of practical achievement as there had been felt to be in Birmingham in the 1870s. At the beginning of the year he had written: 'I believe the English and Scotch democracy will shortly be strong enough to hold their own against all other sections.'[2] The use of the word 'democracy' is significant. The democratic rhetoric that Chamberlain introduces into British politics in 1885 is founded on the assumption that belief in the reality of 'democracy' can be a powerful and cohering political force; and it had been such a force in the Birmingham of Chamberlain's politically formative years.[3]

Nevertheless, there was a marked contrast between rhetoric and conduct. If the language implied the support of coherent majority opinion, the strategy that Chamberlain adopted resembled rather the kind of tactical manœuvre normally indulged in by minority sections. The threat of not joining a future Liberal government suggested a consciousness that he had not succeeded in rallying a majority of Liberals behind his proposals so that it was necessary for him to resort to other, more obstructive methods of inducing the party leaders to take them up.

The Radical programme of 1885 was by no means a completely unco-ordinated assemblage of reform proposals. The themes of local government and land reform that predominated in it were not only inter-connected, for example through the scheme for

[1] Chamberlain to Harcourt, 9 October 1885, Garvin, *Life of Chamberlain*, ii, p. 103. Chamberlain to Dilke, 20 September 1885, Chamberlain MSS., JC 5/24/417.
[2] C. H. D. Howard (ed.), *A Political Memoir 1880–92 by Joseph Chamberlain*, 1953, pp. 142–3.
[3] For examples of his democratic rhetoric in 1885, see Lucy, *Speeches of Joseph Chamberlain*, pp. 132, 153, 160, 188.

the acquisition of estates for subdivision by democratically elected local authorities, but were presented as 'umbrellas' covering reform on a wide variety of subjects. The local government theme was unifying in part because it had been so in Chamberlain's own political experience: it was as the leader of a great local authority that he had put through *his* first major reform programme. In his Ipswich speech of 14 January Chamberlain went so far as to say of local government that in some cases it was more than just 'a means to an end'. It was 'the end itself'. Dilke described local government reform as 'the necessary first step to almost every reform which is pressing at the present time'. 'Temperance reform, taxation reform, the health and recreation of the poor', the removal of Irish discontent, 'all depend upon it.'[1] Chamberlain told Sir Edward Hamilton that he was placing 'Local Government throughout the United Kingdom in the foreground [of his programme]; and social questions must and will follow'.[2] In *The Radical Programme* local government and Ireland were dealt with in the same chapter, for the Radicals intended that the Irish question should be comprehended within the general principle of the extension of local government.[3]

The great change brought about by the Third Reform Bill was the admission of many new rural voters. The farm labourer was the figure on whom all eyes rested in 1885, on whose possible electoral behaviour most speculation centred. The basic problem for Radicals was how to have coherence in a Radicalism that appealed to him and yet was aimed at urban voters as well. Here the theme of land reform was crucial. If developed in the right way, it could have a very useful ambivalence. It appeared basically to involve the interests of rural voters: the farm labourer would get a better deal, and land would be freed from artificial restrictions and made more readily available through the introduction of competition and the breaking up of large estates. But we must not forget that the Radical leaders themselves were overwhelmingly urban—in the constituencies that they represented,

---

[1] *The Times*, 15 January 1885, p. 7; 22 July 1885, p. 11.
[2] Hamilton's diary, B.M. Add. MS. 48640, folio 110 (14 June 1885).
[3] For speeches which illustrate this approach to the Irish problem, see *The Times*, 4 June 1885, p. 8; 10 June 1885, p. 10; 18 June 1885, p. 7.

THE CRISIS OF 1885

in their own occupational and social backgrounds. Although at one time Chamberlain did hope to secure the support of the farmers with his land reform schemes,[1] the Radicals did not in fact get anywhere with them;[2] and, as for the agricultural labourers, a recent analyst of the 1885 elections expresses great doubt as to whether 'three acres and a cow' really was much of a vote-winner.[3] Land reform as presented and interpreted by the Radicals was very much an urban issue—through such themes as the effect of monopolistic ownership of urban land and the flight of farm workers into the towns in causing urban unemployment, housing shortages, and high rents for accommodation, allotments as a form of relief for urban workers in time of distress and unemployment, and the unequal distribution of taxation burdens.[4] But more basic and important than these particular problems was the unifying emotionalism of an attack on the privileged, monopolistic position and selfish behaviour of the landed class.[5] Chamberlain's aim in 1885 was to present policies that were an alternative and a counter to socialism.[6] Land reform served this aim by ascribing the ills of the urban community to influences and classes outside that community. *This* was Chamberlain's 'social'

---

[1] 'It appears to me that the next elections will compel another change of programme. What is the good of bothering about Bankruptcy, or Local Government when our real business is to outbid Chaplin & Co. with the Farmers? But then what will our Whig friends say to Radical proposals as to Tenant Right, Improvements, Rating &c?' Chamberlain to Dilke, 9 September 1881, Dilke MSS., B.M. Add. MS. 43885, folio 151. 'A Tenant Right Bill is essential and would be a great stroke of business. Without it we shall lose the farmers for a certainty.' Chamberlain to Dilke, 4 February 1883, Chamberlain MSS., JC 5/24/341.

[2] Hanham, *Elections and Party Management*, pp. 29–32.

[3] H. Pelling, *Social Geography of British Elections 1885–1910*, 1967, p. 16, and *Popular Politics and Society in Late Victorian Britain*, 1968, pp. 6–7.

[4] For the Radicals' awareness of how the issue could be developed in these terms, see Morley to Chamberlain, 24 December 1882 and 7 January 1883, Chamberlain MSS., JC 5/54/466, 575. Chamberlain's appeal to urban voters on the land reform issue in 1885 can be seen in Lucy, *Speeches of Joseph Chamberlain*, pp. 105, 112, 120, 122, 154, 224, 250. For other examples of this emphasis by the Radicals, see *The Radical Programme*, p. 104, and J. Collings and J. L. Green, *Life of the Right Hon. Jesse Collings*, 1920, pp. 131–2, 179–80.

[5] Cf. F. M. L. Thompson, 'Land and Politics in England in the Nineteenth Century', *Transactions of the Royal Historical Society*, 5th Series, vol. 15 (1965), pp. 23–44. In *Origins of Modern English Society*, pp. 451–3, H. Perkin points to the divisive effect that the land reform issue was now in fact beginning to have among the business classes.

[6] Chamberlain's reaction against socialism is emphasized by Peter Fraser in *Joseph Chamberlain*, Chapter 2.

programme: there was very little else in his programme that concerned the social and industrial problems of the urban worker whom Chamberlain clearly had no wish to treat as belonging to a class on his own.

Another source of emotional unity in the Radical campaign of 1885 was the rhetoric employed by Chamberlain to 'float' it—the rhetoric of democracy, of government by and for the people, of 'natural rights', the greatest happiness of the greatest number, and 'ransom'. It was above all the rhetoric of anti-socialism. The rights that were to be claimed were the rights of individuals, of citizens, not of classes, and they were to be claimed, and 'ransom' paid, in connection not with all property but only with *landed* property which alone Radicals distinguished as being unworked for and 'stolen'. It is doubtful, however, whether Chamberlain's rhetoric gained him much support to compensate for the alienation of moderate Liberals. It did in fact cause a split in the ranks of the Radicals themselves.[1] A rag-bag of Benthamite, French revolutionary, and American democratic slogans, it may have appeared to Chamberlain himself to have a substantial enough relationship to social and political reality, i.e. to the situation in which he himself had held power in Birmingham, but to many Liberals it looked merely a rhetorical gloss on a basically unexciting set of reform policies.

One effect of Chamberlain's Radical campaign was to stir up anti-programme feeling among Liberals. Chamberlain was felt to be raising, and demanding commitment on, too many 'unripe' questions, for example 'free schools'.[2] His rapid progression from the stage of discussion to the stage of forcing commitment on fellow Liberals did not leave in its wake much matured conviction. 'I have no pretension to dictate the policy of the Liberal party', he had said in January. 'I will not try

---

[1] Hamer, *John Morley*, pp. 147–61.

[2] Thus Chamberlain discovered, as Sir E. Hamilton put it, that the 'free schools' question 'may revive all the non-conformist prejudices and difficulties'. Hamilton's diary, B.M. Add. MS. 48641, folios 99–100. Mundella, the party's leading authority on educational reform, made clear to Chamberlain his feelings about the 'unripeness' of this question. Cf. Chamberlain to Collings, 12 October 1885, Chamberlain MSS., JC 5/16/109, and U. Kay-Shuttleworth to Mundella, 2 October 1885, Mundella MSS., folio V.

THE CRISIS OF 1885

to lay down any absolute platform, but to indicate the nature of the discussion which I think may be with advantage pursued.'[1] But by September he did seem to be trying to dictate policy to the leaders of the party—without there being any conclusive evidence that he had succeeded in converting a majority of Liberals to his views. John Bright told Gladstone on 23 October that in his opinion it was 'injudicious' for Chamberlain 'to start "new hares" just now' and to bring up 'new questions on which much discussion is required before any united opinion & action can be expected'.[2] John Morley felt that Chamberlain was being too 'impatient'.[3] Gladstone himself eventually came out against programme politics. 'Nothing would be more easy for me', he said in mid-November, 'than to court popular favour by presenting to you an enormous list of reforms'; but he nevertheless would not do so.[4]

It became clear that Chamberlain was failing to convince a sufficient number of Liberals that he held the key to coherent and effective Liberal political action. The alternatives facing the Liberal party appeared to be growing disunity and incoherence, on the one hand, and reliance on Gladstone's authority, on the other. The appeals which Gladstone began to receive are typified by a letter to him from Lord Dalhousie on 7 September. 'I feel very strongly', wrote Dalhousie, 'that as a party we want strong leading just now, or we may come to grief.' He urged Gladstone to take some kind of initiative, to issue a manifesto or convene a conference of party leaders. 'You can pull us together. Nobody else can.'[5] Gladstone's colleagues began to refer to party unity as dependent on the 'Gladstonian umbrella'. Rosebery, who was chiefly responsible for giving currency to this concept, argued that it was best for the Liberals to 'have no definite programme': 'Let a big Liberal majority be secured on the "umbrella" principle; and out of that, however heterogeneous it may be, it will be possible to evolve certain principles and weld together certain men to carry them into effect.'[6] Harcourt declared on 23 October:

[1] *The Times*, 15 January 1885, p. 7.
[2] Gladstone MSS., B.M. Add. MS. 44113, folio 219.
[3] Hamer, *John Morley*, pp. 156–7.   [4] *The Times*, 18 November 1885, p. 10.
[5] Gladstone MSS., B.M. Add. MS. 44492, folios 70–7.
[6] Sir E. Hamilton's diary, B.M. Add. MS., 48641, folios 37–8 (27 July 1885). *The Times*, 29 September 1885, p. 7.

'We are united because we have a leader in whom we all trust.' A few weeks later, talking again of Gladstone as the basis of party unity, he said that Gladstone 'will give the word, he will be obeyed with implicit obedience'.[1] Already the disposition was appearing, not only to look to Gladstone for a clear lead, but to be prepared to follow this whatever it might be. Once again A. J. Mundella is characteristic of this trend in Liberal opinion. 'I am, *in common with nearly every man I meet*', he wrote to Gladstone after the elections, 'angry, not to say indignant, that any member of our party, except yourself, should presume to prescribe the course to be taken by the Liberals, in view of the present state of political parties.' He urged Gladstone 'to believe that whatever policy you propound will receive the general acceptance of the Liberal party, and that the dissentients, if any, will be few and insignificant'.[2] Chamberlain knew well what he was up against. 'I fancy that a large number, perhaps the majority, of Liberals will support *any* scheme of Mr. G.'s', he wrote.[3]

During 1885 both Radicals and Whigs continued to manœuvre so as to retain contact with Gladstone, so as not to have his authority ranged against them, and so as to get it, if at all possible, on their own side or even under their own control. This recognition of the force of Gladstone's authority and of its weight in the political balance of course helped to enhance it even more. Rosebery observed in May 1885 that all the Ministers were wanting the Ministry to break up 'and yet none want to break away from the rest, dissociated from Mr. G. They each want Mr. G.'s aegis to be spread over them.'[4] In February Dilke had submitted to Chamberlain the following argument against a Radical withdrawal from the government: 'The object of the Whigs is to force us to war with Mr. G. who is strong, & not with Harty whom we shd. break. We therefore play into their hands by going *now*.'[5]

For the Radicals the problem of the disposition of Gladstone's authority was especially acute. Gladstone's influence over

[1] *The Times*, 24 October 1885, p. 10; 11 November 1885, p. 10.
[2] 15 December 1885, Gladstone MSS., B.M. Add. MS. 44258, folios 211–15.
[3] Chamberlain to Dilke, 19 December 1885, Gwynn and Tuckwell, *Life of Dilke*, ii, p. 198.
[4] Sir E. Hamilton's diary, B.M. Add. MS. 48640, folio 66 (16 May 1885).
[5] 3 February [1885], Chamberlain MSS., JC 5/24/99.

Radical opinion was such that they could not afford to have him against them, for then Radicalism would be divided and so as ineffective as ever. As early as 1882 Hartington had predicted that Radicals would be most reluctant to break with Gladstone no matter what it was that he was doing or proposing.[1] Clearly it was essential for Chamberlain in 1885 that he should try to capture and not alienate Gladstone. In September he explained his strategy to Collings and Dilke. 'I do not think it worth while', he wrote, 'to accentuate the differences between us & Mr. Gladstone.' 'In the first place he is squeezable & will probably give way to our views.' But, secondly, it was 'undesirable to have even the remains of his tremendous influence cast against us'. According to Chamberlain, it was possible 'to read between the lines in his manifesto' and interpret it as reasonably close to the Radicals' own programme[2]—'extra powers to local authorities are hinted at— Revision of taxation in favour of the Working classes is distinctly implied—& Free Schools are not finally disapproved'.[3] Thus, by attaching themselves to Gladstone, the Radicals could try to make it appear that they had now taken him over, that his political force was now absorbed in their own. For Chamberlain, who repudiated the whole idea of the Gladstonian 'umbrella',[4] could see the great danger to Radicalism of a Gladstone still 'loose', still having an independent power and appeal. That power and appeal must be at least neutralized and contained, if not harnessed to the chariot-wheels of Chamberlainite Radicalism. Therefore Chamberlain presented Gladstone with a choice between alternatives either of which would have the effect of ending Gladstone's controlling influence over Liberal-Radical politics. Gladstone could accept Chamberlain's programme as the work for his next government and thus forfeit his independence by appearing to accept the control of Chamberlainite Radicalism; or he would have to retire because the refusal of the Radicals to join would render him no longer able to form a government of his own.[5] Chamberlain

[1] Holland, *Devonshire*, i, p. 345.
[2] Chamberlain to Collings, 20 September 1885, Chamberlain MSS., JC 5/16/107.
[3] Chamberlain to Dilke, 20 September 1885, Chamberlain MSS., JC 5/24/417.
[4] Chamberlain to Morley, 26 September 1885, Chamberlain MSS.
[5] Chamberlain to Gladstone, 10 September 1885, Howard, *Political Memoir by Chamberlain*, p. 123.

insisted that Radicals would participate in a Gladstone government only if their land policy was part of its legislative programme, and that in it the Radicals should enjoy 'freedom to speak and vote as we like on questions of free schools'.[1] One cannot help feeling that for Chamberlain the main importance of Gladstone's acceptance of such terms would have been symbolic. It would have represented the abdication by Gladstone of his supreme authority over Radical politics. Chamberlain was in fact later to interpret the taking up of Home Rule by Gladstone as a reaction to these implications in Chamberlain's strategy. Gladstone, according to Chamberlain, was anxious for office but knew that if, on the one hand, he took the side of Hartington he would lose his influence in the country and if, on the other, 'he accepted my proposals he was thereby giving up the initiative and following where he had been accustomed to lead the way'. Home Rule, therefore, represented Gladstone's bid to regain the initiative for himself in Liberal-Radical politics.[2]

The key to the situation was thus clearly felt by all to lie in Gladstone's conduct and strategy. And the key to that lay as ever in Gladstone's instinct for order and proportion in politics. The state of Liberal politics—and indeed of politics in general—in 1885 must have offended deeply against his 'sense of measure'. It was a very messy situation. So many 'unripe' questions were being canvassed. There was no order in the Liberal party, which seemed on the verge of complete disruption. 'Tory democracy' was overthrowing traditional Conservatism, and new policies of 'construction' and 'socialism' were being favoured.[3] The next Liberal government promised to be even weaker than the last if Chamberlain were to get his way over freedom to speak and vote as he liked on education policy. Gladstone could not see his way clearly at all. He would comment on how different the situation was from that which had existed in 1879-80. 'Then he had in view the displacement of a Gov. which he thought had committed great and many

---

[1] Gwynn and Tuckwell, *Life of Dilke*, ii, p. 190.
[2] Howard, *Political Memoir by Chamberlain*, p. 179.
[3] For Gladstone's comments on these tendencies see Morley, *Gladstone*, ii, pp. 412-13, 417, 461-2, 480-1.

wrongs. Now he is opposed to a Govt. which after all is doing little else than following up the policy of its predecessors and in some directions is apparently on the right track.'[1]

Gladstone was not particularly worried over 'free schools' or 'small holdings'. The issue about which—apart from Ireland —he did show great anxiety was disestablishment, which was part of Chamberlain's programme but not one of the policies that he tried to force on Gladstone. The Tories, however, made more of it than of any of the other 'planks' in the Radical programme, and the threat of disestablishment began to create divisions within the Liberal party. Gladstone was a Churchman. For many years disestablishment above all had seemed to him to be the great coming Radical issue. Now, perhaps, it had come, and Gladstone was worried. In this area of political life, the area that meant more to him than any other, there was only confusion and uncertainty. In October 1885 he wrote to Dr. Döllinger about his inability to find a 'common thread' of purpose and policy: while disestablishment was 'remote generally', it was 'not so remote locally'. In both Scotland and Wales it was being vigorously agitated for and seemed likely after the elections to have the support of the majority of the M.P.s elected in each country; but the Welsh Church question in particular could not easily be disentangled from the issue of disestablishment in England where there was 'no chance of a real majority' for it.[2] The local disestablishment agitations introduced a disequilibrium into general Liberal politics. Thus Gladstone opposed pronouncing on Welsh disestablishment on the ground that this 'would tend to seriously disorganize the action of the Liberal Party in the country generally'.[3] As for Scotland, Liberalism there was in a particularly serious state of disorder in 1885, and Gladstone was, after all, a Scottish M.P. and candidate. Not only was there an exceptionally large number of rival Liberal candidatures, but very vigorous efforts were being made to turn Scottish disestablishment into a 'test question' for Liberal candidates.[4]

[1] Sir E. Hamilton's diary, B.M. Add. MS. 48641, folio 102 (14 October 1885).
[2] Gladstone to Dr. Döllinger, 18 October 1885, Gladstone MSS., B.M. Add. MS. 44492, folios 195–6.
[3] Morgan, *Wales in British Politics*, p. 63.
[4] D. C. Savage, 'Scottish Politics, 1885–6', *Scottish Historical Review*, vol. 40 (1961), pp. 120–4.

Scottish Liberalism was split between Churchmen and disestablishers. Gladstone worked to end the divisions in the constituencies and refused to take up disestablishment which he denied was yet 'mature'.[1] Yet Dr. Rainy urged on him that the very interests of party unity made it necessary that he should take it up, since to leave it 'open' would only make matters worse by causing the party to tear itself apart in prolonged controversy. But Gladstone argued that he could not afford to deal with the Scottish question in isolation: he had to think of the wider interests of Liberalism which would be damaged in England if he were to take up any kind of disestablishment policy.[2]

Gladstone's reaction to the growing disorganization of Liberal politics was characteristic: he became increasingly interested in the possibility of discovering a new unifying policy, a policy that would 'organize the action of the Liberal Party'. In 1885 the principal disrupting influence was associated with programme politics. Gladstone left no doubt that he favoured, and believed the remedy for Liberal disorganization to lie in, the other great mode of Liberal action—concentration on a single subordinating issue.

And in Gladstone's thinking on the political situation it was Ireland that began to emerge as the great cause that might control and subordinate all other political questions and thus create order out of the prevailing chaos. Gladstone saw Irish Home Rule as a 'ripening' issue, assessed its significance as such in relation to the condition of Liberal politics, and began to shape his concern with it accordingly. Gradually there was impressed on him the possibility that it might be such a question as he had craved in 1873, one that, if worked into certain shapes, might serve for a time 'to mould the rest'. Awareness of how an initiative on Irish policy could help to control a situation that was getting out of hand can be seen in a letter which Gladstone wrote to Chamberlain on 26 September in answer to an assertion by Chamberlain that he would not join a Liberal administration that was not pledged to act on the three main points of the Radical programme. In this Gladstone discusses various possible developments in the Irish situation

---

[1] Savage, loc. cit., p. 127.
[2] Simpson, *Life of Principal Rainy*, pp. 31-4, 37.

and suggests that these may make desirable the formation of a Liberal government for the purpose of dealing with them and, in particular, with a plan of Home Rule. Parnell might come back with a united party of eighty to ninety, 'bring forward a plan which shall contain in your opinion adequate securities for the Union of the Empire', and 'press this plan under whatever name as having claims to precedence'. Gladstone suggested that such claims 'could hardly be denied even by opponents', and then went on to ask Chamberlain: 'do you think no Government should be formed to promote such a plan unless the three points were glued on to it at the same time? Do you not think you would do well to reserve elbow-room for a case like this?'[1]

By mid-October Labouchere was reporting to Chamberlain that 'evidently the game of the G.O.M. is to endeavour to unite the Party on Irish Legislation'.[2] Chamberlain visited Gladstone at Hawarden and gained the same impression. He reported to Labouchere that Gladstone 'did not conceal that his present interest was in the Irish question, and he seemed to think that a policy for dealing with it might be found which would unite us all and which would necessarily throw into the background those minor points of difference about the schools and small holdings which threaten to drive the Whigs into the arms of the Tories or into retirement'.[3] This was confirmed when Gladstone told Chamberlain a week or so later that 'he had an instinct that Irish questions "might elbow out all others"'.[4] Thus by the end of October 1885 there had clearly emerged from Gladstone's ordering, systematizing political mind the familiar form of the single great question functioning to control and subordinate all else. Even the difficult Scottish situation might be put in order by it. Gladstone concluded his letter of 3 November to Dr. Rainy about Scottish disestablishment by remarking: 'Do not forget the possibility that a question of Irish government may come up with such force and magnitude as to assert its precedence over everything else.'[5] By late November, indeed, Gladstone was expressing

---

[1] Garvin, *Life of Chamberlain*, ii, pp. 97–8.
[2] Thorold, *Life of Labouchere*, p. 238.
[3] Ibid., p. 239.
[4] Gwynn and Tuckwell, *Life of Dilke*, ii, p. 192.
[5] Simpson, *Life of Principal Rainy*, p. 34.

confidence that 'Ireland' would act on all other questions like the sun on a fire in a grate.¹ It was characteristic of Gladstone, when in a messy, confused, or disintegrating political situation, to look for some particular 'question' that might intervene and overlay this situation. He had done so in 1873; and the same instinct can be seen at work in 1894 when, in writing to a colleague about his great anxieties concerning the naval estimates which he felt might make it necessary for him to resign the Premiership, he added a postscript: 'The Lords *may* raise for us another not less urgent question crossing the scent. The unforeseen sometimes does much in politics.'² The 'unforeseen' was certainly to be made by Gladstone to do a great deal in the crisis of 1885-6 when too, as in 1894, Gladstone seemed to be becoming politically redundant.

The elections left the Liberals as the strongest party in the House of Commons, but only by a margin over the Conservatives which was exactly filled by the Parnellites. In alliance with the Irish the Liberals could now turn out Lord Salisbury's government and form one of their own. But they would then be dependent on the Irish and would obviously have to have an Irish policy acceptable to Parnell. This was not a prospect which Chamberlain regarded with any enthusiasm. He and Dilke advocated allowing the Conservatives to remain in office. This would mean that they, and not the Liberals, would become entangled in the Irish question by being dependent on the Irish for retention of office; and it seems also that Chamberlain hoped that his Radicalism, clearly not yet 'matured' or accepted by majority opinion, might be enabled to become so by the reaction that would follow a further period of Tory rule. He seemed to feel that one or two years more were needed for the ripening of his Radical campaign. In late November he suggested leaving the Tories in for two years and then 'going for the Church'.³ By early December he was saying that the Radicals might stand to profit most from twelve months of weak Tory

---

¹ S. Childers, *The Life and Correspondence of the Right Hon. Hugh C. E. Childers 1827–1896*, vol. ii, 1901, p. 234.
² P. Stansky, *Ambitions and Strategies. The Struggle for the Leadership of the Liberal Party in the 1890s*, Oxford, 1964, p. 35. Cf. Gladstone to Harcourt, 5 February 1894, Harcourt MSS.: '[the Lords' action] seems to raise a new and very large question indeed: possibly one large enough to carry us for the *moment* into some new current.' ³ Gwynn and Tuckwell, *Life of Dilke*, ii, p. 193.

government.[1] The strategy of leaving the Conservatives in appealed to other Liberals who dreaded having to hold office dependent on the Parnellites.[2] But there were naturally many Liberals who felt that there was something wrong about not taking office when it was available, for this seemed a breach of faith with their constituents, and who feared that Tory opportunists, under the inspiration of Lord Randolph Churchill, might proceed to give the people the reforms that the Liberals had promised, splitting the Liberal party in the process.[3] After all, Chamberlain himself seems to have hoped for reforms from a weak Tory government under pressure from the Radicals in alliance with Churchill.[4]

But Chamberlain had many enemies who were determined that he would not thus become the arbiter of politics. These men, associated in particular with Leeds Liberalism, engineered the episode known to history as the 'Hawarden Kite' in order to force Gladstone to take the initiative much sooner than he wished and thus ensure that he remained the controlling influence over Liberal politics.

The key figures in this episode were Gladstone's son, Herbert, M.P. for Leeds since 1880, intensely devoted to his father's interests and anxious to thwart those who were trying to end his political influence, and Thomas Wemyss Reid, leading Liberal journalist who was at this time editor of the *Leeds Mercury*. Reid had long been bitterly antagonistic towards Chamberlain. In the 1870s he had alleged that the 'caucus' system was a mechanism whereby the Birmingham Liberals were endeavouring to subvert and take over local Liberal Associations, such as the one in Leeds. His hatred of Chamberlain was intensified by the clashes between Chamberlain and

---

[1] Chamberlain to W. S. Caine, 4 December 1885, Newton, *W. S. Caine, M.P.*, p. 124.

[2] Cf., e.g., T. Wemyss Reid, *Memoirs and Correspondence of Lyon Playfair, First Lord Playfair of St. Andrews P.C., G.C.B., LL.D., F.R.S., &c.*, 1899, p. 352.

[3] These points are made very strongly in a letter from F. A. Channing to Gladstone, 15 December 1885, Gladstone MSS., B.M. Add. MS. 44493, folios 225–8.

[4] This strategy emerges clearly from his speeches in the later stages of the election campaign. Cf. Lucy, *Speeches of Joseph Chamberlain*, pp. 227, 229. In October 1874 Chamberlain had written that Radicals 'have been taught by experience to look on a Conservative Government as one of the best instruments for advancing their views'. Chamberlain, 'The Next Page of the Liberal Programme', p. 418.

W. E. Forster who was also an opponent of the 'caucus' and whom Reid idolized. Reid became almost pathologically suspicious of Chamberlainite intrigues. He was as ready to see them, often where they did not exist, as he was to engage in intrigue himself to counter Chamberlain's alleged subversion.[1] When in 1885 Chamberlain appeared to be making his great bid to take over the party, Reid's reaction was instant and violent. He wrote to Herbert Gladstone on 18 January 1885:

> Forgive me for saying that I find in Mr. Chamberlain's last two speeches the amplest justification for the prejudice I have entertained regarding him ever since he entered upon public life by attacking Mr. Gladstone. In my opinion the man who is capable of making such speeches, at once cowardly & crafty, mean and swaggering, is absolutely incapable of ever developing into even the similitude of a statesman.[2]

In his relations with Herbert Gladstone, Reid concentrated on depicting Chamberlain as, above all, the enemy of W. E. Gladstone, determined to oust him from the Liberal leadership. Herbert Gladstone had been closely associated with Reid and the *Leeds Mercury* since he became one of the M.P.s for Leeds in 1880.[3] He was later to tell of how he too became worried during 1885 about the imminence of Gladstone's supersession by Chamberlain, especially 'if Home Rule was declared to be outside practical politics or postponed'.[4] For to him what Home Rule represented was the continued assertion of Gladstone's controlling influence over the course of Liberal politics. As Herbert Gladstone saw it, the course of action being advocated by the Radicals in December 1885 must have the effect of putting an end to Gladstone's effective leadership of the party. The continuance of this leadership 'depended on the acceptance of a Home Rule policy by the party'. This was his frame of mind when Chamberlain's enemies made contact with him. Lyon Playfair, who had just been elected as M.P. for South Leeds, informed Reid, who clearly encouraged him

---
[1] S. J. Reid (ed.), *Memoirs of Sir Wemyss Reid, 1842–1885*, 1905, pp. 211–22, 318, 333. T. Wemyss Reid to Herbert Gladstone, 27 May 1882, Viscount Gladstone MSS., B.M. Add. MS. 46041, folios 22–5.
[2] Viscount Gladstone MSS., B.M. Add. MS. 46041, folio 60.
[3] See his correspondence with Reid in B.M. Add. MS. 46041.
[4] Viscount Gladstone, *After Thirty Years*, 1929, pp. 286–7.

to inform Herbert Gladstone, that he had learned from Dilke that the Radicals 'were in action for the shelving of Home Rule, which meant the retirement of Mr. Gladstone'.[1] On 13 December Reid wrote to Herbert Gladstone about these alleged intrigues against his father's authority in the party and urged him to counter them by giving the press some guidance as to Gladstone's thinking on Home Rule. 'I need not say', he assured Herbert Gladstone, 'that your confidence would be absolutely respected. I do not ask you to commit your father in any way whatever; but I certainly think that you might be of great use both to him and to the Liberal party just now, if you would give all the assistance you could to those who are anxious loyally to sustain Mr. Gladstone in this great crisis, & who have infinitely greater faith in his power of dealing with the difficulties of the situation than in that of any other man.'[2]

Herbert Gladstone thereupon went up to London and gave interviews to various journalists as the result of which there appeared on 17 December the 'Hawarden Kite' purporting to represent Gladstone's own views on Home Rule. In this respect those who flew it clearly went beyond what Herbert Gladstone had believed was going to be the consequence of his interviews; but he was by no means an innocent in the matter. His aims and those of Reid and his journalistic associates coincided: he and they alike wished to promote on behalf of Gladstone some kind of counter-*coup* that would restore the initiative and effective leadership in Liberal politics to him. The main difference was in motives—Herbert's filial devotion as against Reid's inveterate anti-Chamberlainism.

It is the effect of the 'Kite', however, that is important, and it was undoubtedly the effect that had been foreseen and calculated by Reid and the others who were responsible for it. Gladstone himself remained remarkably unaware of its significance. But he would probably in any event have gone on as he did towards forming a Liberal government for the purpose of bringing in a Home Rule Bill, once he had discovered that there was no prospect that the Conservatives would do this themselves.[3] The 'Kite's' main object and effect

---

[1] Ibid., pp. 307–8.   [2] B.M. Add. MS. 46041, folios 65–8.
[3] Cf. his attitude to 'the Eastern cause' in 1877: 'While there was a hope that the Tories would run true upon it, I for one could have no wish to make it a party

was as an anti-Chamberlain manœuvre. It forced a premature revelation of the initiative which Gladstone was contemplating but which he deliberately refrained from making public knowledge. What Reid and his associates feared was that Gladstone would retire without revealing his 'conversion' to Home Rule if he saw that opinion in the Liberal party was not likely to support him. In fact, what they did was to accelerate a process that Gladstone would almost certainly have embarked on in due course anyway; but from their point of view it was this acceleration that was vital. For they believed that, if the public revelation of Gladstone's position on Home Rule were delayed much longer, Gladstone would lose the opportunity to take the initiative and Chamberlain would assume the direction of Liberal-Radical politics. 'At this time', wrote Herbert Gladstone later, 'everything was going wrong. Excepting Lord Spencer and Lord Granville, the Whigs were consolidating themselves against Home Rule. Mr. Bright was adverse. The Radical leaders were manœuvring for their own position. . . . Whig and Radical leaders were consolidating their position, not against Mr. Gladstone but against Home Rule—which was much the same thing.' What Herbert Gladstone took was, in his own words, 'counter-action' to ensure that his father retained the leadership of the party— by forestalling initiatives by Chamberlain that might have made this impossible.[1]

The 'Hawarden Kite' made Gladstone the centre of political attention, and Irish Home Rule became at once the predominant issue in British politics. Most leading politicians, Conservative and Liberal, took sides for or against it, and Chamberlain found that, in spite of all that he could do, the future of his Radical programme became a distinctly subordinate consideration in most people's minds. Worse than that—Gladstone's commitment to Home Rule undid all that Chamberlain had been working to achieve since the early 1870s. The unity of Radicalism was shattered. And the wrecking factor was Gladstone's great hold over Radical opinion.

question. But nothing is to be hoped from them, and, as in as many other cases, the Liberal party alone is the instrument by which a great work is to be carried on.' Gladstone to Granville, 23 May 1877, Ramm, *1876–1886*, i, p. 42.
[1] Viscount Gladstone, *After Thirty Years*, pp. 307–11.

THE CRISIS OF 1885

There were many reasons why a Radical might decide to support Gladstone and the cause of Home Rule, and just as many why he might decide not to. Opposition to Gladstone in connection with his proposal of a great measure of reform must have seemed to many a betrayal of their own Radicalism; and Gladstone's appeal to their constituents must have weighed heavily with them. To go against Gladstone carried a great risk of putting in jeopardy one's own political future as a Radical. Furthermore, Home Rule could be seen, and was seen, as a genuinely Radical policy, another step in the historic Liberal programme of emancipation, 'liberation', extension of democracy and self-government, assisting people 'struggling rightly to be free'. In terms of the preservation of continuity everything pointed to the correctness of taking Gladstone's side and favouring Home Rule. Indeed, in August 1885, when someone expressed anxiety to Gladstone about Chamberlain's Radical programme, Gladstone's reply had been that he 'need not trouble about it. Ireland was the main question, and C.'s views were not advanced on that.'[1]

Many—for example, Lord Granville and, for a time, John Bright—were attracted by the prospect of getting the Irish Members out of the House of Commons where they had been such a nuisance and a distraction.[2] The Home Rule crusade rallied behind it a most strange coalition of people who strongly disliked the Irish and all they stood for and did, for example Roman Catholicism and land agitation, and people who were very sympathetic to them and their aspirations. There were also those to whom Home Rule appealed as a drastic but essential means of solving the Irish question so that the way would at last be clear for thorough, uninterrupted attention to Radical reforms. Thus Francis Schnadhorst, the great Radical organizer, wrote to Chamberlain in February 1886: 'I do not think there is any love for the Irish about but I am sure there is an eager desire if possible to get Ireland out of the way so that the rest of the Kingdom may secure some attention for its

[1] As reported by Sir T. D. Acland in a letter to G. W. E. Russell, August 1885, quoted in F. W. Hirst, *Early Life & Letters of John Morley*, vol. ii, 1927, p. 263.
[2] For Granville see his letters to Gladstone of 28 December 1885, 12 April and 1 May 1886, Ramm, *1876–1886*, ii, pp. 420, 441, 447. For Bright see G. M. Trevelyan, *The Life of John Bright*, 1913, pp. 446, 448, 450.

pressing needs.'[1] Chamberlain himself acknowledged that two powerful influences working in Gladstone's favour were 'the Liberal feeling in favour of self government' and 'the impatience generally felt at the Irish question & the hope to be rid of it once for all'.[2]

On the other hand, Radicals could oppose Home Rule because, like Chamberlain, they regarded the whole business as very probably an intentional distraction from the Radical programme which, under Chamberlain's leadership, they had worked so hard to promote and which, especially if they were interested in the land question, they had considerable expectations of seeing being given legislative effect. A Radical might also oppose it because it was not a 'constructive' policy, that is, it involved the breaking down of the power of the British State and not the constructive and improving use of that power which Chamberlain had long been advocating as the remedy for social ills, including those of Ireland.

Chamberlain attacked not only Home Rule itself but also the diversion which he alleged it constituted, and he demanded attention to the non-Irish reforms for which he had campaigned in 1885.[3] In other words, he refused to accept what was becoming the basis of the Gladstonian case for Home Rule—that 'Ireland' constituted an obstruction to action on anything else.

But the Radicals were divided as to what strategy they should adopt in response to Gladstone's taking up of Home Rule. On the one hand, Dilke and Labouchere argued that by causing most of the Whigs to secede the Home Rule issue was paving the way for a more Radical party and that therefore the Radicals should make a tactical acceptance of Gladstone's policy in order to be able to remain in the party and exploit this new situation. In May 1886 Dilke urged Chamberlain to vote for the second reading of the Home Rule Bill because,

[1] 13 February 1886, Chamberlain MSS., JC 5/63/9. John Morley advised Robert Spence Watson that an argument that he should employ in order to get the leading 'Lib-Lab' M.P., Charles Fenwick, to speak out in favour of Home Rule was 'that we want to attend to our own business'. Morley to Watson, 7 April 1886, Watson MSS.
[2] Chamberlain to Thomas Gee, 26 April 1886, Gee MSS., N.L.W. MS. 8305 C, folio 15a.
[3] *The Times*, 22 April 1886, p. 10; 12 June 1886, p. 7.

THE CRISIS OF 1885

although 'the dissolution [on the Home Rule issue] will wreck the party', it would nevertheless 'leave *a* party—democratic, because all the moderates will go over to the Tories; poor, because all the subscribers will go over to the Tories; more Radical than the party has ever been; and yet, as things now stand, with you outside of it'.[1] If Chamberlain voted for the second reading, the way would be open, Dilke argued, for him to succeed 'to the head of the party purged of the Whig element'.[2] Labouchere similarly believed that at last the Radicals were in sight of the promised land. He insisted also on the disastrous effects for Radicalism of not working for Home Rule. In late December he wrote in a letter to *The Times* that Radicals should appreciate that the only alternative to Home Rule was coercion which everyone knew the Conservatives were the best party to carry out. Therefore, if the Radicals rejected Home Rule, the Conservatives would hold office. 'Domestic reforms would be neglected, the Radical chariot would stand still.'[3] On 1 January 1886 he wrote to Chamberlain: 'So long as the Irish question is not settled, the Tories must have the pull in the country, and the Radicals must remain discredited and disunited.' For this reason the 'Radical game' ought to be 'to go with Mr. Gladstone on Irish matters, and to use him in order to shunt them and, if possible, the Whigs'. By March Labouchere was convinced that 'there never was such an opportunity to establish a Radical party, and to carry all before it'. 'Is it worth while wrecking this beautiful future, for the sake of some minor details about Irish Government?' 'For my part, I would coerce the Irish, grant them Home Rule, or do anything with them, in order to make the Radical programme possible. Ireland is but a pawn in the game.'[4]

But these enticements entirely failed to move Chamberlain from his resolve to oppose Home Rule. In the first place, he sensed hostility to Home Rule among many of the people on whom the Radicals depended for electoral strength, and he was naturally most unwilling to do anything to alienate them. He referred in particular to the anti-Irish feeling of 'the English

---

[1] Gwynn and Tuckwell, *Life of Dilke*, ii, p. 216.
[2] Ibid., ii, pp. 218–19.   [3] Thorold, *Life of Labouchere*, p. 269.
[4] Ibid., pp. 278–9, 289–90.

working classes' and 'our best friends—the respectable artisans and the non-Conformists'.[1] But even this was probably not the basic reason. At the basis of Chamberlain's political conduct throughout 1886 undoubtedly lay the feeling that to accept the strategy favoured by Dilke and Labouchere would be tantamount to submitting to the continuation of Gladstone's controlling influence over Liberal and Radical politics; and this above all was what Chamberlain was determined not to do. Chamberlain now rejected what had clearly become the basis of Gladstone's authority in the party—his unique capacity for unifying it by holding together diverse sections. He defined Gladstone's practice of this mode of leadership as a main *cause* of division and disunity in the party, and not a remedy for that state of affairs as most Liberals seemed to believe it to be. Dining with the Harcourts early in January 1886, he summed up as follows what he saw to have been the effect of Gladstone's role as the 'universal amalgam':

> The last Cabinet was arranged on the principle of Gladstone being the keystone of an arch, of which he and Hartington were supposed to be the opposing sections and that it was considered to be the sacred duty of the one side always to oppose the wishes of the other and in consequence each side advocated more extreme measures than they really wanted or were willing to accept, and Hartington carried out this principle in his election speeches and when he (Chamberlain) propounded the irreducible minimum of his demands Hartington went about the country denouncing his schemes as Socialistic.

With Gladstone out of the way, far from the party breaking up as everyone feared would happen, there would be a more genuine unity and spirit of co-operation in the party:

> He [Chamberlain] says Hartington must meet him half way and will find him very willing to meet him. He says 'I may have a dozen or twenty things I want carrying out and if Hartington says "I cannot accept such and such a thing" I will relinquish those measures if he will help me to carry the others.'[2]

Indeed, one can go so far as to say that Chamberlain's main aim in 1886 was not so much to destroy the Home Rule policy

---

[1] Thorold, op. cit., pp. 278–9. Garvin, *Life of Chamberlain*, ii, p. 143.
[2] The Diary of 'Loulou' Harcourt, 11 January 1886, Harcourt MSS.

THE CRISIS OF 1885

as to destroy Gladstone's influence. Home Rule seemed to be important to him less as a policy than as a symbol of Gladstone's continuing power to control and shape the development of Radicalism. In a letter to Dilke of 6 May he wrote: 'I feel that there is no longer any security for anything while Mr. Gladstone remains the foremost figure in politics.'[1] He wrote that the most powerful influence causing Liberals to accept Home Rule in 1886 was 'the tremendous personality of Mr. Gladstone himself'. Liberals did not bother to make 'careful personal investigation' of the proposals: 'They have assumed that the details must be all right because they are recommended to them by Mr. Gladstone's great name.'[2] After the election he told Jesse Collings that the situation was 'dominated by the question of Mr. G.'s action'. 'If he retired all would come right pretty quickly. If he remains it is no use issuing manifestoes or anything else.'[3] Thus Chamberlain accepted the argument now often being resorted to by the Gladstonians that there was an obstruction which rendered futile the promulgation of Radical programmes—but with one difference. He identified the obstruction, not as the Irish question *per se*, but as the influence of Gladstone.

What remains now to be investigated is the extent to which Gladstone *was* influenced in taking up the cause of Home Rule by consideration of the effect which his doing so would have on the unity of the Liberal party. It cannot be denied that during 1885 he came to the conclusion that Home Rule was the right solution to the Irish problem 'independently of all questions of party, of support, & of success', that his claim that 'I look at the question in itself' accurately describes the process which culminated in 'conversion' to Home Rule.[4] But this does not mean that he was innocent of any thought about the effect on the party. We have seen how conscious he was in the later stages of 1885 of the beneficial unifying and ordering

---

[1] Gwynn and Tuckwell, *Life of Dilke*, ii, p. 222.
[2] Chamberlain to Thomas Gee, 26 April 1886, Gee MSS., N.L.W. MS. 8305 C, folio 15a.
[3] Chamberlain to Collings, 29 July 1886, Chamberlain MSS., JC 5/16/116.
[4] Memo by Gladstone of conversation with Granville, 6 May 1885, Ramm, *1876–1886*, ii, p. 367. Gladstone to Hartington, 30 May 1885, Morley, *Gladstone*, ii, pp. 437–8.

consequences that might flow from concentration on a great Irish policy. The idea of devotion to a great national cause was an integral part of Gladstone's concept of what a party, and especially the Liberal party, ought to be.[1] Gladstone had been a Peelite, that is he had once been involved in the disruption of a party when many members of it had failed to respond to its leader's initiative on a major issue of national policy. Like Peel in 1846, Gladstone was prepared, in the last resort, to go ahead on his own with such an initiative and ask his party to support him.[2] If only part of it did so, that part would nevertheless thereby transform itself into an organic whole, the kind of party that Gladstone really believed in, the party devoted to a great cause.

There can be no doubt that Gladstone, in spite of his oft-expressed determination not to ruin the party by 'entering into a schism' on Irish policy,[3] began to accustom himself during 1885 to the idea that a split might be not only inevitable[4] but, if it was of a certain kind, desirable and beneficial. In his speech at Edinburgh on 11 November he described himself as 'labouring with all my heart for the unity of the Liberal party' but then defined this unity as having to be 'founded upon common convictions as to the importance of the work to be done'. There might therefore, he said, come 'a point at which our convictions should part, if the questions at issue are of vital importance'. For 'conscientious convictions' were 'higher than

[1] See above, pp. 64–5.
[2] Gladstone was quite clear that this was the order in which the stages of this process would occur. On 14 October 1885 Sir E. Hamilton thus summarized Gladstone's position after talking to him about it: 'If he is commissioned to take the Irish question in hand, he will probably execute that commission or rather try to execute it on some comprehensive scale. Then the question will arise, who will and who will not follow him?' B.M. Add. MS. 48641, folio 99.
[3] Gladstone to Granville, 9 September 1885, 18 January 1886, Ramm, *1876–1886*, ii, pp. 393, 423.
[4] In the letter referred to above, p. 117, n. 1, he is also quoted as saying: 'Acland, we are come to the break-up of the Liberal party.' Other statements by Gladstone as to the extreme probability of a split are to be found in his letter to Granville of 22 January 1885, Ramm, *1876–1886*, ii, p. 326 (where he tells how he has urged Hartington not to force on a split but to await one 'upon matters of principle, known and understood by the whole country'), and the memo. of his conversation with Granville, 6 May 1885, ibid., ii, p. 367 (when he told Granville: 'Under the circ[umstance]s, while the duty of the hour evidently was to study the means of possible accommodation, the present aspect of affairs was that of a probable split, *independently* of the question what course I might individually pursue.').

party motives', and, if the need arose, 'I hope', he said, 'the Liberal party will sever and split rather than sacrifice conscience and principle'. A party ought to be 'an instrument for the attainment of great ends'.[1] In 1877 Gladstone had written: 'I set up the proposition that whatever be the effect on party, it is better that a nation preferring self-government should be self-governed.'[2] To this proposition he now proceeded to give effect. For Gladstone the great cause came first, and a split might be necessary in order that the party might become its instrument. There was not such great inconsistency as might at first sight appear between Gladstone's claim that he was working to maintain the unity of the party and the fact that he himself brought on a split in the party by his decision to take up Home Rule. His behaviour is understandable if we consider his views on party unity. For it followed from these that a split on a clear issue, a single great question, could, paradoxically, be a unifying force. It could have the effect of producing a party more united, more coherent, more capable of effective action.

Two aspects of Gladstone's political thinking were fused in his conduct in this crisis. On the one hand, there was his belief that great national causes, of the kind to which he had devoted much of his career, needed the Liberal party for their fulfilment, the Conservative party having ceased, since a majority of it repudiated Peel in 1846, to be capable of performing this function. On the other hand, there was his belief that the Liberal party needed great national causes to devote itself to if it was ever to be able to subdue the divisive forces within itself. It is in the convergence of these beliefs that is forged the peculiar form which the Liberal party is found to have assumed as it emerges from the crisis of 1885–6.

[1] *The Times*, 12 November 1885, p. 6.
[2] Gladstone, 'The County Franchise and Mr Lowe Thereon', p. 539.

VI The Irish Preoccupation and Liberal Politics, 1886–1890

THE crisis of 1885–6 culminated in the rift in the party between the majority who supported Gladstone and Home Rule and the minority of Liberal Unionists. This rift was hardened by the holding of a general election in July 1886 explicitly on the issue of Home Rule. The result was a great purge of the party and a drastic simplification of Liberal politics. Those who remained within the party did so because of their stand on this one issue. What they believed about all other issues was no longer relevant to the question of whether or not they were true Liberals. The 'true Liberal' was now to be defined and identified on the basis of support for Gladstone's Home Rule policy. After so many years of confusion, there was at last a single, clear test of Liberalism. 'The Liberal creed having been set up in such a simple way with a profession of faith so easy of recognition, the notion of political orthodoxy penetrated the Liberal Organization from one end to the other.'[1] Labouchere expressed very clearly the basic implication of what had happened when he wrote to Herbert Gladstone: 'Your father has created an Irish Home Rule Party, and it will fall to pieces, if the principle of Home Rule be not maintained.'[2]

This development was welcomed by many Liberals, and what they had to say and write about it referred too frequently and too substantially to the basic, long-term problems of Liberal politics to be dismissed as simply reflecting an endeavour to make the best of a bad job. Much stress was laid on the unity and cohesion that now resulted from the party's having one and only one major policy commitment. There was rejoicing that the party was now, as Herbert

[1] Ostrogorski, *Democracy and the Organization of Political Parties*, i, pp. 293, 307.
[2] 3 August [1886], Gladstone MSS., B.M. Add. MS. 46016, folio 113.

Gladstone put it, 'a solid party under one flag, supporting a definite policy'.[1] Ireland, declared Rosebery, supplied Liberals with 'a great cause to arouse us and unite us'. It gave the party 'faith and discipline' and was a defence against 'chaos' in Liberal politics.[2] Sir Walter Foster told the N.L.F. in 1888 that the Irish question had 'done the party good by giving it a platform on which to fight for Liberal principles'.[3] After his return to the Gladstonian fold Trevelyan told Sir Edward Hamilton that he was 'very happy' because 'for the first time in his political life, he found himself among a homogeneous (Liberal) party'.[4] Sir Henry Campbell-Bannerman even thanked the Irish party 'for having invented an Ireland and an Irish question, which had been a source of so much good and so much strength to the Liberal party'.[5]

In comparison to these advantages the loss of power and defeat in a general election were of small importance. If unity and the possession of power were alternatives that could not co-exist for long in Liberal politics—as the history of the governments of 1868-74 and 1880-5 appeared to prove—then far better, it was argued, to be united and out of office than in office but unable to achieve anything. Writing in 1889, G. W. E. Russell suggested that in 1886, 'though we were heavily beaten, our state was, in one main respect, more gracious than it had been in 1885. We were no longer hampered by conflicting policies, or called on to decide between authorised and unauthorised programmes. A plain issue was submitted to us.'[6] Sir Edward Grey referred to the 'general feeling' among Liberals 'that we are less hampered by *impedimenta*, and more ready for action' than in 1885; and Robert Spence Watson said that the party was 'better and stronger for its recent purge'—words which echo Gladstone's remark in 1866 that 'a general election which should somewhat reduce the party would be of great use if it should also have the effect of

[1] Sir C. Mallet, *Herbert Gladstone. A Memoir*, 1932, p. 131.
[2] *The Times*, 28 April 1887, p. 10. Rosebery to Gladstone, 11 August 1889, Rosebery MSS., Box 19.
[3] *N.L.F. Report 1888*, p. 91.
[4] Sir E. Hamilton's diary, B.M. Add. MS. 48648, folio 75 (13 April 1888).
[5] *The Times*, 21 June 1888, p. 10.
[6] G. W. E. Russell, 'The New Liberalism: A Response', *N.C.*, no. 151 (September 1889), pp. 493-4.

purging it'.[1] Significantly in view of his later work for the 'concentration' of Liberal policy, it was this aspect of the preoccupation with Home Rule that appealed most to Lord Rosebery, who was unenthusiastic about, indeed uninterested in, the Home Rule policy itself.[2] The Liberal party now had 'only one principle' and 'union under one leader', and that, he would argue, was better than the frustrating and sterile possession of power. He would describe how there had been times when, although the party was 'enormously preponderant in the House of Commons', it had still been weak because 'it contained many schools of thought and still more numerous leaders'. Liberals had at those times been 'a somewhat disorganized multitude'; now, although fewer in number, they were more 'useful for the purposes that we have at heart'. 'It is quite true', he once said, 'that our numbers are less than 200 in the House of Commons. But then, after all, it is a party so enthusiastic, so devoted to its one leader, it is united by so great and so true a principle, it is based on so firm and so logical a basis, that I, for one, have never been happier or prouder as a Liberal than I am at this moment.'[3] The Liberals, according to Rosebery, were no longer 'a flabby disconnected majority, but a compact minority united by a principle'.[4]

The basis of the Gladstonian Liberals' case as to the relationship of the Home Rule policy to British politics in general, and the principle with reference to which their preoccupation with Irish policy was most often justified, was the notion of an 'Irish obstruction', summed up in the slogan 'Ireland blocks the way'. They claimed that Ireland consumed so much of the time and demanded so much of the attention of Parliament

[1] *"Eighty" Club. Liberalism and Social Reforms. Speech by the Right Hon. John Morley, M.P. on Tuesday, Nov. 19th, 1889*, p. 9 (comments by Grey as chairman). *N.L.F. Report 1888*, p. 91. Gladstone's remarks are quoted in Cowling, *1867*, p. 105.

[2] 'As to Ireland, he [Rosebery] thinks little of it. . . . He says, he takes no interest in the Irish question . . .' Sir E. Hamilton's diary, B.M. Add. MS. 48643, folio 63 (2 April 1886).

[3] *The Times*, 18 August 1887, p. 6; 21 May 1887, p. 14.

[4] Rosebery to Lord R. Churchill, July 1887, quoted in R. R. James, *Lord Randolph Churchill*, 1959, p. 322. On 16 November 1888, Rosebery, talking to Hamilton about the Liberal Unionists, declared that among Liberals, 'instead of regret at losing them, there was pleasure that they had been got rid of, and that there was a prospect of a more harmonious party in the future'. Sir E. Hamilton's diary, B.M. Add. MS. 48649, folio 114.

and government that no satisfactory progress was possible on any other reform question until Irishmen were enabled by the concession of Home Rule to look after their own affairs.

The 'obstruction' theory enabled the Liberal leaders—especially Gladstone who, as always, excelled at this kind of thing—to explain the political situation and put across their policy in terms of vivid imagery. The 'Irish obstruction' was likened to an accident on a railway line that blocked the line and prevented all other trains from getting through until it was cleared. Thus did Gladstone justify the Irish preoccupation to a group of Liberal M.P.s in March 1887:

> Now let us suppose the case of a railway accident. It has encumbered the line with a wreck of carriages and goods, perhaps of passengers. The next train comes up. It cannot move, and half-a-dozen trains accumulate all together, and the passengers in the half-dozen trains are impatient; but suppose one of those passengers was foolish or indiscreet or hasty enough to go and dodge the guard and dodge the engine-driver, and to say, 'It is a monstrous thing to keep my train waiting here. We are long past the time'—and how many public questions are there that have been knocked out of time altogether in consequence of this unhappy dilemma in which we are involved—'I cannot have my train kept waiting; I insist upon your driving on.' That engine-driver or guard, if a sensible man, would say, 'Are you fool enough not to know there is but one thing to do, and that is to clear the line?' And that, gentlemen, literally and strictly is your case. . . . You must clear the line. You must dispose of the Irish question.[1]

Lord Spencer varied the imagery when he called the Irish question an express train that 'stops the line' because it has to be given priority: 'We have other trains laden with precious measures valued by the Liberal party, but they are blocked and shunted until this express train which carries a true and liberal measure for Ireland passes by.'[2] Another image which Gladstone employed was the enclosed garden. The Irish question was a high wall that no one could scale. There was a door in it, but the keys that could open this door 'have been lost or have not yet been found'. Inside the wall was 'a splendid garden' full of trees on which was 'a great collection of ripe

[1] *The Times*, 18 March 1887, p. 10.
[2] Ibid., 27 April 1887, p. 12.

fruit'—in other words, English reforms. But this fruit could be plucked only when the wall was pulled down or the keys found that could open the door. The 'Irish obstruction' must first be removed.[1]

Settlement of the Irish question was depicted as the key that alone would unlock the way to progress on all other questions. 'There would never be any progress in English legislation', Gladstone argued repeatedly, until the Irish question was settled. 'Until you have got rid of it', he would tell Liberals, 'it will ride you like a nightmare, it will possess and absorb the public mind more and more, and the whole course of legislation will be impeded and obstructed in such a way as to yield only the most partial and unsatisfactory results.'[2] The Liberals represented British politics as being in an abnormal state in which the normal work of passing reform legislation had to be suspended. In their explanations there was both a promise and an excuse. According to Shaw-Lefevre in 1889, only when Parliament was 'free from that incubus of the Irish question' would it be able 'to devote its time and attention to those measures of reform on which the democracy of the country had set its heart'.[3] The N.L.F. declared in a manifesto in August 1886 that 'no progress can be made with the ordinary work of the Liberal party'.[4] Campbell-Bannerman insisted that 'until social order was restored in Ireland by some means or other they could not attend to the reforms that were so urgently required both for Scotland and England'.[5] Examples of this kind of explanation for not attending to anything else except the Irish question abound in the speeches of the Gladstonian Liberals from 1886 to 1890.[6] The 'Irish obstruction' was said to render futile even the discussion of other questions.[7]

[1] Speech at Limehouse, 15 December 1888, quoted in P. W. Clayden, *England Under the Coalition. The Political History of Great Britain and Ireland From the General Election of 1885 to May 1892*, 1892, pp. 403–4.
[2] *The Times*, 23 August 1886, p. 6; 25 March 1890, p. 10.
[3] Ibid., 10 October 1889, p. 7.
[4] Ibid., 9 August 1886, p. 10.
[5] Ibid., 20 January 1887, p. 10.
[6] For other examples see *The Times*, 12 January 1887, p. 7 (Bryce); 15 January 1887, p. 9 (Gladstone); 20 January 1887, p. 10 (Shaw-Lefevre); 21 January 1887, p. 7 (Labouchere); 27 April 1887, p. 12 (Spencer); 7 February 1889, p. 6 (Spencer); 4 March 1889, p. 6 (Arnold Morley); and Hamer, *John Morley*, pp. 202–4.
[7] Hamer, *John Morley*, pp. 201, 242. *The Times*, 6 January 1887, p. 7 (Lord Ripon: 'The discussion of the question of land, of local self-government, of the

Gladstone made quite plain his belief that since 1885 the Liberal party had ceased to be a 'normal' party. In a speech at the National Liberal Club in April 1888 he said that he could not remember any period 'when party objects as distinct from national objects have been less in view, and have been less made the aim of combatism, than they have been by the Liberal party during the last two years'. The Irish controversy had 'thrown into insignificance, reduced almost to the absolute point of zero, all those considerations apt to come uppermost in a working party in time when a great public national object is not so prominently before them'.[1] And he left no doubt that this was a development which he welcomed.

For, presented in these ways, the preoccupation with Home Rule became the latest single great question or substitute for system in Liberal politics. It imposed order on the vast range of reform questions in which Liberals were interested. Thus H. H. Fowler saw it as the 'one question which, like Aaron's rod, swallowed up the rest', and justified this description by reference to the argument that 'all questions would either be imperfectly solved or hopelessly arrested' until Ireland was settled.[2] All other questions were now dependent on the securing of Home Rule, and so at last there was injected into Liberal politics an ordering and controlling influence. According to Gladstone, Ireland was the question 'upon which, in truth, all other questions of the highest order now substantially turn'. It was 'the key to the position of every English question and the real helm that steers the ship of politics'. 'English questions are guided and governed by Irish motives', he would say.[3] It had been a long time indeed since Liberal leaders had been able so confidently to maintain that there was a single set of motives guiding and controlling the beliefs of Liberals on 'English questions'.

The Home Rule preoccupation offered a temporary remedy

question of registration, or of election procedure was at the present moment almost a waste of time. There would be no satisfactory arrangement of these matters until they had cleared out of the way the great Irish difficulty. . . .'); 2 June 1887, p. 7 (Spencer: 'He wished he could deal with agricultural and other unexciting topics, but one great question—that of Ireland—now absorbed attention to the exclusion of all others').

[1] *The Times*, 12 April 1888, p. 7.
[2] Ibid., 2 October 1888, p. 7.
[3] *N.L.F. Report 1888*, pp. 62–3. *The Times*, 23 May 1888, p. 7; 2 July 1888, p. 7.

for faddism, a temporary answer to the problem that had plagued the Liberal leaders for many years of fixing priorities among reform demands. The 'obstruction' theory determined priorities. Clearing 'Ireland' out of the way was obviously the first duty of every reformer, no matter what his own special interest was. The sections were at last 'concentrated' and integrated into Liberal politics by being told that it was in the interests of each one to co-operate with the others and with the Liberal party as a whole in clearing the Irish obstruction out of the way. All the sections now had something in common: all alike were frustrated by 'Ireland'. The Home Rule issue thus became what Gladstone had wanted in 1873, an issue that, if 'worked into certain shapes', would 'help to mould the rest, at least for the time'.[1] In the absence of a Liberal creed, this single great question functioned as a substitute, conferring a provisional order on the miscellaneous and otherwise unco-ordinated interests in Liberal politics.

Again and again, Gladstone discussed the Home Rule preoccupation in these terms, using it to 'mould' the sections into conformity and co-operation. For example, in October 1888 he advised Liberals in Scotland that 'the interests of each part of the country will be most solidly provided for by putting forward boldly that great interest of the whole which is so much concentrated in the Irish question'.[2] In March 1890 he said to all Liberals who had 'special and what might be called preferential interests' in particular questions: 'Your first interest is to get rid of the Irish question.' It was, he told them, the subject 'to which, not only in despite of our own special preferences, but for the sake of our special preferences, we must direct our supreme attention'.[3] When in 1890 pressure was put on Gladstone to announce whether Welsh disestablishment was to get priority over Scottish disestablishment or vice versa, he replied that he could not 'exalt Wales as against Scotland, nor Scotland as against Wales' because 'it is impossible at the present period to determine any question of priority, either as between them, or as among the various measures, to which the Liberal party is variously pledged'. The reason was 'the Irish question, which, independently of its own greatness, disturbs

---

[1] See above, p. 65. [2] *The Times*, 2 November 1888, p. 7.
[3] Ibid., 25 March 1890, p. 10.

and obstructs all progress whatever'.[1] According to Gladstone, because of the Irish obstruction there had to continue in a 'state of inaction and, for practical purposes, oblivion' 'perhaps thirty or forty questions of great public importance, many of them of vast public importance, most perfectly ripe for discussion, all of them demanding solution, and all of them having large and intelligent bodies of men pushing them forward'.[2] One cannot imagine that the thought of this alternative to the Irish preoccupation—the uncontrolled 'pushing' of thirty or forty bodies of ardent reformers—was at all appealing to Gladstone. And it is certainly significant that it was during this period that he wrote for the *Nineteenth Century* another series of articles entitled 'Electoral Facts', showing, as had his article of 1878, the beneficial effects on the fortunes of the Liberal party of concentration on a single issue.[3]

In fact, sectionalism was for a time suppressed by the predominance of the Home Rule issue. The influence of the sectionalists in the party was temporarily weakened by the way in which the rift over Home Rule cut right through their ranks. Supporters of particular causes were cut off from one another, and so the strength of the sections was much diminished. In Scotland the vexatious disestablishment controversy was swamped by the emergence of the Irish issue: after all, even in 1885 Dr. Rainy had been prepared to concede that disestablishment might have to be postponed until Ireland was settled.[4] Nonconformists in England too found themselves on different sides of the controversy. Quite a few went with Chamberlain as 'the only statesman of first rank to whom we can look for disestablishment'; but others retained their veneration for Gladstone or accepted that Ireland did block the way.[5] The post-1885 career of W. S. Caine, the ardent advocate of temperance reform, shows how difficult it now was for 'faddists'

---

[1] Gladstone to Thomas Gee, 2 July 1890, Gee MSS., N.L.W. MS. 8306 C, folio 91a.
[2] *The Times*, 18 March 1887, p. 10.
[3] These articles appear in nos. 128, 154, and 175 (October 1887, December 1889, and September 1891).
[4] Savage, 'Scottish Politics, 1885–6', p. 129. Simpson, *Life of Principal Rainy*, p. 42.
[5] Dale, *Life of R. W. Dale*, p. 466. Guinness Rogers, *Autobiography*, pp. 214–16. Guinness Rogers to Gladstone, 4 March 1887, Gladstone MSS., B.M. Add. MS. 44500, folio 148.

to assert the primacy of their sectionalist interests in face of the absorption of political controversy in the Home Rule issue. Much against his will, he was obliged to become categorized primarily in terms of this question.[1] One notes too how the 'Crofters' Party' in Scotland was unable to maintain its independence after 1886 and was absorbed into Home Rule Liberalism.[2] The land reform 'lobby' was divided. In 1888 Liberal Unionists were replaced by Gladstonian Liberals in the presidency and committee of the Allotments and Small Holdings Association in spite of a plea by Jesse Collings that the Association should not be turned into 'a Home Rule Association'. Sir Walter Foster argued that, on the contrary, 'the Association should be supported by either one or the other of the sections of the Liberal party, since at present it suffers greatly from the difference of opinions existing'. Nevertheless, after the Association had been taken over by the Gladstonians, Collings and the Unionists decided to withdraw from it and to set up their own Rural Labourers' League in Birmingham.[3]

The obstruction argument was accepted by various sectionalists as a reason for subordinating their own questions and interests. W. S. Caine, for instance, told temperance supporters in 1887: 'At present there is an obstruction on the line of progress, and until we get that obstruction out of the way all other claims seem likely to be shelved.' He explained thus why, even although he opposed Gladstone's Home Rule policy, he had accepted that 'all other questions are, for the time being, only shadows; the Irish difficulty is the substance':

> It does not rest with a humble member of Parliament to pick and choose those subjects which from time to time are made the burning questions at elections. They are brought to the front by great leaders of governments, in response to public agitation; and as these questions come forward into the range of practical settlement, each in its turn receives, *and ought to receive*, the prime consideration of members of Parliament, often to the exclusion of subjects which are still distant.

Gladstone had done this in 1886; and even politicians who

---

[1] Newton, *W. S. Caine, M.P.*, pp. 179–82.
[2] Savage, 'Scottish Politics, 1885–6', p. 133. D. W. Crowley, 'The "Crofters' Party"', 1885–1892', *Scottish Historical Review*, vol. 35 (1956), p. 123.
[3] Collings and Green, *Life of Jesse Collings*, pp. 196–202.

disagreed with his proposals and would have preferred concentration on some quite different question had to recognize the impact on political life of his having concentrated attention on the Irish issue.¹ Another sectionalist who accepted the primacy of the Irish question was Stuart Rendel, the leader of the Welsh M.P.s. 'Ireland really does stop the way', he wrote in 1892; the Irish would refuse to accept other measures as 'concurrent' with their own, and there was nothing effectual that the supporters of these measures could do to retaliate against this.²

The 'obstruction' theory was from the outset a subject of much controversy. As we shall see, more and more of Gladstone's own supporters came to feel, as Chamberlain did in 1886, that 'Ireland' did not have to be regarded as an obstacle, insuperable save by the concession of Home Rule, to progress on any other matters. Where did the feeling that it did constitute such an obstacle derive from?

It was, of course, mainly the product of the Liberals' experience in office after 1880 and of the events of 1885–6 when the Irish had held the balance between the two main parties and had seemed to be playing them off against each other. 'Ireland' was blamed for what was felt by many Liberals to be a very serious problem: the accumulation of 'arrears of legislation'. Gladstone put it this way in a speech to the N.L.F. in 1891:

... we have the fact of the arrears of public business. You never can overtake the mass of work in which you are already involved, and which increases from year to year, until this terrible Irish controversy is out of the way. The effect of it has been, during the whole of my political life, that a fraction of the population of the United Kingdom, hardly amounting to one-eighth or one-ninth part, necessarily consumes an enormous portion of its legislative time, and makes it impossible for it [Parliament] to perform its proper office.³

One of the most thorough statistical analyses of the Irish 'obstruction' was made by Herbert Gladstone in an article entitled 'Ireland Blocks the Way' published in the *Nineteenth*

---

¹ Newton, *W. S. Caine, M.P.*, pp. 179–81.
² Rendel to A. C. Humphreys-Owen, 11 October 1892, Glansevern Collection: Letters to Humphreys-Owen, folio 612.
³ *N.L.F. Report 1891*, p. 114.

Century for June 1892. He surveyed the business of Parliament year by year, found that Irish affairs took up a 'disproportionate share of the national time', and concluded that 'the handing over of Irish affairs to Irish men in Ireland will save at least 25 per cent.' of this time. This prospect fully justified concentration on Home Rule: 'If the passing of a Home Rule Bill should occupy most of one session, or a considerable part of two, it would be one of the most profitable investments ever made by Parliament.'[1]

That 'Ireland' had absorbed a great deal of Parliament's attention since 1880 cannot be denied. Ireland clearly needed, and had the means of exacting, this attention. But what interests us here is the relationship which was established by the concentration on Home Rule after 1886 between this situation and the general problems of Liberal politics. Was the progress which the Gladstonians claimed that Ireland alone was preventing from occurring itself a myth, and was it one of the functions of the obstruction theory to delay or obstruct its being revealed as such? For the Home Rule preoccupation was closely associated throughout with the maintenance of a faith in 'progress'. The railway line imagery expressed this very well. It involved the assumption that a line of progress did continue to stretch into the future and that what alone prevented Liberals from following it was a mechanical breakdown, a temporary blocking of the line. Once the line was cleared, progress would resume and Liberals would be carried on smoothly and automatically to a single, already established destination. But, of course, in reality, as we have seen, no such line or destination existed. Quite apart from Ireland, there was another and much more fundamental obstacle to onward movement in Liberal politics— the confusion among Liberals as to what 'progress' now meant, their indecision as to what line of action to follow, their inability to agree on what reforms to promote and in what order. Irrespective of its accuracy, the notion of the 'Irish obstruction' did give the Liberals a temporary means of excusing or concealing these basic internal weaknesses. What the Liberal leaders constantly implied in their speeches was that the removal of the obstruction was the key to the re-emergence of coherence and system in Liberal politics.

[1] *N.C.*, no. 184, pp. 899–904.

Confusion would then disappear. Gladstone put it thus: 'It is in the removal of that one great obstacle that the secret of all rational and effectual progress lies.'¹ In this respect the Home Rule preoccupation was part of a growing tendency in Liberal politics. Rather than uniting to promote 'progress' and 'improvement' in any definite way, Liberals were concentrating more and more on the removal of obstacles to 'progress' which itself remained undefined. This masked their inability to discern where progress now lay or to agree on what they as Liberals should be doing to secure it. The removal of obstructions unified Liberals as the positive work of carrying through policies of reform no longer did.

The Irish preoccupation also represented a decision by Gladstone and the Liberals who supported him in favour of concentrated 'single question' politics as against 'programme' politics. The National Liberal Federation, which had been created as a vehicle for Chamberlainite 'programme' politics, was transformed into an agency for organizing concentration on a single question. And this was what most of the Liberal leaders wanted it to remain. They were now constantly on the alert for signs that any kind of programme was being re-created. They were perpetually fearful that the N.L.F. might get out of hand and that 'the active & fussy (& not by any means always *wise* tail) shd. insist on wagging the head'.² The Chief Whip, Arnold Morley, wrote to Gladstone concerning the 1889 meeting of the N.L.F.: 'There will be, I doubt not, a desire to compare what is put forward at Manchester with Salisbury's Nottm. programme. I agree that there is a considerable danger among our friends of attempting to add to the Party programme undigested & ill considered subjects, and a warning against this might not be out of place.'³ But the N.L.F. appeared to be in safe hands. Sir James Kitson from Leeds, its President in the late 1880s, was an outspoken critic both of Chamberlain and of programmes.⁴ The man who succeeded him as President in 1890, Robert Spence Watson, was also a

[1] *The Times*, 25 March 1890, p. 10.
[2] Herschell to Spencer, 14 October 1888, Rosebery MSS., Box 49.
[3] 28 November 1889, Gladstone MSS., B.M. Add. MS., 44253, folios 282-3.
[4] Cf. his remarks at the 1887 N.L.F. conference, quoted in *The Times*, 1 October 1887, p. 6.

strong enthusiast for concentration on single questions. In his presidential address of 1891 he opposed the prevailing mood of the 'Newcastle programme' meeting when he said that in his opinion declarations of policy were becoming too numerous and assuming too much 'of the character of a programme' and that 'some of us look back to the good old time when we took up one great burning question and fought it . . . until we carried it into law'.[1]

His remarks, and what happened at the Newcastle meeting in 1891, show that already the 'obstruction' theory was losing its efficacy for keeping the party in control. What it had introduced into Liberal politics was, of course, only a provisional ordering, a temporary substitute for system. As R. B. Haldane wrote in 1888, the preoccupation with Home Rule had given the Liberals a 'breathing space' for the preparation of new policies and principles, a period during which discussion of these was immune from the pressure of demands for immediate action.[2] Whether, after the ending of this preoccupation and the 'clearing of the way', the Liberals would commence a course of orderly and cohesive reform action or would plunge back into the chaos that had reigned before 1886, depended on how creatively the period of allegedly enforced abstention from commitments to action was used to develop new order in Liberal politics. What we have now to consider is why it was not so used.

The Newcastle programme and its aftermath were to show that little had been achieved via the National Liberal Federation. N.L.F. 'programmes', that is the resolutions passed at each meeting, expanded in a quite indiscriminate way. The original idea that one of the main functions of the N.L.F. was the placing of reform questions in some kind of order of priority seemed largely forgotten, and items were added after 1886 with little evidence of overall control—except that Irish Home Rule remained as first priority. Indeed, the Irish preoccupation was itself in part responsible for the continuing absence of order in the programme. The obstruction argument, since it meant

[1] *N.L.F. Report 1891*, p. 42.
[2] Haldane, 'The Liberal Creed', *C.R.*, vol. 54, p. 474 (October 1888). Hamer, *John Morley*, pp. 200–1.

that nothing could as yet be done about *any* reform question, conferred an air of unreality on the N.L.F. 'programmes' and encouraged the impression that there was no practical disadvantage involved in adding more and more questions to them. The Irish preoccupation, by creating an appearance of system in Liberal politics, gave rise to a sense of false security. Its collapse was to demonstrate just how provisional had been the ordering that it had conferred.

Another reason for the increasingly loose and 'omnibus' character of N.L.F. 'programmes' seems to have been the determination of Francis Schnadhorst, himself now separated politically from Chamberlain with whom he had worked closely for the whole of his previous political career, to return to the original spirit of the N.L.F. which he regarded as having been contaminated by the over-close identification of the N.L.F. with Chamberlain and Birmingham. In December 1886 Schnadhorst told Stuart Rendel that his aim was to secure 'a *complete* representation of the Liberal Party as a whole throughout the Kingdom' and 'to bring to a national character the scattered provincial organizations'. In Birmingham the N.L.F. had 'contracted a provincial character', and Schnadhorst now wanted 'to get rid of the "Birmingham" quality of provincialism'. But in order to achieve this aim Schnadhorst informed members of various sections, for instance the proponents of 'London Municipal Reform' and Welsh disestablishment, that all that was needed to get their questions accepted as 'planks in the Party platform' was for them to participate in the activities of the N.L.F. and be represented at its conferences. Under Schnadhorst's influence the resolutions passed by the N.L.F. became the representation of the ideal of comprehensiveness; and he made promises that no particular section would be 'fettered', i.e. obliged to accept any ordering of questions, as a result of decisions taken at N.L.F. conferences.[1]

In 1887 a wide range of reform proposals was approved of by the N.L.F., but both the 'omnibus' resolution and the Executive's report reduced the meaningfulness of the commitment by pointing out that only an Irish settlement could render the party capable of attending to these.[2] In 1888 there was

[1] Rendel to A. C. Humphreys-Owen, 18 December 1886, Glansevern Collection: Letters to Humphreys-Owen, folio 290.   [2] *N.L.F. Report 1887*, pp. 9, 34.

again a large 'programme' and again this was controlled by one of the resolutions which stated that 'an early settlement of the Irish Question' would 'enable Parliament' to attend to the reforms wanted by the N.L.F. The Report indicated, however, that the Executive Committee was trying to carry out some other process of selection and ordering. According to this Report, an attempt had been made in the choice of questions to form the subjects of resolutions 'to concentrate attention upon questions of pressing importance, with regard to which the mind of the party as a whole has been made up'. It urged local Liberal Associations to bring before the N.L.F. only 'questions of a practical character, with regard to which there is a general consensus of opinion in the party'. It then raised another important issue concerning the form of Liberal policy when it asked all members of the Federation to refrain from regarding the resolutions passed by the annual meetings as constituting political programmes. The problem was then illustrated by the Report itself when it went on to list regional conferences held during the past year under the N.L.F.'s auspices at which resolutions had been passed welcoming and accepting 'the Nottingham programme' of 1887. In his presidential address Sir James Kitson insisted that the officers did not see themselves as 'the founders of a policy or the suggesters of a programme'. Their aim was to ascertain Liberal opinion on current issues and, 'having ascertained it, to aid in concentrating the whole strength and resources of the party upon the promotion of such legislation as was by general consent of the greatest importance'. He expressed concern at the way in which Liberals were pressing for 'the introduction of too many subjects' at the annual meeting and called for more 'ripening' of these subjects beforehand.[1] But the problem was even worse in 1889. The resolutions covered an even wider range of reform issues, and there was an enormous 'omnibus' resolution summing them all up; but there was no reference in it to the Irish 'obstruction', the sole controlling factor of previous years.[2]

The test for determining whether or not a question ought to

---

[1] *N.L.F. Report 1888*, pp. 8–9, 12–14, 17–19, 89.
[2] *N.L.F. Report 1889*, pp. 6–10.

be included among the resolutions submitted to the N.L.F. meetings was said to be its 'ripeness'. The problem was to define this. The distinction was made between questions on which the party had 'made up its mind' and questions that were still 'in the stage of discussion'.[1] If strong feelings continued to be expressed within the party against a particular proposal, then clearly it was not 'ripe' and its supporters would have to go on trying to 'instruct the public mind'. This argument was frequently employed to prevent the submission of resolutions on the eight-hour day. Thus in 1889 Kitson ruled that this subject could not be 'brought there and discussed' but must first be 'threshed out in the country'. The 1890 Report said that, as opinion in the party was still greatly divided on the eight-hour question and 'the facts upon either side are as yet but imperfectly known', it was 'a question in the stage of discussion' and, 'therefore, a good example of one upon which it is impossible for the Federation at present to make any declaration'.[2]

On some questions it was a good deal easier than on others to ascertain 'ripeness'. Gladstone had pointed the way by using as one of his arguments for taking up Irish Home Rule the fact that in the 1885 elections most of the successful candidates in Ireland were supporters of Home Rule. In November 1889 he used similar reasoning to arrive at the conclusion that the time had come when he ought to vote for a private member's motion on Scottish disestablishment: 'He has twice, and in two Parliaments (I think) had majorities, rather large, of the Scotch members present; and every bye-election reinforces them. I seem, as a Scotch member, to have got the declaration of Scotch opinion which I have required.'[3] Such criteria could in time bring Scottish and Welsh disestablishment to the top of the list. With Irish, Welsh, and Scottish questions the Liberal leaders could find much clearer and more quickly accumulated evidence of a 'consensus of opinion' than they could on other, more general questions where the area of opinion to be covered was so much broader. It is not surprising that Welsh disestablishment rose quite rapidly to become

[1] Cf. *N.L.F. Report 1888*, p. 14.
[2] *N.L.F. Report 1889*, p. 130. *N.L.F. Report 1890*, p. 30.
[3] Gladstone to Rosebery, 10 November 1889, Rosebery MSS., Box 19.

acknowledged as the question to be dealt with next after Irish Home Rule. As early as 1887 Liberal leaders were referring to it as 'ripe for settlement' and 'ripe for decision', and at the 1889 N.L.F. it was for the first time given priority over all else except Irish Home Rule.[1] It was, after all, the type of reform that most obviously came next in the pattern of politics established by the preoccupation with Home Rule— the politics of attention to the demands of Celtic nationalism.[2]

Only in these very limited ways, then, was new order in Liberal politics being developed through the work of the National Liberal Federation. But obviously much depended also on the conduct of the Liberal leaders themselves and the extent to which they were prepared to take the initiative in organizing work on the construction of new policy.

From 1886 to 1894 the party was led by a man who deliberately refrained from taking initiatives of this kind and from engaging in the preparation of policy. This was most unfortunate because after the upheaval of 1885–6 what remained of the party was more dependent than ever on Gladstone for its cohesion. His leadership, in association with the Irish policy, was the rallying-point for the many diverse elements of Liberalism. The party as it existed after 1886 was a party shaped in his own image, constructed around his own personal decision to take up Home Rule. It was now a party of men each of whom had decided to support Gladstone on this and many of whom would never otherwise have become advocates of Home Rule. Lord Acton wrote in 1887 of how incalculable now was the force of Gladstone's political authority. It was 'a bewildering problem', he told Gladstone, to try to work out 'where we should be without you, and which wing of the party would predominate apart from the sword which you throw into

---

[1] Morgan, *Wales in British Politics*, pp. 76–7, 80–2, 90–3, 133. *N.L.F. Report 1887*, pp. 9, 73–4. *N.L.F. Report 1889*, pp. 10, 63–4.

[2] 'I see more clearly than ever that Home Rule is not more essentially the Irish national question, than Disestablishment and Disendowment are essentially the Welsh national question.' John Morley to Thomas Gee, 20 August 1890, Gee MSS., N.L.W. MS. 8307 D, folio 210. 'The recent contest has been fought upon the question of nationality........ this very fact, that an election has been contested on grounds of nationality, of itself gives a new place to nationality as an element of our political thought.' W. E. Gladstone, *The Irish Question*, 1886, p. 36.

the scale'.¹ 'Talk of the Liberal party?' John Morley said in 1891. 'Why it consists of Mr. G. After him it will disappear & all will be chaos.'²

But after 1885 Gladstone's leadership constituted a major obstruction to the development of Liberal policy because of the combination of this kind of authority with his refusal to regard it as part of his responsibility to help with this development. In 1885 he had made it plain that at his age he felt no further concern with the 'ordinary exigencies of party' and with the wide range of matters normally attended to by a party leader. If he stayed in politics, it would be only in order to help with the settlement of the Irish question. In August 1885 he told Hamilton that he was 'still determined that to fight the battle of the "outs" against the "ins"—that merely to unfurl the flag of Liberalism *versus* Conservatism—is for him no duty of necessity. He can and will only abstain from retiring if some specific work is put before him—some work with which the nation specifically entrusts him. The only work of such a kind which is likely to present itself is the Irish question . . .'³ This was his comment on complaints that Radicalism was becoming 'too bold and too forward' and that schemes of 'organic change' were being propounded which would 'raise doubtful and difficult controversies': 'I am not going to raise a discussion on that point. I am too old to change the frame of mind, the general frame of mind, with which I look upon political questions, and it is not for me to say whether men's opinions are tending to be too advanced or not.'⁴ Thereafter he expressly absolved himself from participation in the discussion of the new ideas and policies that the party would so urgently need after the Irish interlude, insisting that he remained '*in situ* for the Irish question only'.⁵ 'What are Land Laws and County Gov. to him?' he had asked in 1885. 'They can be just as well & even better dealt with by others.'⁶ The party lacked direction from the top on anything except Irish

---

[1] Acton to Gladstone, 9 January 1887, F. N. Figgis and R. N. Laurence (edd.), *Selections From the Correspondence of the First Lord Acton*, vol. i, 1917, p. 179.
[2] Sir E. Hamilton's diary, B.M. Add. MS. 48654, folio 132 (13 January 1891).
[3] Sir E. Hamilton's diary, B.M. Add. MS. 48641, folios 48-9 (7 August 1885).
[4] *The Times*, 23 November 1885, p. 10.
[5] Gladstone to Acton, 13 January 1887, Morley, *Gladstone*, ii, p. 595.
[6] Sir E. Hamilton's diary, B.M. Add. MS. 48641, folio 110 (16 October 1885).

policy and those policies, such as Welsh disestablishment, which Gladstone felt it necessary to take up for the sake of the Irish policy. Gladstone was too old and too near retirement, too much absorbed in his last great crusade, to take a wider view; but the party of which he remained the leader and which indeed had been virtually fashioned anew by himself suffered as a result.

In October 1886 Andrew Reid asked him to contribute to a symposium on 'The New Liberal Programme'. Gladstone replied: 'I hold on to politics in the hope of possibly helping to settle the Irish question, but the general operations both of party and of particular subjects I am obliged, & intend, to leave in the hands of others.'[1] Writing to Harcourt at this time about the '*superfoetation* of Radical ideas on our side', he remarked: 'I am rather too old to put on a brand new suit of clothes.'[2] Thus from the leader the response to the new 'ripening' ideas was almost entirely negative. He was not disposed to enter into the work of preparing the Liberal future. In October 1886 he explained that he had declined to address the N.L.F. at Leeds on the general policy of the Liberal party 'because I must confine myself to winding up things already begun, whereas this is in the nature of a *commencement* for the party generally'.[3] In October 1887 he told the N.L.F. that he did not wish to give his own views on the various questions that were coming up because of the 'necessary limitations' to his political action and because 'I am not likely to be a responsible person in giving effect to those views'.[4] A year later he told the N.L.F. that they were led 'by one who is himself too conscious ... that he can now but half perform the office of a leader'.[5]

Some of Gladstone's colleagues accepted this assessment of his position, for example John Morley, who wrote in 1891 that Gladstone should not attempt to 'touch other questions': 'He does not understand them, nor the sentiment that makes them important with our people.'[6] But others strongly disagreed. 'Surely', wrote Harcourt, 'it would not be a glorious sunset for

[1] There is a facsimile reproduction of this letter between pp. xiii and 1 of A. Reid (ed.), *The New Liberal Programme Contributed by Representatives of the Liberal Party*, 1886.   [2] Gardiner, *Life of Harcourt*, ii, p. 12.
[3] Gladstone to Spencer, 2 October 1886, Spencer MSS., Misc. Corr. 1886 E–GL.
[4] *N.L.F. Report 1887*, p. 73.   [5] *N.L.F. Report 1888*, p. 77.
[6] Morley to Harcourt, 5 January 1891, Harcourt MSS.

a great statesman with the experience of 60 years to confess that in the whole range of the complicated interests and wants of the British race he had no comprehension and no sympathy with anything except a single question which affected a fraction of them.'[1] Harcourt had to recognize, however, that because Gladstone had 'confined his mind so entirely to one topic' since 1885 he had by 1890 reached the stage where he did not have 'much grasp of anything else'.[2] Some of Gladstone's associates grew very impatient with this consciously abnormal kind of leadership and worried about the effects that it was having on the party. In September 1888 Sir Edward Hamilton discussed the problem with Rosebery, who complained that 'Mr. G. had lost more than ever all sense of *proportion*'; and Hamilton wrote afterwards in his diary:

Where he [Gladstone] is to blame is that, being wholly engrossed in one subject he thinks that at his time of life he need trouble himself about no other. He forgets that he is not only the exponent of a policy for Ireland, but the leader of one of the great parties of the State, in which capacity he ought to give the lead on all political subjects which are on the horizon, and not let all the Labboucheres, Cunningham Grahams [*sic*], & the like 'run riot'. About this I feel very strongly; but it is no easy matter to make Mr. G. himself see things in this light. He feels 'you must take me as you find me; or else get rid of me'.[3]

Meetings of the Liberal leaders to concert strategy or discuss policy were infrequent and usually confined to aspects of the Irish question. The party felt the consequent lack of overall guidance and direction. R. Munro Ferguson, M.P. for Leith Burghs, told Rosebery in May 1887 that 'I believe it would be generally approved by the rank & file that the ex Cabinet should occasionally meet & discuss the best course for the Opposition to take'.[4] Haldane wrote in 1888 that much of the confusion and drift in Liberal politics was attributable to Gladstone's continuing to be Liberal leader while maintaining

[1] Harcourt to Morley, 6 January 1891, Harcourt MSS.
[2] Harcourt to Morley, 30 December 1890, Harcourt MSS.
[3] B.M. Add. MS. 48649, folios 61-2 (23 September 1888). Cf. Hamilton's entry for 17 June 1890: 'Lord Acton thought Mr. G. somewhat ageing, & that want of proportion & perspective was growing upon him.' B.M. Add. MS. 48653, folio 44.
[4] Ferguson to Rosebery, 9 May 1887, Rosebery MSS., Box 14.

that 'he had no expectation' of carrying through anything except Home Rule.¹ In May 1890 James Bryce remarked on 'the odd state the party in the Commons has got into': 'It is not an Opposition at all in the sense of former days, but a number of skirmishers, occasionally, like the Arabs before Mohammed, uniting for a raid upon the enemy, when the old chief appears.'² Asquith saw the absence of normal leadership as responsible both for the existing 'dead-lock' and Liberal disorderliness in the House of Commons and for the lack of concern with 'making provision for the future & looking ahead'.³ But Gladstone himself expressed contempt for what went on in the House of Commons. 'My own opinion', he wrote, 'is that, now as in the Jingo time, our battle is to be fought in the country; that the Parliamentary Debates are not read in the country to any great purpose . . . and that we are under no obligation to waste sense and breath upon an impenetrable majority.'⁴ Harcourt could not agree with this. He replied: 'I am disposed to think that the country still attaches more importance to definite action in the House of Commons than to "excursions and alarums" in the Provinces. They look upon one as real warfare and the other as a Review or sham fight.'⁵

Gladstone's colleagues had the utmost difficulty in persuading him to hold meetings of the ex-Cabinet 'to talk over the business of the time'. In 1890 Rosebery wrote of having 'pointed out & in vain until I am sick of it', 'the inconvenience of an opposition being conducted without previous concert or consultation among leaders'.⁶ The problem was not, however, a new one. It was Gladstone's 'intense dislike' of 'having anything like joint consultation or common action'—manifested, for instance, in connection with the Home Rule issue at the end of 1885 and the beginning of 1886.⁷ There was little place in Gladstone's concept of the role of a leader for prior education or consultation of colleagues and followers.

¹ R. B. Haldane, 'The Liberal Party and its Prospects', *C.R.*, vol. 53, p. 148, (January 1888).
² Bryce to Rosebery, 22 May [1890], Rosebery MSS., Box 64.
³ Sir E. Hamilton's diary, B.M. Add. MS. 48646, folios 62–3 (9 June 1887).
⁴ Memo by Gladstone, 14 November 1890, enclosed in letter to Harcourt of the same date, Harcourt MSS.
⁵ Harcourt to Gladstone, 17 November 1890, Harcourt MSS.
⁶ Rosebery to Bryce, 21 May 1890, Bryce MSS., E 21–2.
⁷ For Harcourt's comments on this see Gardiner, *Life of Harcourt*, ii, p. 178.

Another problem was that Gladstone was increasingly cut off from normal contact with colleagues and with the day-by-day procedures of political life, partly through his increasing physical infirmity—especially his failing eyesight and hearing[1] —and partly because of the tendency of his family and *entourage* to shelter him and minimize such contact. Sir Edward Hamilton complained in 1886 that neither Gladstone nor Mrs. Gladstone would 'see things ... if they present themselves in an unfavourable light'.[2] A year later, Hamilton records in his diary that Harcourt and Gladstone had had a 'turn up' because Harcourt had 'broken out with some home truths, as to Mr. G.'s living too much in the clouds & not hearing what the world says'. Gladstone was living secluded at Lord Aberdeen's house at Dollis Hill, and, as a result, Hamilton wrote, 'nobody can ever get at Mr. G.'[3]

Gladstone's continuing dominance kept the development of Liberal policies and ideas frozen. So long as he was leader, an air of unreality was bound to pervade Liberal politics. The feeling that 'ordinary' politics were in a state of suspension is reflected in Campbell-Bannerman's remark in 1892 that the Liberals were not involved in 'an ordinary case of forming a Government'. 'The Government', he said, 'is being formed for the special purpose of enabling Mr. G. to carry out his ideas: it is in an unusual degree *his* Government.'[4]

In spite of all this, it was frequently claimed by the Liberal leaders that a major consequence of the Liberal schism of 1886 was that the party had become more Radical. This claim, of

[1] 'The principal sign of age that I notice about Mr. G. now is his increased loquaciousness, partly no doubt due to his deficient hearing power.' Sir E. Hamilton's diary, B.M. Add. MS. 48657, folio 90 (11 March 1892). 'One of his greatest failings through life had been his very slow recognition of faces; and now that his sight was failing he was getting worse & worse. In the lobbies for instance he hardly dared to go up & speak to anyone whom he did not know well for fear of making a mistake.' Hamilton's summary of what Gladstone had said to him in conversation, B.M. Add. MS. 48648, folio 33 (25 February 1888).
[2] Sir E. Hamilton's diary, B.M. Add. MS. 48643, folio 78 (10 April 1886).
[3] B.M. Add. MS. 48646, folio 53 (26 May 1887). On 27 July 1887 Rosebery told Hamilton that 'he was sure Mrs. G. was acquiring a greater influence over him [Gladstone] and that Mr. G. was less inclined to listen to others than ever he was'. B.M. Add. MS. 48646, folio 113.
[4] C-B to Harcourt, 14 August 1892, J. A. Spender, *The Life of the Right Hon. Sir Henry Campbell-Bannerman, G.C.B.*, vol. i, [1923], p. 124.

course, contradicted, and was undoubtedly intended to contradict, the conclusion to which Chamberlain's secession had most naturally given rise, that the party was now less Radical. The seriousness and impact of this aspect of the schism could obviously be lessened if attention were focused on the Whigs and class were made to appear the basic cause of the rift. Furthermore, since before 1886 Gladstone had often referred to his determination not to cause a schism in the party or lead one side against another, it was now in his interest to try to make it appear that it was not his own decision to take up Home Rule which was basically responsible for the schism. The leaders felt, or at least said that they felt, that the centre of gravity in the party had shifted leftwards, in other words that the withdrawal of so many Whigs and conservative Liberals more than made up for the loss of Chamberlain and other Radicals. Gladstone wrote in September 1887 that 'the course pursued by Lord Hartington and his friends has given a powerful impulse to Radicalism within the lines of the Liberal party; and it will, I think, be difficult, when the ground is cleared by the settlement of the Irish question, for moderate Liberalism to hold its ground'.[1] Addressing the N.L.F. a month later, he said that the behaviour of the dissentient Liberals had given 'an enormous stimulus to advanced opinions all through the country and throughout the ranks of the Liberal party'. The resistance to Home Rule, together with 'all the influences and powers which that resistance will have brought into action', would be found, when the Irish controversy was at an end, to have enabled 'the advanced Liberals, the Radical portion of the party', to get 'a vastly increased influence' in it.[2] At about this time Gladstone was telling one of his colleagues that the amount of Radical influence in the party in future was going to be determined 'by the duration and intensity' of the opposition to Home Rule. Those who feared the growth of this influence should appreciate that the 'remedy' lay 'in passing Home Rule as quickly as possible'.

To me as a politician [he went on] it is probably nothing, but to me as an individual this advance of radicalism is a matter of great regret. Even Hartington, in his venom against Home Rule, is giving

[1] Gladstone to A. Taylor Innes, 2 September 1887, A. Taylor Innes, *Chapters of Reminiscence*, 1913, pp. 164–5. [2] *N.L.F. Report 1887*, p. 48.

it countenance. When Home Rule is settled, Chamberlain will atone for his defection on this question by greater intensity on others. In 1866 John Mill said the Liberal party were 'a broad church', and it was true. But it will be difficult to keep them so.[1]

Two years later Gladstone was still dwelling on this theme. At the 1889 N.L.F. he explained thus why it was not Home Rule itself on which blame for the 'serious disintegration of the Liberal party' should lie:

> For a long time [before 1886] the wealthy and the powerful had been gradually detaching themselves from the body of the Liberal party and finding their most natural associations in Toryism, in stagnation, and in resistance. For some of them it was a perfect Godsend when Home Rule turned up, and supplied them with a plausible excuse for doing ostensibly or even ostentatiously that which in their hearts they had been longing for an excuse to do.

But as a result of their secession the dissentient Liberals had 'shifted the centre of gravity in the Liberal party', brought about a great change in 'the colour and complexion' of the party, and given a 'great impulse' and a 'large increase of scope' to 'what are called Radical opinions'. The party was no longer Mill's 'Broad Church', covering 'in harmony, men whose political opinions exhibited a considerable variety of shades of colour'.[2]

What is striking about these utterances, especially those made by Gladstone in public, is their ambiguity. It is often very hard to know whether he is disapproving of these trends or welcoming or even encouraging them. What Gladstone above all had to achieve was rapid progress towards an Irish settlement. To 'moderate' Liberals and to wavering dissentients he presented the prospect of an intensification of Radicalism and reaction if the controversy over Home Rule were prolonged. They might not like Home Rule very much, but they should see that the choice now lay between it and the growth of that Radical influence which, he was clearly implying, they would like even less. But at the same time he suggested to Radicals that it was also in their interests to continue to devote themselves

---

[1] Gladstone to Rosebery, 21 November 1887, Rosebery MSS., Box 19. See also Gladstone's letter to Lord Edmond Fitzmaurice quoted in Hammond, *Gladstone and the Irish Nation*, p. 170.
[2] *N.L.F. Report 1889*, pp. 75–6.

to the Home Rule cause because of the beneficial effects of the controversy over it on their own position in the party. Of course, in private there was no ambiguity. Gladstone seemed aghast at the Pandora's box which he had opened and bitterly regretted 'the extinction of the Whigs & moderate Liberals which he considered Hartington's action had rendered inevitable'.[1] On one occasion, talking to Sir Edward Hamilton, Gladstone 'broke forth about the suicidal policy of the moderate Liberals. They had hitherto formed the moderators of advanced radicalism. They were now going to be effaced; & the inevitable consequence will be that extreme views will advance with rapid strides & Radicalism, Socialism, & Bradlaughism will accomplish their triumph far sooner. He deplored the result above everything with real earnestness.'[2]

Gladstone might characteristically be facing both ways, but some of his colleagues were much less ambiguous. Harcourt, for example, told the N.L.F. in November 1888 that the rift between the Whigs and the Liberal party was 'unmuzzling' the party and giving 'an immense impulse to the democratic party'. The Radical secession had not been important, had 'not touched the heart of the Radical party'. The course taken by Lord Hartington and his friends would prove to 'have immensely quickened the pace'.[3]

But who were these Radicals who were supposed to be gaining such influence in Liberal politics? The most conspicuous variety of Radicalism within the party in the late 1880s was that associated with Henry Labouchere, the editor of *Truth* and M.P. for Northampton. Violent in language and extreme in the opinion of most Conservatives, this Radicalism was nevertheless thoroughly traditional in regard to policies and objects of attack and was just as incoherent and ineffectual as previous Radical 'movements' within the Liberal party. Indeed, one important aspect of it, its anti-Socialism, was distinctly conservative. It was the classic Radicalism of those who wished to reduce the power and interference of the State as much as

[1] Sir E. Hamilton's diary, B.M. Add. MS. 48646, folio 18 (13 April 1887).
[2] Sir E. Hamilton's diary, B.M. Add. MS. 48646, folio 30 (1 May 1887). See also folios 37, 132-3 (7 May, 26 August 1887), and B.M. Add. MS. 48651, folio 33 (5 July 1889) for similar observations by Gladstone.
[3] *N.L.F. Report 1888*, pp. 116-17. See also Harcourt to J. Morley, 15 July 1892, Harcourt MSS.

possible.¹ Many Liberals disliked it because of its negativeness and extreme individualism.

After 1886 evidence that any coherent kind of Radicalism was on the way to acquiring dominance in Liberal politics was even harder to find than it had been before 1886. Nevertheless, there was a vacuum in reform politics, and Labouchere, for all his deficiencies, did find himself appealing to a considerable number of rank-and-file Liberals and back-bench M.P.s. Labouchere was a natural 'opposition' Radical.² He professed to want to see the development of the party controlled by the rank and file, not the leaders. In 1886 he called for an extension of the role of the party organization so that 'each individual Liberal elector' could have a hand in shaping the party's programme. The leaders should be merely 'executive officers charged with the task of giving effect to the popular mandate'. 'All impulse must come from below, it will never come from above.' The N.L.F. should become 'the Liberal Parliament', and when the Liberals were in power, 'Ministers should be but the Parliamentary Committee of the Federation'.³ Labouchere proceeded to try to put his philosophy into practice and to take initiatives on behalf of 'the party' without waiting for the leaders. Thus in the Commons in March 1888 he moved a resolution attacking the House of Lords and attracted 162 votes. In the debate he threatened to have the Lords issue made into a test question against 'half-hearted' Liberals in the constituencies.⁴

His principle of getting the party to 'lead' the leaders seemed to have achieved practical effect when Harcourt spoke strongly in favour of the resolution.⁵ Harcourt was becoming increasingly concerned about the effects of the Irish preoccupation on the party. He believed that the party could not afford to remain in this abnormal condition: it must be kept in some kind of

---
¹ See below, pp. 235-6.   ² Cf. above, pp. 51, 96-7.
³ Reid, *The New Liberal Programme*, pp. 6-7.
⁴ *Hansard*, 3rd Series, vol. 323, cc. 763-813.
⁵ Labouchere and the Radicals tried in the late 1880s to 'capture' one of the Liberal leaders, preferably Morley or Harcourt. See Labouchere to Morley, 23 July 1889, in the packet of miscellaneous letters and papers on the Royal Grants issue in the Harcourt MSS., and Morley to Harcourt, 29 May 1889, Harcourt MSS. ('You and I must really have a talk soon about the Jacobyn faction. G.O.T[revelyan] wants us "to place ourselves at their head". I said *I* would certainly see them d—d, before I would lie down in the gutter for them to march over me whenever they took a fancy to that operation.')

relationship with Radical opinion so that it would continue to justify being the 'party of progress' in a two-party system.[1] He seems to have made up his mind from 1886 on to try to relate his own political conduct as closely as possible to the movements of Radical opinion. He was anxious to appear to be growing 'more Radical', and so, for want of anything better, he responded ostentatiously to initiatives taken by Labouchere and other back-bench Radicals. This greatly disturbed his colleagues and the non-Radicals in the party who found Harcourt far too 'squeezable' and opportunistic.[2]

In 1889 the Radicals formed their own parliamentary organization, allegedly covering about seventy M.P.s, with its own Whips. Its purpose was to take initiatives in the House of Commons without reference to the Front Bench, and for a year or so it was responsible for a series of Radical motions and amendments which sometimes embarrassed or even split the Front Bench, for example on the question of Royal Grants.[3] The aim of this group was 'to give real and effective weight to Radical views'; but it soon disintegrated, owing partly to the divisive effect of social questions.[4] The weaknesses and problems of 'the New Liberalism' were acutely analysed in an article in the *Nineteenth Century* in August 1889 by a prominent member of the group, L. A. Atherley-Jones, whose own background undoubtedly put him in a particularly good position to appreciate what was lacking. He was the son of Ernest Jones, the Chartist, who, having felt the Charter, with its purely political Radicalism, to be inadequate, and having tried after 1848 to foster support for Socialism among the working classes, had turned after 1858 to a strategy of close co-operation with middle-class Radicalism.[5] It was a divided heritage. The unification

[1] For his debate with John Morley about this see Hamer, *John Morley*, pp. 228–30.
[2] Cf. ibid., pp. 289–91. Reginald Brett wrote to Rosebery, 7 November 1890, that Harcourt 'is—as Labouchere says in praise of him—squeezable; but what a prospect in a Leader, even if his Leadership is confined to the House of Commons'. Rosebery MSS., Box 6. Rosebery himself, talking about 'the future of Mr. G.'s party', expressed anxiety that Harcourt 'would be so easily squeezable by the extreme Radicals'. Sir E. Hamilton's diary, B.M. Add. MS. 48651, folio 14 (15 June 1889). But, when Hamilton spoke to Harcourt about the party's future, he found that 'in fact he has little real sympathy with advanced men'. B.M. Add. MS. 48652, folio 42 (26 January 1890).
[3] S. Maccoby, *English Radicalism 1886–1914*, 1953, pp. 7 –7.
[4] Atherley-Jones, *Looking Back*, pp. 68–9.
[5] Briggs, *Age of Improvement*, p. 431.

had come through Lib-Labism, and his son was a Liberal M.P. for a thoroughly working-class constituency, Durham North-West. But in 1889 Atherley-Jones seems to sense that the era which his father had helped to inaugurate after 1858 was drawing to a close, that the middle-class Radicalism which had predominated since then was now largely bankrupt. He points out the implications of the desertion of Liberalism by the middle class. Their battle had been 'fought and won'. Even in the North of England 'the strength of middle-class Liberalism is year by year diminishing'. The 'Nonconformist agitation for religious equality', which was almost the last survival of that Liberalism, was dying away; the disestablishment movement was losing its militancy as a result of 'the greater tolerance of the Church and the removal of the more oppressive and invidious distinctions between it and the Nonconformist sects'. Radicals had now to come to terms with the fact that, 'for the first time in the history of English politics', Liberalism was 'almost exclusively identified with the particular interests of the working class'. For traditional Radical causes such as disestablishment and 'free land' had little chance of kindling the enthusiasm of the artisans and the labourers. For this real social reform would have to be taken up.[1]

Atherley-Jones saw other weaknesses in the Radicalism of the late 1880s—'want of leadership', 'the objectionable idiosyncrasies of many of those who affect to speak on its behalf', and the effect of Gladstone's continuing dominance. Another Radical who criticized it was Chamberlain. Laboucherean Radicalism was at the opposite pole to the kind of Radicalism that he had stood for. As a 'constructive' Radical, he found the impracticability of these 'new Radicals' highly distasteful. Home Rule might have made the Liberal party more Radical, but it was a Radicalism that he wanted nothing to do with. He saw Gladstonian Liberalism coming increasingly under the influence of 'anarchists, separatists, and wild spirits of the left'. 'I do not want', he wrote in June 1887, 'to reunite with a party —or faction—controlled by Labouchere, Lawson, Conybeare and Co.' To him the 'new Radicalism' was 'the English imitation of Nihilism, whose only dogma is opposition to all

[1] *N.C.*, no. 150, pp. 186–93.

government and all authority'.¹ In July 1889 he attacked Radicals 'who are destructive in their aims and objects, who have never shown the slightest constructive capacity, who are, in short, nothing more nor less than the Nihilists of English Politics'.²

The minority group of M.P.s which had been able to secure most influence over the shaping of Liberal policy was the Irish Nationalists. From 1886 on they were in alliance with the Liberal party, and an inescapable question of great importance which the Liberal leaders found very difficult to answer was what the future of this alliance was to be. The achievement of Home Rule might well take a considerable time, might even eventually have to be given up as a practicable objective. Would there then be a return to the pre-1886 situation with the Irish detached from and balancing between the two main parties, or could the alliance be made more permanent, covering non-Irish as well as Irish policy? There were many Liberals who wanted Irish representation at Westminster to be maintained even after the concession of Home Rule. Were the Irish votes to be looked upon, or could they be turned into, a permanent addition to the voting force of the Liberal party in the House of Commons? The danger was that too close an alliance might be counter-productive in the sense of alienating English, Scottish, and Welsh voters who disliked the Irish. But for a while it seemed to many sound sense to try to establish control over this voting bloc which might otherwise once again seriously unstabilize British politics, especially Liberal and Radical politics. And there were the pessimists who felt grave doubts as to whether the Liberal party would ever be able again to have a non-Irish majority in the House of Commons. In 1889 Harcourt argued that the Liberals could not 'afford to diminish the number of the Irish votes' in the House after Home Rule because 'we shall want them for a Liberal majority'.³

---

¹ See P. Fraser, *Joseph Chamberlain*, Chapter 7: 'The New Radicalism', and 'The Liberal Unionist Alliance: Chamberlain, Hartington, and the Conservatives, 1886–1904', *English Historical Review*, vol. 77 (1962), pp. 61–2. M. Hurst, *Joseph Chamberlain and Liberal Reunion. The Round Table Conference of 1887*, 1967, p. 101.

² Maccoby, *English Radicalism 1886–1914*, pp. 64–5.

³ Harcourt to Spencer, 25 October 1889, Harcourt MSS. Granville to Spencer, 22 October 1889, Spencer MSS. F. S. L. Lyons, *The Fall of Parnell 1890–91*, 1960, p. 106.

Lord Acton suggested that women should be enfranchised if it could be shown that a majority of them would vote Liberal, because 'since 1886 we have to think very seriously of the future of Liberal politics. We lost our majority by proposing to get rid of the Irish members. How should we have recovered it—in Great Britain—if we had succeeded in getting rid of them?'[1] The Welsh and Scots were understood to feel that all chance of getting their particular measures such as disestablishment passed, would be lost if the Irish votes were removed from the House of Commons.[2] Radicals too, as in the 1830s, looked in their impotence for possible aid from the Irish.[3]

But it was, of course, a complete delusion to see in the Irish any potential for stable participation in a Liberal voting bloc. They were clearly not Liberals in the English sense on many issues, for example education, and their votes were always bound to be guided primarily by considerations of tactical expediency. Appealing as they did to national feeling, the Irish could not afford, nor did they wish, to become too closely integrated in British politics. Lord Herschell once observed that 'the Irish vote could never be counted on, and on all questions with our Liberal touchstones, such as unsectarian education and protection, they would vote against us for a certainty'.[4] Here was no future for the Liberal party: to rely for 'a Liberal vote' on the Irish alliance would be tantamount to placing Liberal politics on a foundation of quicksands. 'I suppose', wrote Labouchere, 'that the notion of keeping the Irish in Parliament for some years [after the passing of a Home Rule Bill] is tempting on account of their votes. But no Govt. can count on them, and they are just as likely to vote Tory as Liberal.'[5]

[1] Acton to Gladstone, 26 April 1891, Figgis and Laurence, *Selections from the Correspondence of the First Lord Acton*, i, p. 235.

[2] John Morley suggested this in January 1893. H. G. Hutchinson (ed.), *Private Diaries of the Rt. Hon. Sir Algernon West, G.C.B.*, 1922, p. 114. Stuart Rendel wrote to Thomas Gee, 15 October 1893, that 'I see the necessity of getting the full Irish vote for Welsh Disestablishment. My view was that we should carry Welsh Disestablishment after Irish Home Rule is assured but before the Irish Representation is reduced or turned aside.' Rendel MSS., 10, folio 42 (draft) [N.L.W. MS. 19458 E].

[3] Thorold, *Life of Labouchere*, pp. 252, 334.

[4] Herschell to Granville, 29 October 1887, Fitzmaurice, *Life of Granville*, ii, p. 492.

[5] Labouchere to Harcourt, 10 January 1893, Harcourt MSS.

VII The End of the Irish Preoccupation

THE Home Rule preoccupation may have brought system into Liberal politics, but the maintenance of this depended on the avoidance of too much discussion of the details of Irish policy. For after 1886 the Liberal leaders found themselves differing more and more from one another on these details, and these disagreements proved to have implications ranging beyond Irish policy and to contain the seeds of later and more fundamental conflicts.

In the first place, there was land policy. The Land Purchase Bills of the Conservative government posed a dilemma for the Liberal leaders. They had, after all, argued in 1886 that a land settlement in Ireland must precede or accompany the establishment of Home Rule. Why then should they not accept what the Conservatives were doing as part of this essential prelude to Home Rule? A few of the younger Liberals, such as Grey and Haldane, adopted this point of view and rebelled against the party leaders by voting for the Conservative measures.[1] But with most Liberals the instinct for 'system', for a clear-cut

---

[1] R. B. Haldane, 'Why I Voted For the Land Bill', *The Speaker*, vol. 1, no. 19 (10 May 1890), pp. 504–5. G. M. Trevelyan, *Grey of Fallodon Being the Life of Sir Edward Grey Afterwards Viscount Grey of Fallodon*, 1937, p. 33. Haldane, *An Autobiography*, pp. 111–12. Grey to Haldane, 8 November 1890, Haldane MSS., MS. 5903, folios 173–4. Morley wrote to Gladstone, 28 October 1888: 'I find, by the way, that there is a view among some of our friends, that we might as well let the gov.mt have their money, on the ground that the more landlords are bought out, the less will be our difficulty when the time comes. Haldane pressed this on me. But I doubt whether it will be a common opinion.' Gladstone MSS., B.M. Add. MS. 44255, folio 278. On 2 April 1890 Morley reported to Gladstone that he had told Lord Spencer: 'If you and I do not vote against the [Land Purchase] Bill, we break with our party: they will go practically solid against it. It may be that we shall be forced to a line of our own on the Land question at some future time. But as we think the present Bill thoroughly bad and dangerous, let us say so, and postpone an evil day.' Gladstone MSS., B.M. Add. MS. 44256, folio 44.

general position, prevailed over the desire to be logical on points of detail. Acceptance of the Conservatives' land purchase policy would have appeared to undermine the case for the necessity of Home Rule.

There was also the very difficult problem of whether or not to maintain the association of a scheme of land purchase with a Home Rule Bill. This had been exploited by the Chamberlainite Radicals who in 1886 denounced the giving to landlords of the money of British taxpayers. Lord Spencer was in 1886, and remained, the most fervent advocate of the 'Twinship'.[1] Another supporter of it was John Morley, whereas Harcourt now became the principal exponent of the Radical point of view.[2] Morley saw a prior or parallel land settlement as essential to make Home Rule a success. Otherwise Home Rule would result in social instability and allegations of the oppression of landlords, which would provide an excellent excuse for British intervention and enable Unionists to claim that Home Rule had failed.[3] The Radicals maintained the Chamberlainite position and, when the Conservatives produced Irish Land Purchase Bills, longed to exploit these as means of asserting the traditional distinction between Liberals and Conservatives. Labouchere denounced as 'a fatal error' the failure to make the second reading of the 1890 Land Bill 'a great Party fight': 'The English Home Rulers may be ready to give Ireland a Parliament, but they object to accepting any monetary liabilities for them, knowing that [the] Irish never pay their bills . . .'[4]

Another question which aroused disagreement with more general implications was that of whether or not Irish M.P.s should remain at Westminster after an Irish Parliament had been set up. And, even if it were assumed that they would be retained, other questions had to be settled, such as how many of them there should be and whether they should have only limited voting rights, for example only on 'imperial'

[1] See his letters to Gladstone, 11 and 12 June and 20 August 1886, and 27 February 1887, Gladstone MSS., B.M. Add. MS. 44313, folios 76, 79–81, 92–3, 114–15.
[2] Morley to Harcourt, 28 July 1887, Harcourt MSS. Gardiner, *Life of Harcourt*, ii, pp. 116–18.
[3] Hamer, *John Morley*, pp. 215–16. See the report of what he told Sir E. Hamilton on the question in Hamilton's diary, B.M. Add. MS. 48654, folios 11–12 (14 October 1890).
[4] Labouchere to Harcourt, 31 December 1890, Harcourt MSS.

questions. Liberal policy on this was affected and complicated by numerous cross-currents. The 1886 Home Rule Bill had provided for the exclusion of the Irish M.P.s, and there continued to be very serious difficulties about any policy of retention, including what would be bound to appear the undermining of the case for Home Rule which relied so heavily on the depiction as an 'obstruction' of the Irish presence at Westminster. Those who were most insistent on exclusion tended to be those who made most of the 'obstruction' theory in their arguments for Home Rule. Sir Edward Hamilton wrote in his diary after a discussion on the subject with John Morley, who was a leading exponent of the 'obstruction' theory:

> He (J.M.) can see no defence for a Bill that gave Ireland a completely free hand as regards the management of her own local affairs & yet allows her to have as large a voice as she now has in English & Scottish matters. He is I think inclined to regard Home Rule as a measure not so much for conferring a privilege on Ireland as for getting rid of an incubus from the legislature in Westminster.[1]

As for partial retention, it would raise a constitutional dilemma as to the status of a ministry which had a majority when the Irish M.P.s were absent but lost it as soon as they returned. On the other hand, total exclusion did make Home Rule look very like that 'separation' concerning the danger of which the Unionists had made so much in 1886.

After 1886 both Harcourt and the Liberal Imperialists—who were alike in saying little about the 'Irish obstruction'—were in favour of full retention, but for widely differing reasons. Harcourt believed that the Irish were needed to make up a Liberal majority;[2] whereas the Roseberyites saw retention as basic to their imperialistic conception of Home Rule. Many Liberals, especially in Scotland,[3] were in favour of Home Rule for imperialist reasons; that is, they hoped that it would prove, if handled and developed in the right way, to form part of a wider scheme of imperial federation. To them retention would be the crucial first step on the road to the creation of a genuine

---

[1] B.M. Add. MS. 48656, folio 118 (19 October 1891).
[2] See above, pp. 152-3.
[3] And Wales: 'You see how the tendency of the Home Rule question is towards Federalism', wrote T. E. Ellis to Herbert Lewis, 21 June 1889, T. E. Ellis MSS., folio 2882.

imperial parliament. Retention also appealed to those Liberals who were anxious to rebut the damaging Unionist claim that Home Rule was in fact the first step in the disintegration of the Empire. Consequently, it is out of this aspect of the Home Rule issue in particular that can be seen developing the Liberal rift over imperialism. For on it two rival concepts of Home Rule—the imperialist and the nationalist—came into conflict. To the young Roseberyites Gladstone's Home Rule, involving, as it did in 1886, the exclusion of the Irish M.P.s, was too 'separatist', too closely identified with the interests of Irish Nationalism. The kind of settlement which they wished to promote would strengthen the imperial idea. Asquith, for example, wanted Home Rule to 'be shown to be both imperial (in the true sense) & democratic', and this, he felt, could be done only by stressing the theme of 'local devolution'. The issue should be generalized. 'If the issue is contracted (as Mr. G. & J. M[orley] wd. narrow it) to one wh. is local, exceptional, & anomalous, we are hopelessly shut in.'[1] Munro Ferguson wrote of the importance of 'Home Rule being an item in the Imperial Federation scheme'. 'If we had only made our start on that line, instead of on the parochial,' he complained in 1889, 'how much healthier matters would be.'[2] Another of the later leaders of Liberal Imperialism, H. H. Fowler, told Rosebery in 1888: 'I am satisfied that the growing feeling in favour of Home Rule (& it *is* growing) is accompanied by a determination, far stronger than in 1886, to resist to the uttermost not only Separation but even the appearance of weakening the supremacy of the Imperial Parliament.'[3]

Differences of this kind meant that unity could be preserved after 1886 only if discussion of detail were avoided and the commitment to Home Rule were kept as general as possible. This was certainly how Gladstone tried to persuade his colleagues to handle the issue. The 1886 Home Rule scheme was declared to be in abeyance; no longer were the Liberals

---

[1] Asquith to Rosebery, second half only of a letter, undated, Rosebery MSS., Box 1.
[2] Ferguson to Rosebery, 30 August 1889, Rosebery MSS., Box 14.
[3] Fowler to Rosebery, 29 December 1888, Rosebery MSS., Box 64. Liberals who supported the movement for Imperial Federation were strongly in favour of the retention of the Irish M.P.s. See J. Saxon Mills, *Sir Edward Cook K.B.E. A Biography*, 1921, pp. 84–5.

committed to any of the details in it. The details of the next Home Rule Bill would be worked out when, and only when, the Liberals were next in office. In the meantime people should be asked to decide for or against the *principle* of Home Rule.

In the late 1880s there was growing impatience within the party about an Irish policy which was so nebulous and yet which was expected to monopolize Liberals' political activity. By late 1888 even John Morley is to be found writing to Robert Spence Watson: 'I feel exactly as you do, about the unsatisfactory position of the Irish question. Mr. G. is the only man who can keep us all together, and he is intensely reluctant to make positive statements.'[1] Furthermore, some of the younger Liberals reacted strongly against the assumption that devotion to Home Rule precluded support for constructive Irish reforms such as those being proposed by Balfour. The attitude that nothing good for Ireland was able, or should be allowed, to issue from the British government or Parliament riled Liberals who believed in the beneficent power of the imperial authority.

Demands grew that the Home Rule policy should be made more positive and substantial, that a new scheme should be worked out. But, of course, this would have to involve decisions on the points of controversy; and, indeed, one of the main sources of pressure for definition was the desire to settle whether Home Rule was to be fundamentally federalist or nationalist. The leaders resisted these demands for as long as possible and kept on insisting on 'the expediency of concentrating the batteries as much as possible on the practicable breach of Coercion and as little as possible on Home Rule'.[2] It was in 1889 that Gladstone began to come under strong pressure to begin the construction of a new scheme, especially from Rosebery who wanted Home Rule turned in an imperialistic direction and also was worried that the nebulousness of the policy was weakening the Irish preoccupation which he still believed was of benefit to the party. He told Gladstone in August 1889 that work on a scheme was essential to 'impart confidence to our scattered congregations, & strengthen followers who are

---

[1] 18 November 1888, Watson MSS. See also Fowler, *Life of Viscount Wolverhampton*, p. 242.

[2] Harcourt to Morley, 8 October 1887, Harcourt MSS. Harcourt to Gladstone, 10 October 1887, Gladstone MSS., B.M. Add. MS. 44201, folio 182.

THE END OF THE IRISH PREOCCUPATION

bewildered as to the scheme of 1886'. He made no secret of his hope that the scheme would 'approximate to the federal principle'.[1] A few months later, Childers, who represented a Scottish constituency, wrote to Gladstone that in his opinion the great question that must be decided was, 'are we to have an Imperial Parliament for all the Imperial affairs of the Empire, with separate Legislatures for England Scotland Ireland & Wales, or is Ireland alone to be dealt with'. He was getting many letters on this point from Scotland where interest in Scottish Home Rule was growing rapidly, and he felt that the 'Federal idea' must be either repudiated or adopted by the Liberal party before the next election.[2] Gladstone, however, refused to accept that it was necessary 'as a condition of settling Irish H. R. to say aye or no on Imp. Federation before the Dissolution'.[3] This was a natural position for him to take at this stage: he wanted to crown his last campaign with success, he had little time left, and he could not afford to complicate the issue with vast new topics of controversy. But other Liberals were just as naturally thinking of the course of Liberal politics *after* Home Rule and were anxious for an Irish settlement that would help to produce the future which they wanted.

These demands produced pressure from the opposite camp for definition of a different kind. John Morley now insisted that the leaders should let it be known that 'we do not intend to put parliament on a federal basis': 'It is to be delegation, and not federation. We shall have to be careful, as Scotland is rather wide awake, but I, for one, am dead against breaking up the old British parliament as it was before the Irish Union.'[4] Scotland was indeed awakening; Scottish Liberal Imperialism, which was to be such a strong force in Liberal politics over the next two decades, was being stirred into life by the prospect of an enhanced role for Scotland in a reorganized and strengthened Empire. In Wales, too, Liberal Imperialism was attracting young Liberal nationalists, such as Tom Ellis, who was to be Rosebery's Chief Whip.[5] Childers warned Gladstone in

[1] Rosebery to Gladstone, 11 August 1889 (draft), Rosebery MSS., Box 19.
[2] Childers to Gladstone, 7 and 10 October 1889, Gladstone MSS., B.M. Add. MS. 44132, folios 292, 295–6.
[3] Gladstone to Childers, 11 October 1889, Gladstone MSS., B.M. Add. MS. 44132, folio 298. [4] Morley to Harcourt, 12 October 1889, Harcourt MSS.
[5] Morgan, *Wales in British Politics*, p. 179.

October 1889 that he did not see how, 'in the present state of Scottish & Welsh opinion', 'saying Aye or No, to the federal idea', could be long deferred. It was at this point that H. H. Asquith, himself a Scottish M.P. and associated with the emerging Liberal Imperialist section of the party, came out with a public call for the production of a detailed scheme of Home Rule. Childers claimed that in this he was 'the exponent of many others'.[1]

The Liberal leaders now met at Hawarden and decided to abandon the policy of 1886. In the next Home Rule Bill provision would be made for a reduced representation of Ireland at Westminster. Harcourt, who had had to leave before this decision was reached, was furious, and demanded that there should be no public discussion of details of Home Rule policy: 'let us confine ourselves *strictly to general propositions*'.[2] 'Nothing', he argued, 'will suit their [the Tories'] book better than to divert public attention to difficulties of detail.'[3] Gladstone was inclined to agree. He felt that the demand for 'further disclosures to the public', at least in so far as it emanated from the Tories, was 'a trap'.[4] Granville advised Gladstone to be reticent: 'Nothing but the pressure of a practical necessity to decide, will produce the perfect agreement which is to be wished for.'[5] The consensus of opinion was clearly in favour of concentrating on securing Home Rule for Ireland and refusing to be committed on the larger question of imperial reorganization—which meant, in effect, settling for a 'contracted' form of Home Rule. Spencer, for example, argued that 'Ireland is enough for the present, & it is so pressing that we ought to concentrate on efforts to get what Ireland wants, & that probably is larger than what any other part of the Kingdom requires'.[6] Asquith, however, argued at once that a decision in favour of some form of retention was 'a complete trans-

[1] Childers to Gladstone, 18 October 1889, Gladstone MSS., B.M. Add. MS. 44132, folio 299.
[2] Harcourt to Spencer, 25 October 1889, Harcourt MSS.
[3] Harcourt to Gladstone, 27 October 1889, Gladstone MSS., B.M. Add. MS. 44201, folios 237-8.
[4] Gladstone to Rosebery, 26 October 1889, Rosebery MSS., Box 19.
[5] Granville to Gladstone, 31 October 1889, Gladstone MSS., B.M. Add. MS. 44180, folios 158-9.
[6] Spencer to Rosebery, 24 November 1889, Rosebery MSS., Box 49.

formation of the scheme of 1886' into the kind of scheme which he and the 'Imperialist' Home Rulers favoured:

under the Bill of '86, the Irish Parlt. was (in effect) to be a body with exclusive legislative powers in Irish matters. The supremacy of the Impl Parlt was to be retained by indirect methods—thro' the Lord Lieut's power of veto &c, & by express restrictions upon the legislative competence of the Irish body. With the retention of the Irish members this is no longer necessary. It cannot be said that a Parlt in wh. Ireland is still directly reptd has no moral authority (even after Home Rule) to legislate for Ireland shd. an extreme case arise. Hence it wd. seem that in any future scheme the Irish legislature should be treated as a subordinate body with delegated powers; in wh. case no question cd. arise as to the continued supremacy of the Impl Parlt.

He predicted, furthermore, that this principle of delegation of local powers from a clearly supreme imperial parliament would be invoked, and could easily be applied, in the cases of Scotland and Wales.[1] And so out of Irish Home Rule would emerge a vast new scheme of imperial reconstruction strengthening imperial connections while according with basic democratic principles.

It was thus with very great difficulty that Gladstone maintained Home Rule as a substitute for system, a unifying and concentrating influence, in Liberal politics. Debate on points of detail constantly threatened to erode the Irish preoccupation from within. But in addition it was under increasing *external* attack from those who, irrespective of their views on whether or not Home Rule was the best solution to the Irish problem, did not believe that it was necessary for Irish policy to monopolize Liberal politics.

---

[1] Asquith to Spencer, 12 January 1890, Spencer MSS., Misc. Corr. A-M. This was in reply to a letter from Spencer concerning a speech in which Asquith had renewed his plea that the Liberal leaders should take the country more into their confidence as to future Home Rule policy. See *The Times*, 7 January 1890, p. 7. Asquith, who clearly spoke for many in dreading the prospect of the next Liberal government's being bogged down for years in interminable wrangles over Home Rule, argued that, if the leaders went to the country with only 'a vague formula', and then, having been elected, produced a Bill, the opposition might say that the people had not voted on this and that therefore the Lords were justified in forcing a second appeal to the constituencies. John Morley, because of his concern about Gladstone's age, came to agree with this and see the need for the early production of a detailed scheme. See Hamer, *Personal Papers of Lord Rendel*, p. 80.

THE END OF THE IRISH PREOCCUPATION

From the outset the 'obstruction' theory was the subject of vigorous debate. According to Gladstone and his followers, *the* obstruction to progress on all other reform questions was 'Ireland', and only the granting of Home Rule would 'clear the way'. But this argument never gained general credence among Liberals. Rejection of it was one of the main causes of divergence between Chamberlain and the Gladstonians. Chamberlain and the dissentient Radicals argued that the real obstruction was Gladstone's decision to take up Home Rule. Once the question was dropped by the Liberals, progress could and would resume. John Bright expressed this attitude well when he wrote in 1887: 'Mr Gladstone stops the way. He insists on an impossible legislation for Ireland, and insists upon it to the exclusion of legislation for the whole Kingdom.'[1] A Radical such as Jesse Collings, ambitious above all to see practical reforms achieved by the Liberal party, could only regard the Gladstonian preoccupation with Home Rule as a *'negation* of political life'. Surely, he wrote, the Liberals as practical men must bring themselves 'to recognise the logic of facts, to admit that the Country for the present at least has declared against Home Rule and to agree to set that question aside, and unite on a platform composed of the other great liberal questions on which as far as I know, all are agreed'.[2] As for Chamberlain, he saw the adoption of Home Rule and the concentration of Liberal politics on it as, in large part, a deliberate diversion, a counter-*coup* by conservative Liberals, including Gladstone, who feared the triumph of his Radicalism. Gladstone, Chamberlain later maintained, had taken up Home Rule because 'there was nothing else for him except my programme' and 'to have adopted that would have been humiliating'.[3] Chamberlain demanded that the Liberals should go on attending to non-Irish questions, and he tried to deprive 'Ireland' of its special, overriding status. Liberals were,

[1] Trevelyan, *Life of John Bright*, p. 443.
[2] Collings to Harcourt, 27 December 1886, Harcourt MSS. Collings wrote to H. H. Fowler on the same day: 'It seems madness to complete the disruption of a party, with so many strong points of policy in common, for the sake of one point on which agreement for the time seems not to be possible; and which if selected as a platform at a General Election, must certainly bring defeat.' Fowler, *Life of Viscount Wolverhampton*, pp. 217–19.
[3] F. W. Hirst, *In the Golden Days*, 1947, p. 169. J. Amery, *The Life of Joseph Chamberlain*, vol. iv, 1951, pp. 511–12.

he would say, 'agreed upon ninety-nine points of our programme; we only disagree upon one'.[1] When Chamberlain sought the reunion of the party early in 1887, he tried to confront Liberals with the alternative of a form of action in which 'all Liberal reform' would not be 'indefinitely adjourned' until the wishes of the Irish had been met. In his *Baptist* letter he condemned keeping the people of England, Scotland, and Wales waiting for the reforms that they urgently needed 'until Mr. Parnell is satisfied and Mr. Gladstone's policy adopted'.[2]

Gladstone's reply to Chamberlain was that what he was doing was not creating the problem of Ireland's monopolizing of the time of Parliament 'but only pointing it out. The fingerpost does not make the road.'[3] He refused, he said, to behave like Chamberlain and 'go about the country, to Highland crofters and others, and to set up hopes that I know must be disappointed, and talk of the impropriety of our allowing the Irish question to monopolize the ground when we allow it simply because we cannot help it'.[4] At times the Gladstonians went further than this and claimed that it was the dissentient Liberals who constituted the basic obstruction to progress in reform politics because of their refusal to help pass Home Rule.[5]

But among those Liberals who did accept Home Rule as the solution to the Irish problem impatience with the Irish preoccupation also began to mount. Ostrogorski comments on how, after all, 'the whole body of Liberalism' could not be made to 'fit into the narrow groove of a single question of Home Rule' and how the spokesmen of various interests, 'far from consenting to keep in the background or to sacrifice themselves to Home Rule', 'maintained that it was only by giving full satisfaction to their demand that the party of progress would justify its name and its *raison d'être*'.[6] Within the Liberal leadership itself the most insistent critic of the Irish preoccupation and exponent of the point of view to which Ostrogorski refers was Sir William Harcourt. He maintained that the party

---

[1] Garvin, *Life of Chamberlain*, ii, p. 278.
[2] Ibid., ii, p. 292. Hamer, *John Morley*, pp. 225–6.
[3] Clayden, *England Under the Coalition*, p. 186.
[4] *N.L.F. Report 1887*, p. 75.
[5] e.g. *The Times*, 6 November 1888, p. 7 (Gladstone).
[6] Ostrogorski, *Democracy and the Organization of Political Parties*, i, p. 310.

existed for something more than Ireland and must show that it did. Perceiving clearly and urgently the problem of the post-Home Rule future of the party, he argued that it was dangerous for it thus to be cooped up within the confines of a single policy and to be a different kind of party from that which was becoming normal and necessary in the two-party system. Again and again in his speeches in the late 1880s Harcourt stressed the abnormality of the state of Liberal politics since 1886. It was abnormal, he suggested, even for Gladstone, who had in fact during his career been responsible for 'many and great reforms which have redounded to the advantage and the benefit of every class of the people of this nation'. By 1889 Harcourt felt that it was essential for someone in the leadership to be reminding Liberals that 'Home Rule is a great, and the first, chapter in the volume of Liberal policy; but it is not the whole of the volume. It is the beginning; but it is very far from being the *finis* of that volume.' At first, he said, it had been necessary, 'before the public mind was satisfied', to attend 'almost exclusively to Home Rule', but now 'it is time that we should bring forward and ripen other great questions which belong to the Liberal creed'. It was the Tories who 'hoped that the question of Home Rule was going to crush out all other questions; that it would enable them to get rid of all other reforms'. It was *their* strategy to use the Irish question 'to divert the people from all questions of reform'.[1]

The problem to which Harcourt was addressing himself was the effect on the party of the reconstruction of 1886. The party seemed to have been forced to revert to a pre-1867 mode of reform agitation, to turn itself into a vehicle, like the Anti-Corn Law League, for the promotion of a single great reform. Was it to resemble the Anti-Corn Law League also in being 'destined to come to an end with the triumph of the particular cause which had called it into life'?[2] This clearly was what concerned Harcourt. The Liberal party after 1885 was perilously close to being an anachronism. Chamberlain had appreciated the importance of creating a framework that would hold the party together and also allow flexibility,

---

[1] *The Times*, 8 February 1888, p. 10; 25 July 1889, p. 6; 24 October 1889, p. 10; 13 November 1889, p. 10.
[2] Ostrogorski, *Democracy and the Organization of Political Parties*, i, pp. 132–3.

response to new issues and problems, and the ability to promote simultaneously a variety of reforms. Harcourt was Chamberlain's heir in his efforts to ensure that the party survived by becoming once again this kind of party, which he defined as 'a house of many mansions'. 'It is a party of progress', Harcourt told John Morley, the arch-advocate of concentrating on single questions; 'and', he added, 'if its advance is checked by insuperable obstacles in one direction it will not dash itself to pieces like a foolish bird, but will go on and prosper in another'. The Liberal party, he would argue, 'exists for something more than Ireland & Irish questions alone'.[1]

A crucial question which the Liberals had constantly to debate among themselves was whether in the interests either of the Home Rule policy itself or of Liberal politics in general, Home Rule should be concentrated on in isolation or should be promoted in association with non-Irish measures. To some Liberals it seemed that a parallel attention to other questions would help to make the Home Rule policy itself more palatable to non-Irish voters and would hasten on the day when the Liberals would have the majority that would enable them to put through Home Rule. The need to adopt such a strategy had been foreseen some years previously by Francis Schnadhorst when he had argued that 'the cry of "Justice to Ireland" *by itself*' would not 'awaken enthusiasm in the English constituencies': 'I think it is necessary that side by side with the claims of Ireland must be put the claims of England & Scotland.'[2] The two leading advocates of this after 1885 were Harcourt and Labouchere—one reason why their names were so often linked. And what is especially significant is that what they argued for was the 'programme' as distinct from the 'single question' mode of reform politics. Labouchere maintained that, since the masses cared very little about justice for Ireland, it must be 'wrapped up' in issues that meant 'justice to themselves'. 'Depend upon it', he wrote in 1888, 'we shall only win on Home Rule by making it a mere portion of liberalism everywhere.'[3] Harcourt came out very definitely in

[1] Harcourt to Morley, 6 January 1891; Harcourt to Chamberlain, 28 December 1886, Harcourt MSS.
[2] Schnadhorst to Chamberlain, 29 January 1883, Chamberlain MSS., JC 5/63/5.
[3] Labouchere to Herbert Gladstone, 9 July [1886], 31 March [1888], Gladstone

favour of programmes. Home Rule and other reforms both could and should be promoted together, he argued. This is how he justified his claim that it was not 'necessary to talk exclusively of Home Rule':

> It is in the nature of every great reform that it carries other reforms with it in the momentum of its progress. *Reforms mutually propel one another.* That is the experience of the past in politics, and you will find that will be the history of the future. . . . We speak of other things. Those other things will help to carry Home Rule, and Home Rule will help to carry those other things. . . . These other things are good in themselves, as Home Rule is good in itself, and in my opinion they will all come together.[1]

By contrast, those who defended the concentration on Ireland often referred to the advantages stemming from dealing with 'one thing at a time'. John Morley, for example, could see in the strategy of adding questions the usual 'dispersive' consequences of programme politics. In his view, what would happen would be that each additional reform taken up would rouse some fresh antagonistic interest, for example the liquor trade or the defenders of the Established Church, and so the progress of any particular reform would be cumulatively retarded.[2]

Harcourt's case was that the unpopularity of, or lack of enthusiasm for, Home Rule, and the Liberal party's apparent unwillingness to attend to other questions, would in any event have the effect of indefinitely postponing the achievement of Home Rule.

> I am not sure [he wrote to Morley] that you will absolutely conciliate the distrustful Britons by telling them that the Irish are to have what they want first and that that is our present care and the poor Britishers will be considered afterwards and their secondary claims accommodated to the Irish requirements when those are satisfied. . . . I don't see that we shall gain much by representing ourselves as looking only to the Irish case and postponing the consideration of British interests. That is really the very thing of which the Infidels accuse us.[3]

MSS., B.M. Add. MS. 46016, folios 95–9, 130. Reid, *The New Liberal Programme*, pp. 1–2, 9–13.
[1] *The Times*, 24 October 1889, p. 10 (my italics).
[2] Cf. Morley to Harcourt, 18 November 1886, Harcourt MSS.
[3] Harcourt to Morley, 29 October 1889, Harcourt MSS.

Apart from these considerations, some of the younger Liberals, especially those who were later to form the Liberal Imperialist section, saw great danger in the absence of any positive policy other than Home Rule and were most concerned to promote planning for the post-Home Rule future. The Irish preoccupation was creating a vacuum in 'official' Liberal politics, and there was a risk that there might be inserted into this, *faute de mieux*, the 'unofficial' schemes of policy, such as Laboucherean Radicalism or Socialism, that *were* being developed and offered at this time. To these young Liberals it seemed only too likely that the ending of the Irish preoccupation might be followed by the disintegration of Liberalism and its replacement by one of these—because nothing else had been prepared. Thus Munro Ferguson noted early in 1887 the demoralizing effect on Liberals of the preoccupation: 'They don't settle down to work. Social questions are not properly grappled with, leading to a serious growth of socialism.'[1] He became more and more concerned that the lack of attention to non-Irish policy was producing an unhealthy growth of 'Communism & ideas of an extreme character'.[2] In an article in January 1888 Ferguson's close friend, Haldane, complained that the Liberal leaders were not 'occupying themselves with any other question than that of Irish Government' at a time when, 'with an extended franchise, not one but many more difficult questions' connected in particular with 'the relations of labour and capital' were impending. The party should be deciding now its attitude on these and thus preparing for the time when the Irish question was out of the way and it would have to fight on its non-Irish policy. There was a danger of having so indefinite and unprepared a policy that the experience of 1880–5 would be repeated—and worse. For, while the party was 'drifting', extreme Socialists were making rapid progress in converting people to their programme.[3] The problem, as Ferguson saw it, was that there was certain to be 'a rush, which no one can help, on our side to get away from Irish affairs & attend to British'.[4] What would be waiting to satisfy this demand for Radical non-Irish policy?

[1] Ferguson to Rosebery, 16 March 1887, Rosebery MSS., Box 14.
[2] Ferguson to Rosebery, 12 May 1887, Rosebery MSS., Box 14.
[3] Haldane, 'The Liberal Party and its Prospects', pp. 145, 148–9.
[4] Ferguson to Rosebery, 7 March 1888, Rosebery MSS., Box 14.

To these Liberals it seemed vital not to let the Irish preoccupation disrupt Liberal politics completely but to preserve continuity with the pre-Home Rule period and, in particular, to carry on the work of developing Liberal policy which Chamberlain had begun. A. H. D. Acland, for example, feeling that much work still needed to be done, and had to be done, to turn Chamberlain's Radical programme into material for practical legislation, began organizing his friends to undertake this work. He surveyed the 'whole field of possible Liberal legislation' and assigned areas of it to them to investigate.[1] Some of the senior Liberals, notably John Morley, whose insistence in works such as *On Compromise* on the importance of preparing 'new ideas' was a strong intellectual influence on these men, were notably sympathetic and helpful. Acland later recalled how 'Morley & one or two more on the Bench in those years & several of us off it did build up matter for the General Election apart from the Irish question—and did take counsel together in order to do it'.[2] The younger Liberals formed a group and tried to begin the preparation of new Liberal reform policies. They were particularly concerned to develop policies of social reform that were both attractive and a 'safe' alternative to Socialism.[3] Another party leader who was sympathetic to them and to whom they looked increasingly for guidance was Rosebery. He became very concerned about the absence of any programme 'beyond the Irish question', which he felt was 'sickening electors'. The problem as he saw it was that 'Mr. G. would attend to & think of nothing else' and that Gladstone had still to be 'accepted on his own terms' because 'the disorganised Liberal-Radical party would go still more to pieces were it not for the ascendant authority of Mr. G.'[4]

As Haldane wrote, this work could best be carried out in 'the breathing space which the question of Home Rule has given

---

[1] J. A. Spender, *Sir Robert Hudson. A Memoir*, 1930, pp. 21–2.

[2] Acland to Asquith, 20 January 1899, Asquith MSS., Dep. 9, folio 170. For Morley's activities and influence see Hamer, *John Morley*, pp. 245–7.

[3] Haldane to Munro Ferguson, 4 November 1889, Haldane MSS., MS. 5903, folios 139–40.

[4] Sir E. Hamilton's diary, B.M. Add. MS. 48646, folios 60, 91 (5 June, 7 July 1887).

us'.¹ But it was no more than a breathing space. Very soon it would have to be at an end. Unfortunately, apart from John Morley, none of the Liberal *leaders* devoted nearly sufficient time or thought to ensuring that it was used creatively. Even Harcourt, for all his talk about the importance of working on non-Irish policy, seemed to feel that the old Radicalism of local option and land reform would be quite adequate as the basis of the Liberal programme of the future. Harcourt saw the necessity of developing policy; but he himself was essentially not a creative and constructive politician, and his instinct was usually to fall back on attack and negativeness. Thus in November 1890 he argued that Gladstone should move a vote of censure on the government's Irish policy specifically rather than a general motion of no-confidence. For if a general motion were proposed the government would say: 'the country approves of our Finance, our Foreign Policy, our armaments etc. etc. As for you, before we dissolve the country must know definitely what is your policy as to hours of labour, disestablishment etc. etc.' 'This general issue', wrote Harcourt, 'seems to me more advantageous to them and less beneficial to us than one which keeps their nose to the grindstone of Coercion.'² Harcourt may have been impatient with the Irish preoccupation; but, when the alternative was the revelation of the confusion and inadequacy of the Liberals' non-Irish policies, he too had to accept its advantages. This is seen again in the crisis that confronted the Liberals shortly after Harcourt had written the letter which has just been quoted.

The Parnell divorce crisis at the end of 1890 and the beginning of 1891 forced on the Liberal leaders an awareness of how 'unripe' reform policy still was, of how little 'maturing' was taking place. Home Rule had been dealt a severe blow, and the Irish preoccupation clearly could not be maintained much longer. But it was in vain that the leaders searched for anything that could provide an adequate substitute. John Morley reviewed the entire range of reform questions in which Liberals at the time were interested and discovered a disquietingly high degree of 'unripeness' and unfitness to 'rally' the

---
¹ Haldane, 'The Liberal Creed', p. 474.
² Harcourt to Morley, 2 November 1890, Harcourt MSS.

party.¹ Lord Ripon made a most penetrating analysis of the inadequacy as a new single great question of the reform of the electoral registration laws. 'I do not think', he wrote, 'that it would call forth any enthusiasm or that it would, standing alone, have go enough about it to secure a good majority.' The problem was that 'Registration Reform is only an improvement of machinery', and the time was past when people would be content with this kind of reform. 'The working classes will, no doubt, be glad enough of a reform which will increase their power. But they will ask what is it going to lead to? What will be the result of it?' Thus the only consequence of the displacement of Home Rule would be that 'a whole series of labour questions would come to the front, which Registration Reform would help forward, but of which it would not take the place even temporarily'.² In other words, no longer was it possible to concentrate the attention of voters on reforms that were merely the prelude to *real* reform; people now wanted to know for what the improved machinery was to be used. But the Liberals did not yet have an answer ready. Clearly Ripon is implying that there is still no substitute for the 'Irish obstruction' as a reason for having to defer giving this answer.

For, apart from reforms for the removal of obstructions and the 'improvement of machinery', there was still little else available for the Liberals to take up except the 'fads'. At the height of its acceptability the Irish preoccupation had only just been containing the impatience of the sectionalists. In 1887 W. S. Caine, who was at this time a Unionist, while nevertheless accepting that there was 'an obstruction on the line of progress' which necessitated the deferring of 'all other claims', went on to say: 'I believe it will not be very long before, somehow or another, we shall get the Irish question settled. We must then take care that ours [temperance] comes next. We have been shunted a little too often, and we must take care that we are not shunted any more.'³ As Ripon appreciated, once the Irish preoccupation was ended, it was

¹ Hamer, *John Morley*, pp. 264–6. See also Sir E. Hamilton's account in his diary for 26 December 1890 of a conversation with Morley about the absence of an alternative 'cry', B.M. Add. MS. 48654, folios 103–4.
² Ripon to Gladstone, 30 December 1890, L. Wolf, *Life of the First Marquess of Ripon K.G., P.C., G.C.S.I., D.C.L., Etc.*, vol. ii, 1921, pp. 199–200.
³ Newton, *W. S. Caine, M.P.*, p. 179.

THE END OF THE IRISH PREOCCUPATION

going to be very difficult to get people to accept any more excuses for inaction in regard to the questions in which they were specially interested. And, as soon as the Parnell divorce crisis broke, the sections began to stir into life again. The Liberal Chief Whip began to receive letters from prominent sectionalists advancing the claims of their own questions to be taken up now.

Arnold Morley saw the basic problem when he commented on the idea of taking up a programme consisting of 'Direct Veto', 'one man one vote', and reforms 'specially affecting the agricultural voters': 'During the last $4\frac{1}{2}$ years such questions have been almost driven off the field by Ireland.'[1] John Morley, who *had* been helping to prepare new policies since 1886, had to confess that he doubted 'whether anything is ripe for action beyond electoral reform'.[2] It is not surprising, therefore, that the only agreement that the Liberal leaders found themselves able to reach in their discussions in early 1891 was that the Home Rule policy was to remain the party's principal preoccupation. To most of them it still seemed the only possible focus of Liberal politics. A. H. D. Acland summed up his impression of the situation as follows: 'How dark it all looks for the moment—The Old Man with no interest in a domestic programme—our other leaders doubtful & if one may [say] so rather ignorant as to what should come next.—We want a man with Chamberlain's gifts to stir our Radicalism a bit.'[3] For even Harcourt, who thought at first that the crisis was the opportunity for which he had long been waiting to overthrow the Irish preoccupation, was forced to acknowledge the difficulties that were involved in replacing it. The 'selection of any particular subject for the first place' instead of Home Rule would, he admitted, 'cause discontent in the camp of those whose hearts like the Temperance people and the Welsh Noncons are mainly set on other topics'. Irish policy would therefore have to remain in first place.[4] Labouchere saw exactly what

---

[1] Arnold Morley to Gladstone, 30 December 1890, Gladstone MSS., B.M. Add. MS. 44254, folios 63–4.
[2] J. Morley to Gladstone, 2 January 1891, Gladstone MSS., B.M. Add. MS. 44256, folio 107.
[3] Acland to Ellis, 1 January 1891, T. E. Ellis MSS., folio 23.
[4] Harcourt to Gladstone, 3 January 1891, Gladstone MSS., B.M. Add. MS. 44202, folios 48–9. See also Harcourt to Labouchere, 1 January 1891, Harcourt MSS.

was needed—a policy that would fulfil the same function as Home Rule had in relation to other Liberal policies. He argued for 'Electoral Reform' on the ground that it was this kind of policy because 'it includes—if properly understood, like the Bible—everything'. It would be possible, in other words, while concentrating on it, to use arguments similar to those that had been used about the 'Irish obstruction', to 'say that no Reforms are possible without the people [being] really represented, whilst all will be, when they are thus represented', or 'that no real reforms, such as are to make people happy, wealthy, and wise, can be passed until the Legislature is democratized'.[1] But Harcourt was not convinced that 'Electoral Reform' was capable of achieving this effect. He felt that 'to give it exclusive prominence would arouse the suspicions and distrust of other important sections'.[2] And so Harcourt executed another typical retreat into negativeness. 'I don't think at present', he wrote to Gladstone, 'it is really possible for us to strike out a very definite line in any direction and for the present at least our action must be mainly directed to attacks on our opponents' policy rather than any very positive development of our own.'[3] For he had reached the conclusion that, as he told John Morley, 'just now it would be quite impossible for him [Gladstone] to publish a class list with order of merit of the rival questions without creating many more jealousies than he would appease'.[4] Once again, for all his insistence on the need to develop the 'British' part of the Liberal programme, Harcourt had to accept, rely on, and maintain the disciplining and controlling effect of the Irish preoccupation:

> Mr. G. suggests [he wrote to John Morley on 30 December 1890] an early *meeting of the Party*. I have written a vehement remonstrance against this to A. Morley. It would be a most dangerous and fatal proceeding. It would necessarily announce a change of front. Everyone would assume it meant that H. Rule was dropped. Each man would insist on his own question being made the *first* and it would be Bedlam and chaos. It must not be thought of.[5]

---

[1] Labouchere to Harcourt, 31 December 1890, 2 January 1891, Harcourt MSS.
[2] Harcourt to Labouchere, 1 January 1891, Harcourt MSS.
[3] Harcourt to Gladstone, 7 January 1891, Harcourt MSS.
[4] Harcourt to J. Morley, 3 January 1891, Harcourt MSS.
[5] Harcourt MSS.

Maintaining the existing arrangement of policies did not satisfy the rank and file at all. Alarm and despondency in the party at the prospect of having to face the electorate with so meagre and unattractive a programme became so great that the leaders found it necessary to associate themselves officially with the resolutions passed at the annual meeting of the National Liberal Federation in Newcastle in October 1891. These resolutions became known as the 'Newcastle programme', and it was widely accepted for some time thereafter that they were the official policy of the Liberal party.

In form there was nothing new about the 'Newcastle programme'. 'Omnibus' resolutions of the same kind as the one which was said to embody it had been passed by the N.L.F. in 1889 and 1890, and in 1887 there had been talk of a 'Nottingham programme'. What was different was the adoption of this 'omnibus' resolution by the party leaders, their willingness to display as party policy binding on themselves this by now traditional recital of reforms favoured by the sections of activists among the Liberal rank and file. In doing this the leaders were responding to a mood in the party; but in their anxiety to find some way of supplementing the Home Rule policy all that they could find to offer was what was perennially available—the 'omnibus' resolution of the National Liberal Federation. Later criticism of the Newcastle programme fastened, as we shall see, on the alleged lack of real belief in it on the part of those who took it up. And, indeed, it was very much the product of panic, of reaction against reliance on Home Rule alone, rather than a definite move towards any clear, positive alternative.

We have seen how the theory of the Irish obstruction unified the party by giving all the sections the common interest of clearing it out of the way.[1] But now the policy which had constituted the means and the prospect of effecting that clearance was severely damaged. Consequently, the sectional causes in all their disunity were exposed once more to view— in the Newcastle programme. The programme was not new at all. It was an accurate representation of the abiding condition of Liberal politics, which only seemed new because it

[1] See above, pp. 129–33.

had been obscured since 1886 by the Irish preoccupation. F. A. Channing described the programme as a 'stereotyped but rather hackneyed list of disestablishment, local option, registration and taxation, each appealing only to special groups', and based on 'the log-rolling which faddists like'.[1] Ostrogorski perceived that no longer was there the 'umbrella' of the Home Rule policy covering all the sections; one unifying form, the programme, had been substituted for another, the single great question: 'Huddled together in the same *omnibus* programme, demands of the most varied character were required to combine and so ensure the unity of the party. The *omnibus* was to take the place of the *old umbrella*.'[2]

The Newcastle programme could unify only by appearing to promise all the sectional interests that something would be done for them and by not putting the reform proposals in any order of priority. Apart from the recognition of Home Rule as having first priority, the crucial problem of the ordering of reform questions was evaded. Characteristic of the approach to this was the putting up of Sir Wilfrid Lawson, the temperance-reform enthusiast, to move the 'omnibus' resolution—an office he had already performed in 1887 and 1889. Lawson made no secret of the fact that, programme or no programme, temperance reform remained paramount for him, made no effort to take account of the feelings of the advocates of the other reforms, and made reference to nothing which suggested that for him the programme had any significance.

The Liberals took office in 1892 without an independent majority. Their dependence on the Irish meant, in association with Gladstone's retention of the leadership, that Home Rule must continue to have priority. But not all the Liberal leaders accepted this, and even those who felt that the party still had a primary and inescapable commitment to produce a Home Rule Bill tended to feel that the interests of the Irish policy itself would best be served by its being associated with non-Irish measures. When forming the government and debating the strategy which it should follow, the Liberal leaders faced the dilemma typical of the position of all minority govern-

[1] F. A. Channing, *Memories of Midland Politics 1885–1910*, 1918, p. 117.
[2] Ostrogorski, *Democracy and the Organization of Political Parties*, i, pp. 316–17.

ments—should they refrain from doing anything beyond what the prevailing circumstances, in particular dependence on the Irish, made practicable, or should they drive ahead with a programme of bold reforms and throw upon others the onus of deciding whether these should pass while at least themselves getting the credit with the electorate and with impatient Liberals for having proposed them?

Harcourt was naturally strongly in favour of tackling a large programme. Although Gladstone showed some sympathy for Harcourt's point of view, this was mainly because of his concern for the success of Home Rule. Harcourt, by contrast, cared nothing about Home Rule and treated it as an irrelevance already. Where Harcourt had perhaps differed most from his colleagues since 1886 was in his lack of belief in, or at least his unwillingness in his speeches to refer to or make much use of, the obstruction theory. As a result, uncommitted by frequent recourse to this argument, he was now much freer than many of his colleagues to take the position that attention to non-Irish questions was possible and could be fruitful even although Irish Home Rule had not yet been secured. He also took little or no account of the need to retain Irish support, and so, in spite of their many differences, was already close to the position soon to be adopted by Rosebery, that the party's overriding need was to develop policies that would enable it to appeal again to a non-Irish majority of the electorate. The opposite point of view was that of John Morley who argued throughout that the vital task was to 'come to some sort of terms with our Irishmen'.[1]

As for Gladstone, he appreciated that 'if we had thrown British questions into the shade we should have had no majority at all'. He could therefore see great risk in relying 'on Home Rule alone for the Session'. The constituencies 'might I think consent to a great deal of temporary sacrifice if they saw us conducting a Parliamentary movement for Home Rule so strong as to have a chance of overawing the House of Lords, but . . . if they saw immediate Home Rule to be out of the question would feel with some justice that we ought not to postpone all their wants with no hope of an equivalent'. On the other hand, non-Irish questions must be dealt with in such

[1] Morley to Harcourt, 28 June 1892, Harcourt MSS.

a way as to avoid the appearance of 'shifting our polarity' away from Home Rule. Home Rule could not be postponed, but neither in all probability could it be carried straight away. Perhaps, therefore, some intermediate Irish policy might be attempted, for example 'to *Drummondise* (so to speak) the administration of Ireland', while satisfaction was given on 'those subjects of Liberal Legislation which would be both *concise* and telling, in the various divisions of Great Britain'.[1]

John Morley was horrified at this: the Home Rule cause depended on Gladstone's leadership, and at his age any further delay was quite unthinkable if the cause was to have any chance of success.[2] But Gladstone addressed himself very seriously to the task of finding 'legislation which shall be at once concise and drastic to help the *British* part of the bill of fare', and suggested 'Death Duties' and 'taxing ground rents'.[3] Morley, who was absolutely committed to giving a Home Rule Bill first priority, tried to check this alarming tendency. He begged Gladstone 'not to worry about either policy or persons until we all meet at the end of the month in London', and then insisted that all would 'really depend on what the Irish can do': 'They are the pivot on which the manœuvring turns, now and for many a long day to come.' Morley was obviously quite clear where *he* wished the 'centre of polarity' of Liberal politics to be. He also strongly disagreed with Gladstone's interpretation of the election results and showed his continuing dislike of programme politics: 'The truth is, dear Harcourt, we have moved much too fast and too far towards the Extreme Left in every subject at once—and quiet sensible folk don't like it.'[4] And so Morley tried to keep Gladstone's attention focused on the single great question, while Harcourt worked hard to move Gladstone in the direction of a programme. On 15 July he wrote to Gladstone to say how much he agreed that 'British subjects must be put well forward', and he argued in favour of a much larger 'British programme' than that which Gladstone was suggesting.[5] They should 'play the parts of

[1] Gladstone to Spencer, 13 July 1892, Spencer MSS.
[2] Hamer, *John Morley*, p. 282.
[3] Gladstone to Harcourt, 14 July 1892, Gladstone MSS., B.M. Add. MS. 44202, folios 157–8.
[4] Morley to Harcourt, 14 July 1892, Harcourt MSS.
[5] Gladstone MSS., B.M. Add. MS. 44202, folios 160–2.

THE END OF THE IRISH PREOCCUPATION 177

"daring pilots in extremity" ' and seek safety in the storm by 'cracking on' and 'running' the ship. No fewer than five major reforms should be proposed for the next session, for the Liberals were now quite definitely given over to programme politics: 'This I think is the *very* minimum of what we should bring forward and is only a fraction of what you [Gladstone] pledged us to at Newcastle.'[1]

Morley advocated quite the opposite strategy, one of 'steaming as slow as ever we can thro' the banks of fog by wh we are surrounded'. Radicals should 'lie low and sing small' and wait to see what the Irish would permit them to do. 'It is in the highest degree dangerous at this stage to say what we will or what we won't do.'[2] As far as Morley was concerned, the Liberals were still 'impotent', still rendered incapable of making progress with non-Irish reform. Liberal politics were still controlled and organized—by the Irish.[3] Gladstone, however, was still thinking of how 'to give for 1893 a just satisfaction to Ireland without spending the Session on Home Rule'. He was trying to devise 'a good though of course incomplete bill of fare for England Scotland Wales (with some aid from Executive Acts) by means of those subjects which will allow of very concise legislation, such as will be most likely to defy obstruction'. But the obstruction was not now 'Ireland': it was the veto power of the House of Lords. This was now in his mind replacing 'Ireland' as the controlling factor in the situation. It necessitated the bringing forward of 'a series of measures which will be challenges to the Lords and which will give us a stronger position with (London and) the country, than Ireland could if alone'.[4]

Harcourt wrote to Gladstone on 19 July arguing that the Irish could be kept 'reasonably satisfied' by the repeal of the Coercion Act and should be told that 'Home Rule cannot be

[1] Harcourt to Morley, 15 July 1892, Harcourt MSS. Harcourt to Gladstone, 16 July 1892. Gardiner, *Life of Harcourt*, ii, p. 179.
[2] Morley to Harcourt, 16 July 1892, Harcourt MSS.
[3] Lewis Harcourt noted in his diary on 29 July 1892 that Morley 'thinks the Irish demands not unreasonable, viz:—that Home Rule shall be introduced in January or February and pressed as persistently as possible, which would not preclude measures like Registration and One Man One Vote being introduced in the intervals. He said "After all, the Irish are our masters and we had better realise it at once." ' Harcourt MSS.
[4] Gladstone to Harcourt, 18 July 1892, Gladstone MSS., B.M. Add. MS. 44202, folios 166–7.

carried without a fresh appeal to the Country and that it is to their chief interest to strengthen us in that appeal' by assisting the passage of non-Irish reforms. He then advocated bringing forward a large number of measures, and advanced in favour of this strategy the kind of argument always used by advocates of programmes. For example, he suggested that it would make Chamberlain's position more difficult because 'he will be forced into the attitude of the opponent of all the Reforms we bring forward and the more numerous these are the more his Toryism will be exposed'. This is the classic argument of the cumulative effect. Similarly he argued that the more measures the Lords rejected, 'the worse for them'. And as for the Liberal party, it would bring order there too because it would make 'all the members of all the sections' 'averse to precipitating an early dissolution', eager in fact to 'do all they can to avert it'.[1]

Other Liberal leaders saw the dilemma. Lord Kimberley noted how, on the one hand, 'everything really depends' on 'the temper of the Irish Nationalists' and, on the other, there was in the Liberal party 'no enthusiasm for Home Rule, and a desire to put forward at once other measures'. 'Of course', he added, 'Home Rule *must* be brought forward'; he could only hope that the Irish would 'allow us free hand enough to enable us to do something at once to satisfy our party'.[2] Lord Ripon agreed as to feeling in the party, and expressed the view that 'a Registration, One man one vote, etc., Bill' should 'precede a Home Rule measure' and that a 'Rural Bill' should be brought in during the same session as Home Rule which should, however, 'have precedence'.[3] One of the major themes of the late nineteenth-century debate on the nature of Liberal policy occurs constantly in the correspondence of Liberals at this time: should Liberals concentrate on the reform of machinery and institutions, or should they be more concerned with the *use* of political institutions? When Harcourt invited the opinions of leading Radicals as to what the new government should do, some, such as F. A. Channing, told him that there must be 'a bold constructive policy all round from the first': 'Mere machinery—Registration & the rest—will do little for us.'

[1] Gladstone MSS., B.M. Add. MS. 44202, folios 171–3.
[2] Kimberley to Ripon, 19 July 1892, Wolf, *Life of Ripon*, ii, pp. 200–1.
[3] Ripon to Kimberley, 21 July 1892, ibid., ii, p. 201.

THE END OF THE IRISH PREOCCUPATION

But to others electoral reform appealed as a theme on which to concentrate partly because it would mean the postponing of awkward questions as to what the machinery was to be used for. Thus W. S. Caine urged 'an Autumn Session for Registration, and even for 1 man 1 vote', and then in the Queen's Speech for 1893 promises of 'payment of Return[ing] Officers expenses, payment of members, & if possible the second ballot'. Were this done, he wrote, 'you can safely ignore all other labour questions, on the plea that you want direct labour representatives by your side in parliament, to tell you what to do'.[1] The same kind of argument, that no social reforms could be properly carried out until the machinery of parliamentary government had been improved and made more democratic, had been employed in connection with the Irish 'obstruction' and was soon to be employed again by Radicals in the agitation against the House of Lords. Some leaders of sections *were* prepared to react to concentration on electoral and registration reform in the way described by Caine—and by Labouchere at the time of the Parnell divorce crisis.[2] Stuart Rendel wrote in January 1893 that he doubted whether it was 'quite right to treat Welsh Disestnt. and Registration Reform as competitors for precedence':

I look on Registration Reform as a sharpening of Liberal tools and upon W. Disest. as work for the tools, sharp or blunt.
I should be slow to object to the claims of Registration Reform to the earliest attention because it is at the root of success with all important measures including Disest.[3]

For Gladstone the problem continued to be how 'to cast the balance fairly between Irish and British claims'.[4] But he was acutely aware of the limitations imposed on Liberal action by the nature of the government's majority and by the instability and unpredictability of the Irish party since the schism of 1891.[5] He was also aware of the practical difficulties of getting non-Irish

---

[1] Channing to Harcourt, 5 August 1892; Caine to Harcourt, 22 July 1892, Harcourt MSS.
[2] See above, pp. 171–2.
[3] Rendel to A. C. Humphreys-Owen, 15 January 1893, Glansevern Collection: Letters to Humphreys-Owen, folio 624.
[4] Gladstone to Harcourt, 22 July 1892 (copy), Gladstone MSS., B.M. Add. MS. 44202, folio 176.
[5] Gladstone to Ripon, 23 July 1892, Wolf, *Life of Ripon*, ii, p. 203.

reforms passed: the subjects would have to be very carefully chosen and would have to be such as 'can be very concisely handled in Bills'.[1] His caution was understandable and is in striking contrast to the unbounding and unthinking optimism of Harcourt. The younger 'Roseberyite' Liberals, too, were from the outset pessimistic about the chances of getting much done through legislation. Beatrice Webb wrote in her diary on 24 December 1892 after meeting Haldane and Asquith: 'All the younger men in the Government hard at work introducing administrative reforms, yet uncertain whether the old gang will not dictate a policy of evading all legislative proposals.'[2] Haldane believed that much could be done by the Home Office, Local Government Board, and Education Department 'by administration only, not legislation', to 'put new life into Liberalism all over the country'.[3]

It turned out that this lack of confidence was fully justified. In spite of the leaders' awareness of the danger of such a course, the first year of this government was taken up principally with the second Home Rule Bill. The government was not allowed much time for non-Irish measures, for the Opposition put up a very strong resistance to the Bill at all stages and its progress through the House of Commons was very long and drawn out. Gladstone, for all his concern in July 1892 for constructing a 'British programme', could not help but become immersed in the Home Rule controversy again. It remained the great cause which alone kept him in active political life. 'I am as fast bound to Ireland', he had to acknowledge, 'as Ulysses was to his mast.'[4] Others of his colleagues, especially Morley and Spencer, felt too that getting a Home Rule Bill through remained an inescapable commitment as the party's first priority. Spencer wrote to Gladstone on 25 July 1892: 'I am altogether with you in your main contention that we are bound to deal with Home Rule in our first Session by pledges, by action at Elections & by the necessity of keeping the Irish with us, which we can only do by showing them that we are in

---

[1] Gladstone to Harcourt, 22 July 1892 (copy), Gladstone MSS., B.M. Add. MS. 44202, folio 176.   [2] B. Webb, *Our Partnership*, 1948, p. 109.
[3] As quoted by Grey in a letter to his wife, October 1892, Trevelyan, *Grey of Fallodon*, p. 60.
[4] Gladstone to Ripon, 23 July 1892, Wolf, *Life of Ripon*, ii, p. 203. Morley, *Gladstone*, ii, p. 731.

earnest in our desire to deal in a comprehensive & satisfactory way with the Irish difficulty.'¹ Spencer contrasted his own and Harcourt's positions when he wrote to Harcourt in January 1893 about 'the Irish measure, for which alone some of us continue in Politics, and which we put before every other measure which has to be brought forward in Parliament. I know that you take the exactly opposite view to this but the Liberal Party as it now exists was formed on these lines and those who have thrown themselves in with the Liberals cannot work in a different direction.'²

But the Irish preoccupation could now be justified much less easily, for the simple reason that the credibility of the obstruction theory had largely evaporated. Very few people now believed, and the Liberal leaders far less frequently maintained, that it was not *possible* for any other questions to be satisfactorily attended to until Home Rule was conceded to the Irish. Even John Morley privately conceded that 'Ireland' no longer constituted an obstruction.³ Home Rule itself as a Liberal policy was drastically reduced in status. It was now just another Liberal policy, and the reason for the particular attention to it now seemed to be Gladstone's relationship to it rather than the problem of the obstruction. There was now an ambiguity in the references of some of the Liberal leaders to the 'obstruction'. Rosebery said in the House of Lords in September 1893: 'We want to get Ireland out of the way in order that the time and energy that it engrossed might be better given to other purposes. . . . We are only too anxious to get the Irish question out of the way, in order to make way for English, Scotch, and Welsh reforms.'⁴ This *could* be given a Gladstonian interpretation: only through the concession of

¹ Gladstone MSS., B.M. Add. MS. 44314, folio 39.

² 6 January 1893, Harcourt MSS. Spencer was one of those who wished to reintroduce the Home Rule Bill in 1894 and try all over again. Sir E. Hamilton's diary, B.M. Add. MS. 48661, folio 24 (8 August 1893).

³ 'J. Morley agreed that nothing was to be feared from Ireland by the Tories . . . The fact is that the Irish are found out. Moonlighting & cattle mutilations & agrarian assassinations won't make a revolution. The Irish will not go beyond this form of resistance & the English know it. The Parnellite schism & the want of money complete the Irish collapse. Coercion can be restored in an instant & the British voters are no longer revolted by it.' Memo. by Rendel of conversation with Morley at Cannes, 21–5 December 1894, Rendel MSS., 2nd Series, folio 681.

⁴ Speech of 7 September 1893, *Lord Rosebery's Speeches (1874–1896)*, 1896, pp. 125, 128.

Home Rule was effective action on non-Irish reforms possible. But, after he had become Liberal leader six months later, Rosebery was to give effect to an alternative interpretation of 'getting Ireland out of the way': ignoring it and acting as though it was the Liberals' preoccupation with Home Rule, and not the Irish question *per se*, that had hitherto constituted the obstacle. Meanwhile, in 1892-3 the party *had* to carry through a measure of Home Rule, but everyone was oppressed and paralysed by the great unreality that pervaded Liberal politics at this time and was caused by the certainty that the Lords would reject the Bill and by the obvious impotence of the Liberals to do anything about this rejection.[1]

Gladstone's intentions were of the best. At the Cabinet on 19 August he made a general statement that 'he thought it of great importance that English measures should be pressed on concurrently with Home Rule'.[2] Nevertheless, in the next few months little was done to give effect to this principle. Two months later, in fact, Gladstone was resisting discussion in Cabinet of any of the Bills for the coming Session because of the uncertainty as to what could be carried at the same time as Home Rule. This enraged some members of the Cabinet. Harcourt, Arnold Morley, Bryce, Fowler, Trevelyan, and Acland met privately and uttered loud 'complaints of Gladstone's idea that the programme for next Session is to be "limited" '. What they wanted was 'a big programme of all questions including Welsh Disestablishment (Suspensory) Bill, Village Councils, Direct Veto, Registration, One Man One Vote, Payment of Election Expenses, London Measures, Abolition of Magistrates' Qualification, Labour legislation including Conspiracy Bill and Railway Hours etc.'.[3] Harcourt took this list to Gladstone who promptly accepted the lot, only to destroy the effect by insisting on 'his reservation as to only producing those which have a prospect of passing'.[4] Once again approval of the wide range of reforms advocated by Liberals was combined with emphasis on the overriding and

[1] Harcourt said to Sir E. Hamilton on 19 December 1892: 'But what I should like to know is the use of considering this & that detail [in the Home Rule Bill]? If a ship is bound to sink, what does it matter whether the cabins are to be fitted up with satin-wood or rose-wood?' B.M. Add. MS. 48659, folio 61.
[2] Lewis Harcourt's diary (19 August 1892), Harcourt MSS.
[3] Ibid. (27 October 1892).   [4] Ibid. (29 October 1892).

paralysing effects of the Irish obstruction. When the Cabinet became immersed in Home Rule, as well as in numerous time-consuming discussions on Uganda, Rosebery and Harcourt began sitting apart at Cabinet meetings on what they called 'the English bench' in protest at the neglect of non-Irish questions.[1] In doing this they were reflecting a new mood in the party, a feeling that England's wants *could* be attended to and that if there was an obstruction now it was the continued preoccupation with Home Rule and not the Irish question *per se*. Thus Harcourt took a deliberately 'English' attitude to the Home Rule Bill. He told Sir Edward Hamilton when the details of the Bill were being worked out that 'what he was bent on doing was to make the Bill palatable to reasonable Englishmen, thus throwing the onus of rejection on the Irishmen: that . . . would be the "euthanasia" of Home Rule, and the most decent way of interring it.'[2] Liberal M.P.s had won the election by promising that English reforms would be dealt with.[3] They were naturally worried when they saw the possibility that these promises might not be fulfilled. Labouchere warned Harcourt on 8 August 1892 that a speech by Gladstone, in which he had said 'that the English reforms were "subordinate" to Home Rule, and that he only lived for Home Rule', had caused 'a good deal of complaint'.[4] Labouchere summed up the mood of the party in a letter to Herbert Gladstone on 27 August 1892. On the one hand, he could find 'no sort of hesitation about Home Rule': 'the Party would vote solidly for pretty well any Bill that may be submitted'. But there was, on the other hand, 'the first law of nature', 'self preservation': 'They have won these elections by dwelling on these English reforms, and they dread the slightest possibility of these not being passed by the House of Commons before the next General Election.'[5] It is not surprising, therefore, that the party became very impatient during the interminable debates on the Home Rule Bill in 1893.[6]

[1] Hutchinson, *Private Diaries of Sir Algernon West*, p. 82.
[2] Sir E. Hamilton's diary, B.M. Add. MS. 48659, folios 28, 60–1 (4 November, 19 December 1892).
[3] Cf., e.g., Channing, *Memories of Midland Politics*, pp. 129, 147.
[4] Harcourt MSS.   [5] Gladstone MSS., B.M. Add. MS. 46016, folios 156–8.
[6] Hamer, *John Morley*, pp. 280–1. 'The 4th clause of the Home Rule Bill was finished to-day. Many of us are very impatient, not to say angry, that our leaders

THE END OF THE IRISH PREOCCUPATION

The final breakdown of the great Irish preoccupation came with the rejection of the second Home Rule Bill by the House of Lords in September 1893 and the decision of Gladstone's government not to make this rejection the subject of an appeal to the country. This decision demolished the old obstruction theory and dethroned the Home Rule policy from its status as a single great question. For behind it was revealed another obstruction on which it itself depended—the veto power of the House of Lords. Home Rule had hitherto been represented as the policy that alone could end the paralysis in reform politics and ensure progress on the various causes in which Liberals had particular interests. This argument could no longer be used. Home Rule was reduced to the level of other reform issues that appealed only to sections or minorities. Like them, it would have to wait until the Lords' veto could be effectively challenged on some issue which did appeal to a majority of the electorate. Until then it too was paralysed. Home Rule for Ireland remained a Liberal policy, but the great change was that it no longer rested on the obstruction theory.

don't get on faster and take stronger measures.' H. J. Wilson to his wife, 23 June 1893, M. Anderson, *Henry Joseph Wilson: Fighter For Freedom 1833–1914*, 1953, p. 60. In March 1893 Labouchere wrote to the chief Whip, E. Marjoribanks, advising him 'that in the coming debate on the Home Rule Bill silence should be the order of the day on the Government side and that only one or two members even of the front Bench should make speeches'. Sir E. Hamilton's diary, B.M. Add. MS. 48660, folio 24 (26 March 1893).

VIII The Liberal Government of 1892–1895

THE sudden removal of the two factors which had disciplined and concentrated Liberal politics over the eight years since 1886—Gladstone's leadership and the preoccupation with clearing the Irish 'obstruction'—restored to view the basic disorganization of Liberal politics. Sectionalism re-emerged, rampant and uncontrollable. The sections again clamoured for priority of attention, and the leaders found the same difficulty as they had before 1886 in placing their demands in any generally acceptable order. They now lacked the means of imposing priority which the Irish 'obstruction' had provided. It was a problem that Gladstone had foreseen. As early as 1890 he was telling Rosebery that 'what he fears in the future for the Liberal party is a number of fanatics contending for precedence for their questions'.[1]

One section that became particularly impatient and even rebellious was the Welsh. The N.L.F. had placed Welsh disestablishment next after Home Rule, and in 1892 the Welsh demanded that the new Liberal government should honour this 'pledge'.[2] Although Gladstone *was* concerned that something should be done for the Welsh, his assurances were not definite enough to satisfy some of the Welsh M.P.s who began to talk about seceding from the party.[3] Gladstone called Welsh disestablishment 'an essential part of the Liberal policy and plans' but refused to give any promises about priority. When in 1894 it was given a low place in the programme so that it clearly had little chance of passing that session, four Welsh

---

[1] Memo. by Rosebery of talk with Gladstone, 30 April 1890, Rosebery MSS., Box 109.
[2] See F. Edwards to Ellis, 22 May 1892, T. E. Ellis MSS., folio 478.
[3] Morgan, *Wales in British Politics*, pp. 122–3.

M.P.s, including Lloyd George, resigned the Liberal Whip and said that they would abstain on Bills which were given what they considered to be unfair priority over Welsh disestablishment.[1] In 1894-5 the Welsh M.P.s were notably restless and undisciplined, partly perhaps because they lost their two leaders of the late 1880s and early 1890s, Stuart Rendel, a close friend of Gladstone, who accepted a peerage, and Tom Ellis, who became Chief Whip. It has been argued that the dissidence of the Welsh M.P.s made a major contribution to the 1895 defeat on the 'cordite vote' which the government made its pretext for giving up office.[2]

Another section which pressed very hard was the advocates of temperance reform. They fought for attention and tried to advance their claims over those of other sections. They claimed that many people had voted Liberal only because it was so clearly the 'Temperance party'.[3] In 1893 the United Kingdom Alliance, the principal temperance organization, noted how the government's 'range of choice' was influenced by 'competition between sections of their own followers', and T. P. Whittaker, M.P., told Alliance members that in this situation they would 'have to show more fight' because 'those who made the loudest demand would be attended to first'. The Alliance advanced various reasons why its demands should receive priority. The government ran the risk, it argued, of losing the votes of the considerable number of temperance reformers who were 'not at all sympathetic with the Government on general questions' but who had voted Liberal in 1892 in the belief that the Liberals 'really intended to pass a Direct Veto measure'. As was habitual with sectionalist organizations, it tried to show that its cause was comprehensive, that it covered all others. Temperance was of 'supreme importance', and, 'when it is being compared with other questions, Mr. Cobden's dictum ought to be remembered—that "the Temperance question lies at the basis of *all* reform" '.[4]

The Liberal leaders, however, found themselves quite

[1] Morgan, *Wales in British Politics*, pp. 139-45.
[2] Stansky, *Ambitions and Strategies*, pp. 158-68.
[3] *Fortieth Report of the Executive Committee of the United Kingdom Alliance ... 1891-92*, pp. 31-3.
[4] *Forty-First Report of the Executive Committee of the United Kingdom Alliance ...1892-93*, pp. 20-1.

unable to elevate the party and the government above the politics of sectionalism. In February 1893 Lord Kimberley remarked that they had 'put all the best things in the Queen's speech we could' and yet 'each thing only pleased certain sections'. 'We had not got, and could not get, anything which stirred the country.'[1] And then, to make matters worse, not even the sections were pleased!

With the Home Rule Bill at last out of the way, the floodgates seemed open. 'Everybody' was observed to be 'anxious to see his own pet scheme pushed to the front during the Autumn Sitting'.[2] The Welsh disestablishers were afraid that 'other questions affecting England or Scotland rather than Wales may gain precedence of that which is nearest to their own hearts', while the Londoners, the temperance reformers, and the advocates of local government reform in rural areas were all demanding urgent attention to their questions.[3] By February 1894 one commentator was describing the 'faddists' as 'exacting and impracticable', while Harcourt was having to plead with Liberals not to become what the Tories wished them to be, 'an army without drill and without discipline, a sort of go-as-you-please army, in which each man manœuvres according to his own ideas'.[4] As soon as he became Prime Minister, Rosebery's post-bag began to fill with letters from impatient sectionalists.[5]

The leaders tried to make the best of the situation and counter the bad impression that the rampant sectionalism was making on public opinion by suggesting that it was, in fact, only a sign of vitality. Asquith, speaking on 27 March 1894, argued that the Liberals were and had to be, 'by the very nature of our principles and by the conditions which hold us together and combine us into common work for common purposes, a party in which the initiative of the individual is largely indulged, and in which there is the greatest possible interchange, not only of opinion but of action'. So long as 'the

[1] Hutchinson, *Private Diaries of Sir Algernon West*, p. 138.
[2] 'The Autumn Session', *The Speaker*, vol. 8, no. 189 (12 August 1893), p. 148.
[3] 'The Welsh Radicals', *The Speaker*, vol. 8, no. 190 (19 August 1893), pp. 175–6.
[4] J. Guinness Rogers, 'The Position of the Liberal Party', *N.C.*, no. 204 (February 1894), p. 192. *N.L.F. Report 1894*, p. 70.
[5] For examples see Rosebery MSS., Box 68, e.g. Sir W. Lawson's letter of 10 March 1894.

different ends upon which the different sections bend their energies and to which they direct their efforts and ends, are in harmony with the principles of our common creed', there was no basis for accusations of 'compromise or of unworthy and faltering accommodation if we give the freest and the fullest liberty of action'.[1] But here, of course, was the essential problem: *were* there principles of a 'common creed' that could harmonize the actions of the sections?

In an article published in November 1894 J. Guinness Rogers, the Nonconformist clergyman, who was throughout this period a most perceptive commentator on Liberal politics, admitted that it had become 'the favourite idea of Tory writers and speakers' that the Liberal party 'is made up of a number of discordant sections each intent on some scheme of its own, and not only indifferent to those of the rest, but in some cases positively hostile to them'. And he referred to a point which must have occurred to many Liberals in connection with the possible effect on the party of the ending of the Home Rule preoccupation when he observed that a case, though one 'more plausible than true', could 'be set up in favour' of the view that the Liberal party was 'little better than a promiscuous mob of those who were interested in the progressive policy of the hour, and would dissolve as soon as the particular measure was carried'.[2]

The sectionalists maintained their pressure. W. S. Caine told Rosebery in November that, if the Direct Veto Bill were 'hung up' and 'not placed among the measures that the government mean to *push* next session', 'the discontent which is smouldering will break out into revolt, and the more fiery spirits in the Temperance ranks will follow the example of America, and form an independent prohibition party', while others 'will sulk in their tents' and thus deprive the party of its 'best and most ardent volunteer workers at election time', its 'most earnest and cultured canvassers'. '*There is nothing left of the Newcastle programme which we can patiently see put permanently in front of us—though we can resent nothing that is only put alongside of us.*'[3] At the meeting of the National Liberal Federation

[1] *The Liberal Magazine*, vol. ii, no. 7 (April 1894), p. 78.
[2] 'Nonconformist Forebodings', *N.C.*, no. 213 (November 1894), pp. 801–2.
[3] 11 November 1894, Rosebery MSS., Box 66.

in January 1895 sectionalists quarrelled among themselves. T. Snape, when moving the resolution on local option, said that he would have liked to see it recognized as the first measure to be dealt with and suggested that the main reason why it was not being so recognized was that the thirty Welsh M.P.s who wanted Welsh disestablishment put first would then have seceded from the party. 'For his own part', he added, 'he thought that ten Welsh parsons were not likely to do as much harm as one publican. . . . He could not understand why a country like Wales, which was first in the matter of temperance reform, was unwilling to give precedence to this question.'[1] In his main speech at the conference Rosebery addressed himself in particular to the problem of sectionalism and the difficulties that the leaders were having in dealing with it. Ministers were, he said, 'subject to a bombardment of correspondence', containing 'appeals, some of them menacing, some of them coaxing and cajoling, but all of them extremely earnest, and praying that the particular hobby of the writer shall be made the first Government Bill'. The impression that this correspondence gave was that 'each article of the programme was equally urgent and supreme, and each article of the programme equally incapable of postponement'. Each section claimed that *it* was 'the backbone of the Liberal party': 'my correspondence makes me feel that there is a multiplicity of backbones in the Liberal party, all preparing to be alienated if certain measures are not pushed forward'.[2]

There was a growing inclination to place the blame for this state of affairs on the Newcastle programme. John Morley predicted that there would be a Conservative majority of 70 to 100 after the next election and that this would be followed by 'the disintegration of the Liberal Party which will not endure the fissiparous effects of its overdrawn programme'.[3] The old arguments against programmes were revived, and there were signs that the pendulum was swinging again, that the

[1] *N.L.F. Report 1895*, p. 94.
[2] *Lord Rosebery's Speeches*, pp. 306–7. Did Rosebery recall that in May 1882 he had written to the then Prime Minister, Gladstone, that 'Scotland is the backbone of the Liberal party, and that, if I am rightly informed, there is some discontent as to her treatment'? Quoted in James, *Rosebery*, p. 130.
[3] Memo by Rendel of conversations with Morley at Cannes, 21–5 December 1894, Rendel MSS., 2nd Series, folio 681.

party was moving into another phase of anti-programme feeling. Haldane told Rosebery in June 1894 that 'the country is sick of dry collections of political platitudes like the Newcastle programme'.[1] The objection began to be raised that an aggregation of reform proposals did not automatically generate an equivalent addition of long-term support for the party. R. J. Price alleged at the 1895 N.L.F. that 'for every reform they carried there was some shedding of members in the Liberal ranks'. Supporters of a particular measure, once it was carried, often tended to 'reconsider their political position' 'for other reasons'.[2] In other words, there was no general Liberal cause or 'system' capable of keeping them involved in Liberal politics. Temperance reformers often admitted as much when they claimed that many people had voted Liberal only because it appeared to be the 'Temperance party'. The motives of expediency which appeared to have governed the adoption of the Newcastle programme also came under attack. 'Mr. G. thoroughly demoralised the Liberal party by the policy of sop-throwing in the two years before 1892', observed Haldane. 'The result was that under his leadership we were rapidly going to pieces.'[3]

What went wrong with the Newcastle programme in practice was that the leaders were completely unable to satisfy the numerous interests which believed that they had been given pledges. Since there had been no ordering of the items in the programme, particular sections were unable to see any reason why they should wait until the demands of others were satisfied. Furthermore, the Liberals aroused against themselves simultaneously all the interests which felt menaced by the proposals in the programme and yet, far from gaining strong compensating advantage in the support of the sectionalists, alienated them by their failure to embody the 'pledges' in satisfactory legislation.[4] The problem was that the Newcastle programme had been given a far too inflated significance, represented as the symbol of a revitalized party, more Radical than ever and capable once more of making progress on a wide front with

[1] 6 June 1894, Rosebery MSS., Box 24.
[2] *N.L.F. Report 1895*, pp. 92–3.
[3] Haldane to Rosebery, 24 April 1895, Rosebery MSS., Box 24.
[4] On this point see Ostrogorski, *Democracy and the Organization of Political Parties*, i, p. 320, and Webb, *Our Partnership*, p. 124.

THE LIBERAL GOVERNMENT OF 1892-1895

domestic reform. Liberal candidates made a great deal of it in the 1892 elections, and some remarkable optimism prevailed as to how much of it could be put through. F. A. Channing, for example, declared: 'Between the stages of Home Rule they could deal with Bills for Registration, Plural Voting, Parish Councils, power to buy land at its fair value—the whole programme of making the world better for the workers.' But during the campaign he did say also that if Home Rule 'and the vital reforms of the Newcastle Programme' were to be carried Gladstone would have to be returned 'by a great majority'.[1] Without such a majority the government simply did not have the resources to carry even a small number of the measures 'promised' at Newcastle.

The meetings of the N.L.F. during the lifetime of this government were not very helpful either; although there was increasing uncertainty as to what should be done about the Newcastle programme. The meeting at Liverpool in January 1893 passed only one policy resolution. This simply 'confirmed' the Newcastle programme and called for the prompt introduction of 'Bills embodying the Reforms which have been declared again and again by this Council to be essential to the welfare of the people of the United Kingdom'. But delegates were not agreed on how much ought to be attempted. On the one hand, J. H. Yoxall, who was to become M.P. for West Nottingham in 1895, demanded 'the widest and fullest interpretation of that programme into actions and acts. A strict limitation of the Newcastle programme would be fatal to the enthusiasm in the ranks.' But R. J. Price, M.P. for East Norfolk, warned that concentration on certain measures was essential: 'It is better not to bite off more than you can chew.'[2] The 1894 meeting at Portsmouth showed that programme politics still reigned supreme in the N.L.F. Not only were there five separate resolutions dealing with major issues of policy but there was also an 'omnibus' resolution dealing with land and taxation reform in particular but referring as well to 'the other Reforms' in the Newcastle programme.[3] And even at the Cardiff conference in January 1895 there were still demands 'that the

---

[1] Channing, *Memories of Midland Politics*, pp. 138, 132.
[2] *N.L.F. Report 1893*, pp. 6, 46, 48-9.
[3] *N.L.F. Report 1894*, pp. 5-7.

Government should not falter until they had done their very best to carry out every point in the Newcastle programme'.[1]

The natural reaction of the Liberal leaders—and many of the Liberal rank and file—to this state of affairs was to think of the possibility of discovering a replacement for the Home Rule policy as a single great and overriding question within which Liberal politics could be concentrated. For, although there was a reaction against preoccupation with the affairs of Ireland, there was not also a reaction against the form of political action which this preoccupation represented. There was a strong feeling in favour of returning to simplified 'single question' politics, and this feeling was expressed in particular in connection with the question of the powers of the House of Lords.

The Lords question was a natural successor to the Irish preoccupation, for it too could be seen and represented as involving an obstruction blocking the way to progress on all other reforms. Gradually during the early 1890s it assumed in the political thinking of many Liberals the status of the next great obstruction which Liberals had to concentrate on removing if anything was to be achieved in connection with any of the reform questions in which they were particularly interested. Gladstone characteristically ranged ahead and saw this as the next issue after Home Rule to receive precedence over all others. In 1891 he told the N.L.F. that, if the Lords threw out the next Home Rule Bill, they 'will raise up a question which will take precedence of every other question, because upon that alone would depend whether this country was or was not a self-governing country'.[2] The language was identical with that which he had been using to promote the Home Rule cause over the previous five years.

As the prospect of chaos after the collapse of the Irish preoccupation loomed closer, the disciplining potential of concentration on the Lords question also became more apparent. The Liberal leaders must surely have appreciated the significance of words such as those of Lloyd George at the N.L.F. in January 1893. After insisting that Welsh disestablishment be the next big reform to be taken up after Home Rule,

[1] *N.L.F. Report 1895*, p. 59.   [2] *N.L.F. Report 1891*, p. 105.

he referred to the Lords in these terms: 'Wales was prepared to forego for a time even the question of Disestablishment to join in the pursuit and lynching of this culprit.'[1] In late 1893 the advantages of concentrating on the Lords question became a common theme with those who were debating the form that post-Home Rule Liberal politics should take. The *Speaker* on 26 August argued that a way of 'settling the precedence of British measures' was to place them in order according to their usefulness in the fight against the Lords.[2] A few weeks later the N.L.F. issued a manifesto recalling Gladstone's statement of 1891 and declaring that the Lords question must soon 'displace for a while all other subjects of reform'.[3]

For Gladstone it was the right kind of single great question. Many diverse questions could be compressed within the simple issue that it raised.[4] He began to develop plans for launching another great crusade, culminating in a dissolution on the issue; but his colleagues, not surprisingly, would not hear of it. Nevertheless, they themselves were prepared to exploit it as a systematizing question. For example, Harcourt told Liberals at the N.L.F. in February 1894 to take as their theme 'that it is not upon one question, or upon two questions, or upon three questions, but upon all questions that the House of Lords is the champion of all abuses and the enemy of all reform'.[5]

In the editorials of the *Speaker* throughout 1894 can be traced the development of this new substitute for system in Liberal politics. On 17 March it wrote: 'English, Irish, Scotch, and Welsh demands—it [the Lords] bars them all, and they can make no progress until it is struck down. It is *the* great question, as Sir William Harcourt said at the Foreign Office. All other questions under its shadow are vitiated by a sense of unreality; they cannot move while it stands still.' The question 'dwarfs and over-rides all other questions', it proclaimed on 7 April; 'all other movements must be subordinated to and absorbed in this'. The special interests and the sections were once more to be 'swallowed up': 'those members of our party who are more especially interested in other movements'—

[1] *N.L.F. Report 1893*, pp. 45–6.   [2] Vol. 8, no. 191, p. 203.
[3] R. S. Watson, *The National Liberal Federation From Its Commencement to the General Election of 1906*, 1907, pp. 151–2.
[4] Hutchinson, *Private Diaries of Sir Algernon West*, p. 270.
[5] *N.L.F. Report 1894*, p. 81.

and of whose sectionalist behaviour the *Speaker* had been complaining for a long time—'may rest assured that victory in this attack will mean victory all along the line'.[1] Because the House of Lords 'stops the way of everything', it supplied the party with 'a cause which will unite all the diverse elements of which it is its pride to be composed'. The 'diverse elements' could now, it seemed, safely be termed the Liberal party's 'pride'; often in the past they had seemed, from the *Speaker*'s editorials, to be its curse. That the Lords question was seen as replacing Home Rule was made quite clear by the *Speaker* on 24 November: 'It "holds the field" to-day, as Home Rule held it in 1886. And it holds it all the more securely and certainly because all other questions, including that of Home Rule, are bound up with it.'[2]

The language is that of the Irish preoccupation adapted to fit the new obstruction; sometimes it seems almost a parody of it. Liberals had grown accustomed to thinking and speaking about the political situation in these terms. The Irish obstruction argument was not abandoned now. Since so much had been made of it and based on it, this would not have been easy. Instead it was adapted. Ireland was said to be an obstruction still—because the greater obstruction of the veto of the House of Lords forced it to be. Thus Gladstone in a speech in September 1893 began quite normally by referring once again to the Irish question as 'a great barrier' between the nation's just demands and 'the measures necessary to give them satisfaction'. 'The Irish Question remained between them and the satisfaction of their wants.' Gladstone was being consistent and showing that he still believed in the Irish obstruction. But then he went on: 'And why did it remain? Who was responsible for its remaining? That was a question which could not be evaded.' And the answer was that 'the responsibility for the painful state of things rested with the House of Lords'.[3] The *Speaker* accepted this: 'The House of Lords has now made itself responsible for Ireland's blocking the way. . . . it is now the House of Lords alone which keeps that difficulty still upon our

[1] Vol. 9, no. 220, p. 295; no. 223, p. 382; no. 229, p. 543 (19 May 1894); no. 230, p. 572 (26 May 1894).
[2] Vol. 10, no. 250, p. 397 (13 October 1894); no. 251, p. 424 (20 October 1894); no. 256, p. 557.
[3] Maccoby, *English Radicalism 1886–1914*, p. 160.

shoulders.' 'The House of Lords is now the prime obstructive. While Ireland blocks Great Britain's way, the House of Lords blocks Ireland's way.'[1] It is significant, however, that Harcourt, who had never been a believer in the 'Irish obstruction', was now most anxious to promote a new and more 'British' version of this obstruction theory as well. In August 1893 he was demanding that there be an autumn session of Parliament for the purpose of providing the opposition with 'plenty of rope': 'The more they obstruct, the more patent will it be that their obstruction is really aimed not against H. Rule but against British measures.'[2]

The Lords issue gave the Liberal leaders a means of unifying the Newcastle programme. They did this by resorting to the strategy of 'filling up the cup', that is binding together a large number of reform measures by sending them up to the Lords to incur a common fate, rejection. Ostrogorski was to analyse the significance of this strategy as being that all the reform interests, 'however different they might be, ought, so to speak, to club together their resentment against the Lords' in order that there might develop 'the semblance of having a common platform'. He argued that the object of the agitation against the Lords was 'to bring about a *state of feeling* in the country on which it appeared easier to reunite the majority of the electorate than on some definite legislative measures'.[3] Certainly, the Lords question did supply an essential ingredient that was missing from the Newcastle programme—a generalized emotion, a spirit of system, a unifying principle. All the interests could be shown to share a common characteristic—ill treatment by the Lords.[4] A crusade against the Lords was welcomed by Liberals as a question which 'deeply concerned' every interest connected with the party and gave Liberals a clear, unambiguous definition of the general issue between 'the aristocracy and the democracy'.[5] J. E. Ellis expressed the prevailing attitude

[1] Vol. 8, no. 196, p. 341 (30 September 1893); no. 198, pp. 398–9 (14 October 1893).
[2] Sir E. Hamilton's diary, B.M. Add. MS. 48661, folios 23–4 (6 August 1893).
[3] Ostrogorski, *Democracy and the Organization of Political Parties*, i, p. 319. See also Stansky, *Ambitions and Strategies*, p. 147.
[4] Asquith argued in this sense at a dinner party in December 1893, whereupon Lord Welby 'shrewdly pointed to the difficulty of focussing all the points'. Hutchinson, *Private Diaries of Sir Algernon West*, p. 228.
[5] *N.L.F. Report 1894*, p. 49 (S. F. Mendl).

when he wrote to Rosebery in 1894 that Ministers should determine to deal decisively with the question because the choice that faced them was between the politics of 'Bills strongly supported by groups' and the politics of a great question supported by 'the party at large'.[1] In fact, of course, the latter would not exclude but rather contain the former. The politics of sectionalism, of catering for minority groups, would continue but would be cohered by a general principle which it was hoped would construct from among the sections a majority of resentment. Labouchere was to argue that a campaign against the Lords had 'this advantage, that it may be pointed out that any special thing wanted, will be obtained, when the Liberal Party has a free hand'.[2]

Obstruction politics remained the Liberals' substitute for system. External forces, not internal disorder or paralysis, could continue to be blamed for the party's weaknesses. Even the same railway-accident imagery was used to describe *this* obstruction. Frank Lockwood told the Eighty Club in November 1894 that

> we want to get this line clear. We have been saying, and a great many people have been telling us, both in the House of Commons and out of the House of Commons, that there are a great many overladen trains which are very much overdue, and ... I take it that this Government has been very much pressed by various sections of its party to consider that their particular train is overdue. Who is responsible for that?

The answer was that it was the House of Lords which was blocking the line.[3] But, as some commentators saw, there remained a more fundamental problem. Andrew Reid, for example, wrote in 1894 that, while it was true that the Liberals were 'at present impotent' because of the Lords and 'may have all the Newcastle programmes in the world, but they cannot do anything with them', this was 'only half the story': 'If the House of Lords was out of the way to-morrow, they would still be impotent. The impotency is within the Liberal

---

[1] 26 July 1894, Rosebery MSS., Box 67.
[2] Labouchere to Harcourt, 17 December 1898, Harcourt MSS.
[3] "Eighty" Club publication: speech by F. Lockwood, 19 November 1894, pp. 6–7. Cf. Stansky, *Ambitions and Strategies*, pp. 135–6. Cf. also the remarks by R. McKenna in *N.L.F. Report 1895*, p. 67.

THE LIBERAL GOVERNMENT OF 1892-1895

party, not without. It has no principles, no ideas, no faith in common.'[1]

One of the main reasons for the prominence of the Lords question in 1894-5 was that Lord Rosebery, after he had succeeded Gladstone as Prime Minister in March 1894, chose it as his concentrating issue. In a great speech at Bradford in October 1894 he presented the Lords question to Liberals as a great comprehensive issue that embraced all other questions. The next election, he said, would be fought not on disestablishment or Home Rule or the liquor question but on one question 'which includes and represents them all—I mean the House of Lords'. It was a question which rendered programmes 'foolish'; programme-makers should recognize that it 'must take precedence of the realisation of all their projects'. But then, like Gladstone, Rosebery believed that even in normal circumstances programmes were 'foolish'. And, like Gladstone also, he uses an argument about an 'obstruction' to persuade others that they should regard them in a similar light. His description of the effect of this obstruction on Liberal politics has many echoes of what Gladstone had said about the Irish obstruction between 1886 and 1893. 'You are bound hand and foot', he told Liberals. 'You may vote, and vote till you are black in the face. It will not change the face of matters at all; still the House of Lords will control at its will the measures of your representatives.'[2] It is significant of Rosebery's Gladstonian approach to the politics of single great questions that he took the initiative in launching his anti-Lords campaign without consulting or 'educating' his colleagues beforehand—with the predictable consequence that, lacking Gladstone's great authority, he could not induce them to follow him.[3]

Nevertheless, Rosebery persevered virtually single-handed in his efforts to get the Liberal party to concentrate on this campaign. Addressing the N.L.F. at Cardiff in January 1895, he urged Liberals to devote all their energies to it. The Lords issue was 'the supreme question of the hour . . . because it covers and underlies simultaneously so many of the questions in which you are interested'.[1] Some of his followers responded

---

[1] A. Reid (ed.), *The New Party Described by some of its Members*, 1894, p. 441.
[2] *Lord Rosebery's Speeches*, pp. 268-70, 277.
[3] Cf. James, *Rosebery*, p. 361.   [4] *Lord Rosebery's Speeches*, pp. 304, 330.

enthusiastically. Haldane saw an anti-Lords campaign as an excellent way of arousing general Liberal 'sentiments', which were, he said, more important than 'ten first class Bills'.[1] In the 1895 election campaign Rosebery presented the question once again as one that 'embraces and involves' all others, that 'involves and concentrates in itself all those other causes' in which Liberals 'specially may bear a particular interest'. As Gladstone had once said of Home Rule, so Rosebery now said of the Lords: 'if you can deal with that successfully, it facilitates dealing with all the others.' To deal with it was the surest way of being in a position to carry the rest. Therefore, all other questions, including those which his chief lieutenants, Morley and Harcourt, were offering at the time, were inferior and subordinate to it:

> If you could relegate the House of Lords to its proper position—relatively to the House of Commons—you would have little difficulty about the other points of reform to which I have alluded. But if you carry one of those other points of reform, you are no nearer carrying the others. Supposing you got a majority of 200 in the next House of Commons pledged to carry the Veto Bill, you would be no nearer necessarily carrying Home Rule. Supposing you got a majority for Irish Home Rule in the next House of Commons, you would not necessarily be nearer carrying one man one vote. But if you carry the annihilation of the House of Lords—as regards its legislative preponderance, which keeps our Party in manacles, you would have gone not half but three-quarters of the way to carrying those other reforms. No, gentlemen, but I dare say some of you may ask: Does the putting forward of the question of the House of Lords imply turning your back on the other great measures that we have at heart? God forbid! It is a means to their end, and not a means of keeping them back. It implies rather this—that the next Liberal Government, whoever may constitute it, and by whomever it may be headed, must take one thing at a time.[2]

This has been quoted at length because it is undoubtedly one of the classic definitions of a single great question combined with the principle of the 'obstruction'. It is a classic instance of how a question of this kind could be used to control sectionalism in Liberal politics. For Rosebery's great objective was to per-

[1] Haldane to Rosebery, 24 April 1895, Rosebery MSS., Box 24.
[2] "Eighty" Club. *The Pressing Question for the Liberal Party*, [1895], pp. 9–13 (report of speech by Rosebery on 2 July 1895).

suade people who were putting their own special questions in the forefront of their own individual Liberal programmes to consider these 'as fitting into and as subservient to the policy of the party with regard to the House of Lords'.[1]

But there were some serious defects in Rosebery's anti-Lords campaign. In the first place, he was perhaps too obsessed with the need to select a 'concentrating' policy and selected one a shade too deliberately without doing the necessary preparatory work first. Secondly, he had not thought out the difficulties associated with converting general anti-Lords 'sentiment' into practical policy that would have the same unifying significance. The Liberal leaders were not at all clear—or agreed—as to what should be done about the Lords, and consequently the 'Lords obstruction' was not nearly such a good 'concentrating' issue for the party as the 'Irish obstruction' had been. In that case a positive remedy—Home Rule—was available to become the focus of debate and action.

Many rank-and-file Liberals favoured the abolition of the House of Lords and rallied to this cause as a simple, clear-cut solution, most suitable for a political agitation. But others could see what a long and perhaps ultimately unsuccessful struggle adoption of this aim would produce and favoured less drastic remedies. The main problem connected with any reform that left the House of Lords in existence was to avoid that kind of 'mending' which would in fact strengthen it by making it representative of a wider area of opinion than had hitherto been the case.[2] The leaders were unable to settle on and announce to the party any definite plan for dealing with the powers of the Lords or with its composition. This did not worry Rosebery, however. What really mattered for him, as we shall see again later in connection with imperialism, was the creation of a frame of mind, a unifying spirit of system in Liberal politics. Not only was he not very interested in details; he was inclined also to regard debate on them as a hindrance to the creation of this general spirit.[3] But his colleagues refused to share this attitude. Campbell-Bannerman wrote to Rosebery

[1] *Lord Rosebery's Speeches*, p. 350.
[2] Stansky, *Ambitions and Strategies*, pp. 135-44. Gardiner, *Life of Harcourt*, ii, pp. 130-1.
[3] See below, pp. 279-81.

in October 1894 that he was 'a little at a loss what to say' about the Lords: 'The day for generalities has passed, and it is only when one begins to think of a possible speech that one appreciates the difficulties of the position fully.'[1] Lord Herschell warned him of how difficult it would be to put 'in a working shape' any scheme for limiting the Lords' veto. An elected second Chamber was not 'within practical range just now': 'The democracy wd. object to its being made too strong, the aristocracy to its supplanting them.' He pointed also to what would happen if a Bill were brought forward. It 'might be passed after great labour & expenditure of time with the certainty of immediate defeat in the H. of Lords'. The peers' justification for throwing it out would be the government's lack of mandate for reform of their House.[2] Harcourt bluntly declared in Cabinet that he was 'a Single Chamber man' and found himself supported in this by Herschell, Asquith, Ripon, and John Morley who were all equally dubious about any scheme for reforming the Lords.[3] Again and again Rosebery's desire to remain at the level of generalities came into conflict with his colleagues' anxiety about details. It was the Irish policy of the late 1880s all over again. Discussion on detail divided Liberals and destroyed the unifying effect of the intended substitute for system. On 5 November Lewis Harcourt recorded in his journal that his father was 'depressed about the H. of L. policy': 'he sees infinite difficulties in propounding the policy. It seems to be inevitable that Ministers should declare in the Debate, when it comes on, whether they are for one or two Chambers.' Four days later at a meeting of the Cabinet, when Harcourt 'said in reference to the H. of L. that R[osebery] had better state his plans of procedure', Rosebery 'did not seem inclined to do so', whereupon Harcourt 'proceeded to take points of R.'s Edinburgh speech seriatim and to point out difficulties

---

[1] 5 October [1894], Rosebery MSS., Box 2.

[2] 12 October 1894, Rosebery MSS., Box 67. In the Cabinet, indeed, Herschell had said 'that the whole idea of an agitation against the Lords was mischievous nonsense'. Diary of Lewis Harcourt, Harcourt MSS. (23 February 1894).

[3] Lewis Harcourt's diary, Harcourt MSS. (31 October 1894). John Morley wrote to R. Spence Watson on 4 November 1894: 'Rosebery says he is for a Second Chamber. Half his colleagues doubt whether the operation of creating one is possible—and your argument is unanswerable, that if you strengthen the H. of L. you weaken the H. of C.' Watson MSS.

and objections to be overcome and some inconsistencies'.[1] When on 23 November Rosebery at last made a definite proposal, namely that the House of Commons should be asked to pass a resolution declaring 'that it would not have its decisions revised by an hereditary and unrepresentative Second Chamber', Harcourt promptly 'objected *in-toto* to this phrasing, as he said it left the door open to acquiescence in revision by a reformed, non-hereditary or representative Chamber, which he is not prepared to admit as a possibility'.[2] In January 1895 Rosebery proposed that a Cabinet Committee be set up 'to consider the form of the action to be taken against the House of Lords'. Once again Harcourt objected, saying that 'the more they discussed their opinions the more they diverged', and, together with John Morley, refused to join the Committee. According to Lewis Harcourt's report of this meeting of the Cabinet, Rosebery then observed that 'it comes to this—that our language about the House of Lords is all a sham', to which Sir William Harcourt's reply was: 'If you choose to put it so I think it is.'[3]

Outside the leadership as well some Liberals were very uneasy about the whole business. After the long period of preoccupation with Irish Home Rule there was little appeal in another time-consuming crusade which was only too likely to prove as unproductive as the eight-year struggle for Home Rule. One Liberal warned against a full-scale campaign against the Lords because, he wrote, it could only be 'at the cost of stopping all the necessary domestic legislation of the three Kingdoms'.[4] Others found difficulty in accepting Rosebery's suggestion that all the problems of Liberalism should be attributed to the Lords. A speaker at the 1895 N.L.F. conference gave this warning: 'Members had by-and-bye to go back to their constituencies, and they would be asked why they had not carried out the pledges they had given. It would be futile to go back and say they had not been fulfilled because of the House of Lords.'[5] There was a growing weariness with the politics of obstructions.

[1] Lewis Harcourt's diary, Harcourt MSS. (9 November 1894).
[2] Ibid. (23 November 1894).   [3] Ibid. (29 January 1895).
[4] H. F. Moulton, *The Life of Lord Moulton*, 1922, p. 81.
[5] *N.L.F. Report 1895*, p. 59 (R. D. Burnie).

The Liberal leaders knew perfectly well that an appeal to the country against the Lords could not be entered upon lightly. It could do more harm than good both to the party and to the cause itself, for the country would very likely reject the appeal and thus strengthen the authority of the Lords for wrecking the future legislative programmes of Liberal governments. Victory was probable only if the Lords were to reject some reform that enjoyed very wide popularity, and this they manifestly were not yet doing. The impotence of the Liberals in face of the obstructive and destructive conduct of the Lords was another consequence of sectionalism, of having in the party programme reforms which appealed only to minority sections or interests. 'Filling the cup' was in fact a desperate attempt to construct out of this situation an anti-Lords majority, section by section. For, when Gladstone had wanted a last crusade under his premiership against the Lords, his colleagues refused to let him have it, appreciating that as yet nowhere near a majority of the population felt indignant with the Lords. 'The plain truth is', Morley told Harcourt in September 1894, 'that we can do nothing with the H. of L. unless they really resist the will of the British constituencies—and this they are not now doing.'[1] Even Rosebery had his doubts about making the Lords question the principal issue at a general election. He said in December 1894 that the serious objection to doing so was that, 'if the Liberal party, appealing to the country on the question of the House of Lords, were beaten, it wd. greatly strengthen the position of the House of Lords'.[2]

The leaders, especially Rosebery, roused rank-and-file feeling in the party on the Lords question without having any clear idea of how they were going to satisfy it. To the ordinary party activist and to many Radical M.P.s strong denunciations of the Lords seemed naturally to lead on to a campaign to abolish it. But Rosebery, a peer frustrated by his own position as a member of a tiny minority in the only House to which he could belong, seemed to wish to reform and 'improve' and increase respect for the House of Lords. In November 1894 Reginald Brett defined Rosebery's 'principal mistake' as 'want of clearness':

[1] 21 September 1894, Harcourt MSS.
[2] C. P. Scott to Rosebery, 8 December 1894, Rosebery MSS., Box 69 (Scott recalls a conversation in which Rosebery said this).

THE LIBERAL GOVERNMENT OF 1892-1895

People could not make out what he was driving at as regards the House of Lords. The House of Lords was on no account to be abolished. Therefore there must be a Second Chamber, and a Second Chamber with some vetoing power; otherwise it would be an absurdity. Then was it to be a reformed House of Lords which he was advocating? In that case, let him say so: a reformed House of Lords might be more evenly balanced as regards parties; but it could hardly fail in some respects to be more powerful than the present Upper House.[1]

It was, of course, fatally tempting for Liberals, leaders and rank and file alike, to unload their frustrations on to this new scapegoat, to sink their differences and seek emotional unification in this new campaign for overcoming an obstruction. But, whereas Gladstone had been ready in 1885-6 with a practical remedy for the problem of the Irish obstruction, Rosebery was not able to provide his followers with a similar practical and constructive outlet for their emotions and frustrations. The emotion built up but was not effectively harnessed or disciplined by the party leadership; and the history of the Liberal party in 1894 and 1895 is characterized by, on the one hand, mounting complaints about the lukewarmness and half-heartedness of the leaders and their failure to follow through their rhetorical assaults on the Lords, and, on the other hand, growing anxiety among the leaders about the uncontrolled extremism of the party on the issue.

At the meeting of the N.L.F. in February 1894 a backbench Liberal M.P., E. J. C. Morton, warned the leaders 'that they were not to be treated as they had been in 1884' when 'they got up steam in the country against the Lords' and then 'owing to the supineness of their leaders the Lords were allowed to escape'. He went on:

They were there to warn their leaders that although they wanted Home Rule, and the Parish Councils Bill, and an Employers' Liability Bill, and the rest of the Radical legislation demanded by the people, yet they were not to allow the House of Lords to get out

[1] Sir E. Hamilton's diary, B.M. Add. MS. 48665, folios 61-2 (21 November 1894). Haldane too felt that Rosebery had failed to define his position on the Lords question 'with sufficient clearness', 'had not got up the constitutional history with enough accuracy', and 'had failed to give the idea that he was really in earnest about the question'. Sir E. Hamilton's diary, B.M. Add. MS. 48665, folio 119 (14 January 1895).

of their present position even by the passage of these Bills. What they wanted above all things was first a quarrel with, and then the destruction of their great national enemy—the House of Lords.[1]

When Rosebery became Prime Minister the next month—a peer instead of the Radicals' favourite, Harcourt—the party revolted, and a strong anti-Lords resolution proposed by Labouchere was passed by the House of Commons.[2] The N.L.F. now flung itself into the anti-Lords campaign, and worked the question furiously right through 1894.[3] This agitation greatly embarrassed the leaders[4] and undoubtedly helped to stir Rosebery to try to take the lead and moderate it. By October Bryce had to warn him of the hold which abolitionist sentiment had gained over the party: 'our Radicals have got so irritated with the Lords that they cannot rid themselves, in thinking of a Second Chamber, of the notion that it would be merely the Lords over again'.[5] The 'leaders' saw their 'followers' getting out of control. Lord Tweedmouth wrote that 'our extreme section have so run away with the project of a Bill that it may be difficult to bring them back to the post again'.[6] Rosebery himself began 'regretting he ever invited the Leeds Conference to give him a lead over the House of Lords'.[7] By the end of the year the leaders were growing very indignant about the extremists, and pressure was put on junior Ministers who appeared to encourage them.[8] When at a Cabinet meeting late in January 1895 all but one of the Commons members of the Cabinet urged the convening of a party meeting 'for purposes of Party unity', Rosebery expressed very strong opposition to the idea. 'He says', reported Lewis Harcourt, 'the Party would ask all sorts of inconvenient questions about the action against the House of Lords "and neither Harcourt

[1] *N.L.F. Report 1894*, pp. 61–2.   [2] James, *Rosebery*, pp. 338–9.
[3] For the Leeds conference which was organized on the question in June 1894, see *The Liberal Magazine*, vol. 2, no. 10 (July 1894), pp. 204–17.
[4] Sir E. Hamilton's diary, B.M. Add. MS. 48664, folio 28 (24 June 1894).
[5] 11 October 1894, Rosebery MSS., Box 66.
[6] Tweedmouth to Gladstone, 20 October 1894, Gladstone MSS., B.M. Add. MS. 44332, folios 276–8.
[7] Lewis Harcourt's diary, Harcourt MSS. (1 October 1894).
[8] For efforts to curb the involvement in the agitation of W. Woodall, who was Financial Secretary to the War Office, see Lewis Harcourt's diary, Harcourt MSS. (28 November 1894), and Campbell-Bannerman to Rosebery, 2 December [1894], Rosebery MSS., Box 2.

nor I should know what to say." W. V. H[arcourt] said "Quite so".[1] Organs of Liberal opinion 'in the country' became just as indignant about the behaviour of the leaders. The *Speaker* complained in an editorial on 11 May 1895 about the failure of some of Rosebery's colleagues to keep the question to the front: 'We cannot have a better battle-horse than this question of the House of Lords, and it is the duty of Liberals to stick to it. Nor ought they to forget that this question, in a sense, contains all the minor questions which are now occupying their minds.'[2]

One of these colleagues was Harcourt, and his attitude was of vital importance because he was leader of the party in the House of Commons. He refused to take any part in Rosebery's anti-Lords campaign, chiefly because it was Rosebery who was sponsoring it. 'You talk of the "House of Lords"', he wrote to Lord Spencer in September 1894. 'I have formed only one clear opinion upon that subject and that is that *the question cannot be undertaken by the existing Govt.* AS AT PRESENT CONSTITUTED.'[3] A month later he told Sir Edward Hamilton that he was 'very pleased that R. has decided, as he has, to take his own line on his own responsibility; because [he] has not the faintest idea what to advise or to say himself on so insoluble a problem'.[4] The question upon which he chose to concentrate was local option which he had viewed since the early 1880s as the best available 'question for the party'. His promotion of local option legislation between 1893 and 1895 constituted, together with his 'death duties Budget' of 1894, the most definite realization that he was able to achieve of his normally vague ideas about making the party and its policy 'more Radical'. But the question caused this government perpetual difficulty, and nothing practical was accomplished. Harcourt professed to be 'convinced that temperance was the only question which really interested the electors'; but Rosebery found that 'Harcourt's views about temperance & the Local Veto Bill are shared by no other member of the Government unless it be John Morley'.[5] Harcourt, however, made it clear that he, together with Morley and Fowler, would refuse 'to appeal to

[1] Lewis Harcourt's diary, Harcourt MSS. (29 January 1895).
[2] Vol. 11, no. 280, p. 506.
[3] 21 September 1894, Spencer MSS.: Corr. with Harcourt, vol. 3.
[4] Sir E. Hamilton's diary, B.M. Add. MS. 48665, folio 17 (22 October 1894).
[5] Sir E. Hamilton's diary, B.M. Add. MS. 48666, folio 115 (30 April 1895).

the country on the House of Lords question', for, whereas 'a large section of the community were enthusiastic' about local option, 'the reform of the Upper Chamber was a dead-letter'.[1] What is especially significant is that Harcourt entirely rejected not only the content but also the form of Rosebery's appeal. He scorned Rosebery's tactics of 'concentration' and 'one thing at a time' as 'absurd' and condemned the idea of a policy that would treat the items of the party programme 'all alike' as subordinated and relegated:

> If the Liberals did get a majority, they would, under R.'s programme, have to deal first with the House of Lords, which (Harcourt says) would involve a further dissolution. He (Harcourt) intends to stick to the old programme & the whole of it: it would never do to disappoint Irishmen, Welshmen, and 'Local Optionists' all alike.[2]

Harcourt thus brought up against Rosebery's single great question the same objections as he had raised concerning the Home Rule preoccupation. He himself preferred to maintain the programme form of Liberal policy while imposing his own italics on part of the Newcastle programme.[3] He put local option first in his own election campaign in 1895, and many believed that both his own defeat at Derby and the defeat of the party were attributable primarily to its unpopularity. Munro Ferguson had reported to Rosebery in April 1895 that Herbert Gladstone 'was very strong against the Local Veto Bill' and that there would be 'a general revolt against Harcourt's policy in the Party before long, if it is not controllable in any other way'; 'If one were in search of the method by which we could be wrecked with the greatest amount of certainty & facility, it would be in following the banner of the U.K. Alliance that success would be met with in the shortest time.'[4] But Harcourt was quite indifferent to such arguments. He told Sir Edward Russell that underlying his local veto policy was the view 'that Party exists for the purpose of promoting measures and that measures are not to be taken up or dropped in reference to the interests of Party'.[5] W. E. Gladstone saw in this

---
[1] Sir E. Hamilton's diary, B.M. Add. MS. 48666, folios 134-5 (21 May 1895).
[2] Sir E. Hamilton's diary, B.M. Add. MS. 48667, folio 60 (4 July 1895).
[3] Gardiner, *Life of Harcourt*, ii, p. 366.
[4] 24 April 1895, Rosebery MSS., Box 15.
[5] Harcourt to Russell, 4 June 1895, Harcourt MSS.

THE LIBERAL GOVERNMENT OF 1892-1895 207

episode an example of the unwisdom of mixing up the politics of sectionalism with governmental Liberal politics. He suggested to Harcourt that in future it might be better if local option were 'propelled by independent action than by a Liberal Government'.[1] Like Gladstone, Rosebery had at least tried to offer a policy that transcended and 'controlled' sectionalism. Harcourt had no such policy available.

During the early months of 1895 a longing to escape from office grew rapidly among the Liberal leaders. Harcourt behaved very much as he had in 1885. To Rosebery's great annoyance he would talk 'loudly in the House before everybody about the coming downfall of the Government to which he wished a speedy end'.[2] Finally, the Cabinet were very pleased to be able to find in the defeat on the 'cordite' vote a pretext for resigning. The Unionists then entered office under Lord Salisbury and promptly dissolved Parliament. In the Liberals' election campaign there was no concentrating issue accepted by the whole party and leadership, in spite of Rosebery's efforts—admittedly not very strenuous—to make the Lords question into such an issue.[3] Harcourt preferred to campaign on local option and John Morley on Home Rule. The will to win was almost entirely absent on the Liberal side; defeat was accepted as very probable and indeed welcomed as a solution to the problems that had plagued the Liberals when in office. 'I can't help feeling that defeat may be good for us', wrote Herbert Gladstone. 'We are plagued with obstinate faddists who are too strong for the leaders, and except for Ireland I could wish to get rid of them through defeat.'[4] Yet again the theme appears of purge and reconstruction through defeat.

[1] Gladstone to Harcourt, 15 July 1895, Gardiner, *Life of Harcourt*, ii, p. 371.
[2] Sir E. Hamilton's diary, B.M. Add. MS. 48666, folio 21 (14 February 1895).
[3] For the Chief Whip's complaints about Rosebery's lack of vigour see T. Ellis to Rosebery, 7 July and 14 August 1895, Rosebery MSS., Box 71.
[4] Mallet, *Herbert Gladstone*, p. 156.

IX The Debate on the Future of Liberal Politics

THE defeat of 1895 led to a strong reaction against sectionalism and programmes. Sectionalism, which Campbell-Bannerman described as a tendency among Liberals to assume superior virtue in 'their own particular ideas, which when they came to examine into them might turn out to be nothing more than their own personal likings or dislikings',[1] seemed to have taken over Liberal politics. The unifying and concentrating influences of the past had not been replaced. As Guinness Rogers noted in an article in January 1898, there was as yet no substitute for the great bond which had for a long time 'held together the various sections of a composite party'—the magic of Gladstone's name and authority. But there was also a change in the style of Liberal politics. The history of Liberalism over the previous fifty years—and here he was obviously thinking in particular of the Home Rule preoccupation—seemed to suggest that the party should not 'be regarded as a standing army, but rather as a changing force which had always to be formed anew for each successive work that had to be done'. The difficulty that was now arising in Liberal politics could be attributed to the emergence of a new 'primary idea' about the nature of the party, that it should be 'a permanent army intent on an immediate victory for righteousness everywhere'. 'The natural result of such a mode of warfare', Rogers complained, 'is to unite all the interests assailed in a compact league for resistance.'[2]

The effects of the adoption of the two contrasting modes of Liberal political activity, the single great question after 1886,

[1] *The Liberal Magazine*, vol. 4, no. 40 (January 1897), p. 549.
[2] J. Guinness Rogers, 'Is the Liberal Party in Collapse?', *N.C.*, no. 251 (January 1898), pp. 148–50.

and the programme after 1891, became the subject of much debate and controversy. To some it seemed that the party had been entirely reconstructed in 1886, had become a different kind of party, and could not break out of this mould without a great risk of indiscipline and disintegration. It had become the party of 'Home Rule for Ireland'; that was its *raison d'être*. The result was that some Liberals came to feel that the party could not now afford to drop Home Rule as its principal policy objective because 'with the exception of Home Rule there was very little difference between the programmes of the two parties'.[1] In 1895 C. P. Scott, editor of the *Manchester Guardian*, warned delegates to the N.L.F. that, if the party did not continue to adhere to the Gladstonian Home Rule policy, it would 'be broken up into hopeless factions and divisions'. A year later he argued that, 'if the Liberal party ever looked back, if it ever faltered or was false to itself upon this great question, the Liberal party would cease to be the Liberal party. It would become a congeries of discredited atoms, and would sink to impotence and into disgrace.'[2]

At times the Irish preoccupation itself was blamed for the lack of discipline and order in Liberal politics. The years after 1885 had been abnormal, and the party was now having to go through the difficult process of recovering its normality. The *Speaker* of 10 February 1894 suggested that the effect of what happened in 1886 was that many Liberals 'lost their reckoning':

> The Liberal party, turned aside, as it seemed, from the native course of its ideas in its effort to end the Irish difficulty, did not appear to be itself.... The interval of doubtfulness was peculiarly favourable to loose thinking and indiscipline. Independent Labour claims, Socialist nostrums, Fabianism, London particularism—all had a rare opportunity to develop at the expense of a general perspective. Weak heads, unable to take a comprehensive view, and ignorant of the essential nature of Liberalism, grew dizzy.[3]

Gladstone's style of leadership, deliberately neglectful of other questions, also came in for blame. According to the *Speaker* of 17 October 1896,

[1] *N.L.F. Report 1893*, p. 39 (J. W. Benn).
[2] *N.L.F. Report 1895*, p. 81. *N.L.F. Report 1896*, p. 62.
[3] Vol. 9, no. 215, p. 154.

The great disruption of 1886 had been followed by a dangerous relaxation of party discipline. . . . Mr. Gladstone had openly avowed that he only remained in public life in order to deal with the Irish question. Those other questions which were to be found in the Newcastle Programme, or which, from time to time, were forced to the front by sections of the party, were regarded as being, in a certain sense, out of bounds. Rightly or wrongly, it was assumed that Mr. Gladstone left his followers with a free hand as to the time and order in which these questions should be dealt with. Nobody has any right to complain if one of the results of this prevalent impression was that a large number of irresponsible persons assumed to direct the policy of the party in accordance with their own personal inclination. . . . The party had got out of hand, and a hundred amateurs were seeking at the same moment to carry it in as many different directions.[1]

It followed from this interpretation of the effects of the Irish preoccupation that the great task now before the party was the re-establishment of what the *Speaker* called 'a general perspective'. Some of the leaders began to do this after Gladstone's retirement by bringing forward new interpretations of the reconstruction of the party in 1886. The tendency now was to play down the role of Home Rule in the schism of that year and to argue that there were other more fundamental causes responsible for it. The causes that particular Liberal leaders emphasized were usually related to their own view as to the form that the development of the party should now take. Thus Rosebery claimed that imperialism had been the basic issue in 1886 and that therefore the restoration of 'normality' in Liberal politics—by which he meant the return of the party to its position as the majority party—depended on the bringing of Liberal policy into alignment with imperialist opinion. Harcourt, on the other hand, argued that the 'effective' issue in 1886 was not 'opposition to the Home Rule policy' but 'fear of the progressive march of Liberal ideas'. The dissentients left the party, not because of Home Rule or imperialism, but because they 'shrank from the dreaded advent of equal justice; they foreboded that privilege was foredoomed; they went away sorrowful because they had great possessions'. '. . . it was not Home Rule that caused us their desertion. It was the whole gamut of the Liberal creed that jarred upon their nerves

[1] Vol. 14, no. 355, pp. 404–5.

and which disagreed with their system. They went forth from us because they were not of us.'[1]

As the *Speaker* implied, the Newcastle programme could itself be seen as a manifestation, a product, of a fundamentally abnormal situation. Only the indiscipline fostered by the Irish preoccupation and Gladstone's abstention from fulfilling the normal functions of a leader had enabled such a vast, unco-ordinated, and incoherent set of reform proposals to acquire the status of party policy. The election defeat of 1895 was seen by many Liberals as attributable mainly to the Newcastle programme. Munro Ferguson thus summarized feeling in the party: 'We have been borne down by the burdens we put on our own shoulders.'[2] The government had had no single policy to concentrate on; instead, its meagre resources had been devoted to trying to satisfy simultaneously all the multifarious commitments in the Newcastle programme. Guinness Rogers deplored that John Bright's 'wise counsel' 'not to try and run half a dozen omnibuses through Temple Bar at the same time was cast to the winds'. But he admitted that it was very difficult to find any alternative mode of action for what was 'a conglomerate party' full of 'opposing cliques and disunited forces'.[3]

As usual, the reaction against programmes was accompanied by a revival of enthusiasm for concentrating on a single great question. The *Speaker* argued that the party 'can only hope to triumph when it next appeals to the country if it is united in good earnest, not in advocacy of a motley group of more or less divergent measures, but in support of some great cause which enlists, not the passive approval, but the whole-hearted sympathy, of the universal party'. 'When all our sections are united on behalf of such a cause, the hour of our victory will be near.'[4] Within the Liberal leadership itself similar views began to be expressed. Lord Herschell wrote that in his opinion the election defeat had taught 'some useful lessons': on the one hand, the wrongness of 'these attempts to please the sections of

[1] *Liberal Magazine*, vol. 2, no. 12 (September 1894), p. 282.
[2] Ferguson to Rosebery, 27 July 1895, Rosebery MSS., Box 15.
[3] J. Guinness Rogers, 'The General Election. I. What Does it all Mean?', *N.C.*, no. 222 (August 1895), pp. 184-5.
[4] Vol. 12, no. 293 (10 August 1895), p. 144.

our party witht. regarding it as a whole'; on the other hand, how much better it would have been if the Liberals had promoted some single cause of the kind 'which wd. have benefited all causes' alike.[1]

There was a very general feeling in the party that programme politics should be repudiated. J. E. Ellis wrote to Rosebery after the elections: 'I hope . . . the Liberal party has done with "programmes" against which I have always protested since 1884 [sic] when they were begun *from Birmingham*.'[2] A Liberal veteran, Lord Playfair, said that 'we went to the country with too many questions'. To him the greatest objection to programmes was their indefiniteness: they mystified and confused people. 'We needed definiteness, and, not having it, we lost.'[3] Sir Edward Russell, a leading Liberal journalist, argued that the simultaneous stirring up of so many vested interests had been a major cause of the election defeat. He advanced the following reason why it was much better to concentrate on challenging only one vested interest at a time:

> Everyone who is associated with a vested interest fights resolutely and desperately for the preservation of it—for self-preservation. On the other hand, the attacking party has no personal interest—it is a fight of principle; and hence the only keen enthusiasm obtainable for the attack is that evinced by men of ideas—men who care for political principles as principles. These are a very small minority. The only chance of overthrowing a powerful vested interest is to have the whole community outside that interest enlisted on your side. But if at the same time you are threatening or attacking other interests, those who benefit by them will not join your army in the attack, but will make common cause with your enemy.[4]

The leaders themselves became more and more convinced that much less attention must be paid to the sectionalists in the future if Liberal governments were ever to achieve anything in the areas of reform in which the sectionalists operated. H. H. Fowler, for example, wrote of that arch- 'faddist', Sir Wilfrid Lawson: 'He more than any one else has delayed Temperance Reform and his present attitude only tends to

[1] Herschell to Rosebery, 11 August 1895, Rosebery MSS., Box 71.
[2] 21 August 1895, Rosebery MSS., Box 71.
[3] Reid, *Memoirs and Correspondence of Lyon Playfair*, pp. 403–4.
[4] Sir E. Russell, 'The Liberal New Year', *C.R.*, vol. 69, no. 361 (January 1896), pp. 138–9.

conserve the position and irresponsibility of the Peers. Faddists are the weakness & the danger of the Liberal Party.'[1]

Writing in the *Progressive Review* of November 1896, Haldane, one of the leading critics of programme politics, described 'the hope that the putting forward of the Newcastle Program would unite the opponents of Conservatism' as 'a piece of folly'. The Liberal leaders had been made 'by well-meaning people' to recite their assent to 'the various articles of the "Credo"', but such assent could be only 'notional and not real'. 'A Faith cannot be artificially manufactured. Let us remember this when next we go program-making.' But the editor then added some comments on Haldane's article by R. Wallace, M.P. for Perth, which showed that sentiment in favour of programmes was by no means extinguished.[2] An increasing number of Liberals was, however, prepared to believe that the swing to programme politics in the early 1890s had been a marked departure from the Liberal tradition which was associated with the promotion of single great causes. A. C. Morton, M.P. for Peterborough, told the N.L.F. in March 1897 that the Liberal party had usually been successful when it had concentrated on 'one or two great questions' but that, 'since 1892 the Liberal party in the country had been practically brought to ruin . . . by a long programme being forced upon the leaders'.[3]

The climax of the reaction against the Newcastle programme came in 1898 with the presentation of the annual report of the N.L.F. to its meeting at Leicester in March. For this included an explicit attempt, inspired chiefly by the President, Robert Spence Watson, to dissociate the N.L.F. once and for all from the programme. The report claimed that throughout its existence the Federation had 'refused to formulate a political programme' since 'Liberalism when rightly understood is too vast and too progressive to permit of the hard and fast formalism of a specific creed'. Then it made a categoric statement: 'No Newcastle Programme was ever framed by the Federation or by anyone connected with it; no programme whatever was presented at the Annual Council Meeting at Newcastle or

---

[1] Fowler to Rosebery, 2 April 1896, Rosebery MSS., Box 73.
[2] *Progressive Review*, vol. 1, no. 2, p. 141.
[3] *N.L.F. Report 1897*, p. 78.

elsewhere or at any other meeting of the Federation, whether Council, Conference or Committee.' Furthermore, it observed, correctly, that there was nothing new in the so-called 'Newcastle Programme': 'All the reforms which were embodied in resolutions had been demanded at previous meetings.' What gave these resolutions their special significance now was

the fact that without reference to any person connected with the Federation, and to the surprise of everyone, our great leader, Mr. Gladstone, instead of, as was anticipated devoting his speech at the great Public Meeting to the subject of Ireland, took up *seriatim* the resolutions which had been passed at the Council Meetings and gave them the weight of his direct approval. The newspapers at once spoke of 'the Newcastle Programme'. For a time the members of the Executive Committee protested, but the name stuck and entered into common use . . .

Thus was the blame transferred to Gladstone—though Spence Watson stressed in his presidential address that Gladstone had himself acted quite innocently, never dreaming that the resolutions would or could become a programme 'in the dangerous sense'.[1]

This report aroused the indignation of Herbert Gladstone who made a strong protest about it to Sir Robert Hudson, the secretary of the Federation. He argued that the Federation 'was & is mainly responsible' for the Newcastle programme and for Gladstone's having taken it up: 'For years every kind of pressure from the officials of the Fedn., organizers, wire pullers, & sectional leaders was put upon him to induce him to give this that & the other the party imprimatur. The Fedn. lent itself to this process, focussed & concentrated the various opinions & movements & his hand was as I think most unfortunately forced.' In his opinion, it was, in any case, an error for anyone 'to try to prove that the Federation has never had anything to do with programmes'.[2] What was undeniable, however, was that there had been a connection between the abnormal nature of Gladstone's leadership at the time and the adoption of this incoherent and 'unripe' programme. Herbert Gladstone himself pointed out that his

[1] *N.L.F. Report 1898*, pp. 40–2, 55.
[2] Herbert Gladstone to Hudson, 9 March 1898, 10 March 1898 (copy), Viscount Gladstone MSS., B.M. Add. MS. 46020, folios 10, 15–16.

father had stressed that 'it was for the future and others rather than the present and himself'. Some years later Professor J. S. Phillimore traced many of the party's difficulties since 1891 to Gladstone's 'great tactical blunder of adopting this programme of the left wing practically *en bloc* in order to reconcile Great Britain to Home Rule'.[1] H. H. Fowler wrote that 'Mr. Gladstone's purchase of H. Rule support in exchange for his apparent approval of a great deal which he loathed is not a pleasant chapter in the History of the Liberal Party'.[2]

How were order, proportion, perspective, cohesion to be re-established in Liberal politics? The programme method had clearly failed. The obvious need was for the creation of some new general and systematic creed of Liberal principles within which the diverse efforts and interests of Liberals and reformers could be cohered in a sense of common purpose. It seemed to many Liberals, especially after the experience of 1892–5, that Liberals would have 'to reconsider their whole position', to find some new basis on which to reconstruct the party.[3] The frustration felt by Liberals who were anxious to do good and achieve reforms that would benefit their fellow countrymen was well expressed by A. H. D. Acland when he wrote in 1893: 'Our position in politics seems to me so strange. Are we straining ourselves and spending so much time to any real purpose? No time is left to think on human affairs or human improvement . . . and all is choked with petty and narrow & personal details.'[4] Herbert Samuel argued at the 1896 N.L.F. meeting that less time should now be spent on detailed measures and more time on the organization of 'broad and great principles'.[5] When he and other younger Liberals of the 'Rainbow Circle' founded the *Progressive Review* in 1896, the problem to which they drew particular attention was the constant fragmentation of Liberal politics caused by the multiplication of schools of

---

[1] *New Liberal Review*, vol. 4, no. 21 (October 1902), pp. 346–7.
[2] Fowler to Harcourt, 26 November 1896, Harcourt MSS.
[3] Morley to Spencer, 28 July 1895, Spencer MSS.
[4] He went on: 'It is a miserably poor way to spend our lives unless we are really working for something which is *real*—some real victories over the vile and the cross grained and the retrogressive in the world's affairs.' Acland to T. Ellis, 23 December 1893, T. E. Ellis MSS., folio 38.
[5] *N.L.F. Report 1896*, p. 83.

thought. 'Where', they asked, 'is the synthesis, the unity of principle and of policy which shall give solidarity of structure, singleness of aim, economy of force, consistency of action to this medley of multifarious effort?' Both the diversity of the panaceas believed in by those Liberals who 'act' and the 'frustrated feelings' of those who found themselves unable to 'act' attested 'the urgent need of a re-formation and re-statement of the principles of Progress in terms which shall include and give due emphasis to the new ideas and sentiments of social justice and of a clear rational application of those principles in a progressive policy and a progressive party'.[1]

Somehow sectionalism had to be transcended and some way found of giving the party once again 'a real existence', an organic unity by making its strength 'superior to that of the more or less adherent sections'.[2] The case for synthesis in Liberal policy was put thus by J. A. Simon in one of the *Essays in Liberalism* brought out by six young Liberals in 1897:

> What is, above all, needed is a more comprehensive grasp of the basis of Liberal policy, both in order to justify the details of its development, and in order to establish the interconnection of its several parts. The increasing complexity of civic life and the consequently increasing subdivision of political interests has left many Liberals ignorant and careless of the broader aspects of their faith. It is easy for each of us to see how his own political hobby is a rigid application of Liberal theory, even if that theory be but vaguely comprehended; but it is difficult to appreciate the justice and importance of applications on which others lay chief stress. And thus we have the unedifying sight of teetotal Liberals negligent of everything but Temperance reform; of a champion of undenominational education hinting repudiation of Home Rule, because, forsooth, certain Irishmen are willing to get what they can for Catholic schools . . .[3]

Substitutes for system had been tried, and some had sometimes proved a temporary success and created a provisional order and coherence; but they all had their defects. 'Obstructions' tended to make the confusion worse than ever: other

---

[1] *Progressive Review*, vol. 1, no. 1, pp. 1–3.
[2] J. F. Moulton to Rosebery, 10 October 1896, Rosebery MSS., Box 73.
[3] Six Oxford Men, *Essays in Liberalism*, 1897, p. 104.

reform issues accumulated behind them, and when they were removed or weakened, as in the early 1890s, there was a breaking of the dam, a great and simultaneous surging forward of these other issues, their adherents being all the more impatient because of the promises made during the period of enforced impotence about the prospects after the alleged obstruction had gone. The sudden removal of what had been the sole ordering influence in Liberal politics could itself accelerate the process of disintegration by its destruction of established relationships. In fact, during this period the leaders at times found themselves obliged to move with desperate haste from one 'obstruction' to another.

Another, and, as we have seen, sometimes related, substitute was the single 'concentrating' question. But what those Liberals who believed in this way of bringing order into Liberal politics had to decide was whether deliberately to select a question to fill this role or whether to wait for one to emerge 'naturally'. For it was clearly not possible to succeed simply by selecting any question at all. It had to be such an issue as would stimulate among the supporters of other reform causes a disposition to accept the non-selection and the subordination of their causes. Home Rule had for a time been such an issue, and clearly the best prospects did lie in some policy that could be presented as involving the removal of an obstruction.

The controversy over the mode of Liberal political action was only part of, and at some points closely reflected, the growing uncertainty as to the nature and purpose of Liberalism and the Liberal party. The traditional Liberal view as to the meaning of Liberalism centred on the idea of enlarging freedom, emancipating the individual, and breaking down hindrances and obstructions, especially those created 'unnaturally', that is by governments and political authorities, to a freer and more 'natural' life.[1] Liberal policies continued to be presented in this context; the removal of obstructions continued to appear the party's *raison d'être*.[2]

---

[1] Cf. L. T. Hobhouse, *Liberalism*, [1911], p. 19.
[2] This argument was often used in response to claims that the Liberal party should now be replaced by a Labour party. See *N.L.F. Report 1891*, pp. 21–2, and Hamer, *John Morley*, p. 305.

Gladstone understood the purpose of Liberalism in this way; but towards the end of his career he sensed that British politics were entering a new era in which the place of Liberalism was extremely difficult to determine. In 1885 he referred to 'a process of slow modification and development mainly in directions which I view with misgiving'. In Liberalism he saw and disliked growing enthusiasm for 'construction,—that is to say, taking into the hands of the state the business of the individual man'.[1] In 1889 he told Rosebery that 'I look back with pleasure to the times of liberation in which my political life was cast, and with doubt to the coming times of construction'.[2] For fifty years, according to Gladstone, 'public life in England had been an almost unbroken struggle for emancipation':

> Every great political movement had been in the nature of opening doors and windows, and once any movement had succeeded, there had been no reaction, no regret. The difference between the gross result and the net result had been small. The gains were gains without discount. But . . . in the next fifty years political labour would be in less fruitful soil and under more ambiguous conditions. There would be much that was empirical and much going forward only to go back.[3]

Rosebery, again, as in so much else, assuming the mantle of Gladstone's heir, took up this theme and used it in the 1890s to explain what was going on in Liberal politics. For example, in a speech at the City Liberal Club in April 1894 he suggested that it was now becoming apparent that the Liberal party had, 'apart from the Irish question, undergone great transformations:'

> The era of liberation, which formed the political capital of the Liberalism of the last half century—and a noble heritage it was— has practically passed away, because liberation is accomplished. What has now to be accomplished is an era of reconstruction. In an era of reconstruction, that dangerous, difficult, and delicate task, many may lend their hand who have felt alienated from the Liberal party in the course of what we believe to have been an era of liberation.[4]

---

[1] Morley, *Gladstone*, ii, pp. 412–13.
[2] The Marquess of Crewe, *Lord Rosebery*, vol. i, 1931, p. 347.
[3] Hamer, *Personal Papers of Lord Rendel*, p. 95.
[4] *Liberal Magazine*, vol. 2, no. 8 (May 1894), p. 114.

He even took up the Gladstonian word 'construction'. The 'enfranchising times of Liberalism' had almost passed, he declared; now 'the time of construction has begun'. This explained why there was so much uncertainty in Liberal politics: 'Constructive legislation must be largely experimental legislation, and experimental legislation is much more liable to disappoint, much more liable to mistakes, much more difficult, much more alive with pitfalls and with obstacles than the mere removing of the disabilities of others.'[1]

The Liberal party had its existence also within a party system, that is it was one of the two major political parties between which voters chose at general elections. Its nature and purpose were, therefore, necessarily formed and changed to a very large extent in relationship to the nature and purpose of the other main party with which it was perpetually being compared. If Conservatism changed, so must Liberalism; and a predominant Liberal political emotion at this time was unease about the 'opportunism' of the Tories, their readiness to take up reform policies to which they had only a short time before appeared to be fundamentally opposed, their disinclination to play the role, which Liberals alleged was traditionally theirs, of wicked opponents of all reform and progress. A. J. Mundella expressed a disquiet that was increasingly characteristic of Liberals when he wrote in 1871: 'The worst feature of the modern politics is, to my mind, the absence of a really honest opposition. It is dangerous work when the professed advocates of Conservatism are prepared to go all lengths for the attainment of power.'[2] Gladstone referred in 1885 to his great anxiety about the condition of Conservatism which under the influence of Churchill and 'demagogy' seemed to be moving far from the Conservatism that he had known in earlier days.[3] Some welcomed this. In 1885 Chamberlain had made much of the Tories' 'power of assimilating even the most advanced proposals' and had even argued that it was possible 'that this

[1] *Liberal Magazine*, vol. 3, no. 26 (November 1895), p. 465.
[2] Mundella to R. Leader, 23 October 1871, Mundella MSS., folio IX.
[3] Morley, *Gladstone*, ii, pp. 412–13, 461. In October 1885 Gladstone told Hamilton that 'Bright like myself deplores the state of the Conservative party more than any thing else. If only that party had men of the old Tory stamp, I would not lift up my little finger to disturb them from office.' Sir E. Hamilton's diary, B.M. Add. MS. 48641, folio 114 (18 October 1885).

country could not be better governed than by a Conservative Ministry in an insignificant minority' and 'under the eyes of a watchful Liberal majority'.[1] Harcourt wrote in November 1886 to John Morley, who regarded Harcourt as the arch-opportunist among the Liberal leaders, that 'the rapid conversion of the Tories to Radical measures quickens the speed of Radical progress. Measures which used to take years to carry are now swallowed by their opponents in as many weeks. This makes it possible and right for us to push forward our programme far more rapidly than in former times.'[2] Harcourt believed that Liberals 'ought to rejoice at this whole conversion of the Tories to their own creed. What can be a more complete vindication of Liberal policy than this clear proof that the Tories cannot dispense with it?'[3] But to many Liberals such an attitude meant placing the foundations of their party on constantly shifting sands. In it lay no prospect of stability or security or sense of clear identity and purpose in Liberal politics. No one was more worried about this than Gladstone to whom opinions such as those expressed by Harcourt represented all that was wrong in 'modern' politics. In 1885 he lamented that the Tories 'cannot see that the further they go, the more extreme must infallibly be the Radical programme, which they professedly so dislike'. The Radicals were bound to try to 'overtrump' the Tories; and so the country would become 'demoralised by the political parties and their bidding one against another'.[4] In a conversation with Sir Edward Hamilton in 1892 Gladstone 'bewailed the present position of parties. It was no longer a fight between Liberals & Conservatives: Conservatives had lost all their principles and had disappeared: it had become a race between two parties, one outbidding the other'.[5] The Home Rule issue, and in particular the coercion

[1] Lucy, *Speeches of Joseph Chamberlain*, pp. 227, 229.
[2] 20 November 1886, Harcourt MSS.
[3] Sir E. Hamilton's diary, B.M. Add. MS. 48645, folio 16 (25 October 1886).
[4] Sir E. Hamilton's diary, B.M. Add. MS. 48641, folios 105–6 (15 October 1885). By 1887 Gladstone was saying that 'all Radical innovations proceeded from the party which styled itself Conservative'. Sir E. Hamilton's diary, B.M. Add. MS. 48646, folio 30 (1 May 1887).
[5] Sir E. Hamilton's diary, B.M. Add. MS. 48657, folios 105–6 (29 March 1892). On 9 February 1893 Gladstone said to Hamilton that the impulse to 'socialistic legislation' came 'mainly from the party that pleased to call themselves Conservative. It was impossible for him to believe that the present Conservatives were the

controversy, after 1885 seemed to some Liberals to re-establish the clear-cut traditional division between the parties.[1] But, the Irish question apart, the inability of Liberals to define clearly what it was that distinguished them from the Tories and justified their claim to be the alternative to them seemed only to be intensifying. Indeed, the Home Rule issue itself can be seen as contributing to the worsening of this confusion, because views on it had become accepted as the *sole* criterion of party allegiance, irrespective of what one's views on other topics might happen to be—and these views seemed to have become very intermingled. In 1888 Arnold Morley noted of one Conservative candidate that he had 'adopted almost the entire programme of the Liberal party, with the one exception of Home Rule'; while John Morley observed that 'the Tories are able to make the fear of Irish H.R. an excuse for any amount of transformation'.[2]

Especially among the younger Liberals and the Roseberyites, the idea gained favour that the old party divisions were now becoming irrelevant, that new issues and new tendencies of thought were creating a need for new political arrangements. Sir Edward Grey wrote in 1896 of how the country was 'bored with both parties'. 'Party lines are faint & confused just now & there cannot be much merit in conforming strictly to them.'[3] Rosebery was to carry this attitude to an extreme by claiming that party division itself was unnatural and unnecessary. After the 1895 election defeat there were, not surprisingly, many who wondered whether Liberalism might not now be played out and whether the existing party system, with the Liberal party as one of the two main parties, might not soon disappear —though there was no clear idea as to what might replace it. James Stansfeld said in April 1895 that he thought that the Liberal party was very probably soon going to be 'succeeded by a Party of the Centre'. What he feared was the development

representatives of the party to which he belonged 50 years ago. Two generations ago they often no doubt made mistakes but they believed in their own tenets. Now they were embarking on a most perilous course, but did not believe in what they advocated.' B.M. Add. MS. 48659, folios 109–10.

[1] Hamer, *John Morley*, pp. 193–4.
[2] Arnold Morley to Gladstone, 29 March 1888, Gladstone MSS., B.M. Add. MS. 44253, folio 176. Morley to Haldane, 29 January 1888, Haldane MSS., MS. 5903, folio 77.
[3] Grey to Rosebery, 6 September 1896, Rosebery MSS., Box 23.

of a system of sections or of groups, as on the Continent, rather than of alternative government parties which were 'composite' in character.[1] H. H. Fowler similarly warned of the danger of 'the system of groups' and argued in favour of a system 'where each party practically represented nearly half the nation'.[2]

There were thus, it seemed, two alternative prospects before the Liberal party according to the development of the party system. Either the party system would be replaced by some different kind of system, such as that of 'groups', to which Liberalism would contribute by the final separation of its component sections, or the party system would remain but with some new principles or bases of division between the parties. It was the latter prospect that particularly worried many Liberals who associated it with the growth of class division and class conflict in politics. In 1898 Fowler predicted 'the disruption of the Liberal party and the ultimate division of parties into the Haves and the Have-nots'.[3]

The fear that party divisions and class divisions might come to coincide became an obsession with many Liberals in the last two decades of the nineteenth century. To them it seemed that such a development must mean the end of the Liberal party in the form in which it had developed during the century. The prevailing view of the traditional nature of the Liberal party can be illustrated from the Report presented to the Newcastle conference of the N.L.F. in 1891. This argues that in Britain 'a Labour party independent of party considerations cannot assume any real magnitude' for the time being because the burning questions which dominate British politics and which have not yet been solved, such as the House of Lords, the 'privileged Church', and the restricted franchise, are questions which 'create dividing lines *in the whole community*' and not the class lines to which the existence of a Labour party must relate.[4] But, if class conflict took over the field of political action, Liberalism would be crushed between the embattled forces of labour and capital which it had traditionally asserted had fundamental interests in common. Developments in Belgium

[1] "Eighty" Club. *The Liberal Party & Labour and European Armaments*, [1895], pp. 18–19.
[2] Fowler, *Life of Viscount Wolverhampton*, pp. 405–7.
[3] Ibid., p. 439.
[4] *N.L.F. Report 1891*, pp. 21–2 (my italics).

caused Liberals considerable alarm at this period. In 1893 Sir Charles Dilke told 'moderate men' to be 'warned by the example of what had recently happened in Belgium, where the moderate Liberals had been promptly suffocated between the two opposing forces of Toryism and Socialism, as they were too pretentious to submit to Tory discipline and too slavish to become frankly democratic'.[1] Rosebery wrote after the 1895 election defeat: 'It is always possible that that may happen here which has happened in Belgium—the elimination of Liberalism, leaving the two forces of Socialism and Reaction face to face.' 'Whether that shall happen here', he added, 'depends on the Liberal Party.'[2] Herbert Samuel told the 1896 N.L.F. that they could find 'in Germany and Belgium instances of the complete collapse of Liberal parties owing to their not recognising fully' the need for them to adopt policies for the promotion of social reform by the use of the power of the State.[3] For all these men what alone Liberalism could stand for was the reconciliation of classes and the prevention of class conflict.

It would, therefore, be fatal for the Liberal party if it came to represent only one class. The essential feature of Liberalism was seen as being that it was a 'national' creed and the basis of a 'national' party. Mundella once wrote that it was 'our natural function' as Liberals to be 'always treading on somebody's toes or at least on their prejudices' because 'we seek the good of the whole and not of a class'.[4] James Bryce was expressing a general feeling among Liberals about the nature of their party when he said in 1894 that their concern was always 'for the welfare of the nation as a whole': 'They had never consented to be the organ of a class, or sought to put forward the interests of a class.'[5] But mainly through the desertion of the party by the middle classes and their flight into Conservatism, the Liberal party nevertheless did seem to be turning into such a party before the Liberals' very eyes. Writing in January 1888,

[1] Gwynn and Tuckwell, *Life of Dilke*, ii, p. 291.
[2] Rosebery to Canon Scott Holland, 21 August 1895, Rosebery MSS., Box 88, letter copy-book, folio 19.
[3] *N.L.F. Report 1896*, p. 83.
[4] Mundella to H. J. Wilson, 6 January 1876, H. J. Wilson MSS., Sheffield Univ. Library, Box 2.
[5] *Liberal Magazine*, vol. 2, no. 2 (March 1894), p. 36.

Haldane commented on the reversal of roles that was taking place: the Tories were becoming the 'national' party, whereas to a very large degree 'the vote which supports Liberalism has become a class vote'. Liberals must take positive counter-action to arrest this tendency. They must adopt policies that would restore them to the old position of receiving support from all classes and thus 'rescue us from the stigma of being a class party'.[1] This was a constant theme with Rosebery and his followers. Asquith believed that, if the Liberal party was to succeed, it must appeal 'to all sober-minded and level-headed men in all strata of the community', and this it could do only by convincing the people that it was a 'national party', 'distinguished in tradition, in principle, in spirit from those to whom it is opposed—a party which neither fears nor favours classes or interests'.[2] Rosebery himself became more and more worried that the effect of Liberal policies, such as Harcourt's death duties Budget of 1894, was to alienate the propertied classes and thus bring about a 'horizontal division of parties'.[3]

Harcourt, on the other hand, saw this as an inevitable trend and one which Liberals should welcome. In his opinion, since the great mass of voters were men with little or no property, a 'horizontal division' would produce, not two fairly evenly balanced parties, but a great preponderance for the Liberal party.[4] Clearly, however, Harcourt and Rosebery had very different situations in mind. Harcourt's vision closely resembled the theme of conflict between 'the classes and the masses' of which Gladstone had been wont to make so much, for example in his appeals to 'the nation' in 1879–80. Rosebery and his followers saw, and wished to avert, the possibility of the conversion of the Liberal party into an exclusively working-class party. Rosebery wished to preserve 'the variety and richness and intellectual forces' of the old party.[5] There was, as he perceived, a weakness in Harcourt's position. Harcourt gave

[1] Haldane, 'The Liberal Party and its Prospects', pp. 146–7, 160; 'The Liberal Creed', p. 465.
[2] *The Mission of Liberalism. A Speech Delivered by the Right Hon. H. H. Asquith, K.C., M.P., at the Hotel Cecil, On July 19th, 1901*, 1901, p. 12.
[3] Stansky, *Ambitions and Strategies*, p. 131. James, *Rosebery*, p. 342. Rosebery to the Lord Chancellor, 27 March 1894, Rosebery MSS., Box 88, letter copy-book, folio 8. Sir E. Hamilton's diary, B.M. Add. MS. 48663, folios 49–50 (28 March 1894).
[4] Stansky, *Ambitions and Strategies*, p. 131.   [5] James, *Rosebery*, p. 342.

no appearance of having fully thought out the consequences for policy of the 'cleavage of classes', and some of the policies about which he was most enthusiastic, such as local option, scarcely encouraged Liberals to 'hope for much enthusiasm or active support from the masses'.

If Liberalism could survive only by continuing to enjoy both working-class and middle-class support, then the crucial feature of Liberal strategy had to be to ensure that the balance between labour and capital, between working class and middle class, between non-property and property, was kept in such a way that efforts to retain or secure support on one side did not produce an alienation of support on the other. This was a very delicate matter, and the Liberal leaders engaged in frequent calculations as to how to arrive at this point of balance. The theory that Liberalism represented the interest of the community as a whole, over and above the interests of labour and capital, and that it was its duty to hold these two in a balance so as to ensure that neither became excessively predominant in the community, was invoked to justify resistance to the turning of the party into a party only of the working class. J. A. Simon wrote in *Essays in Liberalism* in 1897 that, while the historic function of preserving a balance between labour and capital had hitherto meant supporting the workers against the greatly superior power of the employers, 'it is well to remember that a time may come when the very success of this policy may make it necessary to change the form of its expression'. For it was 'only so long as the balance is seriously uneven' and the forces of capitalism much stronger than the forces of labour that 'the weight of Liberalism can be rightly flung exclusively in the lighter scale'. The 'problem of the *limits* to the rights of labour' was no longer a matter of merely theoretic interest to Liberals.[1]

For a time, as John Morley was to note,[2] the Home Rule issue had overlain and concealed the development of these problems and of class division in party politics. The Liberal party had been able to delay deciding on a labour and social policy. Indeed, to some Liberals Home Rule itself was a good issue on which to focus the attention of the new 'democracy' because it was not directly related to people's own 'selfish'

---

[1] *Essays in Liberalism*, pp. 100–1.   [2] Hamer, *John Morley*, p. 318.

class interests. Devotion to securing Home Rule for Ireland, at the sacrifice of attention to domestic reform questions, was 'unselfish' and to be commended. Chamberlain was condemned for having appealed to the instincts of 'selfishness' in 1885 by asking the agricultural labourers 'to use their new votes for their own class advantage'.[1] After the split in the party Arnold Morley, the Chief Whip, said that the Liberal Unionists were appealing to 'selfish interests' when they urged people 'to shelve the Irish question in order that matters more immediately concerning themselves might be dealt with'. It was, he said, very gratifying that such appeals has not been heeded and that 'the first question to which the enlarged English electorate addressed itself was one which did not affect its own interests'.[2] The arguments which some Liberals used about the Home Rule cause read almost like responses to Bagehot's warning in his introduction to the second edition of *The English Constitution* (1872) that politicians had a duty not to raise questions which 'will excite the lower orders of mankind', 'will bind the poor as a class together', and 'will excite them against the rich'.[3] Gladstone's handling of the Home Rule issue involved much emphasis on it as a 'moral' and 'national' cause transcending class and sectional interests. In 1892, for example, he appealed to working men to give preference to Home Rule over the question of the eight-hour day and thus sacrifice their 'own views and apparent interests' to a 'wider and weightier cause'.[4] Gladstone felt intensely about this aspect of the Home Rule cause. To him it was morally superior because people in devoting themselves to it were rising above 'selfish' material interests. Just how deeply he felt can be gauged from a letter which he wrote to John Morley in 1892 on the eight-hour day question:

I am vexed to see portions of the labouring class beginning to be

[1] Acton to Gladstone, 2 February 1885, Figgis and Laurence, *Selections From the Correspondence of the First Lord Acton*, i, p. 199.
[2] *The Times*, 7 December 1887, p. 5. For similar statements by John Morley see *The Times*, 5 May 1892, p. 6; 6 July 1892, p. 11. Hamer, *John Morley*, pp. 192–3. Cf. also J. Guinness Rogers, 'The Middle Class and the new Liberalism', *N.C.*, no. 152 (October 1889), p. 712.
[3] pp. 275–8 of the Fontana edition, 1963.
[4] 'An Appeal to the West Nottingham Miners from Mr Gladstone' (pamphlet reproducing the text of a letter from Gladstone to H. Broadhurst, 1 July 1892), Gladstone MSS., B.M. Add. MS. 44515, folio 86.

corrupted by the semblance of power as the other classes have been tainted & warped by its reality; and I am disgusted by finding a portion of them ready to thrust Ireland, which is so far ahead in claim, entirely into the background. Poor, poor, poor human nature. Let me treat you to Trench's lines:

> That we, who do our lineage high
> Draw from beyond the starry sky,
> Are yet upon the other side
> To earth and to its dust allied.[1]

Although Gladstone and the other Liberals who thought in this way directed their accusations of appealing to 'selfish instincts' mainly at the Liberal Unionists, the Radicals who remained within the Gladstonian fold also frequently expressed the view that the preoccupation with Home Rule was unsatisfactory and should at least be modified because it was not related to the immediate personal interests of the non-Irish voters. Thus L. A. Atherley-Jones remarked on the great indifference of the English masses to 'the woes of Ireland' and argued that Liberals should feel concerned that they were concentrating on a question in which the English 'mechanic or labourer has—so far at least as his vision extends—no personal interest': 'it does not concern him; it is not a question of his right to vote, of his political, social, or religious status'.[2] But the very fact that it was not such a question was the reason why other Liberals welcomed the concentration on Home Rule. Labouchere was another Radical who advanced the kind of argument which represented the very opposite of the priorities in which these Liberals believed. 'Depend upon it', he wrote 'we shall only win on Home Rule by making it a mere portion of liberalism everywhere. . . . What an English elector wants is an issue in which his interests are personally concerned. Let us get every occupier and every taxpayer to realize that they will benefit by a Liberal Administration, and that they are losing by a Conservative Administration, and we shall win.'[3]

The weakening of the Home Rule cause in 1891 and the certainty that the Liberals would have to turn to some other

[1] 22 August 1892, Gladstone MSS., B.M. Add. MS. 44256, folio 234.
[2] Atherley-Jones, 'The New Liberalism', p. 189.
[3] Labouchere to H. Gladstone, 31 March [1888], Gladstone MSS., B.M. Add. MS. 46016, folio 130.

kind of politics forced the Liberal leaders to turn their attention once more to the problem of the relationship between Liberal policy and the 'personal interests' of the mass of voters. Some of them could see what had all along lain behind, and been held in check by, the Irish preoccupation—a flood of demands for attention to labour and social questions. Lord Ripon observed that, if Home Rule were displaced from its position as the main Liberal policy, 'a whole series of labour questions would come to the front'.[1] In the reactions of Liberals to this prospect one sees the first signs of that very uneasy balance between the desire to resist these new pressures and the feeling that it might be more desirable and expedient to appease and contain them which was henceforth to characterize Liberalism. Munro Ferguson reported to Rosebery on 11 February 1891 that there 'has been a great turn from Irish affairs to Labour & Capital' among Liberals in the country; but two months later he was reporting that he found Liberals in Scotland 'disposed to be cautious as to labour legislation'.[2] A letter written at this time by Robert Reid to Schnadhorst about the Newcastle programme shows the same balance of conflicting instincts. On the one hand, he wrote, there should be no resolution at Newcastle concerning 'labour' because the 'proposals of the working men leaders' were not 'sufficiently definite' and because it would not be right 'to create difficulties for those of our own leaders who have strong views or have had them'. Their attitudes must not be changed forcibly but through 'the effect of time'. The furthest that Gladstone should go was to talk in general terms about being 'deeply anxious to remedy the conditions of the poorer workers', ready to 'consider with open mind any sincere proposals', and aware of 'real grievances'. But, on the other hand, there was no doubt that 'a really forward policy in domestic affairs is an absolute necessity'. For, if the Liberals did not 'broadly recognize' the new concern for social reform '& resolutely affirm our willingness to keep abreast of it, the disparity between the evils revealed & our legislative proposals will dispirit our friends & throw a good many into the camp of socialism'. It was important to express 'a friendly disposition to the workmen on labour questions' in order to

[1] Ripon to Gladstone, 30 December 1890, Wolf, *Life of Ripon*, ii, pp. 199–200.
[2] Ferguson to Rosebery, 11 February, 3 April 1891, Rosebery MSS., Box 14.

combat the 'idea that we are wedded to a capitalist or employer point of view as opposed to the point of view of the employed'.¹ In other words, working men had to be persuaded to believe that the Liberals were holding a fair balance. One notes, in particular, the use of the classic Liberal concept of the 'open mind' and the emphasis on the creation of feeling, of a state of mind, rather than on the production of specific policies.

Schnadhorst's own advice to Gladstone on the development of Liberal policy followed similar lines. The Liberals were, he warned, 'in more danger from division now than we have been for some time & I fear the blame is not entirely on the side of the workers'. And yet all that the Liberals could safely offer 'labour' was 'land, Home Rule in the villages & sympathetic references to efforts to reduce the hours of labour'. Nothing definite could actually be done about this last question since opinion on it in the party was so divided; therefore, it was all the more 'necessary that sympathy should be expressed with all efforts to raise the worker'.² Nothing could better express the paralysis that was overcoming the development of Liberal policy.³ Since the two sides of the labour–capital balance had to be kept in harmony, 'sympathy' and expression of feeling had to be substitutes for action which would disrupt that balance. The Irish preoccupation had enabled the Liberals to divorce 'sympathy' from the pressure for commitment and action.⁴ But now they no longer possessed any plausible means of explaining their inability to give practical effect to their feelings.

The demand for the enforcement by law of a maximum working day of eight hours was indeed a crucial issue in this regard and one which caused deep divisions in the Liberal party and leadership. To Gladstone, as we have seen, the

---

¹ This letter, dated 16 September 1891, was enclosed in a letter from Schnadhorst to Gladstone, 21 September, Gladstone MSS., B.M. Add. MS. 44295, folios 253–5.
² Schnadhorst to Gladstone, 25 September 1891, Gladstone MSS., B.M. Add. MS. 44295, folio 258.
³ This paralysis is also evident in one sequel to this discussion. According to F. A. Channing, a proposal that there should be a resolution in the 'Newcastle programme' on railwaymen's hours of work was accepted by Schnadhorst but then 'shelved by timid counsels at Headquarters'. Channing, *Memories of Midland Politics*, pp. 115, 117.
⁴ Hamer, *John Morley*, p. 242.

demand represented 'selfish' class instincts and he condemned it as such in contrast to the Home Rule question.[1] John Morley opposed yielding to it as a surrender of principle for reasons of electoral opportunism.[2] To many the principle that was at stake was basic to the maintenance of the labour–capital balance on which the survival of Liberalism depended. This form of State intervention and regulation would mean the supplanting of the trade unions in some of their principal functions, such as negotiating with employers for better conditions of work, and would thus weaken them by making them so much less necessary for workers who would look instead to the State and to their ability to influence the use of the power of the State through the ballot box. It was felt by many Liberals that the introduction of a shorter working day and other such changes in industrial life ought to come about through negotiation and voluntary agreement between employers and workers rather than be imposed by the State. Some Liberals went to considerable lengths to help keep the State out of this area of industrial life. Sir William Mather, the great Lancashire industrialist, having introduced the eight-hour day in his own works, retired from Parliament in 1895 in order, as he put it, to 'devote myself to the conversion of my co-employers in Lancashire to the new views on shorter hours': 'To avert the growing demand for legislation on the hours of labour of adult men, by causing the employers to meet the demand voluntarily, would be to save Parliament from degradation and our industries from serious perils.'[3] If this could be done, the balance between labour and capital would be maintained, and the Liberal idea of the State, as a superior force embodying the community interest and not having to come down on one side or the other in industrial issues, would be preserved. Harcourt once described the 'principle of Government interference in strikes' as 'questionable' because it involved the need for a government to take one side or the other.[4] All depended, of

---

[1] The letter to Morley quoted above, p. 226, illustrates this.
[2] Hamer, *John Morley*, pp. 258–9.
[3] Mather to Rosebery, 30 June 1895, L. E. Mather (ed.), *The Right Honourable Sir William Mather, P.C., L.L.D., M.Inst.C.E. 1838–1920*, [1925], p. 156. Mather to Harcourt, 27 January 1895, Harcourt MSS. See also Bassett, *Life of John Edward Ellis*, pp. 102–3.
[4] Harcourt to L. V. Harcourt, 12 April 1903, Harcourt MSS.

course, on whether one believed that the free play of forces—here represented by voluntary negotiations—had an ordering effect and would perpetuate harmony and balance. There were Liberals who could see that direct confrontation between employers and unions had to involve recourse to at least the threat of lock-outs or strikes. Labour spokesmen, indeed, accused anti-Eight Hours Liberals of forcing unions into reliance on the strike weapon. More and more Liberals were coming to see class war and industrial strife as inherent in the classical Liberal principles and to prefer the exercise by the State of a stabilizing and class-war-preventing role. Intervention too, as in an Eight Hours Bill, could be in the community interest.

One of the most important of the pressures that were involving the Liberals in 'class questions' whether they liked it or not was the need to find new sources of revenue to meet rising government expenditure, especially on defence. The taxation primarily of land such as many Liberals and Radicals continued to concentrate on advocating maintained the ideological alliance of capital and labour by being aimed at the old enemy of the 'industrious classes', the landed class. But, as Rosebery indicated in his alarmed reaction to the Budget of 1894, the principle of graduating taxation so that the rich paid at a higher rate than the poor—which was the only principle that would ensure an almost indefinitely expandable source of State revenue—did seem to be introducing class distinctions into governmental policy. The principle of avoiding the identification or isolation of classes through the taxation system was understood to be fundamental to traditional Liberal or Gladstonian finance. Many Liberals judged policies according to this criterion above any other. For example, in 1885 A. J. Mundella commented on Chamberlain's 'free education' proposals: 'I am quite ready to propound a scheme if Taxation can be so adjusted as not to press too heavily on any one class. I want *all to benefit by and be interested in* our Educational system, and so to arrange it that no Class Agitation or reaction is likely to follow.'[1] But what was lacking as yet was any scheme for using the increased revenue for social reform. The taking of

[1] Mundella to H. J. Wilson, 25 September 1885, H. J. Wilson MSS., Sheffield Univ. Library, Box 2.

money from the rich to compensate the poor for their poverty and thus level incomes was what many Liberals understood 'socialism' to involve.

To many Liberals it seemed that the vital necessity was to construct a Liberalism that was concerned with social reform and that was ready to meet the emergence of urgent social demands and problems. Typical of these Liberals was the concern expressed by H. H. Fowler in 1887 'that while we play with politics great social questions are rising up which before long may let loose a deluge upon us'.[1] But equally important was to prevent Liberalism from becoming Socialism as the result of this process of adaptation. Liberalism had to offer both an attractive and a viable alternative to Socialism. In particular, it must involve the kind of social reform that would avert the class conflict which Socialism was believed to threaten. A group of Liberals particularly concerned to reconstruct Liberalism on these lines were the young 'Liberal Imperialists' who began to become active in the late 1880s. They and the older Liberals, such as John Morley, who sympathized with what they were trying to do, looked increasingly to Lord Rosebery as the leader to promote this reconstruction of Liberalism. And Rosebery himself gradually became aware of the role that he was being expected to play. In December 1892 he commented thus on a report that he might be prepared to serve as Foreign Secretary in an administration headed by the Duke of Devonshire, the former Lord Hartington:

> He must stick to his own party; especially as they were so devoid of leading power; for the fact was not only Mr. G., but Harcourt & J. Morley were not in touch with the new order of things & ideas. 'Cobden-ism' was coming to an end; new doctrines were being developed; & fresh wants were being created. He did not feel at all sure that the aspirations of the new democracy would be realised; but at any rate experiments on new lines would have to be tried, & tried by those who had loosened their old moorings.[2]

---

[1] As reported in Ferguson to Rosebery, 30 August 1887, Rosebery MSS., Box 14.

[2] Sir E. Hamilton's diary, B.M. Add. MS. 48659, folio 60 (18 December 1892). In August 1891 Morley urged Rosebery to expound 'a practicable socialism'. Viscount Morley, *Recollections*, vol. i, 1917, p. 313.

In 1888 Haldane urged Liberals to begin formulating their attitude to a question that 'may prove to be of profound moment as regards the future of Liberalism': 'the relations of labour and capital'. It was urgent for them to counter the efforts that 'the extreme Socialist party' was making to 'mould the new voters to its wishes'. There must be no class-war Socialism in the Liberal programme, for this would destroy Liberalism by completing the alienation of the middle class; but at the same time Liberals must 'throw off that indifference to the relations of labour and capital which has characterized the Liberal party in the past, and which has allowed a Socialistic party to grow up'.[1] For Haldane the essential feature of the social reform which Liberals would offer had to be that it would retain or win the support of both middle and working classes. Haldane constantly warned Liberals that it would be futile—as well as fundamentally wrong—to try to cultivate working men as a class or voting block or to offer them 'remedies for grievances as a mere exchange for votes'. 'They must', he said, 'remember first that the working man was not altogether a predictable quantity; he was flesh and blood, often with a good bit of Toryism in his composition, and working men could not be counted on as a solid and united body.' What would impress the working class and 'touch their hearts and imagination' was not the putting forward of 'class' measures which they were incorrectly assumed as a body to want but the demonstration by Liberals that 'they were in earnest' and 'believed with their whole soul in what they advocated'—*whatever that might be.* (In this Haldane was reflecting the widespread belief as to the basis of Gladstone's appeal to working men.)[2] The basic proposition which Haldane wished to induce Liberals to accept, and which he believed would halt the trend towards class politics, was that 'a democracy has not got, as is assumed in practice, a body of definite opinions for the expression of which in Parliament it is seeking for delegates, but that it is an assembly of human beings earnestly seeking guidance from those of whose sympathies it is sure'.[3] Liberals must realize that there

[1] Haldane, 'The Liberal Party and its Prospects', pp. 145, 149, 153, 160.
[2] *N.L.F. Report 1897*, p. 96. Hansard, 3rd Series, vol. 328, cc. 638–9 (6 July 1888).
[3] Haldane to Ferguson, 4 November 1889, Haldane MSS., MS. 5903, folio 141.

was no necessity for them to be offering class reforms. Other Liberal Imperialists adopted a similar attitude. Asquith wrote about 'people who are both ignorant and dumb' as regards policies and ideas but who 'are crying for leadership' founded on 'intuition, constructive imagination, and hard-headed audacity'.[1]

In 1889 another prominent member of this group, R. Munro Ferguson, appealed to Rosebery to 'define a policy' that would guide Liberals on the question of relations between labour and capital. He raised one particular problem: 'How far is Liberalism as we understand it, & Socialism, meaning a rapid extinguishing of private property without compensation—to be held as distinct creeds?'[2] The 'Liberal Imperialists' decided to try to find out and, especially in the years 1889 to 1892, they worked at constructing a bridge between Liberalism and Socialism by means of contacts with the Fabians.[3] Another, and related, bridge-building operation was the Progressive party on the London County Council. The danger of the extinction of Liberalism through the emergence of the politics of class conflict was felt to be particularly acute in London, and Rosebery himself was associated with this Socialist–Liberal alliance in London.[4]

Liberal intellectuals searched for a creed or a set of principles that could be used to justify and to direct and control attention by Liberals to social reform and yet at the same time be definitely non-Socialist. T. H. Green had pointed the way with his work on redefining concern for individual liberty so

[1] J. A. Spender and C. Asquith, *Life of Herbert Henry Asquith, Lord Oxford and Asquith*, vol. i, 1932, p. 101.

[2] Ferguson to Rosebery, 20 and 29 September 1889, Rosebery MSS., Box 14.

[3] A. M. McBriar, *Fabian Socialism and English Politics 1884–1918*, Cambridge, 1966, p. 242. B. Webb, *My Apprenticeship*, 1929, p. 352. For Haldane's reaction to the Fabians see his letter to Elizabeth Haldane, 30 January 1891, Haldane MSS., MS. 6010, folio 83, and Ferguson to Rosebery, 1 September 1891, Rosebery MSS., Box 14. It seemed to Haldane that the *Fabian Essays* indicated ways in which traditional Liberal principles and themes could be adapted and brought up to date. He told Rosebery that they placed 'the old antagonism between classes and masses' in 'a new and fuller light': 'Here at last is a spirit in which the relations of labour and capital can be approached anew and more profitably by the statesman, and here is a new context for John Morley's phrase about equality of opportunity.' 6 June 1894, Rosebery MSS., Box 24.

[4] For the impact of class politics on Liberalism in London and the history of the Progressive alliance, see P. Thompson, *Socialists, Liberals and Labour The Struggle for London 1885–1914*, 1967, *passim* and especially Chapter V.

as to place that liberty in a social context and so as to justify State intervention in social problems in the interests of its protection.[1] The aim of reconciling non-Socialist Liberalism with policies extending such intervention underlies much of the Liberal political writing of the period 1886 to 1905: in the articles and books of R. B. Haldane and L. T. Hobhouse, for example; in the *Essays in Liberalism* of 1897; and in *The Heart of the Empire*, published in 1901, in which a group of young Liberal intellectuals set about devising Liberal principles and policies for dealing with the urgent social problems of London. The spirit of their activity is perhaps seen best in the 'Rainbow Circle', a small group of politicians, journalists, and economists, such as Herbert Samuel, Charles Trevelyan, and J. A. Hobson, formed in the late 1890s to debate 'the New Liberalism' and its position with regard to the principle of 'liberty'. They rejected Socialism and aimed at averting a split between Liberalism and Labour: Ramsay MacDonald was associated with them in the years immediately preceding his becoming Secretary of the new Labour Representation Committee.[2] In the first issue of the *Progressive Review*, the short-lived journal which they founded in 1896, they declared that there was an 'urgent need of a re-formation and re-statement of the principles of Progress in terms which shall include and give due emphasis to the new ideas and sentiments of social justice and of a clear rational application of those principles in a progressive policy and a progressive party'.[3]

A year later the *Progressive Review* wrote of the party being split possibly beyond hope of ever being reunited by the issue of the role of the State in regard to social, economic, and industrial problems.[4] Certainly the rise of 'the social question' was tearing apart traditional Radicalism. Bradlaugh, Henry Fawcett, Labouchere, John Morley, and others who had been regarded at least up to the 1870s as thoroughly Radical in the senses in which Radicalism was then principally defined began to appear and be denounced as very conservative when the controversy shifted to demands for State intervention in economic and

[1] M. Richter, *The Politics of Conscience. T. H. Green and his Age*, 1964.
[2] Samuel, *Memoirs*, pp. 24–6. B. Porter, *Critics of Empire British Radical attitudes to colonialism in Africa 1895–1914*, 1968, pp. 156 ff.
[3] Vol. i, no. 1, p. 3.
[4] Vol. ii, no. 12 (September 1897), p. 490.

industrial life. After 1895 there was a rift between those Radicals, such as Labouchere, who wished to continue concentrating on 'manhood suffrage', 'one man one vote', abolition of the House of Lords, and other traditional political reforms of this kind, and those, such as Sir Charles Dilke, who wanted the Radicals to take up industrial questions which appealed to the working classes.

By now there was appearing a fundamental division in the form of the reaction of Liberals against Socialism. With some, such as these Radicals, the reaction was entirely negative. But with others, such as the Liberal Imperialists, the reaction can be called positive in that it involved a concern to out-bid the Socialists, to devise a more attractive alternative that might eliminate and not just oppose Socialism. To them the danger of a purely negative response was that it could have a polarising effect and actually hasten on the development of that class conflict which it was the basic purpose of Liberalism to avert.

The main problem for such Liberals was to find a way of justifying social reform that would prevent it from appearing to be the product of pressure from working-class voters. For such an appearance could destroy Liberalism and help Socialism by accelerating the flight of the middle class into the Conservative fold. Social reform had necessarily to concern itself mainly with the ills of working people. If Liberalism were to survive as a distinctive creed, it had to discover some way of demonstrating to all that such reform was for the benefit of the whole community and was being undertaken not in response to electoral pressure from the working class but under the guidance of the principle of a transcending community interest. Some Liberals were to find in Liberal Imperialism and the related idea of 'national efficiency' the solution to this dilemma.

X Liberal Leaders and the Reconstruction of Liberal Politics

AFTER the 1895 election defeat most of the Liberal leaders shrank from taking any positive initiatives to reconstruct the party or devise any new basis for its policy. The lesson that they seemed to draw from the experiences of 1892–5 was that the party simply would not respond to such initiatives and that therefore they were wasting their time in making them. They felt that now the best strategy was to play a waiting game and rely principally on the effects of reaction against their opponents. They did, and wished to do, little or nothing to develop new policy. Instead they concentrated on attacking the Unionist government and exposing its alleged blunders—only to prove, as in the episode of the South African committee, for instance, that they were not very good even at that. The principal practitioner of this style of leadership was Harcourt who was leader of the party in the House of Commons until the end of 1898 and was widely regarded as leader in the country after Rosebery's resignation in October 1896. Harcourt had little capacity for constructing policy. His main strength was as a parliamentarian and a political campaigner, and his boisterous anti-Tory speeches made him popular with the rank and file. But his speeches contained few positive ideas concerning policy.[1] After 1895 the leadership that he offered the Liberals was entirely negative, possibly because

[1] 'Was not that a fine speech of Harcourts?', wrote Mundella to J. D. Leader, 5 October 1879. 'He has excelled himself in it, yet withal I distrust his Liberalism. If ever he gets into a commanding position, he will turn out a very poor reformer. He may help us to turn out the Government, but he will be slow to deal with *great* reforms.' Mundella MSS., folio IX.

of what had happened when he had taken a positive initiative with the local option policy. Now he seemed to believe that all that the party should have, or could respond to, were stirring anti-Tory speeches, vigorous and larded with boisterous wit, but largely devoid of any effort at constructing positive alternative policy. Harcourt was not a constructive leader. Sir Edward Hamilton made a very accurate assessment of him in his diary entry of 17 June 1885: 'When in opposition he is in his real element. Indeed he ought, if he is to be seen to the fullest advantage, to be in perpetual opposition.' Rosebery described 'slashing attack' as Harcourt's '*forte*'.[1] Harcourt once summed up his own approach to the responsibilities of leadership when he wrote that 'I am a good deal of a fatalist and trouble myself little about forecasts about the future and am quite content to await events, which are never either as good or as bad as we expect'. He was no believer in planning ahead or in trying to shape the course of Liberal politics. 'The only thing I see', he wrote, 'is to go on "pegging away" in season and out of season—picking the mortar out of the Unionist joints—and then one fine day the wall falls down, no one knows exactly why.'[2] He once described himself as having 'always held that a Government is destroyed a great deal more by its own faults than by the exertions of its opponents'; and he was always very ready to allow the Tories to define the nature of Liberal political activity. Thus in 1890 he expressed pleasure that the annual meeting of the N.L.F., at which he was to speak, was to take place after a Tory demonstration: 'It is a good deal easier to attack than to promulgate a programme of our own.'[3] Harcourt was an opportunist, not a planner. He once wrote of having to march out 'like travellers into a country without guide book or map and make our way as best we can *pro re nata*' as 'quite as good a *Plan of Campaign* as any other and often the most successful'.[4] A. H. D. Acland observed that

---

[1] B.M. Add. MS. 48640, folio 116; 48649, folio 8 (9 July 1888).
[2] Harcourt to Labouchere, 12 November 1887, Harcourt MSS.
[3] Harcourt to Arnold Morley, 20 September 1890, Harcourt MSS.
[4] Harcourt to John Morley, 5 January 1890, Harcourt MSS. Morley complained that Harcourt's 'characteristic qualities' were 'sufficient unto the day, etc.', and said that Harcourt's policy was 'always dictated by the exigencies of the hour without regard to the future'. Garvin, *Life of Chamberlain*, ii, pp. 488–9. Hamer, *John Morley*, p. 290.

'Harcourt's H. of C. qualities are great & notable but he has always been a "hand to mouth" man and always will be'.[1]

Seldom had new ideas been so little in evidence in Liberal politics. The leaders had no positive guidance to give the party as to the development of policy. It was fatally tempting to give up the struggle to organize Liberal policy, to stop trying to think about the meaning of Liberalism, and to lapse instead into a simple attitude of opposition to whatever initiatives the Tories chose to make.[2] Liberalism was the opposite of Conservatism. The task of defining the Liberals' identity and of selecting their policy positions was, therefore, in the hands of the Conservatives and was no longer the Liberals' responsibility. The relief of many Liberals at being able to put themselves in this position was very evident: it was a responsibility which they had long been proving themselves quite incapable of fulfilling on their own account. Those who did have definite ideas and wishes as to the reconstruction of Liberalism saw this danger as one of the principal trends that they had to overcome. Sidney Webb, for example, observed how easy it would be after the 1895 elections for the Liberals as the alternative-government party simply to lapse into relying on the almost inevitable turning of the tide, and he warned of the need to combat any disposition of this kind. His view was that those who thought as he did should not work for the party if it was in this frame of mind. The party ought to be allowed to grow weaker until such time as it was 'settled *what* the Liberal leaders mean—what reforms they have really at heart, and in what direction their intellectual convictions impel them to lead'. 'There is no calamity in politics', he wrote, '*against* which I would work harder than a return of the Liberal leaders to office without a definite programme. Every weakness of the Conservative Government, *every success of a Liberal candidate at a by-election*, makes me tremble lest the Liberal

[1] Acland to Ellis, 15 October 1896, T. E. Ellis MSS., folio 44.
[2] '. . . would it not be possible', wrote Labouchere to Lewis Harcourt, 16 June [1895?], 'to arrange a defeat, and then for the Govt. to resign, leaving it to the Unionists to come in and go to the country with their programme, whatever it may be. The Lords will not "fight". Liquor will lose us votes. Home Rule is dead. By the Welsh Church we certainly do not gain votes in England, and Scotland seems to be going against us.' Harcourt MSS. The Liberal government *did* resign after having clearly 'arranged a defeat'; but unfortunately the Unionists failed to oblige with a programme of their own which the Liberals could then attack.

leaders should be thereby encouraged to "wait", and rely on the return of the tide.'[1]

The *Speaker* expressed the predominant feeling among Liberals when it wrote immediately after the elections that 'there will be no need for our leaders to formulate new programmes in order to find some ground on which to appeal to the country when the next general election takes place. Their opponents will furnish them with a cause and a cry.' 'The initiative no longer rests with us, but with our opponents'—such was the constant theme of this leading organ of Liberal opinion. It argued that one advantage of concentrating on opposing whatever the Unionist government did was that there would thereby be most easily re-established 'as clear and distinct as it ever was' 'the dividing line between the two great parties', 'the party of progress and the party of reaction'.[2] Thus 'progress' was to be defined by criteria determined not by the Liberals but by the Conservatives, their policy and conduct being assumed to represent 'reaction' automatically and in all instances.

Some of Rosebery's colleagues and advisers were not very happy about the adoption of so negative a strategy. Lord Tweedmouth warned him that they ought not to 'let the future be left to chance and to what may be evolved out of a period of inaction during which we shall go from bad to worse & the faddists more & more insist on their own projects'.[3] But from others came very different advice. 'A policy of inaction seems to be that which for the present commends itself to the party', reported Wemyss Reid, the editor of the *Speaker*.[4] Haldane told him that all that could as yet be done in Liberal politics was 'clearing the ground'. The country was not yet ready to respond to a 'definite lead'. The Liberals could do no more for the present than 'watch & wait': 'There is plenty of dormant Liberalism, only it is no good trying to waken it up before its time has come. And that is not yet, & will not be until the ground is cleared of the rubbish which covers it.'[5]

---

[1] Webb to Herbert Samuel, 25 January 1897, Samuel, *Memoirs*, p. 28.

[2] Vol. 12, no. 291 (27 July 1895), p. 89; no. 294 (17 August 1895), p. 169; Vol. 13, no. 329 (18 April 1896), p. 410.

[3] 17 July 1895, Rosebery MSS., Box 72.

[4] 5 August 1895, Rosebery MSS., Box 44.

[5] 19 October 1895, 24 August 1897, Rosebery MSS., Box 24.

Rosebery's attitude was itself at first negative to the point of cynicism. He rejected utterly the Gladstonian conception of Liberalism as founded on an almost mystical *rapprochement* with the feelings of the masses. 'The people will come back to us', he wrote. 'Liberalism has always been founded among the masses not on aspiration but on discontent.'[1] Haldane encouraged him in this repudiation of Gladstonian crusading. With 'time & patience', he suggested, 'an accumulation of quieter criticisms' than Gladstone had been wont to make would 'break up' the Conservative government and let the Liberals back into office. There was 'little positive evidence of strong feeling' in the country, but Liberals need not feel that this was a handicap for themselves. After all, Gladstone's arousing of such feeling in 1880 and 1886 had not 'turned out well in the long run' for the party.[2] In his speeches Rosebery urged the strategy of passiveness and inaction on his party. They should 'lie low for a while', he advised, and await the emergence of 'that feeling against the Government which must be the first day-spring of the Liberal reaction'.[3] And privately he endeavoured to work out for himself why such a strategy was the best one to follow. In a memorandum written late in 1896 he argued that demands for 'a definite Liberal policy' were premature and ill advised, for any declaration of positive policy would have the effect both of upsetting the party and of diverting public attention from the government's blunders. The party needed 'some sort of screen' behind which its 'regiments scattered in battle' could be 'reconstructed':

That shelter has been abundantly furnished by the present Government. Their inconceivable blunders furnish an abundant topic for Liberal concentration and attack.

I believe that the best chance for the Liberal party lies much more in reaction from the present Government than in any gospel of its own. The present Government is the first Tory govt. since 1867: weakly and distractedly Tory no doubt, but compelled to be Tory

---

[1] Rosebery to Canon Holland, 21 August 1895, Rosebery MSS., Box 89, letter copy book, folio 19. Rosebery here seems to be repudiating the spirit of Midlothian which sixteen years earlier had inspired his first major involvement in Liberal politics.

[2] 4 April 1896, Rosebery MSS., Box 24. Note again the repudiation of '1880' in particular.

[3] *Lord Rosebery's Speeches*, pp. 380–1, 404–5.

by the brute force of its majority. Since 1867 Conservative Governments have not openly opposed Liberal policy (except in Ireland): they have competed not unsuccessfully at an auction of Liberal measures. Now their majority robs them of all excuse for not being Tory, and, reluctantly I think, Tory they are.

This is an immense advantage to the Liberal party, because it forces real Liberals back to that party . . .[1]

Thus Rosebery too was looking to the Tories to confer once again on the Liberals a distinctive and clear-cut Liberal identity. In their reversion to what was assumed to be an inherent 'Toryness' lay the best hope for the revival of a definite principle of differentiation.

Another party leader, Robert Spence Watson, President of the N.L.F., gave Liberals the same kind of advice. In 1896 he told them that they should not be 'paying attention to the legislation that is to be' but should instead be concerned with 'preparing and formulating the opposition to that which we believe to be bad and reactionary'.[2] But this negative approach to the problem of Liberal revival and reconstruction began to seem profoundly unsatisfactory to many Liberals. The younger Liberals of the *Progressive Review* attacked it strongly. In an article in that journal in September 1897 it was argued that, even though the government had been doing 'unpopular work', and the Liberal party '"manager" has been importunate in urging that it was safer to fight elections on opponents' mistakes, than by attempting to form any definite public opinion', nevertheless the party had 'a mandate from the very nature of things to consider what is its faith, what it is going to do, what it means by progress now'. Once Liberalism had been 'very much more than anti-Toryism', had involved 'directing the force of a convinced public opinion in favour of large measures of a progressive nature'. Now it seemed merely a matter of 'winning majorities (that will not work) on opponents' mistakes'. A Liberal should not 'regard the turn of the tide against the Ministry with unalloyed gladness':

He will remember that the self-same feelings of bewilderment which now prompt the electors to vote Liberal, prompted them to

---

[1] Crewe, *Lord Rosebery*, ii, pp. 522–3.   [2] *N.L.F. Report 1896*, p. 53.

vote Tory at the general election; . . . he will suspect the silence of the Liberal leaders regarding the principles upon which the Liberalism of the future is to be conducted, and their evident joy in seizing upon and running to death the mistakes of the Government, as the tacit confession of wideawake politicians that the party is not at the moment in a position to lay down a positive idea of constructive politics; he will have visions, perhaps, of a Liberal Ministry after the next election, but a Ministry that will plough the sands and consume its time in making apologies for pledges unfilled, and in vainly attacking the constitutional barriers to democratic progress. . . . No one knows what the Liberals can do. If their candidates are returned it is only to protest against the work of the Tory members.[1]

Another protest against negative leadership was made by R. T. Reid in a speech to the Eighty Club in December 1897. He complained that political utterances by Liberals consisted only of attacks on the government and called for an end to the reticence concerning Liberal domestic policy. He condemned the notion that 'we are more likely to prosper upon the faults of our opponents than upon merits of our own'.[2] The response of some of the party leaders was to deny the necessity of prescribing before the Liberals had been called in. But others were becoming conscious of the desirability of some more positive form of preparation for the next period of power. Asquith, for example, appealed to younger Liberals early in 1898 to make use of the party's present freedom from 'immediate responsibilities either of legislation or of administration' to 'form some definite conception of what are the purposes to which in the immediate future our efforts ought to be directed'.[3] A. H. D. Acland was undoubtedly expressing the view of many practical and 'constructive' Liberals when he commented to Asquith in January 1899 on Harcourt's resignation of the leadership that Harcourt had in fact given the party very little leadership, at least in connection with the development of policy. 'The great strength of Mr. G. and of Chamberlain has been that they were always at work out of office especially

---

[1] Vol. ii, no. 12, pp. 485–6.
[2] 'Eighty' Club. *Nothing Venture, Nothing Have*, p. 16.
[3] 'Eighty' Club. *Some Aspects of the Constitutional Problem* (speech by Asquith, 15 February 1898), pp. 15–16.

planning and gathering piles of information from others with a view to the future.'[1]

One reason why so many of the leaders favoured the negative strategy was the tendency among many of the rank and file from 1891 on to identify statements of policy as announcements of 'programmes'. After Newcastle the leaders found it very difficult to say anything about any particular reform policy without enthusiasts for other reforms feeling that the failure at the same time to mention these meant that they had been 'dropped' from the party programme. Leaders were now assumed to be thinking and speaking all the time in terms of comprehensive programmes. The only alternative to constantly arousing unjustified suspicions and offending sensitive groups in the party was to adopt a completely negative standpoint and say nothing definite about anything at all but allow the Tories to select the topics on which the leaders would pronounce. Rosebery was angered to find that his speech to the N.L.F. in January 1895 was seen as representing the declaration of a programme and that as a result there were complaints from the advocates of the reforms to which he had failed to refer.[2] A year later he referred to a 'fatal disadvantage' of programme politics, 'that, supposing there to be thirty-nine articles of the Liberal creed—as there are of other creeds—and you only mention thirty-seven in your recital, you are at once denounced as being unsound on the other two'.[3] In 1897 the N.L.F. itself ran into trouble on this point when a motion was passed at a meeting of its General Committee that 'one of the foremost and immediate objects of the Liberal party' should be reform of the electoral laws. So strong were the protests from the sections about this singling out of one set of reforms that the N.L.F. had to issue a statement denying that any 'programme-spinning' had been involved.[4] The discontent that programme politics gave rise to was almost inevitable, for, although programmes purported to be comprehensive, the 'omnibus' principle being, as Ostrogorski saw,[5] their main unifying factor, nevertheless in practice they could never cover every

[1] Acland to Asquith, 20 January 1899, Asquith MSS., Dep. 9, folios 170-2.
[2] Rosebery to Ripon, 22 January 1895, Rosebery MSS., Box 88, letter copy book, folio 94.
[3] *N.L.F. Report 1896*, p. 110.   [4] *N.L.F. Report 1898*, p. 42.
[5] See above, pp. 173-4.

shade and variety of reform supported by members of the party. Another legacy of Newcastle was the appreciation that programme politics, once embarked upon, were very hard to break away from because of the consequences of appearing to drop something on which a commitment had been given.

After 1896 the leaders were determined to resist the imposition on them by 'the party' of any programme or scheme of political action. They insisted on being allowed complete tactical freedom so that their response to emergencies and to changing circumstances could be as flexible and as little hampered by previous commitments as possible.[1] The great problem then became one of persuading the party to *trust* the leaders. But for this the leaders had to have confidence in themselves and be able to convince their 'followers' that they possessed the authority and the overall view and general understanding that would justify their being given this trust. Frequently the leaders complained about the 'disloyalty' of the party.[2] But some Liberals argued that this was no more than a consequence of disunity and lack of authority in the leadership itself. There were plainly many Liberals who were only too ready to leave decisions as to strategy and the order in which questions were to be dealt with to the leaders, who craved authority and a 'strong hand' at the top.[3] But instead they found leaders who did not believe in themselves and had no sense of purpose either for their own role as leaders or for the party. A. H. D. Acland wrote to Tom Ellis when Rosebery gave up the Liberal leadership: 'It is rather sad for us and men like us with the hopes we brought into public life from Oxford and our homes to have found that those we earnestly desired to uphold & *follow* have through the grave defects you mention given us such a bad time. And of course it must infect the future. All this uncertainty and absence of leading will make more & more pure individualism & anyone will think that to upset the party a bit is not so great a matter.'[4] Followers

[1] On this point see Herbert Gladstone's remarks in *N.L.F. Report 1896*, pp. 85–6.
[2] John Morley, however, called such talk about 'loyalty', 'cant' and argued 'that a leader should enforce adherence, and not expect it as a due'. R. Brett to Rosebery, 16 October 1896, Rosebery MSS., Box 6.
[3] For examples, see *N.L.F. Report 1893*, pp. 30, 44 (Spence Watson, S. Waddy); *N.L.F. Report 1897*, pp. 82, 85 (Lord Battersea, T. Terrell); A. Billson to Rosebery, 26 January 1896, Rosebery MSS., Box 73.
[4] 15 October 1896, T. E. Ellis MSS., folio 44.

blamed leaders, and leaders blamed followers for the disorganized state of Liberal politics. Neither side seemed prepared to grasp responsibility for the positive work of reorientation and reconstruction.

There were those who wished to break this vicious circle and, despairing altogether of their leaders, called for the shaping of policy to be transferred to 'the party'. After 1895 the N.L.F. became the focus for the efforts of Liberals who felt like this. Claiming that it had become shackled to 'official' Liberalism, they demanded that it be 'liberated' so as to become the vehicle of the revitalizing of Liberal politics. For example, they wanted all links between the N.L.F. and the parliamentary party, especially the Whips' Office, to be severed. At the N.L.F. meeting in March 1896 an effort was made to turn the N.L.F. into a 'free' organization by amending the procedural rules to give greater scope for the expression of 'Liberal opinion'. But, whatever the N.L.F. might demand, they had no means of imposing their wishes on the party leaders; and in the reconstruction of policy they proved to be as incapable of 'concentration' as ever.

As the career of Gladstone had shown, the transcending force of a great political personality was indispensable for the effective 'concentration' of Liberal politics. After 1894 the leader who most consciously tried to develop such a personality in order to fill this role was Lord Rosebery.

Rosebery's great theme, the message which he never wearied of preaching to Liberals, was 'concentration', and in his work for the reorganization of Liberalism he sought constantly for the kind of policy that would serve this end. To him, as to Gladstone, the form of Liberal policy was as important as the content because it was the form which made Liberalism an effective and practical political force. It is clear, for instance, that, although Rosebery was very far from being an enthusiastic Home Ruler, he had a very keen appreciation of the way in which the preoccupation with that issue facilitated 'concentration' in Liberal politics in the late 1880s.[1] Every bit as much as Gladstone or John Morley, Rosebery was in favour of organizing and ordering Liberal politics through the single

[1] See above, p. 126.

great question, the substitute for system, which temporarily subordinated or comprehended all other political issues. On one occasion he referred to 'the advantage of being able to concentrate your mind on one or two subjects' and complained that 'what is called popularly a statesman lives in the maelstrom or whirlpool of various questions, all sucking at him in different courses, and he is ignorant to which to give the precedence'.[1] When he himself became party leader, he was very conscious of being in this position and very anxious to find some way of liberating his leadership from it. Addressing the Eighty Club at the beginning of July 1895, he said that the word 'concentration' summed up the lesson that had to be learned from the experience of the 1892-5 Liberal government. And this 'concentration' had to be brought about through a reversion to the 'single great question' tradition in Liberal politics. Large programmes had 'not hitherto been the method by which great Liberal victories have been won'. Concentration on one main issue was best 'for the purpose of a practical appeal to the English-speaking people', and he instanced such Liberal triumphs as 1830 when the cause was 'the great central reform' of Parliament, 1868 when Gladstone focused attention on the question of the Irish Church, and 1880 when 'the main issue of foreign affairs' was 'paramount'.[2] In 1895 *he* offered the cause of the reform of the House of Lords, and in all that he said about it as a political issue the emphasis was not on its content, which remained very vague, but on its form as a potentially disciplining, controlling, and concentrating force in Liberal politics. It was in particular because of this aspect of the Lords issue that he later regretted so much that his advice had not been taken. And, although after the 1895 election defeat he went through a phase of negativism and reliance on anti-Tory reaction, by the late 1890s he was developing a new positive and constructive scheme of 'concentration'. This can be seen in a speech in 1898 in which he blames the prevalent 'public apathy' about politics on the breakdown of the 'single question' tradition. 'Our forefathers', he said, 'were able to concentrate their minds on one particular subject at a time and give it all their energy and all their

[1] *Lord Rosebery's Speeches*, p. 67.
[2] 'Eighty' Club. *The Pressing Question for the Liberal Party*, pp. 9-11.

zeal. For example, for some twenty years they were locked in that great war with Napoleon and the French Revolution which absorbed all their energies, and when that war ceased there came an era of great single questions on which they were able to concentrate all their attention. But now that is all changed.' Men's intelligence was being made 'dazed and blunted and dull' by a great dispersion of interests. Nevertheless, it remained true that apathy disappeared whenever 'the attention of the country is concentrated on a single point'; and this revivifying of politics seemed to be happening now once again—in connection with imperialism.[1]

Although a great deal of his effort after 1894 was to be devoted to freeing the Liberal party from the Gladstonian legacy, Rosebery's style of political leadership—as distinct from the content of the policies that he offered—was very much in the Gladstonian mould.[2] One finds not only the same interest in single great questions that 'concentrate' and subordinate and order, but also an effort to create around himself the same kind of national authority and political personality. As Sir Edward Hamilton's diaries show, Rosebery was fascinated by Gladstone and his political authority and talked often about him, analysing the sources and nature of that authority. 'His admiration for Mr. G. is unbounded', wrote Hamilton after one such conversation. 'He understands the man better than almost anyone else; appreciating to the full his gigantic position and quite alive to his weaknesses.'[3] Rosebery was never a Member of the House of Commons, never a candidate for election to Parliament, never *directly*

---

[1] *The Liberal Magazine*, vol. vi, no. 62 (November 1898), p. 466.

[2] Cf. Sir E. Hamilton's comment on him: 'He is the only man, after Mr G., who has "elastic band" qualifications & could weld together the necessarily heterogeneous elements of the Liberal Party.' B.M. Add. MS. 48640, folio 82 (30 May 1885).

[3] B.M. Add. MS. 48646, folio 22 (17 April 1887). On 4 December 1887 Hamilton wrote after a conversation with Rosebery: 'In talking together we generally get on the topic of Mr G. Rosebery is one of the few men who understand him.' B.M. Add. MS. 48647, folio 82. On 9 July 1888 Rosebery said to Hamilton: 'Like Chatham, Mr G. had that extra-ordinary power of striking the imagination of the public, and at times similar fits of yearning for retirement came upon him.' B.M. Add. MS. 48648, folios 8–9. On 16 August 1891 Rosebery advanced 'the theory that great men founded themselves on other great men, e.g. . . . Mr Gladstone on Canning . . .'. B.M. Add. MS. 48656, folio 57 . . . and Lord Rosebery on Mr. Gladstone?

involved in parliamentary politics and electioneering. But there was one episode in his life when he did come close to this area of political experience and which does seem to have made a deep impact on him as showing what the exercise of political authority and the manifestation of transcendent political personality could achieve—the Midlothian campaign of 1879–80, which he stage-managed for Gladstone.[1] In this he was able to observe at very close range, indeed he contributed to the production of, the phenomenon of a man who was not even the leader of his own party imposing order on politics by focusing attention on his own political personality and arousing national, not merely party, enthusiasm. Was it the Gladstone of Midlothian on whom Rosebery later endeavoured to model himself? Certainly Midlothian did show that supreme political authority and influence did not need to be based on power within Parliament—a power which Rosebery himself, of course, never possessed, and for the mechanics of gaining which he professed nothing but contempt.[2]

Rosebery's aim was to revive Liberalism as it seemed Gladstone had revived it in 1880, by aligning it with an opinion that transcended party boundaries, by making it the vehicle of national feeling. After his retirement from the leadership in 1896 he consciously turned away from the party to appeal to 'the nation' in which he hoped to find a source of new life for Liberalism. Gladstone's career had provided ample proof of how such an appeal could unify and discipline Liberals in Parliament and the party, two institutions for which Rosebery expressed contempt as bases for political action. He himself could have no hope of deriving political authority from influence over Liberal parliamentarians, since his only connection with Parliament was as a member of the miniscule Liberal group in the House of Lords. Instead he strove to make himself a leader of 'national' opinion and attach to himself

[1] Towards the end of his life Rosebery wrote: 'The secret of my life which seems to me sufficiently obvious, is that I always detested politics. I had been landed in them accidentally by the Midlothian election, which was nothing but a chivalrous adventure.' James, *Rosebery*, p. 474.

[2] For his contempt for 'the wire-pulling system' see Sir E. Hamilton's diary, B.M. Add. MS. 48646, folio 21 (16 April 1887). 'I have long thought', wrote Rosebery to Munro Ferguson, 21 July 1899, 'that the House [of Commons] was in the nature of a dangerous and lifelong disease, which one should not catch unless one can see some counterbalancing advantage.' Rosebery MSS., Box 15.

a national, above-party authority. This led him to behave like Gladstone in certain ways, for example in his failure to consult colleagues or party before taking initiatives on national issues.[1] He too did not want to appear to be controlled merely by party considerations. Thus in 1888 he had replied to criticisms from Liberals that he was not speaking out enough and 'asserting himself' as a Liberal leader that this was 'just what he did not want to do'. 'He did not wish [he said] to be too pronounced a partisan. He had two questions at heart—(1) Imperial Federation and (2) reform of the House of Lords—which might be injuriously affected by extreme partisanship on his part.'[2]

Rosebery desired to reach, and to bring Liberalism into an organic relationship with, the 'real' life of the nation which he believed was 'always silently proceeding' beneath 'the storms and strifes of parties'.[3] A few weeks after becoming Prime Minister he wrote that 'I doubt my being long a minister or even a politician' because 'I am sick to death of the eternal babble and bustle of parliament—such endless parade of work with so little done; of the whole system of politics which amounts to so little more than that the outs shall become the ins'.[4] In a speech he defined the kind of opinion which he wished to lead. It was a spirit which he believed to be animating 'the great masses of our artisans, the great masses of our working clergy, the great masses of those who work for and with the poor'. Such people, not connected with 'any existing political organisation', took an attitude towards the politician which might be summed up as: 'A plague on both your Houses, a plague on all your parties, a plague on all your politics, a plague on your unending discussions which yield so little fruit. Have done with this unending talk, and come down and do something for the people.' He expressed himself as being in sympathy with this attitude, and indeed referred to the possi-

---

[1] On this point, see Stansky, *Ambitions and Strategies*, pp. 139, 191. H. H. Fowler once remarked that Rosebery 'must do as Mr G. did: fight his own battle & he will win'. Reported in Wemyss Reid to Rosebery, 18 September 1900, Rosebery MSS., Box 44.

[2] Sir E. Hamilton's diary, B.M. Add. MS. 48648, folios 103–4 (27 May 1888).

[3] *Lord Rosebery's Speeches*, p. 81.

[4] Rosebery to the Bishop of Rochester, 5 April 1894 (copy), Rosebery MSS., Box 66.

bility of there being a new kind of Prime Minister 'who shall not scruple from time to time to come down from the platform of party and speak straight to the hearts of his fellow-countrymen'.[1] His colleagues soon began to feel that he was not behaving as a Prime Minister should. Harcourt told Rosebery's private secretary, George Murray, that in his opinion Rosebery 'spoke a great deal too much in the Country for a Prime Minister'. But, explained Murray, the reason for this was Rosebery's 'idea that he always speaks "as a man and not as a Minister"'.[2] His closest associates encouraged the new Prime Minister to adopt this role. Haldane urged him to make no further speeches 'on the details of current controversies' but instead to 'use words' that would express those ideals which the mass of people 'feel but cannot frame'.[3] What remained to be seen was whether Rosebery could combine behaviour of this kind with exercising the functions of leader of a party. To some it seemed that the débâcle of 1895 was in part attributable to the undue neglect of the party by Rosebery. Reginald Brett warned him that he would have to give up 'mystery and aloofness' as political methods: 'If you are going to carry on the fight, it can only be by conquering first the sympathies and hopes of the rank and file of the remnant of our Party.'[4] This was not the order of priority that Rosebery—or Gladstone, for that matter—ever favoured. In October 1896 Rosebery made his choice, and, giving up the leadership of the party, devoted himself henceforth to becoming a leader of opinion.[5]

Rosebery wished to reinstate the Liberal party as the 'national' party, the party of all classes, reflecting and expressing national opinion. It would then be again what it had been between 1832 and 1886, the party that normally governed 'the nation'. But in order that this should happen the dominance of sectional opinion and the influence of faddism would have to be ended.

[1] *Lord Rosebery's Speeches*, pp. 206–7.
[2] Lewis Harcourt's diary, Harcourt MSS. (26 November 1894).
[3] Haldane to Rosebery, 6 June 1894, Rosebery MSS., Box 24.
[4] Brett to Rosebery, 24 June 1895, Rosebery MSS., Box 6.
[5] John Morley soon came to appreciate what was now Rosebery's order of priority. After the Chesterfield speech he wrote to R. Spence Watson, 25 December 1901: 'R. has no intention whatever of re-joining the party, or of doing anything to contribute to its re-union . . . when he says that his services are at the disposal of the country, he does not mean by the request of the *party*, but of the country at large.' Watson MSS.

The first essential, therefore, was for Liberalism to seek out and associate itself with majority opinion in all things. This was the test that he consistently applied to major issues, for example Home Rule and imperialism. Only by applying this test could Liberals make their movement 'national' once more. For his critics the great objection to such a strategy was that it was scarcely distinguishable from opportunism and would introduce much greater instability into politics. How, they asked, was it possible to differentiate clearly between an open, flexible Liberalism, responsive to movements of popular feeling, and an opportunistic swimming with the tide? Rosebery was clearly over-optimistic about the prospects of finding a coherent, stable, and reasonably permanent majority opinion: time was soon to show that in this respect at least he had backed the wrong horse in imperialism, for example. He himself confessed to Haldane in 1896: 'I think the great difficulty of the age as regards politics is the impossibility of ascertaining the real feeling of the country.'[1]

Rosebery wanted to align Liberalism with majority opinion. He saw in the imperial principle and the devolution of non-imperial questions the means of achieving this and of solving the problem of what was to be done about matters that concerned only minorities. He believed that Liberals had paid too much attention to the interests of minority sections. The time had come to redress the balance and to adopt points of view that corresponded with the feelings of the majority. A good example of conflict between this principle and the Liberal tradition of giving priority to minority rights and interests is to be found in correspondence between Rosebery and John Morley. In 1887 the two men quarrelled over the question of the retention of Irish M.P.s. Morley told Rosebery that he could not

assent to your syllogism: 'Whatever the British public think must be right: The B.p. think full and continuous rep[resentatio]n of Ireld. is right: therefore, it must be right.' As a matter of history, the B. public has never on any important occasion whatever been right as to Ireland. It wd. not be so right as it is now, if Mr. G. had not boldly affronted all its ignorance and prejudice.[2]

[1] Rosebery to Haldane, 1 April 1896, Haldane MSS., MS. 5904, folio 81.
[2] 28 May 1887, Rosebery MSS., Box 35.

After becoming Prime Minister in 1894 Rosebery made clear his opposition to disestablishment, at least as far as England was concerned. He justified the maintenance of the Established Church in England on the grounds that it conformed to the wishes of 'a majority of the nation' and was not engaged in persecuting any minorities. A minority had a perfect right to protest against the Establishment; but, he went on, 'holding as I do the Liberal creed of the rights of majorities, I cannot be inconsistent in maintaining the doctrine I have laid down'. This was, of course, exactly the same position as he was adopting at this time on Home Rule for Ireland and the need to give precedence to the wishes and interests of 'the predominant partner'. Morley's comment on this was that he refused to be 'blind to the undoubted fact that those of our party who are sincerely for disestablishment, in England, or Wales, or anywhere else, scorn the notion of testing their position by considerations of political and secular expediency'. 'Majorities and Minorities don't touch the question, in their minds and consciences.'[1] And, as for Home Rule, when Rosebery asserted that it was 'impossible without a majority in England', Morley reminded him 'that Emancipation was undoubtedly detested by the English majority'.[2] The Liberalism for which Morley and other opponents of Rosebery stood had to be based on considerations other than those of 'Majorities and Minorities'. This, as we shall see, was to be one of the basic issues at stake in the great controversy over imperialism.

Rosebery also shared with Gladstone a tendency to look for the restoration of order in Liberal politics primarily from spontaneous action within the party itself. Like Gladstone, he was opposed to any imposition of order by the leadership or the party machine, and looked instead for a reordering that would develop organically out of a response to some broad movement of public opinion. If the party were disorganized and 'disloyal', as after 1895, he too preferred to stand aside and wait for it to reorganize itself rather than use his power as leader to force

---
[1] Morley to Rosebery, 16 April 1894, Rosebery MSS., Box 36. Rosebery's remarks are to be found in a draft letter to Williamson which Morley returns in his letter.
[2] Morley to Rosebery, 24 May 1893, Rosebery MSS., Box 36.

on it any particular mode of reconstruction.[1] He refused to act merely as a party leader, settling internal differences and trying to hold together the factions; instead he adopted Gladstone's post-1874 resolve to take the lead only in connection with some great national issue which transcended party considerations and linked the party with national opinion. If Liberalism were again to be disciplined and coherent and animated by a unified sense of purpose, then the reconstruction had to come from within and represent some organic force. Again like Gladstone, Rosebery thought of Liberal reconstruction very much in terms of purgation and new growth. It was as if he felt, after the experience of 1894–5, that the same drastic remedy—defeat, purge, and reconstruction on some new basis—was needed now for the crisis of Liberal disintegration as had been applied in 1885–6.

Rosebery welcomed the election defeat of 1895 as possibly 'the best thing that could have happened for the party, which had like a straggling evergreen to be cut down to the roots before it could flourish again'. Defeat was 'a necessary prelude to the resurrection and reconstitution of the party'. 'The Liberal Party had become all legs and wings', he wrote; 'a daddy-long-legs fluttering among a thousand flames: it had to be consumed in order that something more sane, more consistent, and more coherent could take its place. . . . The Liberal Party is purged as with fire. It sees in its purgatory that it must concentrate, and must follow—someone, whomever it chooses . . .'[2] It *might* choose himself. In the meantime he would await the maturing of the process which he summed up as 'purgatory', the emergence, phoenix-like from the fire, of a new organic unity and sense of purpose. He himself would not force on this process. When he gave up the leadership in October 1896, he said that he did so so that the party might be liberated from the restraint of imposed leadership, might be able to 'speak

[1] He was encouraged in this by his friends. Sir Edward Grey used language very similar to that used by Gladstone in 1874: 'These men in the House of Commons won't follow Asquith or Morley or Harcourt any better than anyone else. Leadership is for the present impossible and before the party talks of choosing a leader it must show that it is fit to be led.' Grey to Rosebery, 13 October 1896, Rosebery MSS., Box 23.

[2] Rosebery to Spencer, 12 August 1895; to Lord Farrer, 13 August 1895; to Canon Holland, 21 August 1895, Rosebery MSS., Box 89, letter copy book, folios 12, 16, 19.

once more, naturally and unconstrainedly, with its own voice'.[1] He now said of the party: 'I have thrown it on its own resources. The solid and sensible as well as the high aspiring members of the party must now work out their own salvation, or be wiped out of existence. The party has to be purged from within.'[2] This was to be his attitude henceforth. He was steadfastly to refuse to re-enter regular party politics and become a party leader again until the party itself had carried through this process of working out its salvation.

Rosebery left no doubt as to his own views on the form of 'purgatory' which was needed. It was the eradication of 'Gladstonianism'. While his political style and method closely resembled, and obviously owed much to, Gladstone's practice as Liberal leader, nevertheless Rosebery put before himself as one of his main objectives the destruction of Gladstone's influence and of the various legacies of Gladstonianism in Liberal politics. In this he was, as Chamberlain himself appeared to recognize, pursuing an end very similar to that which Chamberlain had pursued in 1886. For, as he saw it, if any other leader was to be able to establish his own authority over the party and make himself respected by it, then the first essential was to escape from under Gladstone's shadow and create a clear posture of independence, a sharply distinct political identity. As soon as he became Prime Minister, Rosebery made his declaration of independence, the 'predominant partner' statement on Irish Home Rule which cut away the basis of the Gladstonian position on Irish policy by asserting that in the shaping of that policy it was the views of the English, not the Irish, which mattered most and should have the controlling influence.[3] Rosebery made it clear at this time that his aim was to restore the party to its pre-1886 condition.[4] In 1886 the party had become quite explicitly

[1] Rosebery to Grey, 17 October 1896, Rosebery MSS., Box 89, letter copy book, folio 113. Of course, as Munro Ferguson pointed out to him, Rosebery was not really anyway in a position to 'establish any strict discipline' on the party himself, even if he wanted to, because he had so frequently in the recent past forced his colleagues to allow him to have his own way on foreign and imperial policy. Ferguson to Rosebery, 3 October 1895, Rosebery MSS., Box 15.
[2] Rosebery to Corrie Grant, 5 November 1896, Rosebery MSS., Box 89, letter copy book, folio 120.
[3] Cf. Stansky, *Ambitions and Strategies*, p. 103.
[4] *Liberal Magazine*, vol. 2, no. 8 (May 1894), p. 114.

Gladstone's party because it consisted entirely of men who had had to choose to follow him in a particular policy initiative. Rosebery wished to re-create a non-Gladstonian Liberal party. But as leader he was to find that he continued to live under Gladstone's shadow. When he failed to take a strong line in connection with the 'Armenian atrocities' at the end of 1895, Wemyss Reid, the editor of the *Speaker*, wrote to him: 'The old Liberals have not forgotten 1876 & they are clamouring for another Atrocities Campaign with you instead of Mr. G. at its head.'[1] One of Rosebery's principal sources of embarrassment after he had become leader was Gladstone's continuing interest in politics. Rosebery found himself forced into a position rather like that of Hartington in the late 1870s. From time to time the 'retired' leader would insist on taking some line of his own, for example on Welsh disestablishment; and naturally his views continued to be accorded much respect and attention, not least from Unionists who were only too ready to make political capital out of appearances of divergence between Gladstone and Rosebery. Gladstone's re-emergence from retirement in 1896 to speak out on the 'Armenian atrocities' in a way that went completely against Rosebery's policy at the time was the final straw. The force of Gladstone's political influence was frustrating Rosebery's efforts to establish his own independent authority in the party. The frame of mind among influential Liberals against which Rosebery found that he had to contend is illustrated by a report from Wemyss Reid in September 1896 that H. W. Massingham, one of the foremost Liberal journalists of the day, was intending to 'continue to compare you, to your great disadvantage, with Mr. G.' 'How strange it is', remarked Reid, 'that Mr. G. should always be the means of leading shallow people to draw invidious comparisons between him & other men!'[2] Rosebery determined to end this intolerable situation by resigning the leadership, and he made no attempt to conceal the fact that Gladstone's Armenian campaign had been one of the main factors leading him to take the decision to do this. 'I consider that Mr. Gladstone's return to public life is the last straw on my back', he wrote; 'for it gives, quite unconsciously and innocently as

[1] 3 December 1895, Rosebery MSS., Box 44.
[2] Reid to Rosebery, 27 September 1896, Rosebery MSS., Box 44.

regards himself, all the disloyal intriguers in the party a shelter and a rallying-point.'[1] It had given 'discontented Liberals' the excuse 'to pelt me' with Gladstone's authority. Rosebery told a friend of how he had been 'tied to Gladstonian chains' ever since the Midlothian campaigns of 1879–80 and had finally been left in 1894 'with the thankless task of acting as Mr. G.'s political executor and of winding up his political estate'. What was needed now first of all was the creation of a *tabula rasa* in Liberal politics.[2] From this time on Rosebery was to use his own release from official responsibilities to work for a similar freeing of Liberalism from the encumbrances of the Gladstonian legacy.

For Rosebery the two most obnoxious parts of that legacy were the Irish policy and the Newcastle programme. His objection to the latter was, above all, one of form: Rosebery was a 'single question' politician. His objection to the Irish policy concerned content much more. However much it had 'concentrated' Liberal politics in the late 1880s—and of this aspect of it Rosebery had been highly appreciative—it had not been a cause which had aligned Liberalism with 'national feeling'. Indeed, it had concentrated national opinion, expressed as Unionism or imperialism, against the Liberals and reduced them to the status of minority party. Whenever Rosebery listed the great triumphs of the Liberal party and of Gladstone in particular which had been achieved as the result of crusades for single great causes, 1832, 1868, and 1880 had appeared, but 1886 had been conspicuous by its absence. It had been the wrong kind of great question.

After 1893 Rosebery virtually dedicated himself to eradicating the Newcastle programme and its effects from Liberal politics. His friends encouraged him to view Gladstone's adoption of the programme as an aberration in the conduct of a man whose style Rosebery, whether consciously or unconsciously, so largely adopted for his own. Reginald Brett reminded him in August 1894 that 'Mr. G.—until late years—

---

[1] Rosebery to Asquith, 6 October 1896 (copy), Rosebery MSS., Box 1. Cf. John Morley's attitude to Gladstone's continuing influence: 'Tho'' he had retired, still people felt that he was there, and his presence in the body among us gave or preserved a sort of unity. All that is dispersive will now be more dispersive than ever.' Morley to R. Spence Watson, 22 May 1898, Watson MSS.

[2] James, *Rosebery*, p. 392.

never touched a "programme" and never moved outside the path that led to *one* great policy.'[1] And even then, Rosebery would argue, Gladstone had adopted the programme merely in order to serve the ends of his 'great policy'. He would refer to 'the innumerable political propositions lightly accepted by Mr. Gladstone for the promotion of his Irish Policy'.[2] Gladstone had 'endorsed every bill presented to him in his devotion to Home Rule, and his anxiety to enlist every unit on his side'.[3] While thus minimizing the commitment of Gladstone to the programme, Rosebery also frequently sought to absolve himself from any responsibility for or connection with it. In 1891 he had indeed been in semi-retirement. He had not been present at the Newcastle meeting and he had given the programme no endorsement. In December 1895 he protested to the editor of *The Times* concerning allegations that he had been committed to the programme and had tried to promote it. The programme had, he wrote, 'been concocted against my judgment when I was in retirement'. He had joined Gladstone's government in 1892 solely because of his interest in foreign policy, and since becoming Prime Minister had repudiated the Newcastle programme and stated constantly 'in the Cabinet, as well as outside, . . . that I had nothing to do with that Programme'. He had declared repeatedly his 'dislike of this system of Programmes'.[4]

Nobody who had studied Rosebery's speeches since he had become Liberal leader could have questioned these claims. He had established himself unmistakably as the outstanding critic in the party of programme politics. In his election campaign in 1895 he blamed the difficulties that his government had encountered on the Newcastle programme and made it plain that were he to become Prime Minister again he would regard himself as no longer bound by the mandate of 1892. In 1892 the Liberal party had been 'greatly over-loaded with cargo' and had 'landed in Downing Street with an enormous and multifarious programme, and with a very inadequate majority to carry it with'. They had come in, he said, 'on what

[1] 6 August 1894, Rosebery MSS., Box 6.
[2] Crewe, *Lord Rosebery*, ii, pp. 522–3.
[3] Rosebery to Lord Farrer, 13 August 1895, Rosebery MSS., Box 89, letter copy book, folio 16.
[4] Rosebery to Buckle, December 1895 (draft), Rosebery MSS., Box 70.

I may call a mountain range of policy—innumerable peaks; when you had climbed one you saw other ranges in long lines into illimitable space'.[1] When the election defeat came, he knew where the blame should lie. The Newcastle programme had not only helped to turn the Liberal party into 'a mass of fiery fanaticisms, intolerant of each other and impatient of precedence: an army of dervishes each carrying a separate flag'; 'the adoption of every crusade had stirred up an at least equally violent defence of every interest attacked', and so the Liberals had managed to alienate 'every interest in the country'.[2] This was the direct opposite of that 'concentration' in Liberal politics for which he was constantly appealing. He would warn of the 'great danger in too long a programme and in too great a multiplicity of programmes': 'When you want to produce music on the pianoforte you do not strike all the notes at once, and I am inclined to think that, by producing all the articles of a policy, which it may take years to carry out simultaneously, to the people you produce very much the want of harmony which is produced by striking all the notes of a pianoforte at once.'[3] For the future of the party it had to be recognized that the Newcastle programme in its 'bulk and multifarious aggressiveness' 'constitutes an encumbrance—not an inspiration or assistance'.[4]

Rosebery wished to see as much as possible of the Gladstonian past wiped off the slate so that the Liberal party could make a fresh start with principles and policies which were in accordance with the feelings of the majority of electors. Liberalism had to re-establish itself as the national political creed. It remained 'the national spirit of the country', but that spirit was 'dormant in a cave' waiting for the Liberal statesmanship that would re-awaken it and counter the anti-national influences of the Gladstonian Irish policy and of class-war socialism.[5]

[1] 'Eighty' Club. *The Pressing Question for the Liberal Party*, pp. 9–11.
[2] Rosebery to Spencer, 12 August 1895; to Lord Farrer, 13 August 1895, Rosebery MSS., Box 89, letter copy book, folios 12, 16.
[3] *Liberal Magazine*, vol. 3, no. 26 (November 1895), pp. 467–8.
[4] Crewe, *Lord Rosebery*, ii, pp. 522–3.
[5] Rosebery to Professor Knight, 31 October 1897, Rosebery MSS., Box 89, letter copy book, folio 154.

He believed that, if the party could win back those Liberals who had voted Unionist or had abstained since 1886, it could regain its old status as the majority party, the party of the nation. Only a month after becoming Prime Minister he began appealing to the Liberal Unionists by asking them to believe that the chapter in the party's history constituted by the Home Rule preoccupation was now closed. The Liberal party was now becoming a very different kind of party from that which they had left in 1886, and the main reason for this was the growth of 'the idea of interest in our Empire'.[1] His appeal was thus aimed in particular at that body of Liberal opinion which had opposed Home Rule because it was regarded as likely to bring about the disintegration of the Empire. Imperialism was the key to the restoration of the former strength of the Liberal party. Rosebery would argue that the real cause of the split in 1886 was 'the foreign policy of the Government from 1880 to 1885'.[2] Opposition to Home Rule was part of a reaction against the anti-imperialist character of Liberal policy.

Harcourt replied to this that 'the true inwardness of the Liberal secession' was class feeling, the dread felt by the wealthy and privileged at the 'advent of equal justice'.[3] Harcourt suggested that the people whose return Rosebery was proposing and encouraging were those who had left the party because they feared 'the progressive march of ideas'. And it is true that one of Rosebery's main aims was to counter the 'degeneration' of the Liberal party into a class party. The cause of this controversy between Harcourt and himself was the Budget of 1894 which Rosebery said was bringing about a 'horizontal division of parties' in which the Liberals would be mainly a lower class party. In August 1896 he defined 'the process which all true Liberals must have at heart' as 'the restoration of the Liberal party to what it was in richness, variety and strength before 1886'; and in May 1899 he called for a new Liberal party that would embody all the elements of the pre-1886 party.[4] This would include those elements over whose departure Harcourt felt so pleased.

[1] *Liberal Magazine*, vol. 2, no. 8 (May 1894), p. 114.
[2] *Liberal Magazine*, vol. 9, no. 95 (August 1901), p. 388.
[3] *Liberal Magazine*, vol. 2, no. 12 (September 1894), p. 282.
[4] Crewe, *Lord Rosebery*, ii, pp. 523, 559.

Rosebery would refer to post-1886 Liberalism as 'sectional Liberalism'.[1] When Liberals wrote to him about sectional reform questions such as liquor licensing, he would reply that it was his hope to see national solutions to these acceptable to all sides brought in by a 'great party in the State—approaching as nearly as possible to the old Liberal Party before its disruption'.[2] Opinion among Rosebery's political associates as to whether reliance on the return of the ex-Liberals was a realistic strategy for reconstructing the party was divided. Haldane came to believe by 1899 that very soon, 'for every member of the Nat. Lib. Fedn. who is alienated, two will be ready to come over who have voted Unionist for long time past'.[3] Asquith, on the other hand, felt that the appeal to the Liberal Unionists was bad tactics because it was not likely to win over many of the followers of Hartington and Chamberlain but would certainly offend and discourage Liberals who had remained loyal to the party since 1885 and had been violently attacked by the Liberal Unionists for doing so.[4] One Liberal Unionist who had a keen appreciation of what Rosebery was trying to do was Chamberlain himself. Chamberlain was later to observe that 'Rosebery had often had the ball at his feet—e.g. after the "predominant partner" speech. If he had stuck to that, his future would have been certain. We leaders were far too committed, but he would have captured our followers.'[5] In Chamberlain's opinion, Rosebery, when he became Prime Minister, understood 'how to revive the old Liberal Party' and 'tried to do it, in the right way, by his "predominant partner" speech', but, 'having funked', 'destroyed his own handiwork and the Party for ever'. 'I shall never forgive him', was Chamberlain's bitter comment.[6]

[1] *Liberal Magazine*, vol. 7, no. 69 (June 1899), p. 252.
[2] Rosebery to W. S. Haldane, 28 December 1897, Rosebery MSS., Box 89, letter copy book, folio 164.
[3] Haldane to Rosebery, 23 and 29 October 1899, Rosebery MSS., Box 24.
[4] Asquith to Rosebery, 6 May 1899 (not sent), quoted in R. Jenkins, *Asquith*, 1964, pp. 111–12.
[5] Saxon Mills, *Sir Edward Cook*, p. 222.
[6] M. V. Brett (ed.), *Journals and Letters of Reginald Viscount Esher*, vol. i, 1934, p. 210. It is interesting to note that Rosebery told Sir E. Hamilton, 31 March 1893, that he 'felt more in accord' with Chamberlain 'than with almost any other public man'. B.M. Add. MS. 48660, folio 31. In 1894 Chamberlain told Morley, 'that he quaked when Rosebery was made P.M., lest he should fling H.R. overboard, the

effect of which would surely have been to attract masses of Liberal Unionists to the flag of their old party. After R. made his first speech about the predominant partner in the H. of L., he refused an invitation to follow R. at Edinburgh. But when he read the Edinburgh speech, he at once wired to that city that he would come down instantly.' Chamberlain said also that he thought the Liberals' tactics after 1893 'lamentable. We ought to have defied our sections to do their worst.' Morley, *Recollections*, i, p. 296.

XI Imperialism and Liberal Politics

For many Liberals in the 1890s and early twentieth century the absence of a general Liberal creed or system of guiding principles seemed at last to have been remedied. 'Liberal Imperialism' was for them not merely a way of looking at the development of the Empire; it also offered a great systematic and comprehensive concept that unified and guided the conduct of Liberals in many hitherto unco-ordinated areas of policy. It is clear that much of the impact which it made on Liberal opinion, much of the idealism and enthusiasm which it called forth especially among younger Liberals, stemmed from its satisfying a craving for order and system in Liberal politics. It released energies that had hitherto been held in check or even paralysed by the absence of any over-all sense of direction and purpose. One particularly enthusiastic adherent to this new creed, Heber Hart, wrote thus of the Liberal Imperialist: 'His faith is large enough to satisfy the full scope of his aspirations: it provides an enthusiasm for his heart, a system for his mind, and a code for his conscience. . . . His Imperialism dignifies and intensifies every detail of the politics of the home, the school, the factory and the field. His Liberalism is intense because it is elevated into an all-pervading faith.'[1]

The systematic character of Liberal Imperialism was in part a consequence of the Home Rule issue itself. As we have seen, there were many Liberals who remained loyal to Gladstone after 1886 and professed support for Irish Home Rule but interpreted it in an imperialist way as a contribution to a much larger programme of imperial reconstruction.[2] The Home Rule policy stimulated the formulation of general schemes of devolution and Imperial Federation. These combined two unifying Liberal concepts: the traditional concern with the extension of

---

[1] *New Liberal Review*, vol. 1, no. 3 (April 1901), pp. 384, 390.
[2] See above, pp. 155–61.

self-government, and a more modern idealistic imperialism; while also offering a chance for Liberalism to escape from the growing 'Celtic Fringe' influence over the shaping of its policies and to re-establish itself as a national and imperial creed. Rosebery, for instance, began to see in imperial reconstruction a means of bringing Liberalism back into association with the feelings of the 'predominant partner'. In October 1895 he wrote to a Welsh correspondent that 'devolution' might be a remedy for the 'serious and perhaps increasing difficulty in obtaining the time and attention of Parliament for the discussion of subjects which do not directly concern England, but only the other members of the British partnership, unless they happen to involve burning principles of larger application, such as Church Disestablishment, when they encounter the zealous hostility of the English Tory majority, in entire disregard of the wishes of the particular nationality affected'.[1] Martin Conway, an ardent 'Roseberyite', saw in 'federalism' a means of applying Rosebery's principle of 'concentration' and avoiding 'a multiplication of issues' in Liberal politics. The Irish Home Rule policy should be developed, he argued, into a more general scheme for 'devolving upon provincial (perhaps national) assemblies the management of provincial affairs'. This would be the kind of comprehensive policy which, if concentrated on, would simultaneously take care of a large number of the reform questions in which Liberals were interested. For example, 'the federalisation of legislative institutions in the United Kingdom would be a solution of the House of Lords veto as well as of the Irish problems', and as a political issue would, once raised, facilitate the removal 'from the front rank of debated questions' of 'both Welsh and Scottish Disestablishment the settlement of which must necessarily be postponed to that of the major problem'. Other matters that Conway believed could be removed from parliamentary politics by being proposed as business for local assemblies included 'regulation of the liquor traffic', improvements in the conditions of labour, and poor law reform. In this way the all-embracing theme of 'Federalism' could be used either to place within a system or to force the postponement of all 'the various subjects comprised in the late Liberal pro-

[1] Rosebery to J. Hugh Edwards, 29 October 1895, Rosebery MSS., Box 89, letter copy book, folio 28.

gramme'.[1] Munro Ferguson wrote to Rosebery after the election defeat of 1895: 'As to the future. If we unite on H.R. all round & the Lords our programme would be all right. Church, Liquor etc would then be out of the way.'[2] Thus the application of the Liberal Imperial idea began to stimulate the revival of the old comprehensive issue of local government reform. Another Liberal Imperialist, Charles Douglas, argued that 'the policies of devolution and imperialism are part of the same idea'. The efficiency of Parliament would be improved and the paralysis in Liberal politics ended by the removal of the 'perpetual collision of the claims of Imperial questions and local interests'. Therefore, as a Liberal Imperialist he wanted to see the Liberal party make 'constructive devolution' its 'fighting policy'.[3]

There were those who saw in Liberal Imperialism the long-needed and long-awaited Liberal creed that would direct and guide Liberals in a non-Socialist but 'constructive' concern for social reform. It was an alternative to Socialism in that it opposed to a philosophy of class conflict an emphasis on the preservation of an organic and whole community, a true 'Empire', able to face the competition of other Imperial Powers without the fatal handicap of internal division and unrest. Rosebery referred to the rearing of 'an imperial race' as justification for the undertaking of social improvement by the State.[4] Some found in Liberal Imperialism a means of release from paralysing inhibitions concerning social reform. Asquith, for example, saw it as stimulating—instead of frustrating, as most other 'systems' of Liberal thought seemed for a long time

[1] Conway to Rosebery, 19 September 1895, Rosebery MSS., Box 70. Gladstone opposed Scottish Home Rule for the very reasons which Conway here produces in favour of 'federalism'. 'The moment we declare for Home Rule in Scotland', he told the House of Commons on 9 April 1889, 'we are open to the observation that such a question as that of licensing ought to stand over for the consideration of a Scottish Legislature', and the result would be to throw 'into arrear and into the shade every other Scotch question on which the national opinion of Scotland is entitled to bear sway'. Gladstone said that he refused to pronounce in favour of Scottish Home Rule and so enable it 'to be cast in our teeth that by setting forth as ripe for decision the question as to a Scottish Legislature we have pointed out that a Scottish Legislature would be the proper organ for disposing of the subject of Disestablishment'. *Hansard*, 3rd Series, vol. 335, cc. 106–7.
[2] 27 July 1895, Rosebery MSS., Box 15.
[3] *C.R.*, vol. 81, no. 436 (April 1902), pp. 584–5.
[4] For this and other similar statements see B. Semmel, *Imperialism and Social Reform English Social-Imperial Thought 1895–1914*, 1960, pp. 62–3.

to have been doing—all Liberal aspirations and efforts towards social reform.[1] It was a source of inspiration and direction. Sir Edward Cook, one of the leading Liberal Imperialist journalists, believed that 'devotion to the Liberal Imperial idea' and 'devotion to social reforms' were 'logically combined', and tried to make the combination or synthesis the basis of his own work as a creator of Liberal opinion. 'My main effort in journalism', he wrote in 1903, 'has been (1) to influence the Liberal Party in an Imperialist direction; (2) to support social reforms. The political causes which interested me most at the "D[aily] N[ews]", after South Africa and other Imperial questions, were what I called "No Room to Live" and "The Cry of the Children".'[2] One of the main issues of controversy between the Liberal Imperialists and their anti-imperialist critics in the party was whether such a combination was in fact viable. According to anti-imperialists such as Harcourt and John Morley, imperialism must involve a diversion of resources and energies from social improvement at home.[3] But such Liberals were often opponents of State intervention in social and economic problems. There undoubtedly *was* a logical connection between Liberal Imperialism, meaning the use of the power of the British State to 'improve' and 'raise' and 'civilize' other peoples, and a disposition to favour a similar employment of State power with regard to the home population. The connection was in large part forged through Social Darwinian ideas of a struggle for mastery among nations in which that nation would fare best which represented the 'fittest imperial race'. And there was also undoubtedly a connection between antagonism to the increase of the power of the State which is necessarily associated with imperialist policies and adherence to principles of *laissez-faire* with regard to home affairs. Here the link was the systematic concept of 'free trade' which had traditionally comprehended and defined both the nature of Britain's relations with the outside world and the role of the State at home.

These were the two great polarizations or systems of Liberal opinion which seemed to be emerging during the controversy

[1] *The Mission of Liberalism* (speech of 19 July 1901), p. 9.
[2] *New Liberal Review*, vol. 2, no. 7 (August 1901), p. 16. Saxon Mills, *Sir Edward Cook*, pp. 197–8, 206.
[3] Gardiner, *Life of Harcourt*, ii, p. 497. Hamer, *John Morley*, pp. 315–16.

over imperialism. But there were, of course, many Liberals in between; that is, Radicals who wanted the power of the State to be increased but also to be concentrated on home problems, and Imperialists who cared and thought little or nothing about social reform. The problem for the former continued to be how to maintain a viable distinction between themselves and socialists, and for the latter to differentiate themselves from Conservatives. In other words, only the Liberal Imperialists and the 'free traders' were able to claim that they possessed, and had their political practice guided by, a distinctively Liberal system of thought.

The Liberal Imperialists believed that they were supplying the Liberal party with what it most urgently needed, a comprehensive system of ideas, a single basis of unified, systematic principles. What they were offering the party was a 'religion', wrote Haldane.[1] It was not tolerable therefore, in their opinion, that any attempt should be made to perpetuate the Liberal party as an organization that contained the adherents of more than one 'school of thought'. Sir Edward Cook wrote that the effort to follow a policy of compromise between imperialists and anti-imperialists was paralysing the party. In order that Liberalism should be based on 'definite ideals, clear aims, certain views', one of these points of view 'should definitely and unequivocally prevail'.[2] In this respect the Liberal Imperialists were very much in the single-great-question tradition—although, of course, what they believed that they possessed was a system itself and not merely the substitute for system that previous great questions such as Home Rule had constituted. Charles Douglas, writing in 1902, attributed the weakness of the Liberals to 'the lack of any great object of policy which absorbed and united the energies of the party'. He advanced some of the classic arguments in favour of concentration on single great questions: 'Great causes breed great sacrifices. Those who are occupied in securing, together, objects of whose urgent necessity they are convinced, find it easy to forget their differences, and to abandon their prejudices and antipathies as well as more material motives.' Most significantly he referred to the value of the

[1] Haldane to Rosebery, 29 December 1899, Rosebery MSS., Box 24.
[2] *New Liberal Review*, vol. 2, no. 7 (August 1901), pp. 14, 16.

Home Rule policy as this kind of cause. Since it had broken down, there had been 'no such bond of union, no such solvent of differences, in the Liberal party', 'no single project on whose prompt and complete achievement men's minds were so set that their differences were forgotten and their party unity became the instrument essential to an immediate task'. No effective unity in a party could come, Douglas wrote, from the toleration of differences of opinion. There had to be a 'unity of the spirit', a sense of 'an overmastering obligation' and 'personal responsibility for the attainment of public ends pursued in common'. This situation had obtained between 1886 and 1895. Now Liberal Imperialism and 'constructive devolution' could enter the vacuum left by the disintegration of the Home Rule cause.[1]

Rosebery himself now saw the developing rift in the party over imperialism as a great opportunity for the carrying out of the reconstruction and 'concentration' of Liberal politics which he had been advocating since the collapse of the Irish policy. He associated himself with those who insisted that the existence of Liberalism was meaningless unless it was identified with one definite policy or school of thought. He argued that the Liberal party could not be 'a power' again until there was a single set of principles guiding its action. No party could contain two opposed schools of thought as the Liberal party did with regard to imperialism and 'remain an efficient instrument': 'the boat can never advance, for they are rowing in opposite directions. Until the crew make up their mind towards what point they are to row, their barque can never move, it can only revolve.' 'One school or the other must prevail', he declared, 'if the Liberal party is once more to become a force.'[2] Rosebery put this belief into practice by refusing to participate any longer in the activities of a party which continued to contain people with views opposed to those of the Liberal Imperialists.[3]

Once again, as so often in recent Liberal history, there was talk of purging the party and of producing in it the kind of split which would have the paradoxical effect of creating a unified party. Rosebery wrote of the good effect that a 'final cataclysm'

[1] *C.R.*, vol. 81, no. 436 (April 1902), pp. 581–4.
[2] *Liberal Magazine*, vol. 9, no. 95 (August 1901), pp. 415–17.
[3] Cf. his withdrawal from the National Liberal Club. R. Steven, *The National Liberal Club Politics and Persons* [1925], p. 44.

splitting the Radical 'Rump' and 'the Irishry' from 'the Imperialist section' would have 'in the long run'.[1] Haldane maintained that, although there would be two sections to begin with after a split, 'Lord R.'s friends' would be 'from the first not only a large but a growing section', whereas the other section would dwindle steadily; and 'this means that we grow and become the party'. He referred to the Liberal Imperialists as forcing on a 'purgation of the party'.[2] Rosebery, who had a genius for memorable metaphorical presentations of political situations and strategies, produced, and fastened the attention of all Liberals on, the concept of the 'clean slate'. In July 1901 he told Liberals that, in order that they could 'proceed to deal in a new spirit with the new problems of the age as they arrive', they should feel that they were starting 'with a clean slate as regards these cumbersome programmes with which you were overloaded in the past'.[3] In his famous Chesterfield speech of 16 December 1901 his advice to Liberals who wished to regain the country's confidence was that 'you have to clean your slate'. The world had moved on since 1886, and there could not be tolerated on the Liberal slate policies that were 'adapted to 1892 or 1885'.[4]

Finally, in February 1902, the Roseberyites set up their own organization to promote the reconstruction of Liberal policy—the Liberal League. As the deliberate omission from its title of the word 'Imperial' shows, the League was as much concerned with reforming and reconstructing the domestic policy of the party as with imperialism itself.

One of the basic assumptions of Liberal Imperialism was the necessity of identifying Liberalism with the feelings of 'the nation'. Rosebery argued that the Liberal party should move at about the same pace and in the same direction as 'the great mass of the nation is prepared to move'.[4] It was this issue perhaps more than any other that lay at the root of the great quarrel between Liberal Imperialists and anti-imperialists.

---

[1] James, *Rosebery*, p. 413.
[2] Haldane to Rosebery, 25 July 1900, Rosebery MSS., Box 24.
[3] *Liberal Magazine*, vol. 9, no. 95 (August 1901), p. 418.
[4] *National Policy. A Speech delivered at Chesterfield December 16, 1901. By Lord Rosebery*, 1902, pp. 1–2.

Campbell-Bannerman summed up the opposite point of view when he asked: 'Surely it is never meant that we ought to wait until we find out what will be popular and suit the whim of the day?'[1] For the Liberal Imperialists had raised the fundamental question of the extent to which the Liberals should take, or would be obliged to take if they were ever to regain power, the pursuit of electoral success and popularity. During the South African war Rosebery and his followers demanded that the party should adopt positions that were in line with the popular imperialist sentiment of the time. But other Liberals objected that this was based on the principle that Liberalism must change its policies to match every shift of public opinion. They thought that what Rosebery was proposing meant founding Liberalism on the perpetually shifting sands of electoral opportunism. The Roseberyites countered this by arguing that a party which did not *try* to win power was useless and must wither away because people would stop voting for it. The election results of 1895 and 1900 seemed to them to prove that the party's failure to align itself with 'national' opinion was having precisely this effect. Among their opponents there were indeed some such as Harcourt and John Morley who insisted quite categorically that the party must have a firm and stable foundation of principle, that questions of immediate success or failure, popularity or unpopularity, must be disregarded when Liberal leaders were deciding on policy.[2] Campbell-Bannerman, leader of the party from the beginning of 1899, adopted a similar attitude, but one detects in his approach a strain of practicality and realism, an awareness that, since past history had shown the popularity of imperialism to be a periodic and transient phenomenon, adherence to principle in this case was not likely to be—as, of course, it did not prove to be—an electoral disadvantage for very long.

During the South African war the Liberal Imperialists called for the suspension of party attacks on the government. They wanted the Liberals to demonstrate a capacity to put national above party considerations. But, although for a time many Liberals were anxious not to appear unpatriotic and were very uncertain as to whether and to what extent they could safely

---

[1] Spender, *Life of Campbell-Bannerman*, ii, p. 27.
[2] Gardiner, *Life of Harcourt*, ii, p. 372. Hamer, *John Morley*, pp. 302–3.

criticize the government's conduct of the war, there was a growing feeling that there was something unnatural and dangerous about giving up behaving as a party and trying to reduce or blur as much as possible the distinctions between the Liberals and the Unionists. J. A. Spender, the outstanding Liberal journalist, told Rosebery that his 'counsel of no discussion' could not 'be squared with the existence of a House of Commons, party government, by elections, the writing of leading articles, & the making of speeches'. 'If we are not', he wrote, 'to criticise while the war lasts & are to express such approval of present proceedings as will debar us from criticising afterwards, what legitimate function will be open to us when the general election arrives . . .? . . . does the country gain anything from the silencing of criticism to compensate for what it loses from the destruction of party government? Is the Boer war, serious & costly as it is, the kind of national emergency which requires one party to efface itself?'[1]

The critics of the 'Lib. Imps.' laid great stress on the importance of preserving a distinct Liberal identity by maintaining continuity with the Liberal past. To them it seemed that the Imperialists were doing no more than bidding for a 'precarious support by borrowing the opinions and mimicking the practice' of the Liberals' opponents. Adopting the methods and principles of others in hope of enjoying a similar success through employing them 'does not really pay', argued Harcourt, 'because you may be quite certain that people will always go to the real shop for the genuine article, and will not be put off with your margarine imitations'. In Harcourt's opinion it was quite absurd for the Liberals to try 'to go one better than Chamberlain'. To him Rosebery's 'clean slate' meant the destruction of the organic reality of Liberalism: 'All the traditions, the pledges and the faiths of the Liberal Party to be wiped out . . . It is in fact to throw everything overboard in order to get back to office by adopting that which is popular at the moment . . . The whole language is insulting to the whole past of the Liberal Party and a betrayal of its growth in the future.'[2] Harcourt summed up this aspect of the case against the Liberal

[1] Spender to Rosebery, 28 October 1899, Rosebery MSS., Box 75.
[2] Gardiner, *Life of Harcourt*, ii, pp. 477, 536–7. *The Liberal Magazine*, vol. 8, no. 85 (October 1900), p. 484. Cf. Hamer, *John Morley*, p. 323.

Imperialists in a memorandum written after the formation of the Liberal League in 1902:

The Clean Slate

Lord R.'s doctrine thus stated 'To live in the present, to work in the present, with your eye on the present and *not on the past*'.

Why not on the past? The failures and the successes of the past are the best lessons for the present and for the future.

'History is *statesmanship* teaching by example.'

What is the value of a Party or a Policy which has no past or despises it?

This is the doctrine of a Revolutionist not of a constitutional statesman—a chief of a great historical Party.[1]

The anti-imperialist or 'Pro-Boer' section of the party had this in common with the Liberal Imperialists, that they too found objectionable the existence within the party of such a wide range of opinions on imperialism and wished one school of thought to predominate—their own. The difference was that they opposed all notions of the radical reconstruction of Liberal policy and wanted the party to remain firmly based on traditional Liberal principles. They called for respect for the organic evolution of Liberalism. To them revision of policy to take account of changes in the mood of the public smacked too much of opportunism and promised a situation of perpetual flux and instability. But they were as hostile as was Rosebery to the maintenance of a party containing two such radically opposed tendencies of thought. Liberals must be made to choose between them. John Morley wrote in 1901: 'As for our party, I am wholly of Rosebery's mind for once, and regard it as organized hypocrisy of the most futile kind that ever was known in our history.'[2]

When Harcourt resigned the leadership at the end of 1898, the reason that he gave was very like that given by Gladstone in 1875 and by Rosebery himself in 1896—that he did not wish to lead a party rent by sectional disputes.[3] If the party

---

[1] This memo. in the Harcourt MSS. is undated but clearly relates to the events of 1901–2.

[2] Morley to Spencer, 14 August 1901, Spencer MSS.

[3] 'The Liberal Party has a lesson to learn before it can be good for anything.' Harcourt to Arnold Morley, 15 December 1898, Harcourt MSS.

were not agreed on a common basis of action, effective leadership was not possible; and both Rosebery and Harcourt left the leadership in order to work from a much freer position outside it to foster such agreement. Again there is a parallel with Gladstone's working of the question of 'anti-Beaconsfieldism' from 1876 on. But Harcourt was to be the last leader of the party to understand the relationship between leader and party in this way. Not the least remarkable feature of Campbell-Bannerman's leadership was to be his breaking of this tradition.[1]

Like Rosebery, Harcourt believed that the party must choose between the two schools of thought, and he and John Morley set out 'to give Liberal jingoism its quietus for a long time to come'.[2] The anti-imperialists talked about the desirability of reconstructing the party and purging the Imperialist element in it. John Morley wrote in September 1900: 'The Liberal party is where it deserves to be, and I hope the smash will be complete. Then the friends of peace & prudence may try to build another party.'[3] J. E. Ellis wrote that, although 'the outcome politically' of the general election was 'not cheerful', 'I believe in a *purge*—& that our party is getting'.[4] Lord Ripon believed that, if the Liberal Imperialists refused to accept the policy which Campbell-Bannerman laid down with regard to South Africa, 'the Party will be broken up for the moment, no doubt: to be reconstructed on the old principles, and with a clear policy'.[5] Dr. John Clifford, the leading Nonconformist anti-imperialist, advocated the 'dropping' of 'a whole host of "Liberals" so-called' and the creation of a new party 'composed of the most level-headed of the Socialists and the most radical of the Radicals'.[6]

Nevertheless, no final split did occur. One major reason for the maintenance of party unity was the triumph of a particular interpretation of the nature of the party. This we shall analyse in the following chapter. The other major reason was the failure of either wing to carry out a complete separation of itself

---
[1] See below, pp. 293-6.
[2] Morley to Harcourt, 21 December 1898, Harcourt MSS.
[3] Morley to Spencer, 22 September 1900, Spencer MSS.
[4] Ellis to Bryce, 15 September 1900, Bryce MSS., E 14.
[5] Ripon to C-B, 9 November 1900, Wolf, *Life of Ripon*, ii, pp. 259-60.
[6] Sir James Marchant, *Dr John Clifford, C.H. Life, Letters and Reminiscences*, 1924, p. 147.

from the rest of the party. Each wished to help produce a situation where it itself was the party and the other section was merely a faction. It was, as we shall see, much easier for the anti-imperialists, with their emphasis on continuity and tradition, to appear to be in this situation. But in fact both sections remained throughout most anxious not to seem to be behaving sectionally or to be the cause of any split that might develop. Each was determined to extend its influence over, and not allow itself to be separated from, the main body of the party. Many Liberals made the unity of the party their primary consideration and were likely to react strongly against any group which might appear to be initiating the disruption of the party. The aim of each section was to establish its claim to speak for Liberalism. It had, therefore, to try to force its opponents into appearing to be the faction in the situation. The struggle was for the 'centre' of the party, the 'moderates', the rank and file, who wanted to see their party strong and united and holding office once again. These Liberals might be won over to policies or themes which could be seen as related to these objectives, to Liberal Imperialism because it suggested a way in which Liberalism could be brought back into line with 'national' or majority opinion, or to anti-imperialism because in it alone could be found a means of clearly differentiating Liberals from their Unionist opponents. But they would feel nothing but revulsion for any group whose divisive tactics appeared to be postponing indefinitely the chance of a return from the electoral wilderness. The fate of the Liberal Unionists was a precedent skilfully exploited by Campbell-Bannerman and other promoters of party unity to deter either side from breaking away from the party.[1]

The Liberal Imperialists were anxious to present themselves as in the main stream of Liberal political development. They did not want to be branded as a mere coterie or faction out on a limb or in rebellion against 'the party'. They wished to become the party. There was a constant conflict as a result between their natural inclination towards a forceful, militant stance in support of their principles and their fear of alienating other Liberals by an appearance of excessive aggressiveness

[1] Cf. *London Organisation and South African Policy*, 1902, a speech by C-B, 13 January 1902, p. 7.

and factiousness. The desire to appear not to be a faction but a reconstructed form of Liberalism as a whole is reflected in Rosebery's advice that their organization should be called the 'Liberal (Imperialist) League': 'The design of the brackets was to imply that the Liberal Imperialists were the real Liberal Party, which should naturally imply Imperialism. . . .'[1]

The Liberal Imperialist leaders had no desire to break away from the Liberal party and form a new party of their own. They sensed that that way lay impotence and ultimate failure. Theirs was the Fabian tactic of 'permeation' and infiltration of a party felt to be in such an advanced state of decay and with such a complete vacuum where policy and principles were meant to be that capture of it by these tactics would prove to be very easy to accomplish. Setting up a new party would mean throwing away an asset of infinitely greater potential value which was theirs virtually for the taking. R. W. Perks summed up this strategy when he told Rosebery that a reference by Lord Brassey, President of the Liberal Imperial Council, in September 1900 to the Liberal Imperialists' intention to create a new party had been a 'slip': 'My notion has always been to secure sufficient power to capture & control the old.'[2] After the general election of 1900 Perks argued that 'no good purpose' would be served by boasting too much of gains made by 'the "Liberal Imperialist" section', and added that 'the name is not one that I like any more now than at first & I don't think it is popular.' Feeling that the Liberal Imperial Council had become 'rather too assertive & combative', he warned against 'aggressively pushing' it since the Liberal Imperialists' aim must be to capture and reorganize 'existing Liberal institutions', not to promote new organizations.[3] There was even a good deal of uneasiness when the more militant 'Lib. Imps.' published a list of Liberal candidates described as 'followers' of Rosebery. This looked too much like creating a faction within the party.[4] Haldane warned Rosebery in October 1900 that 'the aggression of the Liberal Imperial Council has not done good'. The danger was that it gave their opponents the chance to depict them

[1] Rosebery to Heber Hart, 6 October 1901, Rosebery MSS., Box 89, letter copy book, folio 281.
[2] Perks to Rosebery, 22 September 1900, Rosebery MSS., Box 39.
[3] Perks to Rosebery, 7, 14, 19 October 1900, Rosebery MSS., Box 39.
[4] Wemyss Reid to Rosebery, 23 September 1900, Rosebery MSS., Box 44.

as having voluntarily separated themselves from the party. 'We ought to be . . . defendants & not plaintiffs in ejectment.'[1] H. H. Fowler echoed this when he wrote that what 'Harcourt Labouchere & Co. desire' was that the Liberal Imperialists should be manœuvred into seceding. 'We must smash the talk about secession. . . . *We* represent the majority of the Party. We are loyal to its principles & traditions and we must not allow the idea to spread that we are the authors of a new departure.'[2]

Nevertheless, in February 1902 the Liberal Imperialists did decide to create a new organization for the purpose of promoting the reconstruction of Liberal politics—the Liberal League. It was a hazardous move, and from the start doubts were expressed as to the wisdom of taking it. Asquith thought that the M.P.s 'who agreed with Lord R. . . . should remain in the House of Commons without forming a separate organization, though acting in connection on important questions'. Rosebery showed what risks were involved in any break with 'official' Liberalism when he admitted that he himself 'stood on a very thin edge and that in fact there was little to separate him from the Liberal Unionists more especially if they pursued a liberal domestic policy; and as to that point they had promised to legislate on temperance and education as he had urged at Chesterfield'.[3] The leaders of the League insisted repeatedly that it was in no way intended to be a separate organization or party. Its aim was to 'permeate' local Liberal parties and reconstruct Liberalism from within.[4] Rosebery wrote that the League was 'intended not to cause division, but to permeate and influence'.[5] Asquith was at considerable pains to make the League appear basically a defensive organization, a reaction against sectional intrigue, a bid by many Liberals to defend themselves against attempts to expel them from, and thus disunite, the party. He called it 'a cheap price to pay for the avoidance of what was otherwise inevitable:

[1] Haldane to Rosebery, 30 October 1900, Rosebery MSS., Box 24. Rosebery agreed with this. See his letter to Haldane, 1 November 1900, Haldane MSS., MS. 5905, folio 49.
[2] Fowler to Asquith, 23 June [?1901], Asquith MSS., Dep. 10, folios 3–4.
[3] Draft memo. of meeting at Rosebery's London house, 24 February 1902, Rosebery MSS., Box 106.
[4] Cf. Ferguson to Rosebery, 13 July 1902, Rosebery MSS., Box 16.
[5] Rosebery to C. J. Whitting, 14 August 1902, Rosebery MSS., Box 89, letter copy book, folio 312.

a definite & open split'. 'Nothing', he claimed, 'can exceed the assiduity & ingenuity with wh. Loulou [Harcourt] & his friends are trying to capture for their own purposes our regular organizations e.g. Eighty Club. It is not so much a question of reprisals as of self-protection.'[1] When the League was founded, some sympathizers with Liberal Imperialism were reluctant to make public profession of adherence to it because they were afraid of appearing to be causing a split in the party. One M.P., J. Fuller, explained his position thus to Rosebery: 'To declare at once a split in the party here, & my adhesion to one section would be I think to lose the seat. . . . Until a pronounced C.B.ite candidate appears in the field against me (an unlikely contingency) I shall endeavour not to lay too much stress upon "definite separation".'[2] The Imperialists had to avoid appearing to be the initiators of the disruption of the party, in other words. The way in which each side manœuvred to force the other into this position, especially in Scotland where Liberal Imperialism was strong, is illustrated by a letter sent to Rosebery in August 1902 by T. Gibson Carmichael, one of the leading Scottish Liberal Leaguers. He reported that Lord Tweedmouth was urging the Scottish Liberal Association to 'show no hostility to the league, but rather to let hostility come from us'. The danger was that if there was hostility 'whichever party begins it will turn popular sympathy to the other'. Patience and restraint would soon bring a reward: 'the Young Scots' on the other side were likely to 'break out' very soon, and 'if they do that will strengthen us enormously'.[3]

Rosebery advised members of the League on no account to leave or allow themselves to be driven out of their local Liberal Associations for this would simply mean handing over these Associations to 'the absolute influence of the opposite party'. They must remain within and 'permeate' the party and 'influence it in the only direction which they believe to be sound'.[4] The main object of the exercise soon came to be to secure

[1] Asquith to Spencer, 4 March 1902, Spencer MSS., 1902. A-D. For Asquith's efforts to brand the opposite section as 'aggressive' see his letter to C-B, 15 June 1901, C-B MSS., B.M. Add. MS. 41210, folios 206-7.
[2] Fuller to Rosebery, 22 February 1902, Rosebery MSS., Box 106.
[3] 3 August 1902, Rosebery MSS., Box 106.
[4] *Liberal Magazine*, vol. 10, no. 103 (April 1902), p. 179.

control over local Associations and thus over the selection of Liberal candidates so as to affect the nature of the parliamentary majority on which the next Liberal government would depend. Rosebery hoped that the influence of the Liberal League would help create a Liberal party whose 'soundness' would prevent the reaction against the Tory government from assuming too violent and extreme a form.[1] But it was a race against time. Haldane saw the Liberal Leaguers as engaged in a long struggle 'to educate our party', a struggle which was perpetually liable to be terminated by Campbell-Bannerman's 'tumbling or being tumbled into the possession of office'.[2]

The unity of the party was preserved because *all* sections restrained their aggressiveness. The leaders themselves, while resenting the behaviour of the Imperialists, were determined to give them no excuse for saying that their separation from 'the party' was being forced on them. This would have undermined faith in the 'Broad Church' interpretation of the nature of the party on which, as we shall see in the next chapter, the leaders' position came to depend. Herbert Gladstone argued that Rosebery should be treated 'in a conciliatory spirit' so as to make his own behaviour appear to be 'in the wrong'.[3] In January 1902 Bryce warned Campbell-Bannerman that 'dozens of people would be only too glad to represent you as repelling him [Rosebery] or the Lib. Imps.'. Many 'average Liberals' rallied to Rosebery because they believed that his connection with Liberal politics 'spells unity'; but they 'would hardly follow him if he caused a breach'. Consequently, according to Bryce, 'it seems to make a great difference whether we excommunicate R., or the Lib. Imps., ... or whether they secede from us'.[4] In other words, the various aspirants to influence and authority in Liberal politics would be judged by ordinary rank-and-file Liberals according to the extent to which they *appeared* to be promoting party unity.

The achievement of the Liberal League fell well short of its

[1] Rosebery to Lord Sefton, 11 August 1902, Rosebery MSS., Box 89, letter copy book, folio 311.
[2] Haldane to Rosebery, 7 September 1902, Rosebery MSS., Box 24.
[3] H. Gladstone to C-B, 16 November 1903, C-B MSS., B.M. Add. MS. 41217, folio 35.
[4] 3 January 1902, C-B MSS., B.M. Add. MS. 41211, folios 190-1.

aspirations. It was never a very effective instrument for 're-constructing' Liberalism. It failed, not surprisingly in view of its antagonism to sectionalism and 'faddism', to establish any substantial connection with any other major section of opinion or interest group in the party. Perks in March 1902 wrote with vast optimism of an alliance of 'the Dissenters, the Temperance party, & *Labour*'.[1] But 'Labour' was never touched by the movement, and it and the other two sections to which Perks refers speedily moved from 1902 onwards into an accommodation with the Liberal leadership.[2] The League had an excessively high proportion of leaders, partly because it naturally attracted talented young men who were frustrated by the apparent disorganization and impotence of the party and saw little hope in its existing condition for a fulfilment of their ambitions and a creative outlet for their talents. In part too the League's lack of appeal to rank-and-file Liberals reflected the élitist and even anti-democratic philosophy of some of its promoters. Some who supported it did so because they hoped that it would check the growth of radical and 'democratic' influence over the party's development. W. D. Pearson, one of its wealthiest supporters, told Perks that 'its existence is essential to the Liberal Party if it is going to once more include in it the men of weight and substance who have been alienated from it in recent years; & without whom the Party will never take its proper position or be able to do efficient work'.[3]

The Liberal League was crippled by its dependence on Rosebery's becoming an active Liberal leader once more. Rosebery refused to descend again to the level of party politics. He believed that to do so would mean abandoning that connection with national opinion in which he saw Liberalism's main hope of recovery. But Rosebery's approach to the problem of 'reconstructing' Liberal politics baffled and frustrated many Liberals who looked to him for guidance. He appeared to be concerned primarily with changing the Liberal frame of mind, the entire general scheme of assumptions and attitudes which governed Liberal political behaviour. To him this was the most

[1] Perks to Rosebery, 10 March 1902, Rosebery MSS., Box 40.
[2] See below, pp. 297–314.
[3] Pearson to Perks, 23 September 1904, enclosed in Perks to Rosebery, 24 September 1904, Rosebery MSS., Box 41.

important work that needed to be done, much more important than filling in the details of policy. But many Liberals came to feel that he was too preoccupied with the negative task of 'cleaning the slate'. They began to doubt whether he had any precise and positive reform policy of his own to offer. Munro Ferguson told him in 1899 that there were Liberals in Edinburgh and Glasgow who admired and wished to support him but who also 'wished that they were sure that you were keen on one single domestic reform which you meant to see through'.[1] Such Liberals were not appeased by the Chesterfield speech at the end of 1901. They found Rosebery's reform programme, his list of measures which he wished to see passed, far too threadbare and unspecific and argued that 'you cannot go to the constituencies with a clean slate'.[2] But this was a 'fault' which was inherent in the nature of the exercise in which Rosebery was engaged. He was opposed on principle to programmes, all programmes. He was therefore not going to start constructing one of his own by naming specific reforms that he would take up, especially at the very time when he was trying to change the whole Liberal frame of mind.[3] Going into detail on policy issues would have militated against accomplishment of Rosebery's prime objective, the introduction of the spirit of system into Liberal politics. He wanted to encourage people to understand Liberalism, not as residing in any 'particular measure', but as being 'the frame and the spirit of mind in which we approach great political questions'.[4]

Rosebery's followers thought of Liberal reconstruction in a very similar way. They refused to prescribe programmes or to allow themselves to become preoccupied with the working out of detail. Haldane, writing in the *Progressive Review* in November 1896, described discussion of 'particular problems of reform' as 'of secondary importance' because 'Liberalism in its widest sense is an affair of spirit and not of letter'. 'Our duty', he

---

[1] Ferguson to Rosebery, 26 May 1899, Rosebery MSS., Box 15.
[2] Principal Rainy to Haldane, 25 February 1902, Haldane MSS., MS. 5905, folio 162.
[3] For his refusal to produce a programme see *Some National Questions. A Speech delivered by the Right Hon. the Earl of Rosebery, K.G. at Leeds, On May 30th, 1902*, 1902, p. 3.
[4] *Liberal Magazine*, vol. 11, no. 114 (March 1903), p. 62; vol. 12, no. 130 (July 1904), p. 395.

wrote, 'is, in the first place, to see that we really are Liberals... We need be in no anxiety about programs if we have it in us to rouse the country into the proper frame of mind. To those who seek first the Kingdom of Heaven all things shall be added.'[1] Programmes they saw as representing what was most defective in the frame of mind of the past: the last thing that they wished to do was to fall into the same error. If they did lack a definite and detailed programme, it was not an aspect of their politics that they saw as in any sense a weakness. To them it represented perhaps their main strength in terms of their understanding of what was needed for the recovery of Liberalism. The 'clean slate' idea embodied, according to Asquith, 'the doctrine of selection and concentration'.[2] This was the doctrine which they worked to get established. The question of what was to be selected was of lesser importance. In time, however, some of the Liberal Leaguers began to grow uneasy about the absence of specific detail in the Roseberyite position on domestic policy. Ferguson and others declared their intention of working out 'the details of the two or three constructive proposals in the Chesterfield policy'; and on one occasion Ferguson, Perks, and Haldane urged Rosebery to attend a meeting in favour of the 'Peel proposals' for licensing reform because, in Ferguson's words, he would thereby 'attach some definite policy to the League on this matter, which I believe to be desirable'. 'For if our points are to be few', Ferguson added, 'they should be clear.'[3]

As for the theme of imperialism, the Liberal Leaguers in endeavouring to promote it within the party were struggling against the natural tendency for the Liberals as the opposition party to be associated primarily with the anti-imperialist position. We can see this in a complaint which Munro Ferguson made to Tom Ellis, the Chief Whip, about Campbell-Bannerman's style of leadership only a few months after Campbell-Bannerman had become leader. His complaint was that 'C.B.' had almost at once moved into an opposition stance and thus severely damaged the Liberals' prospects of receiving the credit which properly belonged to them of being the 'true'

[1] Vol. 1, no. 2, p. 141.
[2] *Liberal Magazine*, vol. 10, no. 102 (March 1902), p. 102.
[3] Ferguson to Rosebery, 16 May 1902, 22 January 1903, Rosebery MSS., Box 16.

imperialists: 'After we had held forth on, almost, every platform through the autumn, & in practically the whole of the Press, that to us rather than to the Tories belonged British work upon the Nile—then we come to C.B.'s extraordinary fiasco, the repudiation of E. Grey, the decn. that he had al[wa]ys protested & must continue to protest agst the Nile policy.' To Ferguson what this episode demonstrated was the correctness of the 'too general . . . feeling that the Liberal Party is unfit to govern'.[1] In other words, what he was condemning was the turning of the Liberal party into a party of automatic opposition, a party which could not govern and consider 'the claims of the real issues of national policy' but could only oppose. The Liberal Imperialists' efforts to arouse support for a 'better' kind of Imperialism than that offered by Chamberlain had less appeal for rank-and-file Liberals than straightforward black-versus-white opposition to Toryism and all its works. The problem was always how to differentiate Rosebery's Imperialism from Chamberlain's. The Liberal Imperialists tried hard to make the differences clear, but the arguments were too subtle to appeal to rank-and-file Liberals who as always wanted to feel clearly and unambiguously distinguished from their opponents. The Liberal Imperialists' main aim was to change Liberalism—from within. They cared much less about the present character of Conservatism. But it was to that character, real or imagined, that many Liberals had for a long time been looking to provide them with a definition of their own political *raison d'être*. It is not surprising, therefore, that there was mounting impatience with the Liberal Imperialists for seeming to do more to 'emphasize differences' within the Liberal party than to exploit the 'prevailing feeling' of 'sickness with the government'. Charles Trevelyan told Haldane in December 1901 that there was very strong resentment 'among masses of ordinary Liberals and even Conservatives' against 'the weakness of an attitude almost of acquiescence in all the government does, just because the main policy has the approval of the nation'. Asquith and Grey, he complained, did no more than make 'murmurs of objection, interlarded with attacks on Liberals'.[2] Perks was given by several Liberal agents the

[1] Ferguson to Ellis, 4 March 1899, T. E. Ellis MSS., folio 639.
[2] C. Trevelyan to Haldane, 17 December 1901, Rosebery MSS., Box 24.

following explanation for the loud applause received by 'Pro-Boer' speakers at a meeting of the N.L.F.'s Political Committee in February 1902: 'These men attack the government—they do so vigorously—if we do not attack we cannot exist. . . .'[1] A. H. D. Acland reported to Rosebery that 'middle class opinion in different parts of the North' of England was growing 'very tired' of the 'perpetual emphasising of differences' within the party by Grey and Asquith.[2]

Rosebery's refusal, frequently reiterated and only marginally modified by his association with the Liberal League, to 're-enter the arena of party politics', his determination to 'plough his own furrow',[3] created many difficulties and embarrassments for those who had staked their own political ambitions on his return to Liberal leadership. Ferguson warned him in June 1902 that there were many Liberals who were 'inclined to support the League' but did not want 'to run great risk of being cast off' should they join it only to find that it did not become a going concern because of Rosebery's failure to be an active leader. To throw in one's lot with the League and then see it fail would be to incur 'the equivalent of excommunication'. Already, Ferguson reported, there was 'a scare' in Scotland that Rosebery would 'drop the League': 'The two or three men to whom I spoke in Edinburgh all said much the same thing—"Are we going to be left in the lurch"? Evidently feeling that they had lost all hope of reconciliation with the present Caucus under Tweedmouth, unless the League should chance to come out predominant which would be the end of that Caucus.'[4] This fear helps to explain why the impact of the League on the Liberal party remained so restricted. Many Liberals wanted to be sure that it had a future, and Rosebery's aloofness prevented them from acquiring such confidence.

The League suffered also from the declining enthusiasm for separate Liberal Imperialist activities among Nonconformists. Much of the impetus behind the development of Liberal Imperialism had come from this section of the party. Nonconformists spearheaded the revolt against the Irish preoccupation

---

[1] Perks to Rosebery, 27 February 1901, Rosebery MSS., Box 39.
[2] Acland to Rosebery, n.d. [1901], Rosebery MSS., Box 76.
[3] *Liberal Magazine*, vol. 9, no. 95 (August 1901), p. 415.
[4] Ferguson to Rosebery, 19 June 1902, Rosebery MSS., Box 16.

and the Irish alliance after 1893. An alliance with Roman Catholics and a crusade for a cause that appealed to Roman Catholics only, while offending many Protestants because of their fear of religious intolerance, quickly lost their attraction for Nonconformists once their hero, Gladstone, had retired, and they began to demand changes in the attitude to Irish policy of a party of which they were regarded by many, including themselves, as the 'backbone'. Nonconformist support for Home Rule had, in any event, not itself been unaffected by anti-Irish feeling, by a desire to see reduced the influence of the Roman Catholic Irish M.P.s in the House of Commons and in England's domestic affairs. The Parnell divorce crisis revived the cry that 'Home Rule means Rome rule', and Gladstone's yielding to Nonconformist pressure seemed to indicate that Nonconformists retained a controlling influence over Liberal policy towards Ireland.

The leader to whom Nonconformists came to look in particular was Rosebery. Initial antagonism to him as an aristocrat and owner of race-horses[1] gave way to a realization that he, more than any other Liberal leader, shared their feelings about Home Rule and the Irish alliance. Under the impact of resentment concerning that alliance traditional Nonconformist attitudes, anti-Catholicism, and missionary imperialism, were fused. This combination is seen in such men as R. W. Perks, H. H. Fowler, and T. Wemyss Reid, the biographer and great admirer of that early Liberal Imperialist and opponent of Irish Nationalism, W. E. Forster, all of whom corresponded frequently with Rosebery after 1894 and endeavoured to reinforce the anti-Irish aspects of his politics. They sought to establish close links with Rosebery and to secure him as the leader of a Liberalism that would be based firmly on Nonconformism.[2] As the Irish M.P.s took an in-

[1] James, *Rosebery*, p. 356. In November 1896 Perks found the prominent Nonconformist, the Revd. Price Hughes, strongly hostile to Rosebery: 'he repeats a story which he says comes to him from Mr John Morley to the effect that you alleged that it was your set purpose to shake the Liberal party free from the undue control of the religious communities—& "rest more on the men of the world"!' In 1898 Perks, Guinness Rogers, and Albert Spicer succeeded in blocking a move on the London Nonconformist Council to censure Rosebery for his connection with horse-racing. Perks to Rosebery, 5 November 1896, 1 February 1898, Rosebery MSS., Box 39.

[2] For examples see Wemyss Reid to Rosebery, 5 August and 26 September

creasingly independent line, often opposing their Liberal 'allies', the Nonconformist Imperialists hailed the end of the alliance and the 'death & burial of Home Rule'.[1] Nonconformism had seemingly triumphed in 1890-1. Much of the pressure for the reconstruction of Liberalism and the overthrowing of the Gladstonian Irish policy seemed to stem from a desire to consolidate this triumph and to revive the allegedly traditional primacy of Nonconformism in Liberal politics.

But there were more ways than one of doing this. The 1902 Education Act provided an opportunity for the harnessing of Liberalism to a specifically Nonconformist cause, and the Liberal League rapidly began to appear an embarrassment to those who wished to take advantage of this opportunity. Rosebery himself took up the cause of opposition to the Act, but some of his associates, notably Haldane, refused to do likewise, and their attitude drew down on them the wrath of the Nonconformists.[2] The views of the latter can be exemplified by an article written by W. Robertson Nicoll in the *New Liberal Review* for October 1902. Nicoll was a member of the Council of the Liberal League, but in this article he complained about the holding of a dinner in Leeds to celebrate the by-election success of a Liberal who was associated with the League. The great need now was, he argued, for Liberal unity against the Education Bill, and the League must help in the struggle against the Bill by 'unifying and strengthening Liberalism, not by dividing it and weakening it'.[3]

The Liberal League was not a a separatist organization. Its aim was not to create a new party but to influence and change the old. This being so, permanent aloofness from 'the party' would constitute an admission of futility and lack of purpose. At some point contact had to be established with the main body of the party, proof had to be sought that the League was

1895, Rosebery MSS., Box 44, and Perks to Rosebery, 8 October 1896, 20 May and 4 December 1899, Rosebery MSS., Box 39.

[1] H. H. Fowler to Rosebery, 10 April 1896, Rosebery MSS., Box 73. Reid to Rosebery, 14 May 1896, Rosebery MSS., Box 44.

[2] W. Robertson Nicoll to Perks, 14 October 1902, enclosed in Perks to Rosebery, 14 October 1902, Rosebery MSS., Box 40.

[3] Vol. 4, no. 21, pp. 345-6. In the letter referred to in the preceding footnote Nicoll wrote: 'This is the first question since 1885 on which the rank & file of Liberals have been really united & enthusiastic; & to support the Government in such a matter is high treason.'

succeeding in its objective. The leaders were most anxious to avoid being isolated and turned into a sect or minority faction. But again and again their moderation conflicted with their followers' natural desire for more aggressive and positive tactics. When Rosebery appeared to be showing a conciliatory attitude towards Campbell-Bannerman in November 1902, Ferguson reported to Rosebery that some of the League's 'more active friends' were feeling 'discouraged'; but Ferguson's own view was that Rosebery's attitude was wise tactically as it emphasized 'the great tactical advantage gained' by Campbell-Bannerman's own denunciation of the League.[1]

During 1903 some 'opportunists' began dropping away. Alfred Harmsworth, one of the League's wealthiest and most influential supporters, was reported to have been 'greatly disturbed' when he heard that the King would feel bound to call on Campbell-Bannerman to form a Liberal administration if Balfour resigned. Harmsworth began to wonder 'if he is right in supporting the League'.[2] Rosebery's attitude did not help. He continued to refuse to have anything to do with 'party organizations or party politics'.[3] This depressed his closest colleagues, and Harmsworth argued that, although he remained anxious to support Rosebery's views, it was necessary for him as a newspaper proprietor to have 'a leader & a policy' to fight for.[4] W. D. Pearson wrote to Perks in September 1904 about rumours 'that Lord R. is not desirous of forming a Government': 'It is sad to think of but true that many people have no opinions of their own & in consequence gravitate towards what they think is the winning side. The rumours that Lord R. is retiring from the running make such people commit themselves to the other side—an unnecessary weakening, in my opinion, of our ranks.'[5] In July 1904 Lloyd George commented to Perks on the 'very unreliable men' that Rosebery had around him: 'When they thought he was going to be leader they were all for the League, now they leave him alone &

[1] Ferguson to Rosebery, 13 November 1902, Rosebery MSS., Box 16.
[2] As reported in Perks to Rosebery, 12 May 1903, Rosebery MSS., Box 40.
[3] Rosebery to Asquith, 10 July 1903 (draft), Rosebery MSS., Box 1.
[4] Haldane to Rosebery, 19 July 1903, Rosebery MSS., Box 24. Perks to Rosebery, 23 September 1903, Rosebery MSS., Box 40.
[5] 23 September 1904, enclosed in Perks to Rosebery, 24 September 1904, Rosebery MSS., Box 41.

look after their own skins.' It was not only for Liberal Imperialists that Rosebery was the lost leader: Lloyd George added that he wished that he could 'have a talk with Lord R.' who was 'the only possible man'.[1]

One of the main reasons why Rosebery and the Liberal Imperialists failed in their bid to wipe the Liberal slate clean and effect a fundamental reconstruction of Liberal policy was that rank-and-file Liberals and those who regarded themselves as being in the 'broad Centre' of the party preferred to feel that they retained contact with 'traditional' Liberal principles and policies. Specific aspects of past policy may no longer have appealed to many of them, but there was little sympathy for Rosebery's demand for a complete break with the past and a complete change in the Liberal 'frame of mind'. Campbell-Bannerman expressed very well their instinctive fear that without reference to the past and to the organically developed principles of Liberalism Liberal politics could have no future. In politics there can be no *tabula rasa* or 'clean slate', and belief in such a possibility can be held only by those who, like Rosebery, deliberately and systematically isolate themselves from the normal political life of the country. What might be called the basic Liberal instinct comes out, for example, in the reaction of C. R. Buxton, a young Radical from one of the great Liberal families of the nineteenth century. He felt that it would be 'disastrous to have to throw over the Rosebery-Grey set' in whom he recognized the youthful talent and vigour on which the party was so dependent for the revival of its strength; and yet it was, he wrote, 'much more important that the Liberal *tradition* should be handed on': 'If the party system is to be kept going at all, Liberals must cultivate and cherish their own principles—à la C.B.—not try to find a compromise embodying the merits of both parties. The latter plan can't work unless the whole complexion of our political system is going to change.'[2]

The reference to Campbell-Bannerman is significant. From the outset he based his claim to leadership and authority in the party on the close identification of his own opinions with 'the

[1] Perks to Rosebery, 25 July 1904, Rosebery MSS., Box 41.
[2] V. De Bunsen, *Charles Roden Buxton. A Memoir*, 1948, p. 33.

established principles of Liberalism'. 'I am half surprised', he wrote in 1900, 'to find that as I go on I get more & more confirmed in the old advanced Liberal principles, economical, social, & political, with which I entered Parliament 30 years ago: and if all these gentlemen can't stand my principles they must do without me!'[1] He denied that there was any need 'for us Liberals to make a new profession of faith'. The 'old lines' were quite good enough: 'Any arrangement which involved the leaving out of half our principles, in order to create a new party, a mere sickly shadow of the Government party, would have no support from me.'[2] Campbell-Bannerman spoke for all the 'men of the centre' who, as Wemyss Reid admitted, found 'hateful' the prospect of having to make up their minds as between one extreme and the other and saw no necessity for doing so.[3] The extremes must come to them, not they to the extremes. They represented the continuity, the tradition, the organic reality of the Liberal party. To Rosebery they were an 'organised hypocrisy'; but to the Chief Whip, Herbert Gladstone, who was in daily contact with them in the House of Commons and the constituencies, they were 'the honest middle party, which sympathising with neither extreme, was striving hard to keep the party together as a whole'.[4]

Rosebery's followers did not want to be cut off from 'the Centre', for control over it could alone give them real control over the party. They watched with alarm, therefore, as a Centre–Left alliance appeared to develop under Campbell-Bannerman's leadership.[5] But to many Liberals the strong criticism of imperialism voiced by 'the Left' and by Campbell-Bannerman himself was much more in the Liberal tradition than were the opinions and attitudes of the 'Lib. Imps.'. H. J. Wilson, the veteran Liberal M.P. for Holmfirth, wrote in 1901 of a speech by Sir Edward Grey: 'not a *Liberal* speech in the sense that we used to use the word'.[6] Campbell-Bannerman's

[1] C-B to Spencer, 19 February 1900, Spencer MSS., Misc. Corr. 1900, A-H.
[2] *Liberal Policy and Liberal Principles . . ., 1899* (speech at Hull, 8 March 1899), p. 11. Spender, *Life of Campbell-Bannerman*, i, p. 303.
[3] Reid to Rosebery, 17 July 1901, Rosebery MSS., Box 45.
[4] As reported in Wemyss Reid to Rosebery, 1 and 24 August 1901, Rosebery MSS., Box 45.
[5] Wemyss Reid to H. Gladstone, 5 July 1901, Gladstone MSS., B.M. Add. MS. 46041, folio 158.
[6] Anderson, *Henry Joseph Wilson*, p. 75.

own great appeal to men such as Wilson came from his genuine and strong revulsion against 'Chamberlainism' which invested his attacks on imperialism with an emotional force which was as strong and, for Liberals, as attractive as had been Gladstone's rhetorical denunciations of 'Beaconsfieldism'.[1]

To Campbell-Bannerman Rosebery's statements advocating a 'clean slate' and an end to Liberal 'shibboleths' were 'either idle phrases' or 'a renunciation of Liberalism'. 'I am not prepared', he declared, 'to erase from the tablets of my creed any principle or measure, or proposal, or ideal, or aspiration of Liberalism.'[2] His argument was that it was an illusion to believe that the best way to success lay through imitating the conduct and adopting the policy of one's opponents. The morale and unity and discipline of the party provided the essential foundation for success, and the party in the House of Commons could be strong only if it were 'a party of Liberal men maintaining Liberal doctrines, and ready to apply them and to embody them in Liberal measures adapted to the facts and needs of the new century as occasion may require'. He agreed with Rosebery that for the reorganization of the party it was necessary that Liberals should 'entertain a fixed political faith' and 'remember it and adhere to it and put it in practice'. But only if that faith were made up from the principles of 'traditional policy' could disunity and 'serious differences' within the party be avoided.[3] Campbell-Bannerman felt that mere opposition to whatever a Conservative government happened to be doing at any particular time was not adequate as a basis for party unity: there had to be some more permanent and durable basis, and that could be provided only by what had lasted and survived from the past. In this respect he was rather

---

[1] 'The thing we have to keep going for is Chamberlainism—the vulgarity, recklessness, caddishness, snobbery of it.' 'Is it not extraordinary how J.C. always plays up to the vulgarity & cupidity & other ignoble passions—Equally when he talks of ransom, when he promises acres & cows & pensions, when he annexes goldfields, when he bullies Kruger, when he Mafficks, when he promises preferences & tariffs & wages & work. It is always the same; & he uses the foolishness of the fool and the vices of the vicious to overwhelm the sane & wise & sober.' C-B to Bryce, 29 October 1900, 31 December 1903, Bryce MSS., E 27 and P 6.

[2] C-B to Ripon, 31 December 1901, Wolf, *Life of Ripon*, ii, p. 268. *Present Events and Future Policy . . ., 1902* (speech at Leicester, 19 February 1902), pp. 9–10.

[3] *London Organisation and South African Policy* (speech of 13 January 1902), pp. 3–4. *Liberal Magazine*, vol. 10, no. 103 (April 1902), p. 163.

at odds with his Chief Whip, Herbert Gladstone, who took a more 'practical' and 'opportunistic' attitude. The contrast can be seen in their reactions to Rosebery's Chesterfield speech of December 1901. On the one hand, Gladstone argued that reunification could be achieved if Campbell-Bannerman responded favourably to Rosebery's suggestions on war policy since 'the one all important matter is the war'; but, on the other, C.B.'s reaction was to stress the unacceptability of the general political philosophy of Rosebery's speech: 'All that he said about the clean slate and efficiency was an affront to Liberalism and was pure claptrap. Efficiency as a watchword! ... It [the speech] is not unfavourable to the chance of unity on the war and peace issue: but ominous of every horror in general politics, if it is meant seriously.'[1]

[1] H. Gladstone to C-B, 17 December 1901; C-B to H. Gladstone, 18 December 1901 (copy), C-B MSS., B.M. Add. MS. 41216, folios 171–3.

XII Reconstruction and Recovery 1902–1906

As the observations of C. R. Buxton quoted in the last chapter indicate,[1] the debate among Liberals on the issue of imperialism involved much questioning of the British party system and of the role of the Liberal party within it. The Liberal Imperialists attacked the assumption that the Liberals should be the party of opposition to whatever line of policy the government was pursuing. They believed that in a climate of opinion such as that which existed in the late 1890s Liberals could not afford to observe such conventions of party behaviour and refuse to associate themselves with a particular mood in the country merely because their party opponents had already done this. The lead in the attack on the party system itself was taken by Rosebery. What he advocated was not a new kind of division between parties but an end to all division—and therefore to the Liberal party as it had developed historically. 'Problems', he wrote in 1898, 'are either becoming too large for parties to deal with, or parties, owing to the above or other causes, are becoming too weak to deal with them.'[2] In the South African crisis he called for the relegation of 'Party controversy' and frequently condemned the influence of party politics on national life.[3]

The controversy over imperialism raised also the question of the nature of a political party and the form of its policy, a question which, as we have seen, had been at the heart of so much debate in the party over the previous thirty years. The Liberal Imperialists believed that the Liberal party, indeed any party, in order to be strong and effective, must have a definite, solid, and unified set of policies and principles

[1] See above, p. 287. [2] James, *Rosebery*, p. 403.
[3] Ibid., pp. 411, 431.

on which to base its actions. They insisted that Liberals must strive to establish among themselves a single viewpoint on a wide range of issues, and the viewpoint which they advocated as a systematizing and cohering influence in Liberal politics was 'Imperialism'. To them a party which contained both Imperialists and Little Englanders was doomed to incoherence and paralysis. The Little Englanders agreed with them at least in this. Thus John Morley wrote bitterly in 1900 about Campbell-Bannerman who, in spite of belonging 'entirely to our political school' and having 'all along' 'agreed with us who opposed the war', had accepted a position which involved 'playing fast and loose with all his own real opinions'. Morley had no time for a leader who 'stands shivering and unclad at the cross-roads' and talks 'rubbish about unity', or for a party that refused to take a single, definite stand and pass judgement 'on the jingo pranks of the last five years'.[1] But both sections were opposed by Liberals who adhered to a fundamentally different concept of the nature of the Liberal party, and it is this issue—once again one of form rather than content—that accounts for the divergence between the Liberal Imperialists and the 'Centre' of the party. According to this rival concept, the party was and ought to be what Gladstone had called a 'broad Church'.[2] Its *raison d'être*, and the source of its true and most enduring strength, was its comprehensiveness, the inclusion and representation within it of people of many diverse opinions, the tolerance within its framework of individual initiative and independent thinking. This was the kind of Liberalism which Campbell-Bannerman frequently held up for admiration. Its spirit was well expressed by F. A. Channing when in 1899 he explained thus why he was against the domination of the party by either school of thought on the issue of imperialism: 'The Liberal Party cannot be run for any one man or group of men or any one idea or group of ideas. We can only win by a sympathetic attempt to get differing men & not wholly harmonious ideas to work together.'[3]

The 'Broad Church' Liberals saw Liberal strength as deriving, not from commitment to any one policy or set of ideas but

[1] Morley to Harcourt, 28 July 1900, Harcourt MSS.
[2] See above, p. 147.
[3] Channing to Bryce, 20 January 1899, Bryce MSS., Misc. Engl. Corr. C.

from the representation in the structure of the party of a basic Liberal ideology. Viewed in this way, the many and varied opinions and interests of Liberals were unified through the expression in them of a general Liberal frame of mind. The division over imperialism, which was naturally often referred to by Unionists as evidence of the weakness of the Liberal party, was defended by Liberals as a good thing in itself by reference to this ideology. 'Is it not part of the principles of the Liberal Party', asked Lord Kimberley, 'that we enjoy perfect liberty of speech and thought, and that we never wish to repress it?'[1] Liberals were even encouraged to feel proud of their own quarrelsomeness and inability to agree with one another: these were manifestations of political health, not of decay, as so many Unionists and Liberal Imperialists claimed. The contrast between the two approaches to the problem of organizing Liberal politics comes out clearly in a speech by Campbell-Bannerman in November 1900 in which he compared Liberal Imperialism as 'a section' with 'the whole Liberal Party', a party 'with all its healthful shades of opinion, which, after all, are only indications of a healthy intelligence'.[2] When Campbell-Bannerman addressed the parliamentary party in July 1901, his main theme was that 'the Liberal Party is a party of free speech and independent thought, of comprehensiveness and of tolerance', and that therefore there should be no 'exclusiveness' or 'repression of any genuine opinion' within it.[3] On another occasion he defined the Liberals as, 'above all others, the party of freedom of view': 'No one would desire to impose or think of imposing upon Liberals any rigid discipline of opinion.'[4] The Liberal movement in the country was encouraged to take this view of itself. For example, in 1902 Augustine Birrell, the new President of the N.L.F., reminded delegates to the annual meeting of the long tradition of diversity in the party: 'Mr. Cobden and Mr. Bright—could they have two men of greater dissimilarity of mind? Mr. Gladstone and Mr. Mill approached every question from the opposite poles of temperament. And yet what Liberals those

[1] 'Eighty' Club. *The Duties and Prospects of the Liberal Party* (address by Kimberley, 3 April 1900), p. 11.
[2] Spender, *Life of Campbell-Bannerman*, i, p. 305.
[3] Ibid., i, p. 344.
[4] *A Government of Retrogression* . . . (speech at Ayr, 29 October 1902), 1902, p. 6.

four men were!'[1] Lord Crewe attacked both the Liberal Imperialists and their 'Manchester-school' opponents for elevating 'an imaginary standard of party agreement, both in Imperial and domestic affairs, to which the individuals composing the party never dreamed of aspiring in past years'.[2]

A distinction was, however, constantly drawn between the unifying principle of respect for diversity of opinion and the disintegrating effect of that sectionalism which involved attempting to take over the whole of Liberalism on behalf of one particular opinion or interest and exclude all other opinions and interests. It was in these terms that Liberal Imperialism was condemned. It was acceptable as a tendency of thought within Liberalism, but not as a movement which aspired, as Rosebery constantly said that it did, to become the whole of Liberalism. Campbell-Bannerman described himself as being not 'agst. Lib. Impts. or their opinions', 'only agst. the [Liberal Imperial] Council & its pretensions, which are fatal to the Party'.[3] At the meeting of Liberal M.P.s in July 1901 he said that he disliked and would denounce, not the expression of divergent opinions, but 'organisations established for the purpose of perpetuating and accentuating differences'.[4] It was the traditional Liberal ideal of the free play of opinions producing a more general and organic unity. Campbell-Bannerman argued that in a party so devoted to 'freedom of thought and action' differences of opinion were healthy. What was objectionable was the organization of these differences in such a way that 'the energies of one section are directed in antagonism to another section', for then 'the whole body of honest and earnest Liberals are paralysed for their real work'.[5] Rosebery claimed that the Anti-Corn Law League and the Liberation Society constituted very respectable precedents for the kind of activity in which the Liberal Imperialists were engaged.[6] But Campbell-Bannerman denied that they were in this tradition. In a speech in October 1902 he described the Anti-Corn Law League and the Liberation Society as bodies of men

---

[1] *N.L.F. Report 1902*, p. 68.
[2] *New Liberal Review*, vol. 4, no. 21 (October 1902), p. 327.
[3] C-B to Bryce, 20 November 1900, Bryce MSS., E 27.
[4] *Liberal Magazine*, vol. 9, no. 95 (August 1901), p. 404.
[5] *Liberal Magazine*, vol. 10, no. 103, (April 1902), p. 162.
[6] Ibid., p. 179.

who had strong views on particular questions but who, while working for their own purposes, nevertheless also assisted and harmonized with 'the work of the party at large'. By contrast, 'the common cause' was harmed and paralysed by 'the action of any body of men among us, however amiable and excellent their motives may be, who set themselves in antagonism to other sections or to the main, central mass of the party, and interfere in this way with the work of the whole'.[1] The Liberal Imperialists did want to interfere with the whole; they wished to reconstruct it and in the process to diminish greatly the influence of, if not completely exclude, 'other sections'. The Liberal League was not a single-issue organization in the Anti-Corn Law League tradition at all. As the omission of the word 'Imperial' from its title and the pretensions of its promoters indicate, it was intended to cover the whole field of Liberal politics and change their very nature, to end the regime of tolerance of great divergences of opinion, and to turn the coalition of sections into a movement based on a single, unified set of principles.[2]

It was the 'Broad Church' concept which prevailed. Within it Liberal Imperialists and Pro-Boers were able to reconcile themselves to the continuing existence of a party which included both sections. They had to sacrifice their own views on the *form* of Liberal policy, but at least the triumph of the principle of comprehensiveness over that of exclusion meant that they could maintain their opinions on its *contents*. Most Liberals who identified themselves with the 'Centre' of the party saw no problem about the perpetuating within the party of such differences of opinion. To them such a situation was of the very essence of Liberalism and the tensions which it produced were creative and life-giving.

Each section wished to take over or at least strongly influence the party, not to leave it and organize a separate movement. As, under Campbell-Bannerman's leadership, the party moved closer and closer to the anti-imperialist position, the Liberal

[1] *A Government of Retrogression*, pp. 6–7.
[2] 'I dislike extremely groups in the Liberal ranks, and this last group is not one to promote one special policy, such even as Imperialism, but to lay down the whole policy of the Liberal Party which I for one do not wish to remodel, & I therefore cannot possibly approve of the formation of the new Liberal League.' Spencer to Asquith, 3 March 1902 (copy), Spencer MSS., Misc. Corr. 1902 A–D.

Imperialists had to choose between seeking an accommodation with it under the umbrella of the 'Broad Church' principle and maintaining an isolation from the main body of the party which would leave them without influence over its development. Being very much a group of natural leaders, men of talent and ambition, they preferred the former alternative.

Perhaps the major achievement of Campbell-Bannerman as Liberal leader before 1905 was to bring Liberals to accept that strength and organic unity, rather than disintegration, could result from the co-existence in their party of many different sections and tendencies of opinion. Weakness and disintegration came rather, it seemed, from the internal divisions caused by attempts to impose on the party the dominance of one section or interest or some particular and exclusive definition of Liberalism.

To some it seemed that what the Liberals had always to remember was that they were one of two alternative-government parties. Sooner or later there was bound to be a reaction against the Tory government, and in the British system the Liberals alone could benefit from this—as long as they did appear to be a plausible alternative government. The 1900 general election was the first since the 1867 Reform Act not to produce a swing against the government in office. The rift in the Liberal party seemed to be one major explanation of this. During the election campaign Herbert Gladstone, the Chief Whip, had to admit that his party was not in a fit condition to provide an alternative government.[1] In order that it should be restored to such a condition three principles had to be observed: the avoidance of paralysing internal dissension, which meant adopting the 'Broad Church' concept rather than the long-term Roseberyite remedy of exclusion of all except those who adhered to a particular system or school of thought—a remedy which in the short run would create so much internal strife as to destroy belief in the Liberals as an alternative government; secondly, the rendering of Liberal policy positions in as negative and non-committal and anti-Tory a form as possible; and, thirdly, the creating of an impression among voters that the Liberals were 'practical' in their

[1] *Liberal Magazine*, vol. 8, no. 86 (November 1900), p. 492.

approach to great issues, including those inherited from their own past, such as Irish Home Rule, and could, unlike previous Liberal governments, be relied on to achieve something when in office.

The Liberal leader who did most after 1895 to overhaul and make 'practical' the old Liberal programme was Herbert Gladstone. In 1902 he was to tell the N.L.F. that 'I cleaned my slate and lightened my ship seven years ago' and so did not 'want to be told to do it now'.[1] In fact, he never did clean anything off his slate. That was not his method. What he did try to do was to ensure that the next Liberal government would be able to get reforms through more easily than had been the case with the governments led by his father and that it would not be so hampered by the 'impracticality' and disorderliness of the sections. His approach is best summed up in the description which he himself once gave of his father's 'creed'. It was, he said, '"opportunism" in its best sense': 'Mr. G.'s prevailing motive power was the *recognition of facts* and the endeavour to harmonise them with his principles in order to maintain those principles as far as possible.'[2] Herbert Gladstone's aim, carried out systematically over the ten years between 1895 and 1905, and more particularly after he became Chief Whip in 1899, was to integrate the sections and their causes into Liberalism and to minimize the chances of sectional disruptiveness after the Liberals returned to power. In the late 1890s, for example, he took the lead in trying to free the party from its 1895 commitment, generally felt to have been disastrous for its electoral fortunes, to the policy of Direct Veto. He wanted to ensure that after twenty-five years of 'innumerable speeches', 'attendance at innumerable meetings', and complete absence of practical achievement, a Liberal government would at last find itself able to 'do something practical to diminish the evils of intemperance'.[3] Soon after becoming Chief Whip, he set about trying to organize a 'practical' temperance-reform policy that would appeal not only—perhaps even not at all—to the

[1] *N.L.F. Report 1902*, p. 105.
[2] Sir E. Hamilton's diary, B.M. Add. MS. 48647, folio 51 (30 October 1887).
[3] *N.L.F. Report 1896*, p. 86. Carter, *The English Temperance Movement*, pp. 221–2. Newton, *W. S. Caine, M.P.*, pp. 280–1. *Liberal Magazine*, vol. 5, no. 51 (December 1897), p. 484. H. Gladstone to C-B, 12 April 1899, C-B MSS., B.M. Add. MS. 41215, folio 66.

faddists but would satisfy moderate and 'reasonable' opinion and modify the anti-Liberal stance of 'the trade' at elections, which he believed was a serious handicap to the party.[1] He encouraged Campbell-Bannerman to follow a strategy of exploiting divisions within the ranks of the temperance reformers and playing one section off against another.[2] He also exerted all the influence that he could against the 'temperance faddists' who worked at the local level to deny Liberal candidatures to brewers and to persons who would not accept the Local Option or Direct Veto policy.[3] Gladstone's main aim was to make the Liberals appear once more 'an alternative Govt.', and he was constantly urging Campbell-Bannerman to seek an accommodation with Rosebery.[4] He maintained that the election defeat of 1900 was not caused by any enthusiasm for the government but by the exploitation by Chamberlain of the discredit arising from 'our one central weakness', 'the want of union in the party'.[5] If only the image of the Liberals as a viable alternative government, a party that when in office would not be paralysed but would get things done, could be restored, then they would soon be back in power. Gladstone was therefore, as we have already seen,[6] very ready to grasp at any occasion for re-establishing an appearance of unity, however superficial it might be.

Gladstone was as concerned as was Rosebery to select and concentrate Liberal policy and to eradicate the legacy and spirit of the Newcastle programme from Liberal politics. But whereas Rosebery worked all the time to achieve these ends in the blaze of publicity with a maximum of rhetoric and a minimum of practical effort, Gladstone's tactics were to avoid showdowns and public controversy as much as possible and concentrate on detailed work and negotiations behind the scenes.

---

[1] H. Gladstone to C-B, 19 November 1899, C-B MSS., B.M. Add. MS. 41215, folios 145-7.

[2] H. Gladstone to C-B, 12 and 23 December 1899, C-B MSS., B.M. Add. MS. 41215, folios 169-72, 190.

[3] H. Gladstone to C-B, 3 September 1899, C-B MSS., B.M. Add. MS. 41215, folio 76.

[4] Cf. H. Gladstone to J. A. Spender, 17 December 1901, Spender MSS., B.M. Add. MS. 46391, folio 95.

[5] H. Gladstone to C-B, 9 October 1900, C-B MSS., B.M. Add. MS. 41216, folio 21.

[6] See above, pp. 289-90.

These tactics proved much more effective. Quietly he achieved a great deal and gave the old Liberal coalition of sections and interests one more lease of life. Rosebery's aim was, of course, to eliminate the influence of the sections altogether. He wished to create a new kind of Liberal party. Gladstone very effectively patched up the old and avoided provoking the sections into open rebellion. Paradoxically imperialism helped him in this, as the Home Rule issue had helped his father in the late 1880s, by creating a division of opinion that transcended 'normal' sectional interests and, by cutting across sectional lines, weakened the force of the sections in Liberal politics. Non-conformity was split over imperialism.[1] So was Liberalism in Scotland where Liberal Imperialist electoral activity and efforts at 'permeation' were at a peak and in Wales where traditional issues such as disestablishment were much less in evidence than usual.[2] The sharing of antagonism to imperialism by Liberals and Labour helped Gladstone to reach the electoral agreement of 1903 with the Labour Representation Committee.

A good example of Gladstone's 'practical' approach to the problem of the involvement in Liberal politics of the traditional sectional or 'Newcastle programme' kind of reform issue is a memorandum which he wrote for Campbell-Bannerman in June 1899 on a demand from the Liberation Society that the leaders of the Liberal party should 'make Disestablishment a practical question' and 'give it a distinct and prominent place in the Programme of the Liberal Party, with a view to legislate at the earliest practicable period'. His comments on this constitute a practical application of the lessons of 1891–5:

> We are already face to face with questions of the House of Lords, Home Rule and Temperance—in addition to many other matters of less gravity and difficulty—and we are now asked to load ourselves with another responsibility which will allow our opponents at once to rally and concentrate themselves in opposition. . . . undoubtedly, a Disestablishment policy will cause great enthusiasm and produce much energy in a large section of the Liberal Party: but there is nothing new in that. It has generally been accepted that, if

[1] E. Halévy, *A History of the English People in the Nineteenth Century. V. Imperialism and the Rise of Labour*, 1961 edition, pp. 104–5.
[2] Morgan, *Wales in British Politics*, pp. 179–80.

Disestablishment is to become a practical question, it will become so from action within the Establishment. It may be that the 'crisis'[1] will produce in the near future that action, but, as far as I can see and learn, there is no real evidence of it at the present time.

The Memorandum dwells on the enthusiasm which is created by any mention of Disestablishment at public meetings, and, in particular, the Federation meeting at Hull is quoted. Exactly the same argument has been used with regard to Local Veto.

... It certainly does seem to me that the acceptance of the demand at the present time would plunge us into new and great dangers without any urgent necessity or adequate compensation.[2]

Gladstone also played a major part in modifying and making more flexible and 'practical' the Liberal party's position on Irish Home Rule while at the same time avoiding the showdown with the Irish and the formal abandoning of the policy for which Rosebery called. Gladstone maintained some kind of working association with the Irish, whereas Rosebery sought a formal and public renunciation of the old alliance.

A major question to which many Liberals sought a definite answer was whether or not the Liberals were prepared to take office again as in 1892, dependent on the votes of Irish M.P.s. Asquith and other Liberal Imperialists insisted that they must not do so but must wait until they had acquired an independent majority. Asquith argued that no government could carry on efficiently 'the ordinary every day work of legislation & administration . . . (as I know well from our experience in 92–95) which has not a majority of its own, & is compelled as it approaches every tight place to negotiate with "allies"'.[3] Related to this was the question of whether a definite public pronouncement should be made beforehand by the Liberal leaders as to what they would do if they were to find themselves in such a situation after the next general election. The Liberal Imperialists demanded that Campbell-Bannerman issue a statement committing the party in advance to refuse to take office unless in possession of an independent majority in the House of Commons. Such a statement would, they believed,

---

[1] i.e. the revival of the agitation against ritualistic practices in the Church of England.

[2] 14 June 1899, C-B MSS., B.M. Add. MS. 41215, folios 70–2.

[3] Asquith to J. A. Spender, 5 November 1901, Spender MSS., B.M. Add. MS. 46388, folios 83–4.

itself be an electoral asset whose benefits would much more than compensate for the loss of the votes of the Irish M.P.s who had long ceased to be allies in any meaningful sense. It would signify to the voting public that the Liberals were once again a 'national' party and intended to deal first and foremost with the interests and needs of the non-Irish section of the electorate. The Liberal Imperialists argued that lack of clarity as to what the Liberals might do should the Irish be found to hold the balance of power would cause much damage to the party's cause among non-Irish voters. An independent Liberal majority was more likely to come if the voters knew that the Liberal party had shaken itself free of the Irish alliance.[1] Campbell-Bannerman and Herbert Gladstone refused to give any pledge of the kind demanded by the Liberal Imperialists. But they likewise refused to say that they definitely would take office dependent on the Irish. They emphasized tactical flexibility and allowing the party leaders the maximum of freedom to respond to the particular circumstances in which they would find themselves.

One of the principal objections to the Liberal Imperialists' arguments was that they were Unionist in their implications, as they appeared to involve treating the Irish as political pariahs, fit neither to govern themselves nor to participate in the normal processes of the political system to which they were forced to continue to belong. John Morley gave these reasons for opposing any declaration against taking office dependent on Irish votes:

(1) It is equivalent to saying that the Irish vote is not to count in the parliament: it disfranchises Ireland, and she might as well be excluded.

(2) It means a return to the old way of governing Ireland by a tacit or open understanding between the two English parties united against the Irish party.

This understanding it was Mr. G.'s glory to have banished and broken.

Grey and all Home Rulers who use his language about taking office, ought to realise these two considerations.[2]

---

[1] *Liberal Magazine*, vol. 9, no. 97 (October 1901), p. 504 (Asquith).
[2] Morley to Haldane, 26 August 1898, Haldane MSS., no. 5904, folios 153–4. Cf. Asquith's reply: 'But what is to be said of J. M.'s contention? It amounts to

Closely associated with the problem of future relations between the Liberal and Irish parties was the question of what should be done about the last and greatest of the legacies of Gladstonian Liberalism, the policy of Home Rule for Ireland.[1] Here too the Liberal Imperialists wanted Liberal policy to be clearly defined and unambiguous, whereas Campbell-Bannerman and others favoured vagueness and flexibility. After all that had happened since 1885 the explicit renunciation of Home Rule would have had the most severe effects on Liberal morale, and it is clear that most Liberals had no wish to go this far, though there was also a general feeling that now it could not and must not be the main preoccupation of Liberal politics that it had been between 1886 and 1893. Two of the mainstays of the Gladstonian Home Rule policy had been knocked away. In the first place, the Irish-Liberal alliance was now largely a dead letter and in fact came to seem an electoral liability to many Liberals because of what the Roseberyites referred to as the 'anti-national' conduct of the Irish during the South African war. Secondly, the great assumption on which the argument that Home Rule had to take first place among Liberal policy concerns was based—the existence of an 'Irish obstruction' in British politics—had no validity now, since it was quite clear that no such obstruction now existed even although Home Rule, alleged to be the sole remedy for it, had not yet been conceded. The day when Home Rule could be presented as the great 'concentrating' issue in Liberal politics had now passed.

Many Liberal wanted their leaders to give a definite and unequivocal assurance to the British voters that Home Rule would *not* be among the issues receiving early attention by the next Liberal government. S. F. Mendl wrote that what the British elector really wanted to know before deciding whether or not to vote Liberal was whether the Liberals meant 'to

---

this—that unless you have such a distribution of parties that the Irish have the casting vote, the Irish representation (at least as regards Irish legislation) is "ruled out"! In other words, if we had a Liberal majority over both Tories & Irish, its Acts (quoad Ireland) would not have the same constitutional authority as if the distribution had been such, that Irish votes were needed to carry them into law. This is to my mind new doctrine—with a vengeance.' Asquith to J. A. Spender, 5 November 1901, Spender MSS., B.M. Add. MS. 46388, folios 84–5.

[1] For a full and clear discussion of this question see H. W. McCready, 'Home rule and the liberal party, 1899–1906', *Irish Historical Studies*, vol. 13 (September 1963), pp. 316–48.

scramble into power on a programme of social and other reforms, and, once established there, to fling British reforms to the winds and commence again the weary path we trod in 1886 and 1893, with such ill-success to the cause of all reform, including the reform of Irish government'. The Liberal leaders should renounce 'the Irish policy of Mr. Gladstone' and particularly one of its key features, the precedence given to Home Rule over all other Liberal policies.[1] Augustine Birrell, writing in 1901, a year before becoming President of the N.L.F., described Irish policy as constituting 'a permanent source of paralysis' in Liberal politics. He doubted whether, until the party had made up its mind about its position on Home Rule, the country would be 'much disposed to give heed to speeches . . . about temperance and the housing of the working classes'.[2] As for the Liberal Imperialists, one of Rosebery's main conditions for renewing co-operation with the party leaders was that they should renounce Gladstonian Home Rule; while H. H. Fowler argued that, if 'the Home Rule of 1886, and 1893' were adhered to 'as the cardinal article of the Liberal faith and the infallible test of Liberal orthodoxy', the result would be 'the arrest of Liberal progress and the abandonment of Liberal legislation for a generation' and probably also 'the disruption, if not the destruction of the Liberal party'.[3]

But a compromise was possible, and was achieved, thanks mainly to the 'practical' attitude of Gladstone and Campbell-Bannerman, to their success in bringing the Irish Nationalists to accept that a Home Rule Bill could not be embarked on immediately after the Liberals took office, and to the willingness of most of the Liberal Imperialists to acquiesce in a policy that maintained the formal commitment of the party to Home Rule while introducing much greater flexibility and realism with regard to timing and strategy. Both Campbell-Bannerman and Gladstone insisted on the principle that no policy issue whatever, including Home Rule, should be placed above any other—or below any other—before the time for action arrived. Gladstone argued for a policy half way between the Roseberyite and Gladstonian extremes of complete

[1] *New Liberal Review*, vol. 1, no. 6 (July 1901), pp. 838, 840.
[2] *Liberal Magazine*, vol. 9, no. 95 (August 1901), p. 405.
[3] Fowler, *Life of Viscount Wolverhampton*, p. 472.

renunciation and prior commitment to precedence for Home Rule. On the one hand, he told Liberals, they would not be creating a good impression if they set about asking 'for the confidence of the country on the ground that they have been in error for sixteen years'; but on the other, they had to appreciate that an essential prerequisite for carrying Home Rule was 'a strong Liberal majority' in the House of Commons and that an announced intention of putting a Home Rule Bill first was not likely to secure this for them.[1]

Most Liberal Imperialists who, unlike Rosebery, lived or aspired to live in the world of practical politics, for example as M.P.s with Irish constituents or with non-Irish constituents whose deadliest local opponents for nearly twenty years had been Liberals hostile to Home Rule, were anxious to be provided with some 'practical' compromise, and this was given to them in Asquith's 'step by step' strategy.[2] Once again there was a divergence between Rosebery's absolute approach which reflected his primary intention of changing the whole Liberal frame of mind, symbolized for him by the commitment to Home Rule, and, on the other hand, the instinct of his more politically involved followers for a more positive and practical treatment of the issue. Haldane wrote in January 1902: 'I think that the Scotch & English Lib. electors would be very well disposed to respond to R. if he substituted a more constructive policy for that of Mr. G.'s Bills & did not simply propose coercion.'[3] Liberal Imperialist M.P.s warned Rosebery that they could not associate themselves with his vague and negative Irish policy. Alfred Emmott, for example, wrote to him expressing a

> firm conviction that there is little or nothing to be gained at any rate in the great towns of the North of England from an apparently non possumus attitude on the Irish question. The Liberal Unionist who is willing to return to the Liberal party hardly exists in the constituencies and a reasonable and moderate constructive policy would gain as many votes from the other side, would not play into

---

[1] *N.L.F. Report 1902*, pp. 104–6. *Liberal Policy and Liberal Principles* (speech by C-B, 8 March 1899), pp. 4–6. C-B to H. Gladstone, 26 October 1905, C-B MSS., B.M. Add. MS. 41217, folio 271.

[2] For which see Jenkins, *Asquith*, p. 132.

[3] Haldane to Asquith, 5 January 1902, Asquith MSS., Dep. 10, folios 49–50.

the hands of the little Englanders and yet would contrast favourably with the action of the present Government.[1]

Another Liberal M.P. who was very active on the Imperialist side, J. M. Paulton, suggested to Rosebery early in 1902 that 'the next necessity is some adumbration of a constructive Irish policy, as the Rump will spare no effort to make out that our only aim & idea is coercion'.[2] More and more of the Liberal Imperialists grew concerned over Rosebery's impracticality and extremism on the Irish question—an extremism that, of course, exemplified Rosebery's overriding desire to introduce system into Liberal politics. W. S. Robson wrote:

> We wrecked ourselves by the rudeness of our transition to Home Rule and we are managing our transition back again almost as rudely. We should pay a tribute to the principle while declaring that the method must be altered—or in other words, that we must begin at the near end of the stick with gradually extended Local Government instead of at the far end of the stick, as Gladstone did, with an Irish Parliament.[3]

Soon the tensions became apparent in the Liberal League itself. For example, R. W. Perks wrote to Rosebery in April 1904 describing a League dinner which he had attended. First of all, Lord Arran had made 'a very bold speech—urging the Lib. party to have nothing to do with Home Rule in the interest of Ireland'. But then J. L. Walton, M.P. for South Leeds and a prominent member of the League, repudiated what Arran had said '& made a semi-Home Rule speech'. 'He told me after', added Perks, 'that he had done so because he had so many Irish on his register, & he thought we could not win without the Irish vote!' A third speaker at the dinner was Asquith, and he, according to Perks, 'poured cold water on Walton & said Home Rule was not & could not be part of our programme'.[4] By this he meant obviously the programme for the next election. It was Asquith himself, however, who was chiefly responsible for formulating the principle of working 'step by step' to Home Rule via intermediate measures of

[1] 23 February 1902, Rosebery MSS., Box 106.
[2] 24 February [1902], Rosebery MSS., Box 106.
[3] G. W. Keeton, *A Liberal Attorney-General Being the Life of Lord Robson of Jesmond (1852–1918) with an account of the Office of Attorney-General*, 1949, pp. 105–6.
[4] 22 April 1904, Rosebery MSS., Box 41.

local government and land reform that was accepted by Campbell-Bannerman as official party strategy and which governed the Irish policy of the Liberals between 1905 and 1910. Thus the party preserved its commitment to Home Rule but abandoned the Gladstonian insistence that this reform had to have precedence over all others. The foundation of that insistence—the argument that 'Ireland' constituted the great obstruction in British politics which had to be removed before anything else could be satisfactorily attended to—had long since been undermined.

Another section which Herbert Gladstone strove to reintegrate into the fabric of Liberal politics was Labour. One of the main problems here was the continuing uncertainty as to the status of Labour. Liberals remained unclear as to whether it was just one more section, comparable to the Nonconformists, for instance, within the broad Liberal coalition of sections and interests, or whether it represented something bigger, such as the idea of a balance between labour and capital implied, that had to be handled in a special way. Did Labour now mean the interests of an entire class? This idea had grown much more pausible since 1867 because of the development of the trade-union movement and the greater cohesion of the working class, evidenced in such phenomena as the Trades Union Congress and the creation of 'general' unions covering workers from a wide range of occupations.

After 1886 the Irish coercion issue was exploited by Liberals to forge new links between themselves and British Labour.[1] Every effort was made to get working men to feel that the 'Plan of Campaign' and the other Irish activities against which coercion was used were analogous to trade-union organization in the rest of the United Kingdom and that therefore the Tory coercion represented a potential threat to their liberties as well.[2] Legislation directly in the interests of working men remained anathema to many Liberals—and to many of the older Lib-Lab trade-union leaders as well, as the eight-hour-day controversy showed. The task that faced the Liberal leaders was to avoid anything that looked like class

---

[1] Hamer, *John Morley*, pp. 236–8.
[2] Clayden, *England under the Coalition*, p. 264. *The Times*, 10 October 1889, p. 7.

legislation and yet at the same time maintain a close emotional, even ideological, relationship between Liberalism and Labour. The answer lay in the exploitation from the 1880s through to 1906 of a series of themes—opposition to coercion, anti-imperialism, Chinese labour, tariff reform—which themselves lay outside the realm of working class demands but on which Liberals could assume attitudes which suggested an emotional identification with 'the cause of labour'. On none of these was action needed of the kind which could brand the Liberals as the party of one particular class. At one and the same time the Liberals could depict themselves as upholding the interests of labour because of their opposition to the suppression of tenants' 'trade unions' in Ireland and stress the 'unselfishness' of devotion to a cause which directly promoted the interests of no one class in Britain. There was a distinction between vicarious and direct or 'selfish' promotion of the cause of Labour which Gladstone made plain when in 1892 he appealed to Nottinghamshire miners not to prefer 'an enemy of the Liberals and of the Irish cause' to Henry Broadhurst because of Broadhurst's opposition to eight-hours legislation. They should put the Irish cause first, for they were 'labouring-men and they know that the Irish are, it may almost be said, a nation of labouring men'.[1] Some Lib-Labs not only accepted and welcomed this emphasis on non-'selfish', moral issues but went even further and resented any kind of reference to class interests anywhere at all. In 1881 Tom Burt wrote that the Irish had blundered in trying to arouse opposition to coercion by appealing to trade unions 'to support the Irish tenant-farmers who were fighting a great battle on behalf of the cause of labour'. Such an appeal was based 'too much on narrow, exclusive class grounds': 'class feelings, class distinctions, and class prejudices are fast dying out, and the sooner they are altogether obliterated the better'. He suggested that British working men were much less likely to be influenced by an appeal to 'their sordid material interests' and 'their class feelings and prejudices' than by 'some great chivalrous idea', for example, 'the legislative independence of Ireland'.[2] The tendency to promote the projection of class feeling onto external issues which

[1] Gladstone MSS., B.M. Add. MS. 44515, folio 86.
[2] *N.C.*, no. 50 (April 1881), pp. 613–16.

themselves had nothing to do directly with class relationships in Britain can be seen in the issue of anti-imperialism. Criticism of British policy in South Africa effected a rapprochement between anti-imperialist Liberals and Labour both through attacks on the behaviour and influence of certain capitalists and through the Liberals' campaign on behalf of the cause of 'free Labour' in the Chinese labour controversy.

In 1900 Labour appeared to make a clear break with the Lib-Lab tradition when the Labour Representation Committee was set up by certain trade unions and Socialist societies to promote the representation of the working class in Parliament. Its creation marked the culmination of a long period of criticism by Labour of the failure of the Liberal party to provide Liberal candidatures for representatives of Labour. The basic concept on which Lib-Labism rested was that of the balance between capital and labour. This concept seemed to be negated by the giving of the overwhelming majority of Liberal candidatures to men regarded as representative of one side only of the balance, capital. Many Liberals remained extremely reluctant, however, to acknowledge Labour as a separate force to be given representation as such within the general framework of Liberal politics. Nominations were given by local constituency Associations, and here it very rarely happened that middle-class Liberals were prepared to sponsor working-class candidates simply because they were from the working class. A national view of the problem had somehow to be introduced; otherwise from 1900 on the traditionally unified Lib-Lab vote was likely to be split in many constituencies with normally Liberal seats falling to the Unionists on minority votes as a result.

In 1903 Herbert Gladstone made a secret electoral pact with Ramsay MacDonald, Secretary of the L.R.C., whereby the Liberals agreed to give Labour a free run in certain constituencies and Labour would stand aside in others. From the Liberal point of view, the purpose of this pact was to convert Labour from a disruptive and disintegrating influence to a constructive force in Liberal politics.[1] On the Labour side, it meant an acknowledgement that the L.R.C. was something rather less than a 'normal' parliamentary party aspiring to form the government. Its aim was simply to increase the number of working-class M.P.s

[1] Cf. Herbert Gladstone's remarks in *N.L.F. Report 1903*, p. 99.

and to make the voice of the Labour interest more frequently and effectively heard in Parliament. By agreeing to a pact the purpose of which was to preserve intact the Lib-Lab vote, it showed that it not only was but wished to continue to be a section within the broad coalition of Liberalism. Its limited aspirations meant that it could continue to fit into a general but more explicitly and formally organized pattern of Lib-Lab politics. In a sense, what Labour was doing was going back to the original spirit of Lib-Labism and reviving in a more durable and concrete form a concept which they felt had been allowed to decay, not by themselves, but by the Liberals. From the Labour point of view, it was the Liberal party which had been becoming a class party, especially at the local level where candidates were chosen; and so in the end Labour took counter-action to restore certain traditional features of Liberalism, especially its comprehensiveness, its avoidance of identification with the interests of any one class, and its devotion to the maintenance of a harmonious relationship between capital and labour. The emergence of the Labour party between 1900 and 1906 represented no clear break with Liberal ideology. Although Socialist societies contributed to the creation of the party and were given membership of the L.R.C., the party itself was committed to no programme or creed until 1918 and its M.P.s continued on most political issues to conduct themselves and to vote in a clearly 'Lib-Lab' fashion.

Another problem affecting the recovery of the party on which the Liberal leaders had to make up their minds was the extent to which they should commit themselves beforehand on the items of reform to be included in the legislative programme of the next Liberal government. Having had ample opportunity to appreciate the disadvantage of such commitments, they were very anxious to leave themselves as free as possible so that they would not be harassed after entering office by unruly sections alleging betrayal of pledges. Shortly after becoming party leader, Campbell-Bannerman argued that it was 'impossible for us to lay down any fixed programme for our action at the time when it becomes again in our power to act':

Priority must depend upon the circumstances of the day, upon the feeling of the nation, upon the temper of the party, and, above all things, upon the amount and the quality of the party majority....

It may be a masculine majority, great in stature, strong of limb and muscle, fit for a great enterprise; or it may be a feminine majority, equally excellent in heart, clear in mind, and full of generous emotions, but lacking the physical power to move great legislative weights. No, until we know what it is, or what it is likely to be, we cannot definitely assign its duties.[1]

Herbert Gladstone told the N.L.F. in 1902 that the selecting of issues to be made the subject of legislative action 'must be the work of a responsible Government'. He refused to 'put any one question before another' but preferred to 'put them all behind one thing, and that is the duty of getting rid of the [Tory] Government'.[2] As late as 1905 he was saying that he hoped that the Liberal leaders would continue to refuse to indicate 'to which measure priority would be given': 'so far as the laying down of a policy for the Liberal party was concerned, he confessed he did not think there was very much importance in it, provided the country knew the general lines of such a policy'.[3] The N.L.F. itself became more and more cautious, increasingly prone to pass merely negative, anti-government resolutions rather than the resolutions embodying positive policy commitments and definitions of priority which it had gone in for in the past.

The implication of all this seemed to be that the voters would vote Liberal even although no precise programme was being placed before them. Following the experiences of 1892 and 1895, there was now a reaction against specific commitments, a feeling even that it might be electorally advantageous not to offend sections or interests in advance by narrowing down the potential area of legislative action. The Liberals were again, it seemed, as in the late 1870s to rely on negative factors to get them as the alternative government back into office when positive initiatives, as in 1874 or 1886 or 1892 or 1895, had failed.

This tendency towards vagueness with regard to Liberal policy and emphasis on opposition to the policies and initiatives of others was, of course, vastly accentuated by the reaction among Liberals to the various issues raised by the Tory

[1] *Liberal Policy and Liberal Principles* (8 March 1899), p. 6.
[2] *N.L.F. Report 1902*, p. 104.
[3] *Liberal Magazine*, vol. 13, no. 137 (February 1905), p. 6.

government and by Chamberlain after 1901. The Liberal party began to re-emerge as a plausible alternative government as Liberals began to sink their differences in face of the common enemy. Herbert Gladstone saw in this process a solution to the problem of order in the Liberal programme. In June 1903 he sent to Campbell-Bannerman a list of 'questions on which candidates frequently ask me for guidance', and added: 'Fortunately there is no question of priority—Chamberlain, the Educ[atio]n Bill, & the Land Bill have settled that.'[1]

The Education Bill of 1902 began a dramatic movement away from preoccupation with imperialism among some of the more militant Liberal Imperialists, and, as there were numerous militant Nonconformists on the 'other side', for example Lloyd George, Liberal reunion was powerfully facilitated. The Liberal Imperialists were split: Haldane's support for the Bill angered many of the Nonconformists among them. As Halévy has shown,[2] anger against the Bill gave Nonconformists a strong incentive to work for the return of the Liberal party at the next election. They therefore wished to see a Liberal party that was united and that included as much Nonconformist influence as possible. Sectional organizations, such as the Liberal League, which detached this influence from the main body of the party, were now regarded with disfavour by them.

Asquith hailed the Education Bill crisis as creating the opportunity 'for a new campaign in which the forces of progress, with set purpose and with united ranks, would march to a certain and a not distant victory'.[3] Rosebery himself came out strongly in support of the Nonconformists, and was commended for this by R. W. Perks, one of the leading Nonconformist Imperialists, who thought that the line which Rosebery was taking was '*absolutely right*'. It recognized, he wrote, that the Nonconformists 'are really the motive force of provincial Liberalism'.[4] Even Haldane acknowledged the wisdom of Rosebery's decision to align himself with the Nonconformists:

No one who had the responsibility of giving to a great party advice

---

[1] 24 June 1903, C-B MSS., B.M. Add. MS. 41216, folio 282.
[2] *Imperialism and the Rise of Labour*, p. 209.
[3] *Liberal Magazine*, vol. 10, no. 110 (November 1902), p. 566.
[4] Perks to Rosebery, 1 January 1903, Rosebery MSS., Box 40.

as to the line it must follow could have given any other advice than to distinguish itself from the Government, & not least over the Education Bill. I do not take a sanguine view of the value as an asset of Nonconformist support, but it could not be let go to the other camp. . . . The Education people may blaspheme, but they are not prescribing medicine for a patient with a gaping wound.[1]

Campbell-Bannerman's reaction was likewise to appreciate the importance, after the confusions of the 1895–1901 period, of rediscovering a principle of clear differentiation between the parties. By March 1903 he was speaking of 'a chasm yawning' between the parties 'on almost every public question'.[2]

When Chamberlain launched his campaign for tariff reform, pressure for the ending of internal Liberal differences, and the integration of Liberal Imperialism into the total Liberal effort grew even stronger. Lord Crewe warned Rosebery not to let 'the defence of Free Trade . . . fall into the hands of those whose Imperial imagination is as defective on the one hand as J.C.'s is excessive on the other'.[3] By July 1903 Edward Grey was telling Rosebery that there was a strong desire among Liberal Leaguers for active involvement in the Free Trade struggle, and was urging Rosebery himself to join the Free Trade Union.[4] When a prominent Liberal Imperialist M.P., Alfred Emmott, did join the Union, he was denounced by some of the more extreme 'Lib. Imps.' for doing so; but at the same time Munro Ferguson had to tell Rosebery that Emmott's action demonstrated how the Union was getting 'the backing of your best supporters'.[5] He discovered 'a very prevalent disposition' among adherents of the League 'to wind it up on any good opportunity', even 'though several of us think it wd. not be safe to do so—until a new Govt. is formed at any rate'. He lamented that the development of the Free Trade cause seemed to have ended any prospect of their being able 'to reconstitute the Party' by means of the Liberal League.[6] Instead, the old Liberalism was reconstituting Liberal Imperialism, making it over into its own image, and causing its devotees

[1] Haldane to Rosebery, 4 November 1902, Rosebery MSS., Box 24.
[2] *Liberal Policy . . ., 1903* (speech at Leeds, 19 March 1903), p. 12.
[3] 29 May 1903, Rosebery MSS., Box 78.
[4] 13 July 1903, Rosebery MSS., Box 23.
[5] 25 July 1903, Rosebery MSS., Box 16.
[6] 23 August 1903, Rosebery MSS., Box 16.

to want to take up the old weapons again and fight the traditional campaigns rather than forge new weapons for the battles of a new era, as had been the original purpose of the Liberal League. Thus Fowler called on Rosebery to take the lead in 'the Free Trade battle' and sink his differences with Liberals who were strong Free Traders but had not followed his line on Imperialism and Liberal reconstruction.[1] J. A. Spender analysed what had happened in a letter to Rosebery in October 1904. Chamberlain, had, he wrote, 'raised the one question in all politics which obliterates—at least for the time being—the original politics of the L[iberal] L[eague]': 'Asquith, Grey etc., have been drawn back into the official party by the necessity of fighting J.C., & the Liberal League which was founded on the politics of three years ago has lost its reason for existing.'[2] Lewis Harcourt wrote to his father: 'I can't help thinking that Chamberlain, besides destroying the Tory party, may break up the Liberal League. Many of their recruits must be Fair Traders and protectionists.'[3]

To some extent it was once again a triumph of form over content. But then the form of Liberal political activity had, as we have seen, always been a matter of prime concern for the Liberal Imperialists. The appeal of a transcending, subordinating, and above all 'concentrating' theme was very strong. Rosebery himself began to describe the Free Trade issue to Liberals in terms very similar to those that he had used about, for instance, the House of Lords question in 1894–5: 'Remember that in all these questions in which you are most interested—education, licensing, all the social questions on which the Liberal party have set their hearts—all these are defeated if Free Trade is defeated.'[4] H. H. Fowler, another Liberal Imperialist who had always put great emphasis on the need for selection and concentration of Liberal policies, echoed him. In a speech to the Eighty Club in June 1904 he impressed on Liberals the importance of 'concentration and unity' with regard to a question 'which is supreme and which involves all others'. The defeat of Free Trade would, he said, deal 'a mortal blow' at every cause in which Liberals were interested. The

[1] Perks to Rosebery, 30 January 1904, Rosebery MSS., Box 41.
[2] 22 October 1904, Spender MSS., B.M. Add. MS. 46387, folio 50.
[3] 31 May 1903, Harcourt MSS.
[4] *Liberal Magazine*, vol. 12, no. 127 (April 1904), p. 150.

question 'lies at the very root not only of Liberalism but of our national prosperity and our national progress'.[1]

Abundant similar statements can be found in the speeches of Liberal leaders at this time exhorting all Liberals to rally and unite in the defence of Free Trade. The National Liberal Federation told Liberals that, while 'the education question, the temperance question, the land question, and all branches of social reform' would retain their place in the minds and hearts of all Liberals, nevertheless the Tory party's adoption of '"Protection" as their rallying cry' made it necessary for Liberals to put this 'vital question' 'in the very forefront of the fight'.[2] It was not the fault of the Liberals if all else were subordinated to this one issue—just as a similar development had been beyond their control in 1886. When the young Radical, G. M. Trevelyan, wrote to Campbell-Bannerman complaining of this trend, Campbell-Bannerman replied in what he felt was 'a re-assuring tone' that 'it is not we who wish to let everything be swallowed up in fiscal controversies'.[3] The theme had a unifying effect: Imperialists and Pro-Boers, differing on the content of Liberal policy, could still agree on its proper form. Thus John Morley now argued that, 'whatever issues might present themselves, until they had secured free trade, all the other questions would lie dormant'.[4] Certainly strenuous efforts were made to use the issue to subordinate and control two major disorganizing influences in Liberal politics—Home Rule and Nonconformist sectionalism. Co-operation in the common task of defending Free Trade was sought from Unionist Free Traders, many of them Liberal Unionists, and Nonconformists were asked by Campbell-Bannerman to modify their position on the Education issue in order to facilitate the organization of this co-operation.[5] Herbert Gladstone resorted to the alleged primacy of the Free Trade cause to secure the subordinating of local particularisms in the interests of the Liberals' 'general position'.[6]

[1] 'Eighty' Club. *The Khaki Government How it fares in June 1904*, 1904, pp. 7–8.
[2] *Liberal Magazine*, vol. 12, no. 135 (December 1904), pp. 688–9.
[3] C-B to Spencer, 7 October 1903, Spencer MSS., Misc. Corr. 1903 A–BE.
[4] Hamer, *John Morley*, pp. 344–5.
[5] Cf. C-B to Bryce, 15 January 1904, Bryce MSS. P 6.
[6] H. Gladstone to C-B, 21 December 1903, 14, 18 January 1904, C-B MSS., B.M. Add. MS. 41217, folios 53, 77, 82.

Epilogue
Liberalism after Gladstone and Rosebery

LIBERALS of the late nineteenth century who thought about the historical development of their party and its place in the British political system were quite certain about one thing: ever since the first reform of Parliament, in 1832, the Liberal party had been the governing party of the country, the party which normally controlled a majority of seats in the House of Commons. Tories might occasionally hold office, but soon, as in 1846 or 1880, the claim of the Liberal coalition to represent the basic feelings of the majority of the electors was again vindicated. And at first to many Liberals what happened in 1886 did not constitute any fundamental disruption of this continuity. The Liberal majority was seen to continue to exist: the Conservatives could govern only because of the support which they received on one particular issue from a section of the Liberal party. And 1886 represented the greatest example of all of the dominant Liberal influence over the course of politics: a Liberal initiative transformed the Tories into the Unionists and defined their major purpose for at least a decade.

Nevertheless, as the years passed, another aspect of 1886 became increasingly apparent. By 1900 it was the Unionists who seemed to be the normal governing party and the Liberals who had been relegated to the position of the pre-1867 Conservatives, holding office only for brief and unsatisfactory periods and while in a minority in the House of Commons. The Liberal party was not reunified. Liberals grew uncertain as to the nature and purpose of their political existence. More and more began to think of themselves, at first usually unconsciously, as belonging to a movement of opposition rather than a movement the main concern of which was with the uses of power. There was a growing tendency, which reached its culmination in the years 1901–6 and which the Liberal Imperialists challenged with so little success, to define the essence of Liberal politics as opposition to whatever the Unionists happened to be doing. No Liberal leader reflects this more clearly in his style of leadership than Harcourt who gladly allowed the course of Liberal politics to be shaped by the initiatives taken by the Liberals' opponents and whose own occasional initiatives were either frustrated, as with the reform of London government, or unrelated to a wider scheme, as with the 1894 Budget, or hopelessly unpractical, as with temperance reform.

Throughout the period which we have been examining there was an oscillation among Liberals between two impulses: the desire to assert Liberalism in a positive way without reference to the nature of Conservative politics, and the inclination to allow the political identity of Liberals and the course of their political activity to be determined primarily by their Conservative opponents. Gladstone was the great advocate and practitioner of the positive assertion, believing that 'the Liberal Party as a rule draws its vital breath from great Liberal measures'.[1] He sought to revive Liberalism in great waves of enthusiasm for Liberal causes. But the difference between his approach and that of some of his colleagues is well illustrated by the contrasting interpretations which he and Lord Granville placed on the political situation in 1877. Gladstone claimed that by-election successes showed the effect of a great Liberal cause in rallying and cohering Liberal feeling in the country; but Granville saw them as part of a 'normal' reaction which had not been brought about by anything which the Liberals had done: 'Having lost some 70 seats at the general election, owing to the unpopularity which a strong reforming Gov[ernment] creates, and from other exceptional circumstances—after a short lapse of time we were sure to get back some of our normal majorities in boroughs.'[2] Gladstone's own positive initiatives tended to be followed by lapses into a basic anti-Toryness. In spite of Gladstone, the

---
[1] Gladstone to Harcourt, 18 May 1883, Harcourt MSS.
[2] Granville to Gladstone, 2 March 1877, Ramm, *1876–1886*, i, p. 32.

crusade on issues of foreign and imperial policy had become largely negative in spirit by 1880; and after 1886 the Home Rule issue was deliberately submerged in a campaign against 'wicked' Tory coercion. Even Chamberlain was inclined at times, as in the late 1870s and 1885, to look to the Tories to provide Radicals and Liberals with a clarification and definition of their political purpose.

But the Tories became less and less willing to play this game. Liberals were most distressed to find that their opponents could not be relied on to behave automatically and unmistakably in a 'wicked' and 'reactionary' way. They did not provide a fixed standard of conduct against which Liberals could match themselves and derive a clear impression of Liberal purpose. The bewilderment of Liberals is seen in the fact that no word was more often used by them in this period to describe the Conservatives than 'opportunist'. Liberals felt themselves to be on quicksands in seeking to make Tory behaviour the means of defining their own identity. Constantly present just under the surface of the Liberal preoccupation with Home Rule after 1886 is the feeling that only this issue clearly differentiates Liberals and Conservatives and places Tories in the recognizable and 'traditional' role of oppressors. The alternative is 'opportunism'.

Not surprisingly, in view of what happened in 1886, many Liberals came to see Gladstonian crusades or positive assertions of Liberalism through single great causes as dangerous. The reaction after Gladstone's retirement in 1894 provides ample proof of the prevalence of this belief.[1] They also saw them as unnecessary. There is no doubt that Harcourt's strategy of waiting on the course of events represented the style of leadership that most Liberals preferred when in opposition. The existence of a swinging electoral pendulum had become noticed. Regularly at every election there was a reaction against the party which had won power at the previous election. There were now two alternative-government parties, and, since people voted, it seemed, within this framework rather than in relation to the merits of the parties as political movements, all that Liberals needed to do was to wait

[1] See above, pp. 208–10.

patiently and 'without fussing'—a favourite phrase of Harcourt's—for the pendulum to return in their direction. But gradually the swing of the pendulum slowed down: in 1900 it stopped altogether.[1] There was much talk of the advent of a new system, and some Liberals panicked, arguing that the Liberals would have to take account of the Unionists' discovery in association with imperialist sentiment of the secret of permanent tenure of office. But others kept their nerve, and faith in the alternative-government concept reasserted itself to be apparently triumphantly vindicated in 1906.

The negative Harcourtian strategy would have done very well had the only problem been that of securing power. But there was also the question of how the Liberals were to use power once they had gained it. It was here that the weakness of Liberalism appeared to be most marked. Liberal politics in this period are characterized both by a decline in the ability of the Liberals to use power coherently, constructively, and fruitfully and by a growth in awareness of their decline, a crisis of confidence. In the first place, there was the record of the governments themselves: the difficulties of the period after 1870, the almost total loss of each year's legislative programme from 1880 on, the chaotic state of government policy and strategy between 1893 and 1895. Then there was the decline of these three governments to the point where the Liberal leaders were desperately anxious for any excuse to enable them to hand over the responsibilities of office to their opponents. In January 1874 Gladstone told Granville that 'it might be a godsend if some perfectly honourable difference of opinion among ourselves on a question requiring immediate action were to arise, and to take such a course as to release us collectively from the responsibilities of office'.[2] By May 1885 Sir Edward Hamilton was describing 'almost every individual minister', and especially Gladstone, as 'madly keen to get out'; and the Cabinet was discussing whether, 'in view of all the difficulties present & prospective', the government should 'ride for a fall' on some question in the House of Commons.[3] There is much evidence that it did precisely this soon after-

[1] Cf. J. Mackintosh, *The British Cabinet*, 1962, pp. 197 ff.
[2] 8 January 1874, Ramm, *1868–1876*, ii, p. 438.
[3] Sir E. Hamilton's diary, B.M. Add. MS. 48640, folio 51 (7 May 1885).

wards and deliberately courted defeat.[1] When the government had resigned, Harcourt came into Hamilton's room 'rubbing his hands with delight'.[2] The rot set in very early after the Liberals had taken office in 1892. 'Loulou' Harcourt noted in December 1893 that 'the sentiment of Ministers is rapidly growing like that of the Government of 1885 at the end, when their only desire (in 1885) was to get out of office in any way they could'.[3] In writing this he was undoubtedly recording the mood of his father who from this time on, and especially after the elevation of Rosebery to the Premiership, made no secret of his strong desire for the termination of the government's existence. The 'cordite' vote of June 1895 produced almost exactly the same reaction as the defeat of the Gladstone government ten years previously. Had ministers had any desire at all to remain in office, the vote could easily have been reversed. But the will was entirely lacking. The only subject of debate was whether they should resign or seek a dissolution of Parliament.

The way in which Liberals came to feel about their situation can be seen in the prevalence in analyses of the state of Liberal politics from the early 1880s on of the themes of impotence and obstruction. Explanations of the Liberals' inability to get anything done abounded and soon dominated the thinking of the Liberal leaders and of many of their followers. Liberals were depicted—by themselves as well as by their Tory critics—as powerless and paralysed. The old faith in progress became confined within the politics of the removal of obstructions, each one of which, it was alleged, prevented progress from occurring in every sphere of political life.

Defeat and powerlessness became for many Liberals good in themselves, situations to be sought after rather than avoided, as would be normal with a political party. Gladstone and Rosebery are the most notable examples of the tendency among Liberals to seek a cure for the problems of their party in a process of defeat, purge, and reconstruction. The party seemed to have to undergo a series of phoenix-like transformations. In characteristically vivid imagery Rosebery would describe how the dross

[1] L. P. Curtis, Jr., *Coercion and Conciliation in Ireland 1880–1892. A Study in Conservative Unionism*, Princeton and London, 1963, pp. 19–23.
[2] Sir E. Hamilton's diary, B.M. Add. MS. 48640, folio 98 (9 June 1885).
[3] Lewis Harcourt's diary, Harcourt MSS. (27 December 1893).

that accumulated needed to be periodically burned away so that once again the essence of Liberalism, concentrated and coherent, could emerge free of contamination. From this point of view experiences such as those of 1886, 1895, and 1899–1902 were not disasters but were vital for the restoration of what Rosebery called 'health' in Liberal politics.

The object of any purgation was to establish Liberalism on a more definite and unified basis. Many were anxious that Liberalism should be 'concentrated'—to use the word favoured by Rosebery and the Liberal Imperialists—into a new creed or set of views on issues of policy. Thus at various times those who opposed Home Rule for Ireland or who held 'Little England' views on imperial policy were defined as deserving to be removed from influence in the Liberal party by persons whose overriding aim was the 'concentration' of Liberal politics. Among the Liberals of the late nineteenth century there was much looking back to the days when Liberal political action did seem to have been controlled by a single 'idea'—'Free Trade' or 'utility' or 'Liberty'.

The great problem was always how to arrive at a creed that was comprehensive and flexible enough to include the political interests and feelings not only of active reformers with particular causes to promote but also of that half of the electorate on the winning of whose votes the Liberals depended for the gaining of power. This was where the single great issue involving the removal of an obstruction to progress made such a strong appeal to the Liberal leaders. It could be used to explain the *whole* political situation and to concentrate the attention and energies of people whose primary interest was in progress in particular parts of that situation.

But 'obstructions to progress' were essentially substitutes for systems. For a system itself that might underlie and cohere Liberal politics Liberals were again and again thrown back on a basic liberal creed, the creed of 'the open mind' and intellectual 'liberty', according to which diversity of opinion and multiplicity of interests were admirable and of the essence of Liberalism. This was the creed against which Rosebery and the Liberal Imperialists in the end rebelled. Rosebery demanded an end to the entire regime of 'open-mindedness'. And it is this as much as their imperialism which explains the failure of the Liberal imperialists to secure a predominant influence over the Liberal party. To many Liberals it was not just their imperialism that was alien to the Liberal tradition. Their view as to the proper form of Liberal political activity also seemed profoundly 'un-Liberal' in so far as implied in it was a completely different ideology. Campbell-Bannerman reasserted the old creed and succeeded in persuading Liberals that they were united, not divided, by their propensity for individualism and diversity of opinion. He was the first leader of the party to seek to come to terms with this aspect of Liberal politics, the first leader to try to make Liberals stop worrying about 'fragmentation' and 'incoherence'. His task was, of course, eased considerably by the fact that he was leader at a time when the Conservatives were behaving in a way long regarded as characteristically Liberal. Campbell-Bannerman was able to diminish the obsession of Liberals with their own sectionalism and disunity because the record of the Balfour government seemed to prove that these were not after all a peculiarly Liberal disease.

With the return of the Liberals to office in December 1905 and their triumph in the general election held in the following month, a new era in Liberal politics seems about to begin. The age of Gladstone and Rosebery is at a close. Gladstone and Harcourt are dead, Spencer is incapacitated, and Rosebery is now a completely isolated and futile figure, thrust to the outer margin of the political world by the decision of his closest supporters to join a Liberal government organized on principles completely opposed to the reconstruction of Liberalism which the Liberal League had advocated. Nevertheless, it would be quite incorrect to regard 1905 as a turning-point at which there was a clean break with the past and a disappearance of the problems which have been analysed in the preceding pages of this book. These problems persist and in some cases, as with the House of Lords and the Irish question, eventually became much more serious and urgent than they had ever been before. Some sectional interests, especially those associated with Nonconformity and the great moral causes of the Victorian era, continue their decline in influence and importance; but others, notably Labour and the women's suffrage movement, assume an altogether new dimension and move outside the limits of sectional Liberal politics.

In January 1906 the Liberals found themselves with a substantial majority over all other parties combined. Thus the problem of whether to take office dependent on the votes of the Irish M.P.s did not have to be faced, and the influence of the Irish was temporarily neutralized. It was as if twenty-five years of confusion, disunity, and schism had been erased. Rosebery's prayer for a return to the kind of party that had existed prior to 1886 had been answered but without any need to resort to Rosebery's drastic methods for promoting Liberal revival. But 1906 represented a reversion to 1880 in more senses than one. It was a Liberal triumph, but once again in the very causes of this triumph can be detected also the seeds of failure. The Liberals were again swept in on a tide of reaction against the policies and conduct of their Conservative opponents, not of enthusiasm for the policies that they themselves had to offer. The Liberal programme was almost as threadbare as had been the programme of 1880, and its importance was, as then, made little of during the election campaign. The mood of the campaign was deliberately and essentially negative and marked the culmination of the strategy followed by the leaders since 1901 of blurring over the disagreements within the party and concentrating on rallying a majority of resentment against the initiatives and innovations of the Unionists.

Just as in 1880, there flowed from this campaign no clear indication whatsoever as to the uses which the Liberals should make of the power which they had thus won. It was impossible after 1880 for Gladstone to make resistance to 'Beaconsfieldism' the basis of a legislative programme. So now in 1906 the economic *status quo* had been secured by the simple process of defeating the Unionists in the general election. No further action was needed.

The first three years of the new Liberal government can consequently be interpreted as belonging to that phase of Liberal history which has been the subject of this book. A series of reform measures was produced of the late-nineteenth-century kind, appealing exclusively to minority sections and interests—Welsh and Scottish farmers, temperance enthusiasts,

Nonconformists, the trade union movement. The Liberal government seemed, in spite of its vast majority, to lapse remarkably quickly into the same state of incoherence and lack of common purpose as had characterized the governments of 1880–5 and 1892–5. In May 1907, talking with Beatrice Webb, Haldane analysed this condition in a way which related it directly to the atmosphere of the general election itself. The Liberal Parliament was the creation of that election —'no constructive ideas, merely objections to other people's ideas'. The public seemed to be 'moved more by impatience of what was than by any clear notion of what state of affairs they desired to being about' and the government reflected this exactly, being made up, as Beatrice Webb remarked, of men, 'either with no settled opinions, or with contrary opinions on the questions with which they had to deal', so that the Cabinet was 'an incoherent body—intensely individualistic— each man for himself'.[1] Of course, both Haldane and the Webbs, in their enthusiasm for Roseberyite reconstruction, had endeavoured to promote a very different kind of Liberal politics; but the 'Broad Church' principle of party unity had triumphed, and Liberal leaders seemed united only in their toleration of divergences of opinion.

The old complaints as to absence of 'concentration' began to be heard again. Viscount Wolverhampton, who, as H. H. Fowler, had so often criticized wide legislative programmes in the past, now condemned Campbell-Bannerman for 'allowing so much legislation to be promised and attempted'; and Sir Almeric Fitzroy found John Sinclair, Campbell-Bannerman's close associate, very much in agreement with him when in 1908 he observed that the tendency to raise too many questions was at the root of the government's difficulties: 'the area of attack was immensely widened, and in proportion the dissatisfaction of their own supporters was excited, in some quarters by the alleged inadequacy of their proposals, in others by the slowness with which they gave effect to them'.[2] The criticism bears an uncanny resemblance to that which began to be voiced after the 1868 and 1892 governments had been in office for a couple of years.

[1] B. Webb, *Our Partnership*, pp. 379–80.
[2] Sir A. Fitzroy, *Memoirs*, vol. i [1925], pp. 369, 360.

L. T. Hobhouse, writing in 1911, called for 'fuller cooperation among those of genuine democratic feeling and more agreement as to the order of reform': 'At present progress is blocked by the very competition of many causes for the first place in the advance.' There needed to be 'less of the fanatics of sectarianism and more of the unifying mind'. 'Devolution' remained a possible solution to this problem—and Winston Churchill presented to his Cabinet colleagues in the same year as Hobhouse was writing an elaborate scheme for the devolution of parliamentary business[1]—but beyond that what Hobhouse principally had to suggest was the passion that is kindled by 'the vision of justice in the wholeness of her beauty'.[2] Such a passion had been incited by Gladstone in 1880 and 1886 and by Campbell-Bannerman in his attacks on the conduct of the South African war. Gladstone had called it the politics of 'virtuous passion'. But only in one area did it seem possible that this government might be able to revive Liberal emotions of this kind. The great causes of the past—anti-imperialism, women's emancipation, Irish Home Rule, temperance—had either turned sour or now aroused passions that seemed to Liberals very frightening and un-virtuous. The one exception, it seemed, might be the House of Lords.

Between 1906 and 1908 the House of Lords simply repeated its performance of 1893–5 and rejected or drastically amended nearly all the Bills put forward by the Liberal government. It could do so with impunity because the reforms contained in these Bills catered only for sections and were contemplated by the mass of the population with at best utter indifference. An appeal to the people against the peers' rejection of such measures would run a very grave risk of failure and consequent vindication of their veto power. As a result, by 1908 the Liberal government, desperate to get legislation passed, is having to move not merely to challenge the veto power of the House of Lords but also to cast off the nineteenth-century legacy of sectionalist reform on which rested the impunity with which that power was being exercised. In 1909, with Lloyd George's Budget, the conflict moves into the arena of

---

[1] Quoted in H. J. Hanham (ed.), *The Nineteenth-Century Constitution 1815–1914. Documents and Commentary*, Cambridge 1969, pp. 131–3.
[2] Hobhouse, *Liberalism*, pp. 249–51.

social and fiscal reform, and a new era of Liberal politics seems to be born. The Lords are challenged because, it is alleged, they are resisting policies which affect the welfare and interests of the mass of the people, not just of temperance enthusiasts or the Irish or militant nonconformists.

At first, in fact, the Lords question assumed once again in the rhetoric of the Liberal leaders the traditional form of the single great question, based on its being an obstruction which prevented progress on anything else. *It* became the ordering and controlling influence in Liberal politics. Lloyd George called it the 'one great dominant question', 'one that will absorb all others', and Asquith asked Liberals to consider the Lords' veto 'as the dominating issue in politics—the dominating issue because in the long run it overshadows and absorbs every other'.[1] It was felt to be the issue which now kept the sections related to a general Liberal purpose. Reginald McKenna suggested to the Webbs in 1907 that the Lords' rejection of Bills was all that there was 'to bind Liberal and Labour together'.[2] Of course, the Lords did their best to ensure that this was not so by exempting from their massacre of Liberal legislation the Trade Disputes Bill of 1906.

But there was a difference. This time the Liberals found themselves drawn on by the implications of the Lords' rejection of the 1909 Budget to doing something about the obstruction. It is now generally accepted by historians that initially the Budget was not intended to be a challenge to the Lords to force them into this kind of showdown but was seen as the only way now open to the Liberals to bypass the Lords' veto and secure reforms *while it continued to exist*. The Lords' decision to reject the Budget transformed the situation. The Liberal party was making a decisive entry at last into the arena of social reform, and it is natural that the leaders were extremely reluctant to associate this with a major and time-consuming constitutional conflict. But the Lords' success in requiring the government to go to the country on the issue of the rejected Budget made it essential that the constitutional issue itself be faced. Thus the controlling effect of the

[1] M. Gilbert (ed.), *Lloyd George*, New Jersey, 1968, pp. 38–9. V. Bonham Carter, *Winston Churchill As I Knew Him*, 1967 edition, p. 173.
[2] Webb, *Our Partnership*, p. 385.

concentration on the Lords' obstruction was of brief duration. The Liberal leaders had to immerse themselves in the working out of the detailed provisions of a Parliament Bill. This, we can now see, was another turning-point in the history of the party. From the early 1880s until 1911 the predominant theme of Liberal politics had been the removal of obstructions to the progress of reform legislation. It was a preoccupation which Liberals had often publicly lamented but which they had just as often been prepared to exploit and even welcome and perpetuate because of its unifying influence on Liberal politics. The Parliament Act of 1911 and the Home Rule Act for Ireland which seemed bound to follow three years later promised to remove at long last from the path of Liberal progress the two main obstructions with which Liberals had been preoccupied. Liberals seem to have been too exhausted to notice, but now their leaders would no longer have available to them the excuse that they could not attend to demands for reform because of the existence of these great obstructions. The crucial question ought to have been whether concentrated and fruitful attention to reform policy would at last be resumed. But by 1914 all that the House of Lords seemed to have been an obstruction to was Irish Home Rule and Welsh disestablishment. And national insurance, old age pensions, employment exchanges, and the other social reforms of the post-1908 era were enacted without any need to resort to the machinery for overcoming its veto. As befitted an anachronistic institution, the House of Lords continued to be active principally in relation to those policies which were the Liberal party's inheritance from the previous century.

As the nineteenth-century issues faded from the scene or, like the Irish question, became transmuted into hideous and frightening new forms, it was hard to see what was the distinctive ground that Liberalism alone occupied and which entitled it to be one of the two main parties in the State. Since the days of T. H. Green Liberals had been trying to work out a distinctively Liberal approach to social politics, but it is quite clear that after 1905 it was not social reform that aroused the enthusiasm of the Liberal rank-and-file but the traditional causes—opposition to imperialism and militarism, Home Rule, temperance, the agitation against the landowners, and so forth. Social reform was rather the work and the enthusiasm of the great 'outsiders' such as Lloyd George and Winston Churchill—neither of whom fitted comfortably into the *established* order of Liberal politics—plus Fabian Socialists and strong-minded civil servants, such as the Webbs and Morant.

Since 1868 the Liberals had existed as an alternative-government party, one of two main parties; and this basic fact of their existence had often been enough to float them out of severe internal difficulties and confusions, simply because they were there when the electorate grew dissatisfied with their opponents' conduct of office, and because they were able to define their purpose as the opposite of what the Conservatives were doing or proposing. But now their position in the political spectrum was changing. They were no longer on one side but in the middle, and they seemed to be less an alternative to the Conservatives than an alternative to the entirely different type of party politics which the confrontation of Labour and Conservatives threatened to introduce. The purpose of the Liberals seemed more than ever to be to prevent the development of the politics of class antagonism. Lloyd George warned that the Labour movement, if it detached itself from Liberalism, might frighten 'the great middle classes of this country' into 'positive hostility' and reaction 'by a purely class organization to which they did not belong'.[1] Winston Churchill saw the Liberal party as a force 'against the twin assaults of capital & Labour', and advocated the abandonment of *laissez-faire* as the only way of averting 'savage strife between class and class'.[2] Liberals had to appeal to people from whatever class who were afraid of the development of class conflict and make them appreciate that to support either the Tories or Labour was to contribute to such a development.

There were two possible reactions to this situation, and both can be seen emerging in the critical years 1909–10 when the entire fabric of traditional Liberalism appeared to be dissolving. On the one hand, Liberals could endeavour to reassert the main traditional Radical understanding as to the fundamental socio-political cleavage in Britain, and this Lloyd George

[1] Gilbert, *Lloyd George*, p. 33.
[2] R. S. Churchill, *Winston S. Churchill*, vol. ii, 1967, pp. 72, 325.

briefly did in his rhetorical assaults against the landlords in 1909. He drew a distinction between, on the one hand, the parasitic landlords flourishing on their 'unearned increment' and, on the other, the millions of people who did the work of the country. In the latter category employers and working men were undifferentiated. The old Gladstonian rhetoric was revived. Churchill called the Parliament Bill 'territory conquered by the masses from the classes', and claimed that the peers were hostile because they hated 'a government representative of and resting on the middle and working classes, a government supported by nonconformists and trade unions'.[1] The rhetorical passion was intense but it proved to be no basis for a durable revival of Liberalism which, as the 1910 elections showed, had lost its majority in England. Lloyd George had plans in 1913 for a great new campaign on the theme of land reform, but the relevance of the land question to the problems of urban society was now seeming more and more marginal.

The other reaction was to abandon the struggle and replace the traditional alternative-government party by a great centre force in politics that would leave the dangerous extremes isolated and impotent. By 1910 this was the direction in which Lloyd George was looking and he proposed to the Conservative leaders that a coalition government be formed with compromise policies on most of the great issues of the day. The attempt of 1909 to create a new emotional unity in Liberalism seemed to have failed. As the result of the first election of 1910 the Liberals were now dependent on the votes of Labour and the Irish, and the nineteenth-century handicap of dependence on sectional influences was re-created. Gladstone had controlled these influences by his great crusades which in his opinion lifted Liberalism on to an altogether higher and essentially 'national' and non-partisan political plane. The purpose of Lloyd George's proposal was similar. It too was a way of neutralizing the sectionalists—and in his scheme he particularly refers to Labour, the Irish, and the 'teetotal faddists'.[2] Traditional Liberal politics were to be dissolved and replaced by what Churchill called *'une politique d'apaisement'*. Churchill

---

[1] R. S. Churchill, op. cit., ii, pp. 358, 328.
[2] P. Rowland, *The Last Liberal Governments: The Promised Land, 1905–1910*, 1968, pp. 308–11.

argued that now 'all the outworn controversies of the Victorian period had been honourably settled and cleared out of the way'.[1] When, seven years later, Lloyd George did become the leader of a coalition government, he was to say: 'The old hide-bound Liberalism was played out; the Newcastle programme had been realised.'[2] For, although at the time the project was not supported, it can now be seen as the beginning of the end of the attempt to maintain Liberalism in its traditional form.

The main subject of this book has been sectionalism and the efforts of the Liberal leaders to control or subdue it. These efforts may have been necessary in order to maintain the effectiveness of the Liberals as an alternative-government party, but one may argue that they contributed also to the sapping of the vital essence of Liberalism. Without enthusiasm for temperance reform or disestablishment or Irish Home Rule, what *was* Liberalism? The assumption was always that Liberalism needed to take up social reform in order to make itself relevant to contemporary needs. But the distinctive Liberal rationale for social reform, that it was needed in order to avert class conflict and 'socialism', could just as well be expressed in that defensive, protective reaction which was causing the middle classes to desert Liberalism for Conservatism, especially when the existence of a Labour Party was polarizing politics along class lines. The formation of a coalition with the Conservatives was perhaps the only way of 'saving' the Liberals in these circumstances, but it was a 'solution' which destroyed both the Liberal party as a separate force and the Liberal idea in so far as it facilitated the emergence of Labour as an alternative-government party. There is no evidence that before 1914 social reform was able to arouse among Liberals that enthusiasm, that 'virtuous passion', which had characterized their devotion to the great causes of the nineteenth century. The Liberals could not live with sectionalism, but nor could they live without it.

[1] Churchill, *Winston S. Churchill*, ii, pp. 349, 360.
[2] T. Wilson (ed.), *The Political Diaries of C. P. Scott 1911–1928*, 1970, p. 257.

Appendix
Biographical Notes

THE following are biographical details relating to the Liberals who are principally referred to in this book. I have attempted to place them in categories according to what seems to me to have been their predominant function or role in Liberal politics. In some cases the Liberal moved into or out of another category during the period which has been the subject of this book. I have marked the names of such Liberals with an asterisk and indicated what the other category was.

1. *Leaders*

BRIGHT, JOHN (1811–89): President of the Board of Trade, 1868–70; Chancellor of the Duchy of Lancaster, 1873 and 1880–2. Resigned from Cabinet in 1882 in protest against bombardment of Alexandria. Opposed Home Rule from 1886 on. Hated political programmes, strongly advocated concentration on one issue at a time as in the days of the Anti-Corn Law League. To disappointment of some Nonconformists, failed to act as leader of their section within the party.

BRUCE, H. A. (1815–95): Home Secretary, 1868–73; created first Baron Aberdare, 1873. South Wales mine-owner and iron-master.

BRYCE, JAMES (1838–1922): M.P. for Tower Hamlets, 1880–5, and South Aberdeen, 1885–1906. Chancellor of the Duchy of Lancaster, 1892–4; President of the Board of Trade, 1894–5; Chief Secretary for Ireland, 1905–6. Background: academic (professor of law; writer on constitutional history). Major political interests the Eastern question, sympathy with 'nations struggling to be free'—took keen interest in Southern Africa and took Boer side in war of 1899–1902. Relied on heavily to expound constitutional intricacies of the Irish Home Rule question.

CAMPBELL-BANNERMAN, SIR HENRY (1836–1908): M.P. for the Stirling Burghs, 1868–1908. Financial Secretary at the War Office, 1871–4, 1880–2; Secretary to the Admiralty, 1882–4; Chief Secretary for Ireland, 1884–5; Secretary of State for War, 1886, 1892–5, Leader of the Liberal Party, 1899–1908. Prime Minister, 1905–8. The rapid removal of so many who were above him in the party hierarchy brought to the leadership in 1899 a man who was, for a leader, unusually close in his political attitudes and instincts to 'the Plain' (see below, category 5)—note, e.g., his contempt for 'clever' men (Balfour, Rosebery, Haldane), his lack of fanatical devotion to any policy issues, his deep emotional reactions against very general tendencies in Conservative politics. Largely at a loss when it came to finding positive policies for the party.

CHILDERS, H. C. E. (1827–96): M.P. for Pontefract, 1860–85, and for Edinburgh South, 1886–92. First Lord of the Admiralty, 1868–71; Chancellor of the Duchy of Lancaster, 1872–3; Secretary of State for War, 1880–2; Chancellor of the Exchequer, 1882–5; Home Secretary, 1886.

CREWE, MARQUESS OF (1858–1945): Lord President of the Council, 1905–8; Colonial Secretary, 1908–10; Secretary of State for India, 1910–15. Became prominent in Liberal leadership after 1895 (he had been Irish Viceroy—as Lord Houghton—between 1892 and 1895). Influence strongly in favour of party unity based on the 'Broad Church' concept.

FORSTER, W. E. (1818–86): M.P. for Bradford, 1861–86. Vice-President of the Council, 1868–74; Chief Secretary for Ireland, 1880–2. Forfeited much Nonconformist support as a result of his Education Act of 1870, and failed to win Liberal leadership in 1875. Broke with Liberal leadership in 1882 over issue of conciliation of Irish Nationalist and agrarian agitation, and opposed Home Rule in 1886. Early example of a Nonconformist Imperialist (interested in Imperial Federation). Leading antagonist of Chamberlainite Radicalism and of the 'caucus' system.

GLADSTONE, W. E. (1808–98): Prime Minister, 1868–74, 1880–5, 1886, 1892–4.

GOSCHEN, G. J. (1831–1907): M.P. for the City of London, 1863–80, and for Ripon, 1880–5. President of the Poor Law Board, 1868–71; First Lord of the Admiralty, 1871–4. Moved further and further to the right after 1874 and stood out as one of the last determined and doctrinaire Liberal opponents of the extension of the franchise. Did not participate in Gladstone's second administration, opposed Home Rule in 1886, and joined a Conservative Cabinet in 1887.

GRANVILLE, EARL (1815–91): Foreign Secretary, 1851–2, 1870–4, 1880–5; Colonial Secretary, 1868–70, 1886. Close confidant of Gladstone's. Appears to have been a convinced convert to Irish Home Rule. Took little interest in domestic policy.

HARCOURT, SIR W. V. (1827–1904): M.P. for Oxford, 1868–80; for Derby, 1880–95; for West Monmouth, 1895–1904. Solicitor-General, 1873–4; Home Secretary, 1880–5; Chancellor of the Exchequer, 1886, 1892–5. Leader of the Liberal party in the House of Commons from Gladstone's retirement in 1894 until his own resignation in December 1898. Reluctant and unconvinced supporter of Home Rule—anxious to relegate the policy as soon as possible. Normally in favour of concern with domestic reform on a wide front, but never succeeded in crystallizing this concern into any definite scheme. More comfortable attacking Toryism or Unionism or imperialism. Own policy initiatives seldom enjoyed success. Highly irascible —alienated his colleagues who came to regard him as quite impossible as a leader. His son, LEWIS (or 'LOULOU') HARCOURT (1863–1922), devoted himself to his father's interests as his private secretary and did not commence an independent political career until 1904.

HARTINGTON, MARQUESS OF (1833–1908): Postmaster-General, 1868–70; Chief Secretary for Ireland, 1870–4; Secretary of State for India, 1880–2; Secretary of State for War, 1882–5. Leader of the Liberal party in the House of Commons, 1875–80. By 1885 generally regarded as leader of the 'Whig section'. Showed little enthusiasm for organizing and cohering the party; inclined, as in 1875 or 1885 or 1886–7, to let a process of disintegration take its natural course. Very reluctant interest in any development of policy. Opposed Home Rule in 1886 and was thereafter one of the leading Liberal Unionists. Succeeded father as eighth Duke of Devonshire in 1891.

HERSCHELL, LORD (1837–99): M.P. for Durham, 1874–85. Solicitor-General, 1880–5; Lord Chancellor, 1886, 1892–5. A much respected lawyer whose death in 1899 was regarded as a great loss for the party.

KIMBERLEY, LORD (1826–1902): Lord Privy Seal, 1868–70; Colonial Secretary, 1870–4, 1880–2; Secretary of State for India, 1882–5, 1886, 1892–4; Foreign Secretary, 1894–5. Leader of the Liberal party in the House of Lords after 1891.

LOWE, ROBERT (1811–92): Chancellor of the Exchequer, 1868–73; Home Secretary, 1873–4. Created Viscount Sherbrooke, 1880.

*MORLEY, J. (1838–1923): M.P. for Newcastle upon Tyne, 1883–95; for Montrose Burghs, 1896–1908. Chief Secretary for Ireland, 1886, 1892–5; Secretary for India, 1905–10. Can be said to have passed through three other categories before becoming a leader: (i) journalist and editor—editor of the *Fortnightly Review*, 1867–82, and *Pall Mall Gazette*, 1880–3; (ii) 'single-cause' Radical, associated with the National Education League and the Liberation Society, 1870–6; (iii) 'general' Radical after 1876, closely allied with Chamberlain. Broke with Chamberlain in 1886 when he decided to support Gladstone on Home Rule. Became one of leading advocates of Home Rule. Later a strong anti-imperialist and 'Pro-Boer'. Always opposed programmes and favoured concentration on single questions.

*MUNDELLA, A. J. (1825–97): M.P. for Sheffield, 1868–85; for Sheffield Brightside, 1885–97. Vice-President of Committee of Privy Council for Education, 1880–5; President of the Board of Trade, 1886,

APPENDIX: BIOGRAPHICAL NOTES

1892–4. Notable as a provincial Liberal and as one of the Liberal industrialists most concerned to develop 'Lib-Labism'. Especially in early 1870s was associated with sectionalist causes, e.g. National Education League, but rapidly evolved into a 'general' Radical. By the 1880s he could well be classified as belonging to 'the Plain' because of, e.g., his devotion to Gladstone, his concern for practical administrative achievement, and his dislike of sectionalism.

RIPON, MARQUESS OF (1827–1909): Son of Viscount Goderich who was Prime Minister briefly in the 1820s. First held office in 1859 and did not finally retire from office until 1908. Lord President of the Council, 1868–73; Governor-General of India, 1880–4; First Lord of the Admiralty, 1886; Colonial Secretary, 1892–5; Lord Privy Seal, 1905–8. A convert to Roman Catholicism in 1874; later a strong supporter of Irish Home Rule. A notably liberal Indian Viceroy. Took a more general interest in Liberal policy after 1886 and was particularly anxious for a more positive agricultural policy.

SELBORNE, EARL OF (1812–95): as Sir Roundell Palmer, M.P. for Richmond, Yorkshire, 1861–72. Lord Chancellor, 1872–4, 1880–5. Opposed Irish Home Rule in 1886. A High Churchman who took a very strong line on questions relating to disestablishment, etc.

SPENCER, EARL (1835–1910): the fifth Earl. Lord Lieutenant of Ireland, 1868–74, 1882–5 (on the latter occasion with a seat in the Cabinet); President of the Council, 1880–2, 1886; First Lord of the Admiralty, 1892–5; Liberal leader in House of Lords, 1902–5. Supported Irish Home Rule in 1886. Twice a possibility for the Liberal premiership—in 1892, when Gladstone, if asked by the Queen, would have recommended him, and in 1902–4, when he was starting to look a possible compromise leader in view of the Liberal Leaguers' opposition to C.B. He was then, however, incapacitated by illness. Of great importance to the Liberal promotion of Home Rule because he was widely respected and had presided over a coercionist regime in Ireland. A fine example of the historic Whig devotion to duty.

2. *Whigs and Party Organizers*

BIRRELL, AUGUSTINE (1850–1933): M.P. for West Fife, 1889–1900, and for North Bristol, 1906–18. President of the Board of Education, 1905–7; Chief Secretary for Ireland, 1907–16. Succeeded Watson as President of the N.L.F. in 1902.

*ELLIS, T. E. (1859–99): M.P. for Merioneth, 1886–99. Deputy Whip, 1892–4; Chief Whip, 1894–9. In the late 1880s he emerged as the leader of the younger Welsh Nationalists, but his career was transformed when he accepted appointment as a Whip in 1892 and he had to move away from sectional politics to the general problems of Liberalism. He was a Liberal

Imperialist, a close friend of Rosebery, Asquith, and Acland, and an admirer of Rhodes. This interest facilitated the transition.

GLADSTONE, H. J. (1854–1930): M.P. for Leeds, 1880–5, and for West Leeds, 1885–1910. Liberal Whip, 1881–5; Financial Secretary at the War Office, 1886; Under Secretary at the Home Office, 1892–4; First Commissioner of Works, 1894–5; Chief Whip, 1899–1905; Home Secretary, 1905–10. Youngest son of W. E. Gladstone. Extreme devotion to father led to 'Hawarden Kite' indiscretion in Dec. 1885. Did notable work between 1899 and 1905 in integrating the Liberal sections.

HARRIS, WILLIAM: One of the leading Birmingham Radicals. Became Secretary of the reorganized Birmingham Liberal Association in 1868, and later played a prominent part in the organization of the N.L.F.

HUDSON, SIR ROBERT (1864–1927): associated with the N.L.F. from 1882 on; became Secretary of the N.L.F. and the Liberal Central Association in 1893.

KITSON, SIR JAMES (1835–1911): later Lord Airedale. M.P. for Colne Valley, 1892–1907. President of the N.L.F., 1883–90. An iron and steel manufacturer. Leading Liberal in Leeds—one of strongest antagonists of Chamberlain after 1885.

MORLEY, ARNOLD (1849–1916): M.P. for Nottingham, 1880–95. Chief Whip, 1886–92; Postmaster-General, 1892–5. Son of Samuel Morley.

SCHNADHORST, F. (1840–1900): prominent in the Central Nonconformist Committee, the National Education League, and the Birmingham Liberal Association, before becoming the first Secretary of the N.L.F. in 1877—took Gladstonian side in 1886 and remained Secretary until 1893. He was an outstanding organizer but not always scrupulous about his methods as the controversy about his securing of financial support for the party from Rhodes was to show. Seems to have had little influence on policy.

TWEEDMOUTH, LORD (1849–1909): as Edward Marjoribanks, M.P. for North Berwickshire, 1880–5, and for Berwickshire, 1885–94. Liberal Whip, 1886–92; Chief Whip, 1892–4. Succeeded to father's title in 1894. Leader of Scottish Liberalism—master-minded resistance to the Liberal League in Scotland and became the *bête noire* of the Liberal Imperialists there. Lord Privy Seal and Chancellor of the Duchy of Lancaster, 1894–5; First Lord of the Admiralty, 1905–8.

WATSON, ROBERT SPENCE (1837–1911): outstanding figure in Newcastle upon Tyne Liberalism. President of the N.L.F., 1890–1902. Never entered Parliament.

WOLVERTON, LORD (1824–87): as G. G. Glyn, M.P. for Shaftesbury, 1857–73. Chief Whip, 1867–73. One of Gladstone's leading advisers.

3. Sectionalists and 'Faddists'

This section includes Liberals who were associated particularly with one cause or group or interest in the party. Some of them, notably the Lib-Labs, were certainly not 'faddists' and in their behaviour tended to merge into 'the Plain'.

ARCH, JOSEPH (1826–1919): M.P. for North-West Norfolk, 1885–6, 1892–1902. Notable for his work on behalf of agricultural labourers. A staunchly Gladstonian Lib-Lab.

BROADHURST, H. (1840–1911): M.P. for Stoke-on-Trent, 1880–5, for Bordesley, 1885–6, for West Nottingham, 1886–92, and for Leicester, 1894–1906. Under-Secretary at the Home Office, 1886—first working man to be a member of the Government. The leading Lib-Lab of the day—was Secretary of the Parliamentary Committee of the T.U.C., 1875–90, and a strong Gladstonian. Put up a strong resistance to Eight Hours Bills.

BURT, THOMAS (1837–1922): M.P. for Morpeth, 1874–1918. One of the first two working men M.P.s. Secretary at the Board of Trade, 1892–5. Trade union leader in North-East of England (mining). A Lib-Lab—opposed Eight Hours Bills.

CAINE, W. S. (1842–1903): M.P. for Scarborough, 1880–5, for Barrow-on-Furness, 1886–90, for East Bradford, 1892–5, and for Camborne, 1900–3. A Baptist who devoted most of his career to the promotion of temperance reform. Appointed a Civil Lord of the Admiralty in 1884 but his official career was soon terminated as a result of his opposition to Home Rule in 1886. He strongly supported Chamberlain for a few years but rejoined the Liberal party in 1890 mainly because of his concern for the temperance question. Found much difficulty in re-establishing himself in Liberal politics.

CLIFFORD, DR. JOHN (1836–1923): outstanding Baptist clergyman—led opposition to the 1902 Education Act.

DALE, DR. R. W. (1829–95): one of the leading Birmingham Liberals. The Congregationalist Minister at Carr's Lane Chapel. Inclined in early 1870s to press Nonconformist interests very strongly. Opposed Home Rule in 1886 but worked for Liberal reunion.

GEE, THOMAS (1815–98): Nonconformist leader in North Wales. One of the leaders of the anti-tithe agitation in the late 1880s. A Methodist minister and a (Welsh-language) publisher in Denbigh.

HOWELL, GEORGE (1833–1910): M.P. for Bethnal Green North-East, 1885–95. One of the leaders of the Reform League in the late 1860s. Secretary of the Parliamentary Committee of the T.U.C., 1871–5, and an outstanding practitioner of Lib-Labism.

APPENDIX: BIOGRAPHICAL NOTES

LAWSON, SIR WILFRID (1829–1906): M.P. for Carlisle, 1859–65, 1868–85, and for Cockermouth, 1886–1906. Fanatically devoted to temperance reform, but anti-imperialism was an important subsidiary interest.

LEWIS, J. HERBERT (1858–1933): M.P. for Flint Boroughs, 1892–1906, and for Flintshire, 1906–18. A supporter of Cymru Fydd. Strongly opposed the South African war. Was a Liberal Whip, 1905–9.

LLOYD GEORGE, DAVID (1863–1945): M.P. for Caernarvon Boroughs, 1890–1945. In the 1890s an extreme Welsh sectionalist, but opposition to the South African war and the Education Act of 1902 made him a leader of two other groupings in the party as well (anti-imperialism and Nonconformity), and by 1904–5 he was well on the way to becoming a leader of the party as a whole.

MIALL, EDWARD (1809–81): M.P. for Bradford, 1869–74. A former clergyman. Founder and editor of the *Nonconformist*. A leading figure in the Liberation Society.

NICOLL, W. ROBERTSON (1851–1923): former Free Church minister in Scotland. As editor of *The British Weekly*, 1886–1923, a very influential Nonconformist journalist.

RAINY, DR. ROBERT (1826–1906): Principal of Free Church College, Edinburgh, 1874–1901.

RENDEL, STUART (1834–1913): M.P. for Montgomeryshire, 1880–94. Granted a peerage in 1894. Welsh parliamentary leader and friend of Gladstone.

RICHARD, HENRY (1812–88): M.P. for the Merthyr Boroughs, 1868–88. A Congregationalist minister. Secretary of the Peace Society, 1848–85, and a leading advocate of international arbitration, as well as of numerous Nonconformist causes.

ROGERS, J. GUINNESS (1822–1911): Congregationalist minister (in London, 1865–1900). Wrote a great deal on Nonconformist questions and Liberal politics.

*STANSFELD, JAMES (1820–98): M.P. for Halifax, 1859–95. Career followed orthodox course until early 1870s and in 1871 he entered the Cabinet as President of the Poor Law Board. But then his career underwent a dramatic change and he devoted himself to the repeal of the Contagious Diseases Acts. In 1886 he supported Gladstone over Home Rule and replaced Chamberlain as President of the Local Government Board; but he never succeeded in re-establishing himself as a Liberal leader.

WHITTAKER, T. P. (1850–1919): M.P. for Spen Valley from 1892. Temperance reformer.

APPENDIX: BIOGRAPHICAL NOTES 337

*WILSON, H. J. (1833–1914): M.P. for Holmfirth, 1885–1912. Leading Sheffield Liberal. Enthusiast for most of the leading sectionalist causes, especially temperance reform and the repeal of the Contagious Diseases Acts. Gradually merged into 'the Plain'. Opposed eight hours legislation and the South African war.

4. General Radicals

These are Radicals who wished to see Radicalism predominate in the Liberal party but sought a Radicalism broader than that connected with particular causes of the kind favoured by the 'faddists'. They tended to be strongly opposed to sectionalism.

ATHERLEY-JONES, L. A.: M.P. for Durham North-West from 1885. Son of the Chartist Ernest Jones. A barrister. Keen advocate of the enfranchisement of women.

BRADLAUGH, C. (1833–91): M.P. for Northampton, 1880–91.

CHAMBERLAIN, JOSEPH (1836–1914): M.P. for Birmingham, 1876–85. President of the Board of Trade, 1880–5; President of the Local Government Board, 1886. Mayor of Birmingham, 1873–6. In early career associated with particular reform interests, notably the National Education League; but from 1872 on devoted himself to fostering and organizing a general Radical movement. Opposed Gladstone over Home Rule in 1886.

COLLINGS, JESSE (1831–1920): M.P. for Ipswich, 1880–6. A leading Birmingham Liberal and faithful supporter of Chamberlain. A Liberal Unionist from 1886 on. Special concern was the welfare of agricultural labourers and land reform generally.

CONYBEARE, C. A. V. (1853–1919): M.P. for Camborne, 1885–95. Known as an extreme Radical. Imprisoned in connection with activities in Ireland in the late 1880s. Took active interest in development of Labour politics and was for a few years after 1888 a Vice-President of the Scottish Labour Party.

DILKE, SIR CHARLES W. (1843–1911): M.P. for Chelsea, 1868–86, and for Forest of Dean, 1892–1911. Under-Secretary at the Foreign Office, 1880–2; President of the Local Government Board, 1882–5. Official career abruptly terminated by divorce scandal, 1885–6. Supported Home Rule. Later an independent Radical back-bencher with close links with the Labour M.P.s.

FAWCETT, HENRY (1833–84): M.P. for Brighton, 1865–74, and for Hackney, 1874–84. Postmaster-General, 1880–4. Blind political economist. Extreme advocate of *laissez-faire*.

APPENDIX: BIOGRAPHICAL NOTES

LABOUCHERE, HENRY (1831–1912): M.P. for Northampton, 1880–1906. Journalist-editor of *Truth*. Political gossip, go-between, and intriguer.

MORLEY, SAMUEL (1809–86): M.P. for Bristol, 1868–85. Proprietor of the *Daily News*, one of the leading Liberal newspapers. A very wealthy mill-owner. A Nonconformist who was opposed to direct action by the Nonconformist section. Gave much money to the Reform League and strongly supported Lib-Labism.

SHAW-LEFEVRE, G. J. (1831–1928): M.P. for Reading, 1863–85, and for Bradford Central 1886–95. Secretary to the Board of Trade, 1868–70; Secretary to the Admiralty, 1871–4; First Commissioner of Works, 1880–3, 1892–4; Postmaster-General, 1883–5; President of the Local Government Board, 1894–5. Associated with Chamberlain and Dilke in the early 1880s. Supported Home Rule.

TREVELYAN, G. O. (1838–1928): M.P. for Tynemouth, 1865–8, for Border Burghs, 1868–86, and for Bridgeton (Glasgow), 1887–97. Civil Lord of the Admiralty, 1868–70; Parliamentary Secretary to the Admiralty, 1881; Chief Secretary for Ireland, 1882–4; Chancellor of the Duchy of Lancaster, 1884–5; Secretary for Scotland, 1886, 1892–5. Prior to 1886 was best known for his long fight for the extension of household suffrage to the counties. In 1886 he followed Chamberlain in opposition to Home Rule but a year later changed his mind and returned to the Liberal party. His career never recovered.

5. 'The Plain'

I take this term from John Vincent (*Formation of the Liberal Party*, p. 25) who uses it to describe the 'centre' of the parliamentary party, the 'ballast' of 'politically nondescript' backbenchers who amounted to about half the party in the 1860s. Their principal characteristics may be defined as follows: (i) they function as the disinterested 'jury' in Liberal politics, judging the schemes and policies that others bring forward; (ii) they are impatient of sectionalism and faddism; (iii) they put their main emphasis on party unity and favour the 'Broad Church' concept; (iv) they also emphasize practical achievement. It will be noted that some of those listed here did in fact hold office. What distinguishes them from category 1 is the way in which they carry over into their governmental activity the attitudes of 'the Plain'. Among the leaders Campbell-Bannerman and Mundella approximate most closely to these attitudes, especially the emphasis on party unity and on gettings things done.

ACLAND, A. H. D. (1847–1926): M.P. for Rotherham, 1885–99. Vice-President of the Council, 1892–5. Was an Oxford don before entering Parliament—strongly affected by the idealistic Liberalism current at the time. Main concern educational reform. Became very impatient with the squabbling leaders of the party and retired from politics a disillusioned man. Strong instinct for practical achievement.

APPENDIX: BIOGRAPHICAL NOTES

BUXTON, S. C. (1853–1934): M.P. for Peterborough, 1883–5, and for Poplar, 1886–1914. Under-Secretary at the Colonial Office, 1892–5; Postmaster-General, 1905–10; President of the Board of Trade, 1910–14.

CHANNING, F. A. (1841–1926): M.P. for East Northants, 1885–1910.

COLMAN, J. J.: M.P. for Norwich, 1871–95.

ELLIS, J. E. (1841–1910): M.P. for Rushcliffe, 1885–1910. A supporter of most Liberal causes (U.K. Alliance, National Education League, opposition to C.D. Acts, Liberation Society).

EMMOTT, A. (1858–1926): M.P. for Oldham, 1899–1911. Joined the Liberal League but became increasingly anxious about its opposition to Home Rule in view of the large number of Irish voters in his constituency.

LOCKWOOD, SIR FRANK (1846–97): M.P. for York, 1885–97. Solicitor-General, 1894–5.

MORTON, A. C.: M.P. for Peterborough, 1889–95, and for Sutherlandshire, 1906–18. Died 1923.

MORTON, E. J. C. (1856–1902): M.P. for Devonport, 1892–1902.

PLAYFAIR, LYON (1819–98): M.P. for the Universities of Edinburgh and St. Andrews, 1868–85, and for South Leeds, 1885–92. Postmaster-General, 1873–4; Vice-President of the Council, 1886. A distinguished scientist.

PRICE, R. J. (1854–1926): M.P. for East Norfolk, 1892–1918.

RATHBONE, WILLIAM (1819–1902): M.P. for Liverpool, 1868–80, for Caernarvonshire, 1880–5, and for North Caernarvonshire, 1885–95. A leading Liverpool Liberal. Member of one of the city's great mercantile families.

REID, R. T. (1846–1923): M.P. for Hereford, 1880–5, and for Dumfries, 1886–1905. Solicitor-General, 1894; Attorney-General, 1894–5. Lord Chancellor, 1905–12 (as Lord Loreburn). One of the leading 'Pro-Boers'.

TREVELYAN, C. P. (1870–1958): M.P. for Elland, 1899–1914. Son of G. O. Trevelyan.

WALLACE, R. (1850–1939): M.P. for Perth, 1895–1907.

YOXALL, J. H. (1857–1925): M.P. for West Nottingham, 1895–1918. General Secretary of the National Union of Teachers, 1892–1924.

APPENDIX: BIOGRAPHICAL NOTES

6. Liberal Imperialists

i.e. those Liberals who became primarily associated with Liberal Imperialism, usually via the Liberal League (founded in 1902).

ASQUITH, H. H. (1852–1928): M.P. for East Fife, 1886–1918. Home Secretary, 1892–5. Was one of the Liberal League's Vice-Presidents but drew back from the brink and was foremost among the leading 'Lib.-Imps.' in re-establishing working relations with the other Liberal leaders. Took a very prominent role in the campaigns against the 1902 Education Act and tariff reform. Very ambitious. A talented lawyer capable of speaking well to any brief. Minimal emotional involvement in politics.

BRASSEY, LORD (1836–1918): President of the Liberal Imperial Council. Had been a Liberal M.P., 1868–86, and was then created a baron. Held office as Civil Lord of the Admiralty, 1880–4. Immensely wealthy (son of the great railway contractor).

CONWAY, MARTIN (1856–1937): a celebrated art critic and explorer. Later became a Unionist M.P. (1918–31). Was created first Baron Conway of Allington in 1931. Strong anti-democratic beliefs.

DOUGLAS, CHARLES (1865–1924): M.P. for North-West Lanark, 1899–1906. Later turned Unionist.

FERGUSON, RONALD CRAUFORD MUNRO (1860–1934): M.P. for Ross and Cromarty, 1884–5, and for Leith Burghs, 1886–1914. Created Viscount Novar, 1920. Governor-General of Australia, 1914–20. A close confidant of Rosebery and a totally committed Liberal Imperialist whose career as a Liberal never re-established itself after the decline of the Liberal League. He later turned Unionist and served in Unionist governments, 1922–4, as Secretary for Scotland. He was Rosebery's private secretary at the Foreign Office, 1892–4. He later took the lead, with Haldane, in trying to organize a separate Roseberyite Liberal organization in Scotland and became one of C-B's principal *bêtes noires*. He was a large landowner in Scotland.

FOWLER, H. H. (1830–1911): M.P. for Wolverhampton, 1880–1908. Son of a Wesleyan minister. Had been Mayor of Wolverhampton in the 1860s. Under-Secretary at the Home Office, 1884–5; Financial Secretary to the Treasury, 1886; President of the Local Government Board, 1892–4; Secretary of State for India, 1894–5; Chancellor of the Duchy of Lancaster, 1905–8; Lord President of the Council, 1908–10. Created Viscount Wolverhampton, 1908. Life-long opponent of programmes and advocate of 'concentration' in Liberal policy. Became strong critic of the Home Rule policy.

FULLER, J. M. F. (1864–1915): M.P. for Westbury, 1900–11. A foundation committee member of the Liberal Imperial Council. Governor of Victoria, 1911–14.

APPENDIX: BIOGRAPHICAL NOTES

GREY, SIR EDWARD (1862–1933): M.P. for Berwick, 1885–1916. Under-Secretary at the Foreign Office, 1894–5; Foreign Secretary from 1905. A Vice-President of the Liberal League.

HALDANE, R. B. (1856–1928): M.P. for East Lothian, 1885–1912. Secretary of State for War, 1905–12. A Vice-President of the Liberal League. Keen interest in philosophy, especially Hegelian.

HART, HEBER L. (died 1948): a lawyer who was Recorder of Ipswich, 1915–36. An unsuccessful Liberal candidate in 1910.

PAULTON, J. M. (1857–1923): M.P. for Bishop Auckland, 1885–1910. A journalist. Hon. Secretary of the Liberal League. Was one of Asquith's private secretaries, 1893–5.

PERKS, R. W. (1849–1934): M.P. for Louth, 1892–1910. A Wesleyan. Treasurer of the Liberal League and one of its principal organizers. Known as 'Imperial Perks'.

ROBSON, W. S. (1852–1918): M.P. for Bow and Bromley, 1885, and for South Shields, 1895–1910. Solicitor-General, 1905–8; Attorney-General, 1908–10. Created Baron Robson of Jesmond, 1910. A member of the Liberal League.

*ROSEBERY, EARL OF (1847–1929): Foreign Secretary, 1886, 1892–4; Prime Minister, 1894–5. First Chairman of the London County Council, 1889. President of the Liberal League. After 1895 he changes completely and refuses to undertake any further responsibilities as a leader of a party which contains adherents to several schools of thought.

SAMUEL, HERBERT (1870–1963): M.P. for Cleveland from 1902. Under-Secretary at the Home Office, 1905–9; Chancellor of the Duchy of Lancaster, 1909–10.

WALTON, SIR JOHN LAWSON (1852–1908): M.P. for South Leeds, 1892–1908. A member of the Liberal League. Attorney General, 1905–8.

7. Liberal Newspapermen

COOK, SIR EDWARD T. (1857–1919): edited the *Pall Mall Gazette*, 1890–2, the *Westminster Gazette*, 1893–6, and the *Daily News*, 1896–1901. Sympathized strongly with the Liberal Imperialists and was ejected from the *Daily News* in the 'Pro-Boer' take-over.

HARMSWORTH, ALFRED (1865–1922): the later Lord Northcliffe. Had founded the *Daily Mail* in 1896 and the *Daily Mirror* in 1903. Took some interest in Liberal Imperialism but only so long as it appeared to be a going concern. He greatly admired Rosebery but eventually despaired of him as a political leader.

HOBHOUSE, L. T. (1864–1929): eminent sociologist and philosopher. Was on the staff of the *Manchester Guardian* at the time of the South African war.

MASSINGHAM, H. W. (1860–1924): editor of the *Daily Chronicle*, 1895–9, and then ejected because of his 'Pro-Boer' tendencies. Later edited *The Nation*. Closely associated with the Fabians in the 1890s.

REID, THOMAS WEMYSS (1842–1905): editor of the *Leeds Mercury*, 1870–87. Founded the *Speaker* in 1890 and edited it until 1897. Managed Cassell's publishing firm, 1887–1905. Great admirer of Forster and Rosebery.

RUSSELL, SIR EDWARD (1834–1920): editor of the *Liverpool Daily Post*. M.P. for Bridgeton (Glasgow), 1885–7.

SCOTT, C. P. (1846–1932): M.P. for Leigh, 1895–1905. Editor of the *Manchester Guardian* from 1872. Took a very strong 'Pro-Boer' line at the time of the South African war.

SPENDER, J. A. (1862–1942): editor of the *Westminster Gazette*, 1896–1922. Emphasized party unity.

8. *Secretaries and Confidants*

ACTON, LORD (1834–1902): the eminent historian. Close friend of Gladstone.

BRETT, REGINALD (1852–1930): M.P. for Penryn and Falmouth, 1880–5. Private Secretary to Lord Hartington, 1878–85. Opposed Home Rule, but withdrew from party politics and became closely connected with the Court. Was secretary for the Office of Works, 1895–1902, and from 1902 on played a major role in the formulation of defence policy. Succeeded father as second Viscount Esher in 1899.

HAMILTON, SIR EDWARD WALTER (1847–1908): Gladstone's private secretary, 1880–5. A Treasury official from 1885 until 1907 but retained close links with Gladstone and other leading Liberals.

WEST, SIR ALGERNON (1832–1921): had been a civil servant since 1852. Was Gladstone's private secretary, 1868–72, and unofficial head of Gladstone's secretariat, 1892–4.

Select Bibliography

In this bibliography are listed only those manuscripts and printed sources which proved to have particular relevance to the themes of this book.

A. *Manuscript Collections*

Earl of Oxford and Asquith Papers, Bodleian Library, Oxford.
Viscount Bryce Papers, Bodleian Library, Oxford.
Sir Henry Campbell-Bannerman Papers, British Museum.
Joseph Chamberlain Papers, University of Birmingham Library, Birmingham.
Sir Charles Dilke Papers, British Museum.
Thomas E. Ellis Papers, National Library of Wales, Aberystwyth.
Thomas Gee Papers, National Library of Wales, Aberystwyth.
Viscount Gladstone Papers, British Museum.
W. E. Gladstone Papers, British Museum.
Glansevern Collection, National Library of Wales, Aberystwyth.
Earl Granville Papers, Public Record Office, London.
Viscount Haldane Papers, National Library of Scotland, Edinburgh.
Sir Edward Hamilton Papers, British Museum.
Sir William Harcourt Papers, Stanton Harcourt, Oxfordshire.
A. J. Mundella Papers, University of Sheffield Library, Sheffield.
Lord Rendel Papers, National Library of Wales, Aberystwyth.
Marquess of Ripon Papers, British Museum.
Earl of Rosebery Papers, National Library of Scotland, Edinburgh.
Earl Spencer Papers, Althorp, Northamptonshire.
J. A. Spender Papers, British Museum.
R. Spence Watson Papers, Hampstead, London.
H. J. Wilson Papers, Central Library, Sheffield.
H. J. Wilson Papers, University of Sheffield Library, Sheffield.

B. *Journals, Pamphlet Collections, etc.*

Hansard's Parliamentary Debates

'Eighty' Club—annual reports of addresses given at meetings.
Liberal Publications Department—pamphlets containing reports of speeches, etc.
National Liberal Federation—reports as follows:
Proceedings Attending the Formation of the National Federation of Liberal Associations; with Report of Conference, held in Birmingham, on Thursday, May 31st, 1877.

Annual Report—the First to the Tenth, Presented at Meetings of the Council from 1879 to 1887.
Proceedings in Connection with the Annual Meeting, 1888 to 1905.
Reports of the Executive Committee of the United Kingdom Alliance.

The Times
The Contemporary Review
The Fortnightly Review
The Liberal Magazine. A Periodical for the Use of Liberal Speakers & Canvassers
The Liberator—A Monthly Journal of the Society for the Liberation of Religion from State-Patronage and Control
The New Liberal Review
The Nineteenth Century
The Progressive Review
The Speaker

C. *Contemporary Commentaries and Collections of Essays and Articles*

ADAMS, F., *History of the Elementary School Contest in England*. 1882.
CLAYDEN, P. W., *England Under the Coalition. The Political History of Great Britain and Ireland from the General Election of 1885 to May 1892*. 1892.
[ESCOTT, T. H. S. and others], *The Radical Programme*. 1885. New edition, Harvester Press, 1971, with introduction and notes by D. A. Hamer.
HOBHOUSE, L. T., *Liberalism*. [1911]
JEPHSON, H., *The Platform. Its Rise and Progress*. 1892.
LUCY, H. W., Diaries of Parliaments in the late nineteenth and early twentieth centuries.
MASTERMAN, C. F. G. (ed.), *The Heart of the Empire*. 1901.
OSTROGORSKI, M., *Democracy and the Organization of Political Parties*. Vol. i. 1902.
PHILLIMORE, J. S., and HIRST F. W. (edd.), *Essays in Liberalism*. 1897.
REID, A. (ed.), *The New Liberal Programme Contributed by Representatives of the Liberal Party*. 1886.
—— *The New Party Described by some of its Members*. 1894.
—— *Why I am a Liberal: Being Definitions and Personal Confessions of Faith by the Best Minds of the Liberal Party*. [1885]
SAMUEL, H., *Liberalism, An Attempt to State the Principles and Proposals of Contemporary Liberalism in England*. 1902.
SAUNDERS, W., *The New Parliament, 1880*. 1880.
WATSON, R. S., *The National Liberal Federation from its Commencement to the General Election of 1906*. 1907.

D. *Biographies, Journals, Diaries, Collections of Letters, etc.*

(Place of publication London unless otherwise indicated)
Aberdare, Lord
    Letters of the Rt. Hon. Henry Austin Bruce, G.C.B., Lord Aberdare of Duffryn. Printed for private circulation, Oxford, 1902.

SELECT BIBLIOGRAPHY

Acton, Lord
>FIGGIS, J. N., and LAURENCE, R. V. (edd.), *Selections from the Correspondence of the First Lord Acton*. Vol. i. 1917.
>PAUL, H. (ed.), *Letters of Lord Acton to Mary, Daughter of the Right Hon. W. E. Gladstone*. 1904.

Arch, Joseph
>*Story of his Life, told by himself.* 1898.

Argyll, Eighth Duke of
>*Autobiography and Memoirs.* 1906.

Asquith, H. H.
>*Memories and Reflections 1852–1927.* 1928.
>JENKINS, R., *Asquith*. 1964.
>SPENDER, J. A., and ASQUITH, C., *Life of Herbert Henry Asquith, Lord Oxford and Asquith*. 1932.

Atherley-Jones, L. A.
>*Looking Back, Reminiscences of a Political Career.* 1925.

Birrell, A.
>*Things Past Redress.* 1937.

Bright, John
>AUSUBEL, H., *John Bright, Victorian Reformer*. New York, 1966.
>READ, D., *Cobden and Bright, A Victorian Political Partnership*. 1967.
>STURGIS, J. L., *John Bright and the Empire*. 1969.
>TREVELYAN, G. M., *The Life of John Bright*. 1913.
>WALLING, R. A. J. (ed.), *The Diaries of John Bright*. 1930.

Broadhurst, H.
>*Henry Broadhurst, M.P. The Story of his Life.* 1901.

Bryce, James
>FISHER, H. A. L., *James Bryce (Viscount Bryce of Dechmont, O.M.)*. 1927.
>IONS, M., *James Bryce and American Democracy*. 1968.

Buxton, C. R.
>DE BUNSEN, V., *Charles Roden Buxton, A Memoir*. 1948.

Caine, W. S.
>NEWTON, J., *W. S. Caine, M.P. A Biography*. 1907.

Campbell-Bannerman, Sir H.
>SPENDER, J. A., *The Life of the Right Hon. Sir Henry Campbell-Bannerman, G.C.B.* [1923].

Cavendish, Lady F.
>BAILEY, J. (ed.), *The Diary of Lady Frederick Cavendish*. 1927.

Chamberlain, J.
>FRASER, P., *Joseph Chamberlain, Radicalism and Empire, 1868–1914*. 1966.

GARVIN, J. L., and AMERY, J., *The Life of Joseph Chamberlain*. 1932–68.
HOWARD, C. H. D. (ed.), *A Political Memoir 1880–92 by Joseph Chamberlain.* 1953.
LUCY, H. W. (ed.), *Speeches of the Right Hon. Joseph Chamberlain, M.P. With a sketch of his Life.* 1885.

Channing, F. A.
Memories of Midland Politics 1885–1910. 1918.

Childers, H. C. E.
CHILDERS, S., *The Life and Correspondence of the Right Hon. Hugh C. E. Childers 1827–1896.* 1901.

Churchill, W. S.
BONHAM CARTER, LADY V., *Winston Churchill As I Knew Him.* 1965.
CHURCHILL, R. S., *Winston S. Churchill.* Vols. i and ii. 1966–7.
JAMES, R. R., *Churchill: A Study in Failure 1900–1939.* 1970.

Clarendon, Lord
MAXWELL, SIR H., *The Life and Letters of George William Frederick, Fourth Earl of Clarendon, K.G., G.C.B.* 1913.

Clifford, Dr. J.
MARCHANT, SIR J., *Dr John Clifford, C.H. Life, Letters and Reminiscences.* 1924.

Collings, J.
COLLINGS, J., and GREEN, J. L., *Life of the Right Hon. Jesse Collings.* 1920.

Colman, J. J.
COLMAN, H. C., *Jeremiah James Colman. A Memoir.* 1905.

Cook, Sir E. T.
MILLS, J. SAXON, *Sir Edward Cook, K.B.E. A Biography.* 1921.

Courtney, Leonard
GOOCH, G. P., *Life of Lord Courtney.* 1920.

Crewe, Lord
POPE-HENNESSY, J., *Lord Crewe, 1858–1945, The Likeness of a Liberal.* 1955.

Dale, R. W.
DALE, A. W. W., *The Life of R. W. Dale of Birmingham.* 1898.

Dilke, Sir C. W.
GWYNN, S., and TUCKWELL, G. M., *The Life of the Rt. Hon. Sir Charles W. Dilke, Bart., M.P.* 1917.
JENKINS, R., *Sir Charles Dilke. A Victorian Tragedy.* 1958.

Ellis, J. E.
BASSETT, A. T., *The Life of the Rt. Hon. John Edward Ellis, M.P.* 1914.

Esher, Lord
>   Brett, M. V. (ed.), *Journals and Letters of Reginald Viscount Esher*. Vol. i. 1934.

Farquharson, R.
>   *In and Out of Parliament, Reminiscences of a Varied Life*. 1911.

Fawcett, H.
>   Stephen, L., *Life of Henry Fawcett*. 1885.

Fitzroy, Sir Almeric
>   *Memoirs*. [1925].

Forster, W. E.
>   Reid, T. Wemyss, *Life of the Right Honourable William Edward Forster*. 1888.

Fowler, H. H.
>   Fowler, E. H., *The Life of Henry Hartley Fowler, First Viscount Wolverhampton, G.C.S.I.* 1912.

Gladstone, Herbert
>   *After Thirty Years*. 1929.
>   Mallet, Sir C., *Herbert Gladstone, A Memoir*. 1932.

Gladstone, W. E.
>   *A Chapter of Autobiography*. 1868.
>   *The Irish Question. I.—History of an Idea. II.—Lessons of the Election*. 1886.
>   Hamilton, Sir E. W., *Mr Gladstone*. 1898.
>   Magnus, P., *Gladstone, A Biography*. 1954.
>   Morley, J., *The Life of William Ewart Gladstone*. 1903. The edition quoted in this book is the two-volume edition of 1905.
>   Ramm, A. (ed.), *The Political Correspondence of Mr. Gladstone and Lord Granville 1868–1876*. 1952. Camden Third Series vols. lxxxi–lxxxii.
>   Ramm, A. (ed.), *The Political Correspondence of Mr. Gladstone and Lord Granville 1876–1886*. Oxford, 1962.
>   Tollemache, L. A., *Talks with Mr. Gladstone*. 1898.

Goschen, G. J.
>   Elliot, A. D., *The Life of George Joachim Goschen, First Viscount Goschen 1831–1907*. 1911.

Granville, Earl
>   Fitzmaurice, Lord E., *The Life of Granville George Leveson Gower, Second Earl Granville, K.G. 1815–1891*. 2nd edition, 1905.
>   See also Gladstone, W. E.—Ramm, A.

Grey, Sir Edward
>   *Twenty-Five Years 1892–1916*. 1925.
>   Trevelyan, G. M., *Grey of Fallodon. Being the Life of Sir Edward Grey, Afterwards Viscount Grey of Fallodon*. 1937.

SELECT BIBLIOGRAPHY

Haldane, R. B.
    Richard Burdon Haldane. An Autobiography. 1929.
    Koss, S. E., *Lord Haldane: Scapegoat for Liberalism.* New York, 1969.
    MAURICE, SIR F., *Haldane 1856–1915. The Life of Viscount Haldane of Cloan, K.T., O.M.* 1937.
    SOMMER, D., *Haldane of Cloan. His Life and Times 1856–1928.* 1960.

Harcourt, Sir William
    GARDINER, A. G., *The Life of Sir William Harcourt.* 1923.

Hartington, Lord
    HOLLAND, B., *The Life of Spencer Compton, Eighth Duke of Devonshire.* 1911.

Hirst, F. W.
    In the Golden Days. 1947.

Hudson, Sir Robert
    SPENDER, J. A., *Sir Robert Hudson, A Memoir.* 1930.

Innes, A. Taylor
    Chapters of Reminiscence. 1913.

James, Sir Henry
    ASKWITH, LORD, *Lord James of Hereford.* 1930.

Kilbracken, Lord
    Reminiscences of Lord Kilbracken G.C.B. 1931.

Kimberley, Lord
    DRUS, E. (ed.), *A Journal of Events During the Gladstone Ministry 1868–1874, By John, First Earl of Kimberley.* 1958. Camden Miscellany vol. xxi.

Labouchere, H.
    THOROLD, A. L., *The Life of Henry Labouchere.* 1913.

Lawson, Sir W.
    RUSSELL, G. W. E. (ed.), *Sir Wilfrid Lawson: A Memoir.* 1909.

Lloyd George, D.
    DU PARCQ, H., *The Life of David Lloyd George.* 1912–13.
    EDWARDS, J. H., *David Lloyd George, the Man and the Statesman.* 1930.
    GEORGE, W., *My Brother and I.* 1958.
    GILBERT, M. (ed.), *Lloyd George.* New Jersey, 1968.
    JONES, T., *Lloyd George.* 1951.
    MORGAN, K. O., *David Lloyd George. Welsh Radical as World Statesman.* Cardiff, 1963.
    TAYLOR, A. J. P., *Lloyd George Rise and Fall.* Cambridge, 1961.
    THOMSON, M., *David Lloyd George.* 1948.

MacColl, Canon M.
    RUSSELL, G. W. E. (ed.), *Malcolm MacColl Memoirs and Correspondence.* 1914.

Masterman, C. F. G.
    MASTERMAN, L., *C. F. G. Masterman. A Biography.* 1939.

SELECT BIBLIOGRAPHY

Mather, Sir W.
    MATHER, L. E. (ed.), *The Right Honourable Sir William Mather, P.C., L.L.D., M.Inst.C.E., 1838–1920.* [1925].

Morley, John
    Recollections. 1917.
    HAMER, D. A., *John Morley Liberal Intellectual in Politics.* Oxford, 1968.
    HIRST, F. W., *Early Life & Letters of John Morley.* 1927.
    KOSS, S. E., *John Morley at the India Office, 1905–1910.* New Haven, 1969.
    WOLPERT, S. A., *Morley and India, 1906–1910.* California, 1967.

Morley, S.
    HODDER, E., *The Life of Samuel Morley.* 3rd edition, 1887.

Moulton, Lord
    MOULTON, H. F., *The Life of Lord Moulton.* 1922.

Mundella, A. J.
    ARMYTAGE, W. H. G., *A. J. Mundella 1825–1897. The Liberal Background to the Labour Movement.* 1951.

Pease, A. E.
    Elections and Recollections. 1932.

Perks, R. W.
    CRANE, D., *The Life-Story of Sir Robert W. Perks Baronet, M.P.* [1909].

Playfair, Lyon
    REID, T. WEMYSS, *Memoirs and Correspondence of Lyon Playfair, First Lord Playfair of St. Andrews, P.C., G.C.B., L.L.D., F.R.S., &c.* 1899.

Rainy, Dr.
    SIMPSON, P. C., *The Life of Principal Rainy.* 1909.

Rathbone, W.
    RATHBONE, E. F., *William Rathbone, A Memoir.* 1905.

Reid, T. Wemyss
    REID, S. J. (ed.), *Memoirs of Sir Wemyss Reid, 1842–1885.* 1905.

Rendel, Stuart
    HAMER, F. E. (ed.), *The Personal Papers of Lord Rendel.* 1931.

Richard, H.
    MIALL, C. S., *Henry Richard, M.P. A Biography.* 1889.

Ripon, Lord
    WOLF, L., *Life of the First Marquess of Ripon, K.G., P.C., G.C.S.I., D.C.L., Etc.* 1921.

Robson, W. S.
    KEETON, G. W., *A Liberal Attorney-General. Being the Life of Lord Robson of Jesmond (1852–1918) with an Account of the Office of Attorney-General.* 1949.

Rogers, J. Guinness
    An Autobiography. 1903.

Rosebery, Lord
>CREWE, MARQUESS OF, *Lord Rosebery*. 1931.
>JAMES, R. RHODES, *Rosebery. A Biography of Archibald Philip, Fifth Earl of Rosebery*. 1963.

Russell, Lord John
>GOOCH, G. P. (ed.), *The Later Correspondence of Lord John Russell 1840–1878*. 1925.

Rylands, P.
>RYLANDS, L. G., *Correspondence and Speeches of Mr. Peter Rylands, M.P. With a Sketch of his Career*. 1890.

Samuel, Herbert
>*Memoirs*. 1945.

Scott, C. P.
>HAMMOND, J. L., *C. P. Scott of the Manchester Guardian*. 1934.
>WILSON, T. G. (ed.), *The Political Diaries of C. P. Scott 1911–1928*. 1970.

Selborne, Earl of
>*Memorials*. Part II. *Personal and Political 1865–1895*. 1898.

Smith, Goldwin
>HAULTAIN, A. (ed.), *A Selection From Goldwin Smith's Correspondence Comprising Letters Chiefly To and From His English Friends, Written Between the Years 1846 and 1910*. [1913].
>WALLACE, E., *Goldwin Smith. Victorian Liberal*. Toronto, 1957.

Smith, Samuel
>*My Life-Work*. 1902.

Spender, J. A.
>*Life, Journalism and Politics*. 1927.
>*The Public Life*. 1925.
>HARRIS, WILSON, *J. A. Spender*. 1946.

Stansfeld, J.
>HAMMOND, J. L., and B., *James Stansfeld, A Victorian Champion of Sex Equality*. 1932.

Trevelyan, G. O.
>TREVELYAN, G. M., *Sir George Otto Trevelyan. A Memoir*. 1932.

Watson, R. Spence
>CORDER, P., *The Life of Robert Spence Watson*. 1914.

Webb, Beatrice
>*My Apprenticeship*. 1929.
>*Our Partnership*. 1948.

West, Sir Algernon
>*Recollections 1832 to 1886*. 1899.
>HUTCHINSON, H. G. (ed.), *Private Diaries of the Rt. Hon. Sir Algernon West, G.C.B.* 1922.

Wilson, H. J.
  ANDERSON, M., *Henry Joseph Wilson: Fighter for Freedom 1833–1914*. 1953.

E. *General Works*

(Place of publication London unless otherwise indicated)

ARNSTEIN, W. L., *The Bradlaugh Case, A Study in Late Victorian Opinion and Politics*. Oxford, 1965.
BEALES, D., *From Castlereagh to Gladstone 1815–1885*. 1969. One of the very few textbooks since Ensor to survey the 1867–85 period.
BEALEY, F., and PELLING, H., *Labour and Politics 1900–1906. A History of the Labour Representation Committee*. 1958. Very useful on the relations between Liberals and Labour and H. Gladstone's efforts to reach an understanding.
BEATTIE, A. (ed.), *English Party Politics*. 1970. Documents.
BEER, S. H., *Modern British Politics, A Study of Parties and Pressure Groups*. 1965. Brief but interesting comments on pre-1914 Liberalism—including a discussion of the N.L.F., its programmes, and their influence.
BELL, P. M. H., *Disestablishment in Ireland and Wales*. 1969. Disappointingly little on the place of the disestablishment movement(s) in general Liberal politics.
BRIGGS, A., *History of Birmingham*. Vol. ii. 1952.
—— *Victorian Cities*. 1963. New ed., 1968. Especially valuable on Birmingham Liberalism.
BULLOCK, A., and SHOCK, M. (edd.), *The Liberal Tradition from Fox to Keynes*. 1956. Documents with a useful introduction.
BUTLER, J., *The Liberal Party and the Jameson Raid*. Oxford, 1968. Very detailed analysis of how the Liberal leaders mishandled the Jameson Raid controversy of 1896–9.
CARTER, H., *The English Temperance Movement: A Study in Objectives*. 1933. A new study is very much needed.
CLARK, G. KITSON, *The Making of Victorian England*. 1962. A few remarks on the development of Liberalism, 1867–85 (see also his introduction to Shannon).
COWLING, M., *1867 Disraeli, Gladstone and Revolution. The Passing of the second Reform Bill*, Cambridge, 1967. A mass of information about, and interpretation of, the state of the party and the leadership in 1867.
CROSS, C., *The Liberals in Power*. 1963. A brief journalistic account of 1905–14.
CURTIS, L. P., Jr., *Coercion and Conciliation in Ireland 1880–1892. A study in Conservative Unionism*. Princeton, 1963. Some material on the Liberals—an essential supplement to Hammond.
DANGERFIELD, G., *The Strange Death of Liberal England*. 1936. Very highly coloured and over-dramatized account of the years 1910–14.
DERRY, J. W., *The Radical Tradition, Tom Paine to Lloyd George*. 1967. Essays on Chamberlain and Lloyd George.
ENSOR, R. C. K., *England 1870–1914*. Oxford, 1936. Still indispensable as the only textbook covering this period.

GILBERT, B. B., *The Evolution of National Insurance in Great Britain. The Origins of the Welfare State.* 1966. By far the best source on Liberals and social policy in the late nineteenth century as well as after 1905.

GWYN, W. B., *Democracy and the Cost of Politics in Britain.* 1962. Useful material on the Liberal party's finances.

HALÉVY, E., *A History of the English People in the Nineteenth Century.* Vol. v. *Imperialism and the Rise of Labour.* 1961 edition. Vol. vi. *The Rule of Democracy 1905–1914.* 1961 edition. He used no manuscript sources and few memoirs and so the account is mainly from the outside; but it remains essential reading, especially for 1905–14.

HAMMOND, J. L., *Gladstone and the Irish Nation.* New impression (with introduction by M. R. D. Foot), 1964, of the 1938 edition. A classic.

—— FOOT, M. R. D., *Gladstone and Liberalism.* 1952. A brief introduction.

HANHAM, H. J., *Elections and Party Management. Politics in the Time of Disraeli and Gladstone.* 1959. Deals with period 1868–80. Outstandingly useful on, *inter alia*, Liberalism in the constituencies, party organization, sectionalism, and Lib-Labism.

—— *Scottish Nationalism.* 1969. Some useful points on the Liberals and Scotland.

HARRISON, R., *Before the Socialists. Studies in Labour and Politics 1861–1881.* 1965. Excellent studies of Lib-Labism.

HURST, M., *Joseph Chamberlain and Liberal Reunion. The Round Table Conference of 1887.* 1967. Exhaustive examination of a few months. Abundant quotation from letters of Liberal leaders.

HYNES, S., *The Edwardian Turn of Mind.* Princeton, 1968. Some analysis of Liberalism under strain. Interesting section on C. F. G. Masterman.

JENKINS, R., *Mr. Balfour's Poodle. An Account of the Struggle between the House of Lords and the Government of Mr. Asquith.* 1954.

KELLEY, R., *The Transatlantic Persuasion, The Liberal-Democratic Mind in the Age of Gladstone.* New York, 1969. Interpretation of Gladstone based on secondary sources—attempts a psycho-analysis of Gladstone.

KINNEAR, M., *The British Voter, An Atlas and Survey since 1885.* 1968. Maps and commentary on general elections.

LLOYD, T., *The General Election of 1880.* 1968.

LYND, H. M., *England in the Eighteen-Eighties. Toward a Social Basis for Freedom.* 1945. Very useful on policies and political ideas.

LYONS, F. S. L., *The Fall of Parnell 1890–91.* 1960. Includes a thorough analysis of the reactions of the Liberal leaders.

McBRIAR, A. M., *Fabian Socialism and English Politics 1884–1918.* Cambridge, 1962. Material on the interaction of the Fabians with Liberalism.

McCALLUM, R. B., *The Liberal Party from Earl Grey to Asquith.* 1963. Brief survey.

MACCOBY, S., *English Radicalism 1853–1886.* 1938.

—— *English Radicalism 1886–1914.* 1953. Industrious compilations of material from pamphlets and newspapers. Interpretation of little value.

—— (ed.), *The English Radical Tradition 1763–1914.* 1952. Documents.

MACKINTOSH, J. P., *The British Cabinet.* 1962. A fair amount of useful information on Liberal governments and party politics.

MANSERGH, N., *The Irish Question 1840–1921*. 1965. Essays on the Irish policies of the Liberal leaders.

MORGAN, K. O., *Wales in British Politics 1868–1922*. Cardiff, 1963. The most thorough study yet attempted of one of the sectional interests in Liberal politics.

PELLING, H., *America and the British Left from Bright to Bevan*. 1956. Discusses the controversy surrounding the development of the Liberal 'caucuses' and the N.L.F.

—— *Modern Britain 1885–1955*. 1960. Very slight.

—— *The Origins of the Labour Party 1880–1900*. Oxford, 2nd edition, 1965. Of considerable value for Liberal politics as well.

—— *Popular Politics and Society in Late Victorian Britain*. 1968. Very stimulating essays on the working class and social reform, Labour and imperialism, and relations between Labour and the Liberals in the 1905–14 period.

—— *Social Geography of British Elections 1885–1910*. 1967. Perhaps over-ambitious attempt to examine every constituency. A large amount of rather miscellaneous information on Liberal politics.

PERKIN, H., *The Origins of Modern English Society 1780–1880*. 1969. Some useful insights into the class relations and attitudes underlying Liberalism.

POIRIER, P. P., *The Advent of the Labour Party*. 1958. Covers much the same ground as Bealey and Pelling.

PORTER, B., *Critics of Empire, British Radical Attitudes to Colonialism in Africa, 1895–1914*. 1968. Analyses Liberal views on imperialism at the turn of the century.

READ, D., *The English Provinces c. 1760–1960, A Study in Influence*. 1964. Sections on Birmingham Radicalism, the N.L.F., and the Liberation Society.

RICHTER, M., *The Politics of Conscience. T. H. Green and his Age*. 1964. One of the best studies of Liberal thought in the late nineteenth century.

ROBINSON, R., GALLAGHER, J., and DENNY, A., *Africa and the Victorians. The Official Mind of Imperialism*. 1963. Detailed examination of Liberal imperial policy after 1880.

ROVER, C., *Women's Suffrage and Party Politics in Britain, 1866–1914*. 1967. One of the causes that many Liberals supported.

ROWLAND, P., *The Last Liberal Governments: The Promised Land, 1905–1910*. 1968. Narrative account with little new to say—Halévy and Ensor remain supreme.

SCHREUDER, D. M., *Gladstone and Kruger. Liberal Government and Colonial 'Home Rule' 1880–85*. 1969. One of the few thorough studies of the 1880–5 government.

SEMMEL, B., *Imperialism and Social Reform, English Social-Imperial Thought 1895–1914*. 1960. A brief discussion of Liberal Imperialism.

SHANNON, R. T., *Gladstone and the Bulgarian Agitation 1876*. 1963. Unmatched as an anatomy of Liberalism in all its manifestations. Essential also on Gladstone and the development of Radicalism.

SOUTHGATE, D., *The Passing of the Whigs 1832–1886*. 1965. Mainly narrative—lacking in analysis (cf. Vincent or Norman Gash on the Whigs).

STANSKY, P., *Ambitions and Strategies. The Struggle for the Leadership of the*

Liberal Party in the 1890s. Oxford, 1964. Clear analysis of the post-Gladstonian chaos.

STEVEN, R., *The National Liberal Club, Politics and Persons.* [1925].

TAYLOR, A. J. P., *The Trouble Makers, Dissent over Foreign Policy 1792–1939.* 1957. Studies of the anti-imperialist Radicals.

THOMPSON, P., *Socialists, Liberals and Labour. The Struggle for London 1885–1914.* 1967. Meticulous and very valuable.

THORNTON, A. P., *The Imperial Idea and its Enemies.* 1959. Some discussion of Liberal attitudes to the Empire.

VINCENT, J., *The Formation of the Liberal Party 1857–1868.* 1966. See Preface to this book.

—— *Pollbooks. How Victorians Voted.* Cambridge, 1967. Some exciting ideas as to the nature of nineteenth-century Radicalism.

WEBB, R. K., *Modern England from the Eighteenth Century to the Present.* 1969. A good recent textbook.

WILSON, T., *The Downfall of the Liberal Party 1914–1935.* 1966. A few remarks on pre-1914 Liberal politics (cf. H. Pelling's criticisms of these in *Popular Politics and Society*).

F. *Articles in Learned Journals*

ADAMS, W. S., 'Lloyd George and the Labour Movement', *Past and Present*, no. 3.

CROWLEY, D. W., 'The "Crofters" Party, 1885–1892', *Scottish Historical Review*, vol. 35 (1956).

DUNBABIN, J. P. D., 'Parliamentary Elections in Great Britain, 1868–1900: a Psephological Note', *English Historical Review*, vol. 81 (1966).

GLASER, J. F., 'English Nonconformity and the Decline of Liberalism', *American Historical Review*, vol. 63 (1958).

—— 'Parnell's Fall and the Nonconformist Conscience', *Irish Historical Studies*, vol. 12 (1960).

GOODMAN, G., 'Liberal Unionism: the Revolt of the Whigs', *Victorian Studies*, vol. 3 (1959).

HAMER, D. A., 'The Irish Question and Liberal Politics, 1886–1894', *Historical Journal*, vol. 12 (1969).

HERRICK, F. H., 'The Origins of the National Liberal Federation', *Journal of Modern History*, vol. 17 (1945).

HOWARD, C. H. D., 'Joseph Chamberlain and the Unauthorised Programme', *English Historical Review*, vol. 65 (1950).

HOWARTH, J., 'The Liberal Revival in Northamptonshire, 1880–1895: a Case Study in Late Nineteenth Century Elections', *Historical Journal*, vol. 12 (1969).

INGHAM, S. M., 'The Disestablishment Movement in England, 1868–74', *Journal of Religious History*, vol. 3 (1964).

KELLAS, J. G., 'The Liberal Party and the Scottish Church Disestablishment Crisis', *English Historical Review*, vol. 79 (1964).

—— 'The Liberal Party in Scotland 1876–1895', *Scottish Historical Review*, vol. 44 (1965).

KELLEY, R., 'Midlothian: a Study in Politics and Ideas', *Victorian Studies*, vol. 4 (1960).

McCREADY, H. W., 'The British Election of 1874: Frederic Harrison and the Liberal Labour Dilemma', *The Canadian Journal of Economics and Political Science*, vol. 20 (1954).

—— 'British Labour's Lobby, 1867–75', *The Canadian Journal of Economics and Political Science*, vol. 22 (1956).

—— 'Home Rule and the Liberal Party, 1899–1906', *Irish Historical Studies*, vol. 13 (1963).

McGILL, B., 'Francis Schnadhorst and Liberal Party Organization', *Journal of Modern History*, vol. 34 (1962).

MAEHL, W. H., 'Gladstone, the Liberals and the Election of 1874', *Bulletin of the Institute of Historical Research*, vol. 36 (1963).

MORGAN, K. O., 'Gladstone and Wales', *The Welsh History Review*, vol. 1 (1961).

ROACH, J., 'Liberalism and the Victorian Intelligentsia', *Cambridge Historical Journal*, vol. 8 (1957).

SAVAGE, D. C., 'Scottish Politics, 1885–6', *Scottish Historical Review*, vol. 40 (1961).

SPINNER, T. J., 'George Joachim Goschen: the Man Lord Randolph Churchill "Forgot" ', *Journal of Modern History*, vol. 39 (1967).

THOLFSEN, T. R., 'The Origins of the Birmingham Caucus', *Historical Journal*, vol. 2 (1959).

THOMPSON, A. F., 'Gladstone's Whips and the General Election of 1868', *English Historical Review*, vol. 63 (1948).

THOMPSON, F. M. L., 'Land and Politics in England in the Nineteenth Century', *Transactions of the Royal Historical Society*, 5th Series, vol. 15 (1965).

WESTON, C. C., 'The Liberal Leadership and the Lords' Veto 1907–10', *Historical Journal*, vol. 10 (1967).

Index

The location of biographical notes is indicated in square brackets

Aberdeen, Lord, 145
Acland, A. H. D. [338], 15, 168, 171, 182, 215, 238–9, 243, 245, 283
Acton, Lord [342], on Gladstone, 65, 78, 140, 143 n.; on future of Liberal party, 153
Allotments and Small Holdings Association, 132
Anti-Corn Law League, xii, 14, 43, 45, 164, 294–5
Arbitration, 15, 15 n.
Arch, Joseph [335], 12
Argyll, Duke of, 34, 75–6, 78
Arran, Lord, 305
Asquith, H. H. [340], on the state of the party, 144, 187; and Home Rule, 157, 160–1, 161 n., 304; and the House of Lords, 195 n., 200, 325; on nature of Liberal party, 224; on need for leadership, 234; on preparation of policy, 243; and Liberal Imperialism, 261, 265, 276, 281–3, 313; opposes dependence on Irish, 300, 301 n.; and 1902 Education Bill, 311; also referred to, 180, 243, 254 n.
Atherley-Jones, L. A. [337], on Radicalism in the 1880s, 150–1; on indifference of the masses to Ireland, 227

Bagehot, Walter, 11, 51, 226
Balfour, A. J., 158, 286
Baptist, The, Chamberlain's letter to, 163
Bath, 1872 by-election at, 6, 69 n.
Belgium, the fate of Liberalism in, 222–3
Benthamites, 41
Birmingham, the 'caucus' in, 10, 50, 113; Liberalism and Radicalism in, 10, 11, 45, 47, 101, 104, 212; the N.L.F. and, 137
Birrell, Augustine [333], 293, 303
Bismarck, 96 n.
Bradlaugh, Charles [337], 235
Brassey, Lord [340], 275
Brett, Reginald [342], on Harcourt, 150 n.; and Rosebery, 202–3, 251; on Gladstone and programmes, 257
Briggs, Asa, 10
Bright, John [330], and the 1870 Education Bill, 35; on Chamberlain's 1885 campaign, 105; and Irish Home Rule, 116–17; argues that Gladstone 'stops the way', 162; on the Conservative party in 1885, 219 n.; also referred to, 40 n., 63, 65, 89, 95, 211, 293
Broadhurst, H. [335], 12, 82, 307
Bruce, H. A. [330], 37, 60 n.
Bryce, James [330], and Radicalism in late 1870s, 81–2; on organization of legislative programmes, 85, 87; on the party in the Commons in 1890, 144; on the House of Lords issue, 204; on nature of Liberal party, 223; and Liberal Imperialists, 278; also referred to, 182
Budgets, of 1894, 205, 231, 260, 316; of 1909, 324–5
Bulgarian agitation of 1876, 66–7, 80
Burt, Thomas [335], 12, 307
Butler, Mrs. Josephine, 69 n.
Buxton, C. R., 287, 291
— Edward, 21 n.
— Sidney [339], 15

Caine, W. S. [335], 24, 92, 131–2, 170, 179, 188

Campbell-Bannerman, Sir Henry [330], and temperance reform, 21 n., 298; and the Irish preoccupation, 125, 128; and the House of Lords question, 199; on sectionalism, 208; on Liberal Imperialism, 270, 287–90, 294–5; and imperialism, 270, 324; as leader of the party, 273, 287–9, 292, 296, 321; efforts of to preserve party unity, 274, 278; the Liberal Imperialists and, 281–2, 286; and the 'Broad Church' idea, 292–4; and dependence on the Irish, 301; and Home Rule, 1900–6, 302–3, 306; and Liberal policy, 1900–6, 309, 312, 314; also referred to, 145, 299, 323

Candahar, 86

Carmichael, T. Gibson, 277

Cavendish, Lady Frederick, 82

Chamberlain, Joseph [337], on the Whigs, xiv; and Labour, 12, 44–5, 44 n.; and the reform of party organization, 29, 47–8, 164–5, 252; and Radicalism in the 1870s, 41, 43–7, 51–6, 59; and programmes, 45–6, 99, 99 n., 103–4; Birmingham experience of, 45, 47, 101–2; and the N.L.F., 46–7, 50–2, 51 n., 54–6, 135, 137; and the Liberal party in the 1870s, 54–5; and Gladstone, 55–6, 76, 106–8; and attack on Beaconsfieldism, 81; rift between John Morley and, 81–2, 96, 96 n.; and legislative work of 1880–5 government, 86; and parliamentary reform, 94; Radicalism of, 95–7, 96 n., 101; and the Radicals, 1880–5, 95–6, 96 n.; Irish policy of, 96, 118; and local government reform, 98, 102; 1885 Radical campaign of, 99–118, 99 n., 104 n., 168, 226, 231; and land reform, 103; rift between Gladstone and, 108, 118–21, 162, 255; strategy of in late 1885, 112–16, 113 n., 220–1; the Hawarden Kite aimed against, 113–16; reasons of for opposing Home Rule, 118–21; and the Irish preoccupation and 'obstruction', 121, 133, 162–3; Nonconformists and in 1886, 131; significance of secession of, 146–7; and Radicalism after 1886, 151–2; Acland looks back to, 168, 171, 243; Harcourt wants to out-bid, 178; Rosebery and, 261, 261 n.; imperialism of, 271, 282, 289, 289 n., 312; tariff reform campaign of, 311–13; also referred to, x–xi, 89, 261, 298, 317

Channing, F. A. [339], 174, 191, 229 n., 292

Chartism, 12, 150

Childers, H. C. E. [331], 159–60

'Chinese labour', 307–8

Churchill, Lord Randolph, 78, 113, 219

— Winston, 324, 327–8

Clifford, Dr. J. [335], 273

Cobden, Richard, xii, 43, 186, 293

Coercion in Ireland, significance of Liberal campaign against, 158, 169, 220, 306–7, 317; also referred to, 177, 181 n., 304

Collings, Jesse [337], 55, 107, 121, 132, 162, 162 n.

Colman, J. J. [339], 7, 9

Conservative party, in 1885, 109, 111–12; Chamberlain advocates leaving in office, 112–13, 113 n., 219–20; and Home Rule, 115–16, 119, 160, 164, 220, 315, 317; Irish policy of after 1886, 154–5; the distinction between the Liberal party and, 155, 219–21, 223, 240–3, 316–17, 327; Liberal concern about trends in, 219–21, 219 n., 220 n., 317; the concentration on opposing after 1895, 237–43, 316; becomes the governing party, 315; disorganization of after 1901, 321; Lloyd George's proposal for coalition with, 328; also referred to, 148, 187

Conservatism, Gladstone on, 57, 219; relationship between Liberalism and, 219, 223, 239, 282, 329; also referred to, 108, 219

Contagious Diseases Acts, movement for repeal of, 2, 3, 20 n., 25, 37, 42 n., 69 n., 89, 94

Conway, Martin [340], 264

Conybeare, C. A. V. [337], 151

Cook, Sir Edward [341], 266–7

Cowper, H. F., 73

Crewe, Marquess of [331], 294, 312

Crimean War, 38

Crofters' party, 132

Dale, R. W. [335], 6, 49, 53

INDEX

Dalhousie, Lord, 105
Death duties, 176, 205, 224
Democracy, and Birmingham Radicalism, 45–7, 101, 104; as ideal on which reform of party organization was based, 46–7, 52; Haldane on, 223
Devolution, the Liberal Imperialists and, 263–5, 268; Churchill's proposal for, 324
Devonshire, Duke of, *see* Hartington, Lord
Dilke, Sir Charles [337], on priority for parliamentary reform, 42; Radicalism of, 95–6; on Radicals in the early 1880s, 95–6; and local government reform, 98–102; and Radical strategy, 1885–6, 106, 112, 115, 118–20; on danger of extinction of Liberal party, 223; and Radicalism in the 1890s, 236; also referred to, 80, 87, 121
Disestablishment (*see also* Irish Church, Scottish disestablishment, and Welsh disestablishment), 3, 7–8, 20–2, 26, 44–5, 75, 82–3, 96, 96 n., 109–10, 131, 151, 169, 174, 197, 253, 264, 299–300, 329
Disraeli, B., 34
Dissenters, *see* Nonconformists
Döllinger, Dr., 109
Douglas, Charles [340], 265, 267–8

Education Act of 1870, 5–6, 35–8
Education Act of 1902, 285, 311–12, 314
Eight hour day, 139, 226, 229–31, 306–7
Eighty Club, 277
Elections, of 1868, 34–5, 247; of 1874, 44, 59–60, 66, 316; of 1880, 79–80, 86–8, 95, 247, 249, 322; of 1885, 100, 112, 139; of 1886, 124; of 1892, 183, 191; of 1895, 207, 211–12, 221, 223, 237, 239–40, 247, 254, 258–9, 265, 270; of 1830, 247; of 1900, 270, 275, 296, 298, 318; of 1906, 321–3; of 1910, 328
Ellis, J. E. [339], 25, 195, 212, 273
— T. [333], becomes Liberal Whip, 23, 186; and Liberal Imperialism and 'federalism', 156 n., 159; also referred to, 245, 281
Emmott, Alfred [339], 304, 321

Essays in Liberalism, 216, 225, 235

Fabians, 209, 234, 234 n., 327
Fawcett, Henry [337], 82, 235
'Federalism', the Home Rule issue and, 156 n., 158–60; Liberal Imperialism and, 264
Fenwick, Charles, 118 n.
Ferguson, R. Munro [340], asks for meeting of ex-Cabinet, 1887, 143; on Home Rule and Imperial Federation, 157; on the Irish preoccupation, 167; on the Local Veto Bill, 1895, 206; on the 1895 election defeat, 211; on labour policy, 228, 234; on Rosebery's leadership, 255 n.; suggests new programme in 1895, 265; and Liberal Imperialism, 280–1, 283, 286, 312
Fitzroy, Sir Almeric, 323
Forster, W. E. [331], 8 n., 35, 114, 284
Fortnightly Review, 81
Foster, Sir Walter, 125, 132
Fowler, H. H. [340], on the House of Lords question, 98, 205; and the Irish preoccupation, 129; and Home Rule, 157, 303; on faddism, 212; on the Newcastle Programme, 215; on the future of the party system, 222; on the emergence of 'great social questions', 232; on Rosebery, 250 n.; and Liberal Imperialism, 276, 284; and the Free Trade issue, 313; on C.-B.'s government, 323
— William, 42 n.
Free trade, 266, 312–14
Free Trade Union, 312
Fuller, J. [340], 277

Gee, Thomas [335], 31
Germany, Liberalism in, 223
Gladstone, Herbert [334], and the Hawarden Kite, 113–16; and the 'Irish obstruction', 133–4; and temperance reform, 206, 297–8; on 1895 elections, 207; on the Newcastle Programme, 214; and the Liberal Imperialists, 278, 290; and the maintenance of party unity, 288, 298; and the 1900 elections, 296, 298; overhauls the Liberal programme, 297–300; on his father's politics, 297; and Irish policy after 1895, 299–301,

Gladstone, Herbert (*cont.*):
303–4; and Labour after 1900, 306, 308; refuses to make policy commitments, 310–11; and Free Trade, 314
— Mrs., 145 n.
— W. E. [331], historians and, ix–x; considers form of policy, xiii, 246; and formation of the Liberal party, 11; and 1868–74 government, 34–5, 52, 60 n., 318; and 1868 elections, 34–5, 64, 247; popular appeal of, 34–5, 75, 233; on the era of 'liberation', 37, 218; retirement of, 1874–5, 39, 60–3, 66, 254 n., 272; on the Birmingham 'caucus', 50; and the Eastern question, 1876–80, 55–6, 64–8, 115 n., 256, 316; hold of over Radical opinion, 56, 75–8, 80, 116–17; Chamberlain and, 55–6, 76, 100, 106–8, 110–11, 114, 120–1, 162–3; Radicalism and, 56, 74–8, 95, 100, 106–8, 114, 116–21, 151; and the N.L.F., 56, 80; reasons for dominance of over Liberal party, 34 n., 70–1, 76–7, 78 n., 246, 249; and the unity of the party, 57–78; on the nature of the Liberal party, 57–9, 115 n., 147, 292; and sectionalism, 57–9, 63–4, 67–9, 69 n., 74, 83 n., 89–90, 130–1, 185, 206–7, 299; and strong parties, 59; and the 1874 election defeat, 59–60, 66; detachment of from party, 60–3, 73–4; tendency of to take initiatives without consulting party or colleagues, 60, 74, 122, 122 n., 144, 197, 250–1; and order in the party, 59–65, 253–4; party leadership of, 57–78; aims of in politics after 1875, 63, 254; seeks wider 'frames of reference' for Liberalism, 63–6; seeks to align Liberalism with national opinion, 63–8; seeks a great cause, 1873–4, 63–6; attitude of to party, 64–5, 122–3; and the split in the Liberal party in 1886, 65, 121–3, 122 n., 146–7; seeks a great cause, 1875–80, 66–8; campaigns of against 'Beaconsfieldism' (including Midlothian), 66–8, 79–83, 86, 88, 108, 224, 249, 256–7, 273, 289, 316–17, 322; aware of proportion and relationship, 68–73, 69 n., 90, 108; strives to systematise, 69–73; and Peel, 69, 122; absorption of in single issues, 69–73, 69 n.; and Rendel, 30, 186; and Welsh disestablishment, 30, 109, 130–1, 142, 185, 246; and the Irish preoccupation, 73, 124–48, 192, 198; and friendships, 73, 73 n.; the Whigs and, 74–8, 106; and disestablishment, 75, 109–10; ambivalent political position of, 74 n., 75, 75 n., 78 n.; Liberal reliance on, 76, 78, 105–6; becomes Prime Minister in 1880, 77; holds party together, 78, 120, 208, 248 n.; 1880–5 government of, 79–98, 120, 318–19; and the 'Irish obstruction', 79, 87, 90–1, 127–31, 133, 135, 161–3, 177, 194, 197, 203; and obstructions, 79, 90–1; and retirement after 1880, 84, 141; and temperance reform, 88–9, 207; and Scottish disestablishment, 90, 109–11, 130–1, 139, 265 n.; and the 1885 elections, 100; and the 1885 political crisis, 105–12, 116–17, 121–3, 219 n.; adoption of Home Rule by, 108, 110–12, 114–23, 122 n., 124, 132–3, 139–40, 142, 162, 203, 252, 255–6, 263, 301; and Liberalism in Scotland, 109–10; seeks a single concentrating issue, 1885–6, 110–12, 121–3; and the House of Lords question in the 1890s, 112, 112 n., 177, 192–4, 202; the Hawarden Kite and, 113–16; on purging the party, 125, 254, 319; Nonconformists and, 131, 284; leadership of after 1885, 140–5, 143 n., 145 n., 168, 210–11; party's dependence on after 1885, 140–2, 168; and Radicalism after 1885, 141–2, 146–8; on the effect on the party of the 1886 schism, 146–8; and Irish policy after 1886, 157–60, 168, 174–83; and Liberal policy, 1891–3, 172, 175–80, 183, 190–1; and the Newcastle Programme, 177, 214–15, 229, 257–8; 1892–4 government of, 182–3; retirement of, 1894, 185, 197, 210, 256, 257 n.; Rosebery and, 218, 246, 248–50, 248 n., 250 n., 253–8; and the state of Conservative politics, 219–20, 219 n., 220 n.; and changes in party politics, 220; on Home Rule as a 'moral' issue, 226–7; and the eight hour day question, 226–7, 229–30, 307; leadership of assessed after

INDEX

1894, 241, 243, 317; preference of for single great questions, 246, 258, 316, 328; and the 'Armenian atrocities', 1896, 256; and Scottish Home Rule, 265 n.; Herbert Gladstone on 'creed' of, 297; and the politics of 'virtuous passion', 324

Goschen, G. J. [331], 8 n., 39

Graham, R. B. Cunninghame, 143

Granville, Lord [331], 40, 57, 62, 67, 76, 78, 97, 116–17, 122 n., 160, 316

Green, T. H., 234, 326

Grey, Sir Edward [341], and Irish policy in the late 1880s, 58, 154; on the Liberal party after 1886, 125; on parties in the 1890s, 221; on difficulties of leadership, 254 n.; criticism of by Liberals after 1895, 282–3, 287–8; and Irish policy after 1895, 301; and the Free Trade issue, 312–13

Haldane, R. B. [341], and Irish policy in the late 1880s, 58, 154; and the Irish preoccupation, 136, 167–8; on Gladstone's leadership, 143; on labour and social policy, 167–8, 233–5; and the 1892–5 government, 180; on the Newcastle Programme, 190, 213; and the House of Lords question, 198, 203, 203 n.; on absence of a Liberal 'Faith', 213; sees Liberals becoming a class party, 223–4; and the Fabians, 234 n.; on policy after 1895, 240–1; and Rosebery, 251; and Liberal Imperialism, 261, 267, 269, 275, 278, 280–1, 323; opposed to programmes, 280–1; and the 1902 Education Act, 285, 311; and Irish policy after 1900, 304; on the Liberal government, 1906–7, 323

Halévy, E., ix, 311

Halifax, 25

Hamilton, Sir Edward [342], on Gladstone, 84, 145, 145 n., 248 n.; on Harcourt, 238; on the break-up of the government in 1885, 106, 318; on Rosebery, 248, 248 n.; also referred to, 99 n., 102, 104 n., 122 n., 125, 126 n., 141, 143, 143 n., 145 n., 148, 150 n., 156, 183, 205, 220

Hammond, J. L., ix

Hanham, H. J., ix, 8, 83 n.

Harcourt, Lewis [332], 177, 200, 204, 277, 313, 319

— Sir William [331], on leadership in 1875, 39, 53; warns Whigs not to leave Gladstone, 77; and the Liberal campaign of 1879–80, 80; and the legislative programme after 1880, 86–7, 87 n., 92–3; and reform of London government, 86, 92, 316; and temperance reform, 89, 94, 97–8, 198, 205–7, 225, 316; wants reforms for 'the party', 97; and Gladstone's leadership, 105–6, 142–3, 145; sees increase in Radicalism after 1885, 148–50; and the Irish preoccupation, 149–50, 163–6, 168, 171–2; and reform in the late 1880s, 149–50; regarded as an opportunist, 150, 150 n., 220, 238 n.; favours retention of Irish M.P.s, 152, 156; and the Radicals after 1886, 149–50, 149 n., 150 n.; and Irish land purchase, 155 n.; and Home Rule after 1886, 160, 183; demands a wider programme, 163–6, 169, 220; tendency of to lapse into negativeness, 169, 172, 237–8, 316; and policy, 1891–2, 171–2, 176–80; and the Irish obstruction, 175, 195; and Irish policy in the 1890s, 175, 177–8, 181, 182 n., 183; and sectionalism, 187; and the House of Lords question, 193, 200–1, 204–6; fails to become leader, 1894, 204; and the 1894–5 government, 207, 319; on the schism of 1886, 210, 260; on the changed nature of Conservatism, 220; 1894 Budget of, 224, 260, 316; on class division and parties, 224–5, 260; on strikes, 230; Rosebery on, 232; leadership of, 1896–8, 237–8, 254 n., 317; as a leader, 237–8, 237 n., 316–18; on Rosebery, 251; and imperialism, 266; and Liberal Imperialism, 271–3, 276; resigns leadership, 1898, 272, 272 n.

Harmsworth, Alfred [341], 286

Harris, William [334], 48 n., 53

Harrison, Royden, 9, 14

Hart, Heber [341], 263

Hartington, Lord [332], and temperance reform, 28; becomes leader, 1875, 39, 61, 64; as leader, 1875–80, 40, 40 n., 256; and the N.L.F., 50;

INDEX

Hartington, Lord (*cont.*):
and Gladstone, 77–8, 107; and the Radicals, 77–8, 107–8; and the political crisis of 1885, 106–8, 120, 122 n.; Gladstone on post-1885 behaviour of, 146, 148; also referred to, xiv, 8 n., 148, 232, 261

Hawarden Kite, 113–16

Heart of the Empire, The, 235

Herschell, Lord [332], 153, 200, 200 n., 211

Hobhouse, L. T. [342], 235, 324

Hobson, J. A., 235

Houghton, Lord, 69 n.

House of Lords, and the 1868–74 government, 35; significance of Liberals' concern with, 42, 179, 192–6, 222; Radicals and in the 1880s, 98, 149; Gladstone and, 112, 112 n., 177, 192–4, 202; and Home Rule, 1892–3, 161 n., 175, 182, 184, 192, 194–5; the Liberal government and, 1892–5, 178, 184, 192–207, 200 n.; the agitation against, 1893–5, 192–207; Rosebery and, 197–207, 203 n., 247, 250, 313; as an issue after 1895, 236, 265, 299; 'federalism' and, 264; as an issue after 1905, 321, 324–6

Howell, George [335], 9, 11–12

Hudson, Sir Robert [334], 214

Hughes, Revd. Price, 284 n.

Hume, Joseph, 82

Imperial Federation, 156–7, 157 n., 159, 250, 263

Imperialism (*see also* Liberal Imperialism), Radicals and in the 1880s, 96; and Irish Home Rule, 156–7, 159–60, 161, 263; Rosebery and, 199, 210, 252, 260, 268–71; Liberal enthusiasm for, 263; and 'devolution', 265; and social reform, 265–6; the Liberal controversy over, 266–73, 291–4, 318, 320; the Liberal League and, 269, 275, 281–2; C.-B. and, 270, 288–9; Liberal opposition to, 281–2, 288, 295, 326; Nonconformists and, 284, 299; Labour and, 307–8

Ireland (*see also* Obstructions), as an interest connected with Liberal politics, 2, 18–20, 22–3, 25, 37, 39

Irish Church, disestablishment of, 20, 35, 37–8

Irish Home Rule, the Liberal preoccupation with, 42, 110, 118, 128–34, 136, 140, 152–3, 159, 161–7, 169, 171–2, 183, 188, 192–5, 198, 201, 208–9, 211, 220–1, 225–30, 246, 267–8, 299, 302, 320; Gladstone and, 91, 108, 110, 114–23, 139, 143–4, 147–8, 162, 257–8; reaction of Liberals and Radicals to in 1886, 117–21, 118 n., 140, 147, 260, 284; and the 'Irish obstruction', 118, 126–7, 133–4, 156, 162–3, 181–4, 199, 217, 302, 306, 326; the rift in the party over, 123–5, 131–3, 140, 146–7, 151, 210–11, 260, 299; Rosebery and, 126, 181–2, 197–8, 246, 252–3, 255, 260, 261 n., 284, 300, 303–5; the N.L.F. and, 136–7, 140, 174; post-1886 debate on details of, 154–61; and imperialism, 156–61, 263; the Liberals and, 1891–4, 169, 172, 174–84, 187, 191–2, 194–5, 227–8, 284–5; the Liberals and after 1894, 207, 209, 216, 264, 284–5, 297, 299–306, 314; the Newcastle Programme and, 174, 211, 215, 258; and party division, 220–1, 317; the 1905–14 government and, 306, 324, 326

Irish land purchase, 58, 154–5, 154 n.

Irish Members, the question of the retention of, 152–3, 155–61, 157 n., 252

Irish party, relations between Liberals and, 18–19, 20 n., 26 n., 30, 112, 152–3, 178–9, 284, 300–2, 322, 328

Irish question, Liberals and, 1880–5, 90–1; 1885–6, 110–21; the Liberal preoccupation with, after 1885, 124–84

James, R. Rhodes, x

Jenkins, Roy, x

Jones, Ernest, 150

Kelley, Robert, 72

Kimberley, Lord [332], 178, 187, 293

Kitson, Sir James [334], 135, 138–9

Labouchere, Henry [338], and Home Rule, 111, 118–20, 124, 165, 183, 183 n., 227; Radicalism of, 143, 148–51, 149 n., 235–6; and the retention of Irish Members, 153; and Harcourt, 150, 150 n., 165; and Irish land purchase, 155; and Liberal policy, 1891-2, 171-2, 179, 183; and the House of Lords question, 196, 204, 236; also referred to, xi, 239 n., 276

Labour (*see also* Lib-Labism), as a sectional interest, 4-5, 9-13, 18-19; the relations between capital and, 13-18, 225, 228-34, 234 n., 306; and the National Education League, 44; representation of, 179, 308; and Liberal Imperialism, 279; the Irish question and, 306-7; Liberal policy and, 306-8; and Liberal politics after 1905, 322, 325

Labour party, 1, 4, 222, 309, 327-9

Labour Representation Committee, 235, 299, 308-9

Land reform, 101-4, 103 n., 128 n., 132, 141, 151, 169, 328

Land Reform Association, 48 n.

Lawson, Sir Wilfrid [336], and temperance reform, 88-9, 92, 94, 98, 174, 212; also referred to, 24, 40 n., 65, 151, 212

Leeds, 16, 113

Leeds Mercury, 113-14

Lewis, J. Herbert [336], 23

Liberal Imperial Council, 275, 294

Liberal Imperialism, in Scotland and Wales, 159, 277; as a Liberal creed, 263-8; and Home Rule, 263; and 'devolution', 264-5; and social reform, 265-6; and Liberal politics, 268-9, 274-7; Nonconformists and, 283; C.-B. and, 294

Liberal Imperialists, and retention of Irish Members, 156; and Home Rule, 156-60, 167, 302-5; concern of for reconstruction of Liberalism, 232-4, 291-2, 295, 320-1; anxious to avert class politics and counter Socialism, 232-4; and social reform, 266; and Imperialism as a creed, 267; aim to take over control of the party, 269, 272, 274-6, 282, 292, 294-5, 320; and Liberal policy, 269, 271-2, 287, 316; and the South African War, 270, 273; and the Liberal League, 276-7; the Liberal leaders and, 278; and imperialism, 282, 291-2; and Rosebery, 286-7, 304-5; and Liberal politics after 1902, 295-6, 304-5; and the Irish alliance, 300-1; and the 1902 Education Act, 311; and the Free Trade issue, 312-13; failure of, 320-1

Liberalism (the connection between Liberalism and other aspects of British political life can be traced under many other headings in the index), absence of a creed or general theory of, x, 40-1, 188, 196-7, 215-16, 263, 267; and opposition to class conflict, 14, 222-3, 231-2, 327, 329; sectionalism, 'faddism', and, 24-33, 43, 57-9, 83, 187, 208, 212-13, 294-5, 299, 324, 328-9; and democracy, 46, 50, 52; as based on ideal of free play of ideas and forces, 48, 231, 294, 320; and 'liberation', 91, 117, 217-19; debate on whether inspired by positive or negative impulses, 241, 316-17

Liberal League, formation of, 269, 272, 276; significance of title of, 269, 275, 295; aims of, 276-9, 285, 295, 321; and the Liberal party, 276-9, 285-6; failure of, 279-83, 285; and reform policy, 280-1; and imperialism, 281; Rosebery and, 276, 283, 286; Nonconformists lose enthusiasm for, 285, 311; decline of support for, 283, 286; and Irish Home Rule, 305; and the Free Trade issue, 312-13; Spencer against, 295 n.

Liberal party (the connection between the Liberal party and other aspects of British political life can be traced under many other headings in the index), coalition nature of, 1-2, 19, 299; as an alternative government, 1-2, 19, 239, 296, 298, 317-18, 327-8; as a federal alliance, 18, 20; and Liberal governments, 35; and the Liberal leaders, 53-4, 149; as the national, majority, or normal governing party, 59, 64, 68, 122, 223-4, 251, 257, 260, 315; and the development of class politics, 147, 151, 210, 223-5, 260; as a 'Broad Church', 147, 165, 267-8, 292-3, 295-6, 321; the theme of purging and reconstructing, 207, 254, 268-9, 273, 319-20; and social reform, 225, 228, 232-6; why did not

INDEX

Liberal party (cont.):
split over imperialism, 273–8; and power, 318–20; changed position of after 1905, 327
Liberal Unionists and the Irish preoccupation, 132, 162–3, 226–7; effect of secession of, 126 n., 146–7; the question of re-gaining, 260–1, 261 n., 304; Rosebery and, 260–1, 261 n., 276; and the Free Trade issue, 314
Liberation Society, 19, 20 n., 22, 22 n., 32–3, 48 n., 77, 299
Lib-Labism, 2, 10–14, 18, 151, 306–9
Lloyd George, D. [336], as Welsh Radical, 32, 186; and the House of Lords question, 192, 325; and Rosebery, 286–7; and the 1902 Education Act, 311; 1909 Budget of, 324; and social reform, 327; and Labour, 327; and the landowners, 328; proposes a coalition, 328–9; on end of 'old Liberalism', 329
Local government reform, 98, 101–2, 107, 128 n., 187, 306
Local option, 21 n., 26, 28, 88–9, 92, 98, 169, 174, 189, 198, 205–7, 225, 238, 300
Local veto, *see* Local option
Lockwood, Frank [339], 196
London, the question of reforming the government of, 86–7, 92, 137, 182, 187, 209, 316; Socialists and Liberals in, 234
London County Council, 234
London Nonconformist Council, 284 n.
Lowe, Robert [332], 8 n., 38, 71, 84

McCord, Norman, xii
MacDonald, Alexander, 11
— J. Ramsay, 235, 308
McKenna, Reginald, 325
Maehl, W. H., 65
Magnus, Sir Philip, ix–x
Manchester School, 41
Marjoribanks, E., *see* Tweedmouth, Lord
Massingham, H. W. [342], 256
Mather, Sir William, 230
Mendl, S. F., 302
Miall, Edward [336], 7
Midlothian, Gladstone's 1879–80 campaigns in, 68, 86, 241 n., 249, 249 n., 257

Mill, John Stuart, 11, 49, 51, 70, 147 293
Morgan, K. O., 23
Morley, Arnold [334], 135, 171–2, 182, 221, 226
— John [332], on the Welsh 'party', 23; prefers concentration on one question, 25, 43, 165–6, 246; on absence of system, 41, 71; and Radicalism in the 1870s, 44, 81, 81 n., 96, 235; and Bryce's proposals, 1878, 81–2; rift between Chamberlain and, 81–2, 96, 96 n., 105; and the House of Lords question, 98, 200–2, 200 n., 205; and disestablishment, 96 n., 253; and the role of the State, 96 n., 235; and the 'Irish obstruction', 118 n., 156, 177, 181; and Gladstone's leadership, 141–2; and Welsh disestablishment, 140 n.; and the Radicals in the late 1880s, 149 n.; and the retention of Irish M.P.s, 153 n., 156, 252; and Irish land purchase, 154 n., 155; against 'federalism', 157, 159; and Home Rule policy in the late 1880s, 157–9, 161 n.; and the Irish preoccupation, 166; and the preparation of new policy in the late 1880s, 168–9, 171; and the Liberal Imperialists, 168, 232; and Liberal policy, 1891–2, 169, 170 n., 171, 175–7, 177 n., 180; and the Newcastle Programme, 176; and Irish policy after 1893, 181 n.; predicts disintegration of party, 189; and the 1895 elections, 198, 205, 207; and Harcourt, 220, 238 n.; on the Conservative party, 221; on class politics, 225; and the eight hour day, 230; and Rosebery, 232, 232 n., 251 n., 284 n.; Rosebery on, 232; on Liberalism and minorities, 252–3; on the leaders and the party, 245 n.; on Gladstone's death, 257 n.; and imperialism, 266; and the pursuit of electoral success, 270; and the rift over imperialism, 272–3, 292; and dependence on the Irish, 301, 301 n.; and the Free Trade issue, 314
— Samuel [338], 13, 15–16
Morton, A. C. [339], 213
— E. J. C. [339], 203
Mundella, A. J. [332], and Lib-Labism, 13, 15–17; on the nature of

INDEX

Liberalism, 64 n., 219, 223; loyal to Gladstone, 76, 106; and 'free schools' in 1885, 104 n., 231; also referred to, 26 n., 40 n., 42 n., 82, 82 n., 237 n.
Murray, George, 251

National Education League, 5–8, 44–6, 48 n., 69 n.
National Liberal Federation, as extra-parliamentary organization, 39, 51 n., 55; foundation of, 46, 56–7, 67, 80; aims and principles of, 46–54, 48 n., 74, 80, 100, 136; and the Whigs, 47, 50; and the Liberal leaders, 52–4, 149; negativism of, 1879–80, 56, 80; and the Irish preoccupation, 128, 136–8; and programmes in late 1880s, 135–6, 138; and Liberal policy after 1886, 136–40, 185; reaction against Chamberlain's influence over, 135, 137; Labouchere and, 149; Newcastle meeting of, 1891, 173, 213–14, 222 (*see also* Newcastle Programme); 1895 meeting of, 188–92, 197; 1893 meeting of, 191; 1894 meeting of, 191, 203; and the House of Lords question, 193, 204; and policy after 1895, 244, 310; post-1895 attempt to increase independence of, 246; and the Free Trade issue, 314
Newcastle Programme, 1891, origins of, 173, 211, 213–15; nature and purpose of, 173–4, 190; the 1892–5 government and, 177, 189–92, 206, 258–9; sectionalists and, 188, 190; the debate on, 189–90, 210–15, 258–9; effect of on Liberal politics, 189–90, 211, 244–5; the House of Lords question and, 195–7; and labour policy, 228, 229 n.; Rosebery and, 258–9, 298; H. Gladstone and, 298–9; Lloyd George on, 329
Nicoll, W. Robertson [336], 285
Nineteenth Century, 8, 67, 131, 133–4, 150
Nonconformists, revised attitude to sectionalism, 7–9, 28, 30; and the 1870 Education Act, 5–7, 26, 35–7; and the elections of 1880, 83; and Home Rule, 120, 131, 284–5; and Liberal Imperialism, 279, 283–5, 311; and Irish policy after 1894, 283–5; and the Education Act of 1902, 285, 311

Nonconformity, 2–9, 20–1, 151, 299, 314, 321
Nottingham, 16

'Obstructions', the Liberal preoccupation with, 90–2, 134–5, 196, 201, 216–17, 319–20, 326; 'Ireland' as, 90, 118, 126–38, 156, 162–3, 170, 172–3, 175, 179, 181–5, 192, 194–7, 199, 203, 217, 302, 306, 326; the House of Lords as, 184, 192–203, 324–6
Ostrogorski, M., xii, 163, 174, 195, 244

Palmer, Roundell, *see* Selborne, Lord
Palmerston, Lord, 34 n.
Parliament, obstruction of the business of, 90–1, 98, 126, 128, 133–4; Gladstone and, 144; Home Rule and the future of, 156–61; Liberal Imperialism and, 264–5
Parliament Act of 1911, 326, 328
Parnell, C. S., 29, 31, 112, 163, 169–71
Paulton, J. M. [341], 305
Peace movement, 3
Pearson, W. D., 279, 286
Peel, Sir Robert, 59, 69, 122
Peelites, 37, 122
Perks, R. W. [341], 275, 279, 281–2, 284, 284 n., 286, 305, 311
Phillimore, J. S., 215
Playfair, Lyon [339], 114, 212
Price, R. J. [339], 190–1
Programmes (*see also* Newcastle Programme), in Liberal politics, 99, 174; of 1885 (Radical), 99–104, 107–12, 116–19; reasons for favouring, 99; opposition to, 99, 104–5, 135–6, 166, 176, 189, 208, 211–13, 244, 257–9, 280–1; Chamberlain and, 99–102, 99 n.; Gladstone and, 105, 110, 197, 257–8; the Irish preoccupation and, 121, 135, 165–6; the N.L.F. and, 135–8, 173–4, 213–14, 244; Harcourt and, 165–6, 176–8, 206; Rosebery and, 197, 199, 247–8, 257–9, 280; the Liberal Imperialists and, 280–1
'Progress', obstructions to, 90–2, 134–5, 319–20
Progressive Party, 234
Progressive Review, 213, 215, 235

Radicalism, and class relations, 14, 151, 327; state of in 1870s, 41–2, 46; Chamberlain and, 41, 43–7, 50–6, 95–7, 99–101, 107–8, 112, 119–21, 151–2; reformed party organization and, 46–7, 50–4; and the power of the State, 51, 95–7, 148–9, 151–2, 235–6; Gladstone and, 56, 76–7, 95, 107–8, 116–17, 120–1, 141–2, 146–8, 151, 162, 220; in early 1880s, 94–6; and Home Rule, 95, 108, 116–21, 146–8; in 1885, 99–112; and the schism in the party, 145–8; in the late 1880s, 148–52, 167, 171; Harcourt and, 149–50, 169, 205, 220; decline of, 150–1, 235–6
Radical Programme (1885), 99, 102
Radicals, devoid of general theory, xi, 41; and Gladstone, 74–8, 81, 106–7; dissatisfied with Irish preoccupation, 89, 162, 227; campaign of in 1885, 99–108, 112–13, 220; strategy of in Dec. 1885, 112–16, 113 n.; and Gladstone's adoption of Home Rule, 116–19; also referred to, xii, 12, 40 n., 41–4, 51, 55, 81, 87, 95–6, 98, 146–53, 149 n., 150 n., 155, 177–8, 202, 204, 235–6
Rainbow Circle, 215, 235
Rainy, Dr. [336], 89, 110–11, 131
Ramm, Agatha, 84
Rathbone, William [339], 33
Reform Act of 1867, 34, 38, 52
Reform Acts of 1885, 93–4, 102
Reform League, 9
Reform Union, 48 n.
Registration, as a reform issue, 128 n., 170, 174, 177 n., 178, 182, 191
Reid, Andrew, 142, 196
— Robert [339], 228, 243
— T. Wemyss [342], and the Hawarden Kite, 113–16; also referred to, 240, 256, 284, 288
Rendel, Stuart [336], and Wales, 30–3, 153 n., 179; and the Irish preoccupation, 133; and Irish representation, 153 n.; retires, 186
Richard, Henry [336], 8 n., 83
Ripon, Lord [333], 128 n., 170, 178, 200, 228, 273
Robson, W. S. [341], 305
Roebuck, J. A., 15
Rogers, J. Guinness [336], 8–9, 28–9, 188, 208, 211, 222, 284 n.

Rosebery, Lord [341], as a Whig, xiv; and arbitration, 15; and Gladstone, 105, 143, 145 n., 168, 248–9, 248 n.; and the Irish preoccupation, 125–6, 158, 168, 183, 246; and Irish Home Rule, 126, 158–9, 181–2, 246, 253, 255, 257, 284, 300, 303–4; on lack of leadership after 1886, 144; on the rift in the party in 1886, 126, 126 n., 210, 255, 260–1; and Harcourt, 150 n., 204–7, 238, 319; and 'federalism', 159; and the Liberal Imperialists, 168, 232, 234; wants policies that appeal to the majority, 175, 252–3, 259; and the Irish 'obstruction', 181–2; sectionalists and, 1894–5, 187–9, 244; and the House of Lords question, 197–207, 200 n., 203 n., 247, 250, 313; and programmes, 197, 244, 257–9, 269, 280; Gladstonian style of, 197, 246, 248–50, 248 n., 250 n., 253–5, 257; and imperialism, 199, 248, 252, 260, 270, 282; and Scotland, 189 n.; on the era of 'liberation', 218–19; on party conflict, 221, 291; on future of Liberal party, 223–4; and the 1894 Budget, 224, 260; and the L.C.C., 234; why remains as Liberal leader, 232; post-1895 negativism of, 241–2, 247, 253–5; resigns leadership, 245, 251, 253–7, 272; calls for 'concentration' of policy, 246–8, 259, 264, 268, 298, 320; stresses the form of policy, 246–8, 257; tries to eradicate Gladstonian legacy, 248, 255–7, 259; and the Midlothian campaign, 241 n., 249, 249 n.; dislikes parliamentary politics, 248–50, 249 n.; aims to appeal to national opinion, 249–54, 257; and Imperial Federation, 250; and retention of Irish M.P.s, 252; and disestablishment, 253, 264; attitude of to order in the party, 253–5, 255 n.; belief of in purge and reconstruction, 254, 319; refuses to re-involve himself in party politics after 1896, 251 n., 253–5, 279, 281, 283, 286–7, 303–4, 321; Chamberlain on, 255, 261, 261 n.; under Gladstone's shadow, 255–7; and the 'Armenian atrocities', 256; and the Newcastle Programme, 257–9, 298; appeals to Liberal

INDEX

Unionists, 260; and 'devolution', 264; on imperialism and social reform, 265; demands reorganization of Liberal politics, 268–9, 272–3, 294, 298, 319–20; and the rift over imperialism, 268, 276–8; and the 'clean slate', 269, 271–2, 280, 289–90; and the South African War, 271, 290–1; attitude of to party after 1896, 272, 288; and the Liberal League, 275–9, 283, 286, 294; and domestic policy, 276, 280–1; the Liberal leaders and after 1900, 278, 289–90; aims to change Liberal frame of mind, 279–81, 287, 299, 304; Nonconformists and, 284–5, 284 n.; and the Irish alliance, 284, 300; and the 1902 Education Act, 285, 311; Lloyd George and, 286–7; and the Free Trade issue, 312–13; also referred to, xi, 143, 157, 185, 188, 190, 196, 212, 218, 228, 283
Rural Labourers' League, 132
Russell, Sir Edward [342], 206, 212
— G. W. E., 125
— Lord John, 34 n.

Salisbury, Lord, 78, 99, 112, 135, 207
Samuel, Herbert [341], 215, 223, 235
Schnadhorst, F. [334], 46, 50, 117, 137, 165, 228–9, 229 n.
Scotland, as an interest in Liberal politics, 2, 18–22, 31; Liberalism in, 20–2; and Irish Home Rule, 156, 159–61; Liberal Imperialism in, 159, 277, 283, 299; also referred to, 132, 153, 165, 189 n., 228
Scott, C. P. [342], 209
Scottish disestablishment, 32, 89–90, 109–11, 130–1, 139, 264, 265 n.
Scottish Home Rule, 91, 159, 265 n.
Scottish Liberal Association, 277
Selborne, Lord [333], 61, 70, 75, 77
Shannon, R. T., ix, 56, 66, 76
Shaw-Lefevre, G. [338], 128
Sheffield, 15–16
Simon, J. A., 216, 225
Sinclair, J., 323
Smith, Goldwin, 75
Snape, T., 189
Socialism, Gladstone and, 108, 148, 220 n.; Liberal Imperialists and, 167–8, 233–4, 265; also referred to, 12, 104, 148, 150, 209, 223, 232–6, 232 n., 259, 267, 273, 309, 329
South African War, 271–2, 324
Southgate, D., ix
Speaker, The, 193–4, 205, 209–11, 213, 240
Spencer, Lord [333], and Irish policy, 116, 127, 154 n., 155, 160, 161 n., 180–1, 181 n.; on Liberal League, 295 n.; also referred to, xiv, 205, 321
Spender, J. A. [342], 74, 271, 313
Spicer, Albert, 284 n.
Stansfeld, James [336], 24, 89, 94, 221
Stansky, P., ix
State, role of, trade unions and, 12, 14; Liberals and, 91, 217–18, 223, 230–1, 235, 265–7; Radicals and, 95–7, 96 n., 118, 148, 235–6, 267

Tariff reform, 307, 312
Taxation, 102, 107, 174, 176, 231
Temperance reform, the movement for and Liberal politics, 3, 13, 18, 20 n., 21, 25, 98, 102, 131–2, 170–1, 174, 186–90, 205, 212, 216, 279, 297–9, 316, 322, 324, 326, 329
Tenants Compensation Bill, 92
Tholfsen, T. R., 10
Thompson, A. F., 62
Times, The, 119, 258
Trade Disputes Bill of 1906, 325
Trade Union Congress, 16, 306; Parliamentary Committee of, 12
Trade union movement, 12–16, 18, 230–1, 306–8, 323
Trevelyan, C. [339], 235, 282
— G. M., 314
— G. O. [338], 85, 125, 149 n., 182
Tweedmouth, Lord [334], 183 n., 204, 277, 283

Uganda, 183
United Kingdom Alliance, 3, 37, 186, 206

Vincent, John, ix–xii, xiv, 10, 20, 34 n., 78 n.

Wales, as a section in Liberal politics, 2, 18, 20–3, 29–33, 185–6, 189; and the Irish preoccupation, 130; and the Irish party, 31, 152–3; and imperialism, 156 n., 159–61, 299

Wallace, R. [339], 213
Walton, J. L. [341], 305
Watson, Robert Spence [334], 15, 49, 118 n., 125, 135–6, 158, 200 n., 213, 242
Webb, Beatrice, 180, 323, 325
— Sidney, 239
Welby, Lord, 195 n.
Welsh disestablishment, 20–2, 30–3, 109, 130, 137, 139–40, 140 n., 142, 153 n., 179, 182, 185–7, 189, 192–3, 256, 264, 299, 326
Welsh Home Rule, 23–4, 91
West, Sir Algernon [342], 21 n., 73
Whigs, as leaders, xiv, 37; as a section, xiv, 39; and the N.L.F., 47, 50; and Gladstone, 76–8, 106; and the Radicals, 95, 100, 118–19; and Home Rule, 116, 118; secession of, 118–19, 146, 148
Whittaker, T. P. [336], 186
Wilson, H. J. [337], 20 n., 25, 25 n., 26 n., 183 n., 288
Wilson, Trevor, ix
Wolverton, Lord [334], 62
Women's suffrage, 3, 153, 322
Woodall, W., 204 n.

Yoxall, J. H. [339], 191

www.ingramcontent.com/pod-product-compliance
Lightning Source LLC
Chambersburg PA
CBHW070009010526
44117CB00011B/1478